Lucy Loved Me

By Paula Stewart
A Memoir

Lucy Loved Me by Paula Stewart, A Memoir

Published in the USA by:
BearManor Media
P O Box 71426
Albany, Georgia 31708
www.bearmanormedia.com

ISBN: 978-1-62933-226-0
BearManor Media, Albany, Georgia
Printed in the United States of America
Book design by Robbie Adkins, www.adkinsconsult.com

To Ava and Jake,
my adorable redheaded grandkids

Foreword

In 1970 I reviewed *Dinah East*, a risqué comedy that held that Mae West was a man in drag and furthermore had an affair with Edith Head, Hollywood's most famous costume designer. Mae approved Edith for her gowns for the classic *She Done Him Wrong* with the admonition, "I like 'em tight." West also had approved Cary Grant for her leading man, thus launching all three of them into legendary Hollywood status.

I found the film amusingly camp. Its producer, Paula Stewart called me up to thank me, and we would be friendly ever since. As a singer, actress and comedian, she would appear in ten Broadway shows, and play Polly Peachum in the celebrated long-running off-Broadway revival of *The Threepenny Opera*. She also performed with both her first husband Burt Bacharach, and then her second, comedian Jack Carter.

By the time I met Paula, a glamorous blonde with a hearty sense of humor, and as it turned out, a steely resilience, she was already moving away from performing and finding success in interior decorating and, more lucratively, real estate investments. Her vintage Spanish Colonial home in the Beverly Flats was worthy of a movie star, and she entertained in style. I remember one dinner party at which the guest of honor was, of all people, Thomas Noguchi, Los Angeles' colorful, controversial "Coroner to the Stars." She told me recently that she "never saw show business as an 'end-all.' I thought money was more important."

She had a handsome Palm Springs home, also a vintage Spanish Colonial, that she'd purchased from the Florsheim shoe store family, completely furnished right down to the luxurious bath towels, each embroidered with a large "F." Paula was riding high-- but also for a steep fall when a brief third marriage cost her all her real estate holdings.

That's when Lucille Ball came to the rescue. With a painful end to her marriage to Desi Arnaz, Lucy decided to take her career in an entirely new direction and made her 1960 Broadway debut in the musical *Wildcat*, in which she played an indomitable prospector determined to strike oil in Texas. She cast Paula as her younger sister--and became the best friend Paula ever had. Paula in turn introduced her to comedian Gary Morton, who would become Lucy's cherished husband for the rest of her life.

Paula's account of the 29 years of their steadfast give-and-take friendship, Lucy Loved Me, reveals how strong and mutual their loyalty to each other was; they really were there for each other when each needed the other's support, and they had lots of fun along the way. Writing in an admirably conversational style--it reads like having a long talk with Paula. She provides a unique portrait of how Lucille Ball--caring, loving, direct, and stalwart—really was as a person. I saw enough of them together to find Paula's view of her best friend to ring true. Lucy invited Paula to stay in her guesthouse at her splendid traditional-style Paul Williams designed home at the corner of Roxbury and Lexington in Beverly Hills. Jack Benny lived next door and Jimmy Stewart across the street. Lucy also put her on salary as a fitness instructor. I then became an occasional visitor.

In 1978 while she was shooting the successful family comedy, costarring Henry Fonda, *Yours, Mine and Ours*, I knew that Lucille Ball was not Lucy Ricardo offscreen but a woman who took her work very seriously. "Drama is what I do for a vacation," she said, and also told me how Buster Keaton had taught her the importance of props, making sure they always worked. I also knew what a gracious woman she could be. At a huge house party given by Barry Diller and Diane von Furstenberg, I received word that Lucy wanted to meet me--I have never figured out how she could know I was there in the first place. She gave me a heartfelt thank you for the fresh review I wrote of a favorite film of hers, also costarring with Fonda, *The Big Street* (1942), a sentimental Damon Runyan story about a busboy entranced by a hoity-toity nightclub singer made remarkably affecting by the sheer talent and skill of its stars. Lucy explained that, much to her disappointment, it had opened as a second feature and went virtually unreviewed.

I found that Lucy and Paula were so close and relaxed with each other that you could really believe they were mutually devoted sisters. With the disappointment of her last series, *Life with Lucy,* behind her, Lucy seemed restless, having been a workhorse all her life, yet not necessarily feeling up to trying to get back in the saddle. She chain-smoked and played backgammon as much as she could. Lucy was hardly without friends, but she obviously cherished Paula's companionship. Gary played lots of golf and tried his hand at producing, and while tender and attentive with Lucy, who clearly adored him, he was gone a lot. It did cross my mind that Lucy might have felt pretty lonely without Paula's presence. In several months Paula was back on her feet and living not too far away in an apartment building with an extraordinary Chinese exterior, owned by her friend, celebrity decorator Phyllis Morris, and Paula kept in close touch with Lucy right up to the end.

Lucy was a wonderful hostess, amusing and unpretentious, and she and Paula together were fine company. One time Lucy remarked with genuine pride and awe that "Katherine Hepburn had once had dinner in this house." I thought to myself, "Why wouldn't Ms. Hepburn be happy to have dinner with America's greatest comedienne?" (She had appeared in one of Hepburn's timeless comedies, the 1937 *Stage Door.*) When Paula and I were alone I commented on a stunning black-and-white 8-by-10 photograph of Lucy placed on a cabinet in her large family room. Paula said, "I had that framed to remind her of her beauty—she never thought of herself as beautiful."

Outside, Lucy's home and garden were the epitome of elegance and formality. Inside it was the opposite, with a completely undecorated look, everything comfortably inviting and well-organized, but largely nondescript. Paula was at least semi-serious when she said she thought the house had been filled with *I Love Lucy* set furnishings. I thought that said something about Lucy's authenticity, but the few upgrades Lucy allowed Paula to make were nice touches.

One major change Lucy forbade Paula was changing the top of her dining room table. When Lucy invited me and a friend to dinner, I must admit I was surprised that her dining room, furnished with a white and gold French Provincial dining room set, featured a large table with its top covered in white Formica. Lucy explained to Paula that to change the top would only make more work for the elderly Chinese couple who oversaw the upkeep of the large house and prepared delicious meals.

That dinner proved to be the highlight of my times with Lucy and Paula--which included my friend John Gaby playing backgammon with Lucy--only to never let him lose to her.

After dessert, Lucy stood up and asked, "Wanna hear a funny story?" (As if anyone would say no.) She told it in her best Lucy Ricardo mode.

"I was the only girl in Hollywood who did not want to play Scarlett O'Hara in *Gone with The Wind*, but RKO said I had to go out to Culver City and meet David O. Selznick. I didn't want to, and I begged not to have to go, but the studio said I had to.

"So, I put on my best wool suit and got into my new roadster to drive over. Then it started to rain, and I tried and tried to get the top up. But it would never go up! So, I arrived soaking wet! What am I going to do!! What am I going to do!! But Marcella Rabwin (Selznick's executive assistant) calmed me down, got me to take off my suit and dry it out by the fireplace and pulled me together to meet Mr. Selznick."

Anyone fortunate enough to have been acquainted with the remarkable and vivacious Mrs. Rabwin would know that she was just the person to handle a movie actress in wet clothes. She was the wife of Dr. Marcus Rabwin, the longtime Chief of Staff of the Cedars of Lebanon Hospital, who oversaw its merger with Cedars-Sinai in 1962. Marcella Rabwin became a Beverly Hills civic leader, helping found the city library, and so dedicated saving the landmark Greystone Mansion until she suffered a minor stroke. When Lucy finally was ushered in to meet Selznick and repeated her plea to not have to test for Scarlett, he took her to heart. Years later Lucy and Desi would take over Selznick International Studio.

"My office would be David O. Selznick's office, and I found a telegram on his desk for me. I opened it up and it read, 'Congratulations, David O. Selznick.' "

- Kevin Thomas, retired LA Times film critic

Introduction

Writing this memoir was not easy. Throughout the years, I've made many attempts, all ending up in file cabinets that contain the minutia of my existence. Paint chips of a multi-colored life. Bits and pieces to remind me of each chapter. Dog pedigrees, my grandmother's Singer sewing machine, tiny Minox bulbs that recall my father's passion for cameras which I inherited. And of course, a treasured backgammon table and Bakelite doubling cube. But, before I give them a decent burial, their closure deserves some sort of tribute or eulogy; what they meant to me and the reason I saved them in the first place. Surely, the most valuable are things related to Lucy. I probably wouldn't be here today if our lives hadn't crossed. Lucy guided me as mentor, mother, sister and soulmate. We were destined to know each other and bonded together in some karmic way. There were so many coincidences in our different yet similar lives. I've recounted them in this memoir.

Paula Stewart

Dear Steve

All the best, wishing you success with your latest production —

Paula Stewart

Lucy Loved Me

I
Wildcat

1960

Free Again.

At least for now, no more eight shows a week, a grueling commitment to that demanding mistress, THE THEATER, whose main caveat is "The Show Must Go On." Forget that you have a raging fever, strep throat, or ears so stopped up you can hardly hear the orchestra, let alone the person next to you with whom you are singing a duet. Being one of the lucky few who worked constantly in musicals, I can assure you that it is a prison sentence and yet you love your jailer despite the torture. Actors, surely have to be the greatest masochists of all.

From A to Z, a musical review that unfortunately only lasted from A to B, had just closed. It starred Hermione Gingold, an acclaimed English performer, with hysterical sketches by Woody Allen and fabulous songs by Fred Ebb. It gave me a chance to finally display my comedic ability in a number about a jilted biker that actually stopped the show. I was touted as a new comedy star. Yes, free at last.

Currently unemployed, I could now return to the pleasures of debauching at PJ Clark's or the Village Blue Note, and maybe catch up on some fellow actors' performances in other shows. I could spend guilty days learning some gourmet recipes at Dione Lucas' Cooking School, or visit the new auction houses, offbeat antique shops, and a rare visit to the unemployment line. Theater performers in those days did not make exorbitant salaries. You were a performer because you loved the art, not because you were going to get rich.

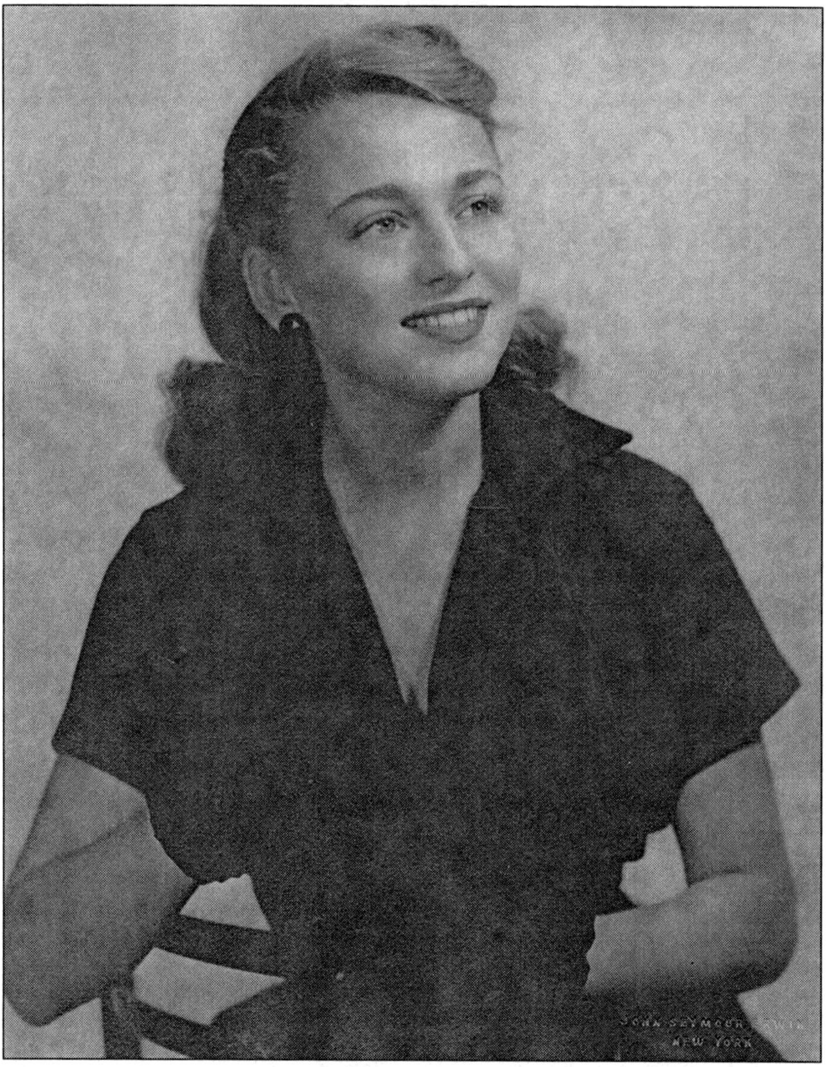

One of my first professional photos. Early 50s.

What drives actors is not money; it's the milk of applause connecting us with that big tit out in the dark, the live audience, giving us our manna, night after night. Then after opening night, it's the same old thing again—eight shows a week with one day off. So when my phone rang at the ungodly hour of 9 a.m., I was sure someone was dead...or would be soon. It was my agent, Gus Shirmer. Before I could express my feelings on the subject, he blurted out the news.

"Paula, you have an audition tomorrow at the Alvin at one o'clock for the part of Lucille Ball's sister in *Wildcat*."

"First, who the hell is Lucille Ball and second, I don't brush my teeth before noon." After years of working nights in the theater, my life was reversed. My body clock was on the graveyard shift, starting to live when others were going to sleep.

"Do NOT tell me you don't know who she is. What rock have you been living under? She's the biggest name in television and now she's taking on Broadway!"

I know this will sound nuts, but I really didn't know who Lucille Ball was. Allow me to explain...

I began my life in the theater around the age of nineteen after dropping out of Northwestern University with the National Touring Company of *Brigadoon* in 1949.

I was lucky enough to work nearly nonstop throughout the 1950s in numerous productions: *Carousel* with Gordon MacRae and also with Howard Keel; *Seventeen* with Milton Berle; *Little Me* with Donald O'Connor; *Kismet* and *The Threepenny Opera*

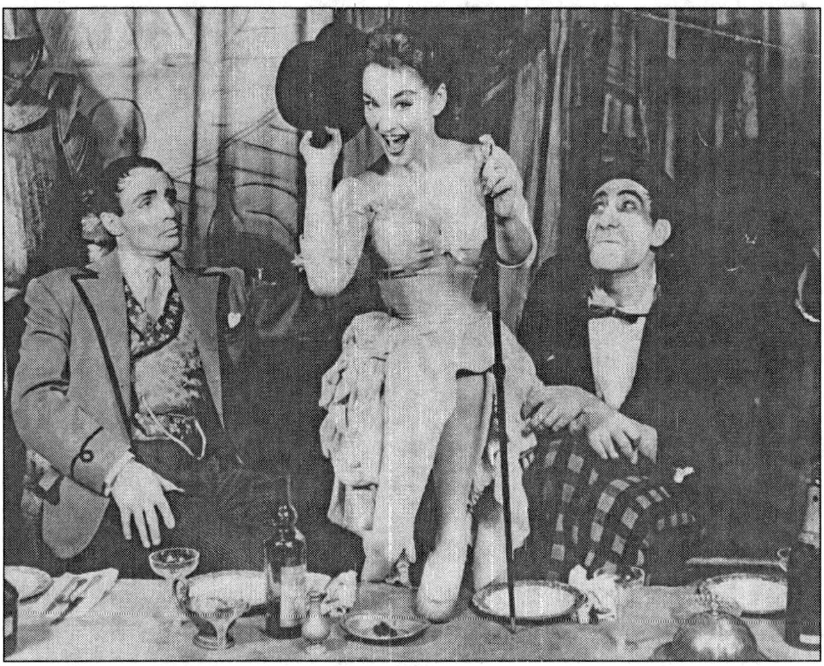

Jim Mitchell, Joe Ely and I. Song: "The Bide-A-Wee in Soho" from The Threepenny Opera*—at the time off-Broadway's longest running show.*

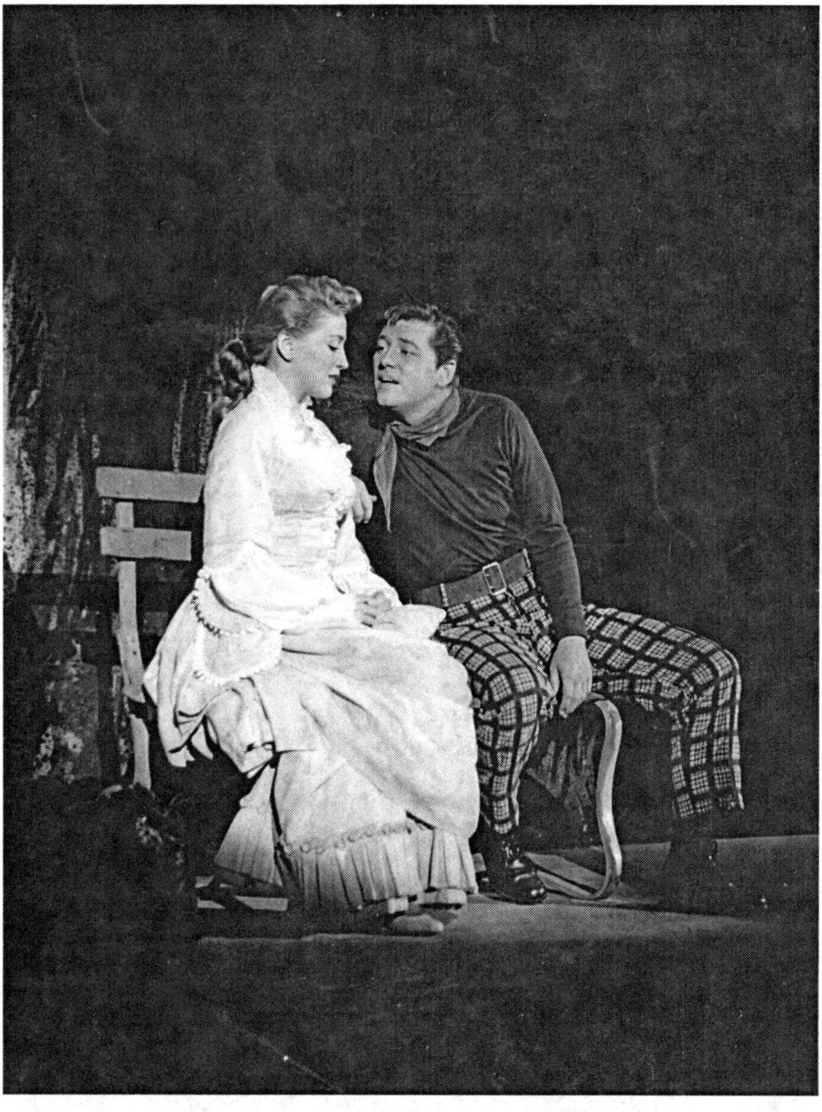

Gordon and Sheila MacRae were a lovely couple and remained dear friends.

with Ed Asner, Jerry Orbach and Jim Mitchell. How fortunate for me that in 1954 this Stanley Chase-Carmen Capalbo production passed its 500th performance establishing a new record as off-Broadway's longest running attraction.

Yes, *I Love Lucy* had been the number one show for years on television, and Lucy's break-up with Desi Arnaz was front-page

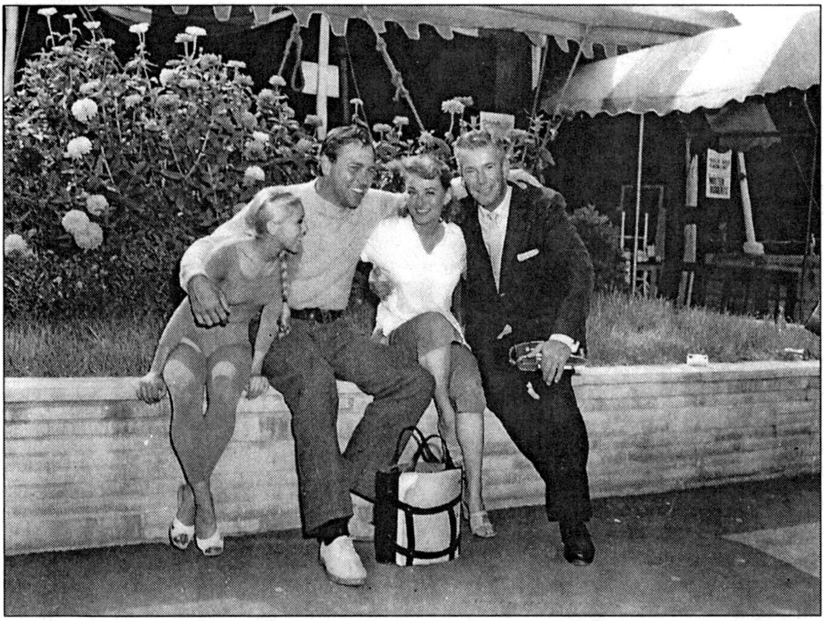

Howard Keel, another one of my obsessions, flanked by Sondra Lee and I during Carousel *rehearsals. I don't remember the gentleman on the right holding my polaroid camera. I only had eyes for Howard.*

news, but I lived in the dedicated world of theater, working nonstop in summer stock and had recently closed a run of *The Most Happy Fella* at the New York City Center. On top of that, I had just been included in an amazing production at the City Center honoring major stars.

I was consumed with theater. I had no time off to even think about watching TV, or what was happening in the rest of the world of entertainment. I was just too busy. I slept all day, worked all night and, occasionally was out until the wee hours seeing friends perform off-Broadway or in clubs. When I got home, I fell into bed. The tiny black and white television I owned was used to hold up my favorite fake plant.

"Oh alright, tell me about it." I knew better than to argue with Gus.

"It's a musical remake of Richard Nash's *The Rainmaker*. Michael Kidd is directing and choreographing. Nash wrote the book and Cy Coleman composed the music."

"Wow...big names," I thought, still half asleep. Michael Kidd was a top choreographer in the film business having worked with

N. Y. CITY CENTER OF MUSIC AND DRAMA, INC.

presents the

CITY CENTER Showcase

OPERA · DRAMA · BALLET · LIGHT OPERA

MONDAY EVENING, APRIL 27, AT 8:30 P.M. (1959)
N. Y. CITY CENTER THEATRE, 131 W. 55th STREET

JEAN DALRYMPLE, *Co-ordinator*
DANIA KRUPSKA, *Director* — WATSON BARRATT, *Decor and Lighting*
JULIUS RUDEL, *Music Director*
HIRAM SHERMAN, *Compere*

Program

1. Overture
Conducted by Julius Rudel
2. Ballet .... *"The Dancing Lesson" from "The Princess"*
Violette Verdy
Conducted by Mario Braggiotti
3. Opera .... Duet from *"Wuthering Heights"*
Phyllis Curtin, John Reardon
Conducted by Julius Rudel
4. Theatre .... *"The Time of Your Life"*
Franchot Tone, Lonny Chapman, Paula Laurence,
Len Doyle
5. Light Opera .... *Two songs by Kurt Weill*
Lotte Lenya
6. Theatre .... *"The Teenagers"*
Mike Nichols and Elaine May
7. Ballet .... *"Western Symphony"*
Ensemble

INTERMISSION

8. Light Opera .... *"Abbondanza" from "The Most Happy Fella"*
9. Light Opera .... *"Happy to Make Your Acquaintance" from "The Most Happy Fella"*
Norman Atkin, Paula Stewart
10. Theatre .... *Scene from "A Streetcar Named Desire"*
Tallulah Bankhead, Sandy Campbell
11. Opera .... *Sextette from "Street Scene"*
Jacquelynne Moody, Jack De Lon, Arthur Newman,
Arnold Voketaitis, Beatrice Krebs, Andrew Frierson
Conducted by Samuel Krachmalnick
12. Light Opera .... Divertissement
Larry Adler, Paul Draper
13. Light Opera .... *"You Can't Get A Man With A Gun"*
"I Can Do Anything Better Than You Can" from "Annie Get Your Gun"
Martha Raye, David Atkinson
14. Ballet .... *"Stars and Stripes"*
Melissa Hayden, Jacques d'Amboise

Wow, so thrilled to be in this company!

movie stars like Fred Astaire and Gene Kelly. Cy Coleman had composed hits like "Witchcraft" sung by Frank Sinatra.

"You play her crippled sister."

"A cripple—in a musical? Where's the humor in that?" Obviously there would be no dance solo for me.

"Just be there... and have Burt play for you."

"I can't, it's his birthday." Burt Bacharach or "Happy" as I called him, was my ex-husband, composer/pianist.

"Burt's out of town," I told Gus, "but I'll be there."

Auditions were never a problem. I rather liked turning nervousness into energy. I called my back-up accompanist, Phil Della Penna, and he met me at the Alvin at 12:30 p.m. He was always late but knew all my songs. I filled him in that Lucille Ball was starring in the show.

"Lucille Ball is doing the show?!" He acted like she was the Pope and I was from Mars. At that moment I felt embarrassed at my being so uninformed. We waited a short time, and then my name was called. I walked to center stage while Phil went toward the piano stage right. As usual, the director, composer and their flunkies were down about the fifth row in the dimly lit theater. We exchanged brief "hellos." My old pal Cy Coleman was there and blew me a kiss. Then we got down to business.

Phil began with a flourish. I was confident—my voice sounded great—in an empty theater I reverberated like Merman. It was not unusual for me to have applause afterward, but this time, I was met with stony silence. They all got up as a group and retreated to the back of the theater to talk. They stayed there too long for my liking. Finally, Michael Kidd came down to the apron with a sheepish look on his face.

"Paula, I'm sorry, you're too much like Lucille Ball," he said.

Huh?! At the time, I had no idea what a compliment that was, but I did begin to realize she was someone very special to command all this deference. I started thinking maybe I needed to get out more. Truth be told, I was grateful because I didn't want the part anyway. Who wants to limp through a musical, especially after I'd just garnered rave reviews in *A to Z*, had received congratulatory

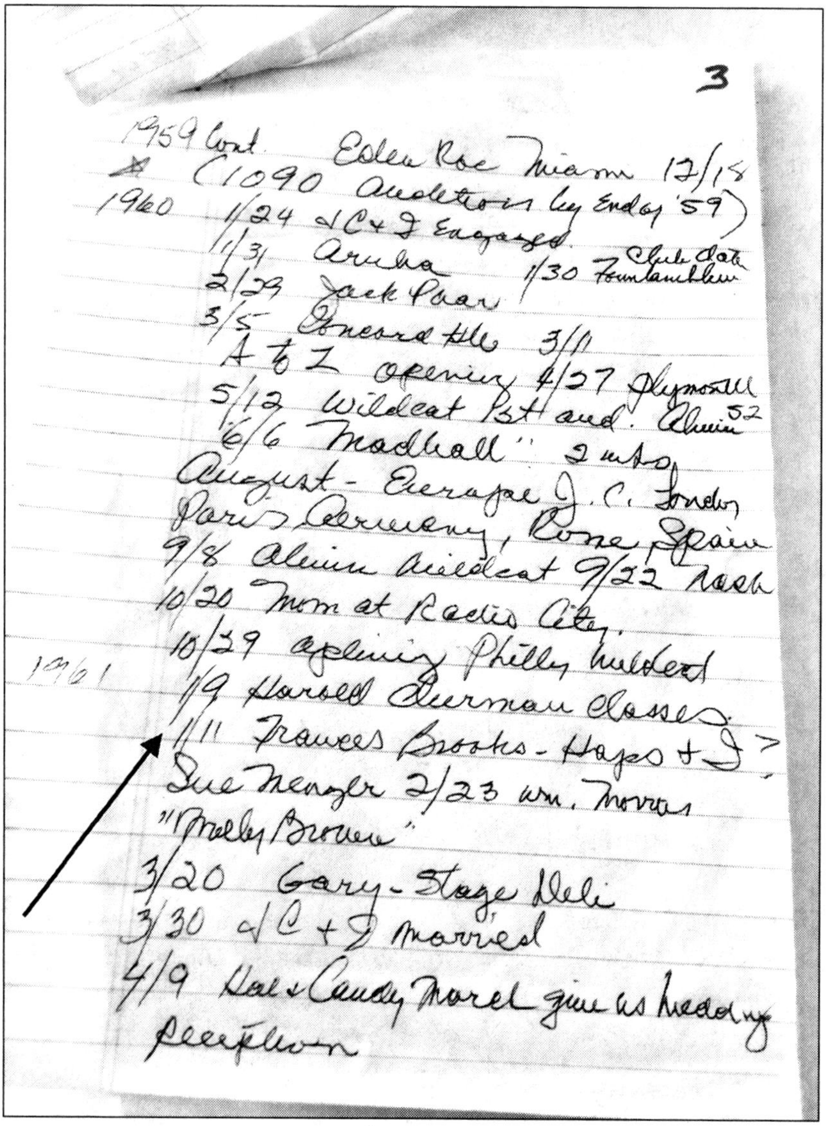

3

1959 Cont. Eden Roc Miami 12/18
(1090 auditions by End of '59)
1960 1/24 JC + I Engaged.
1/31 Aruba 1/30 Fountainbleau Club date
2/29 Jack Paar
3/5 Concord Hotel 3/11
A & Z opening 4/27 Plymouth
5/12 Wildcat 13th and Alvin 52
6/6 "Madhall" 2 wks
August - Europe J.C. London
Paris Germany, Rome, Spain
9/8 Alvin Wildcat 9/22 Nash
10/20 Mom at Radio City
10/29 opening Philly Wildcat
1961 1/9 Harold Auerman Classes
1/11 Frances Brooks - Haps + I >
Sue Mengers 2/23 Wm. Morris
"Molly Brown"
3/20 Gary - Stage Deli
3/30 JC + I married
4/9 Hal + Candy Morel gave us wedding
reception

Highlights of my crazy A to Z life. Even engaged to Jack, Burt (Happy) and I are still performing together for the Duke and Duchess of Windsor at the home of Frances Brooks.

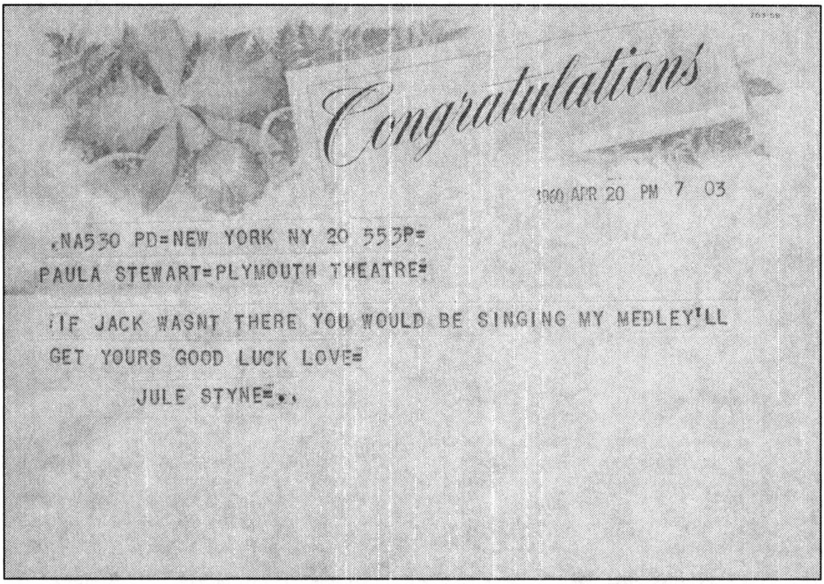

Congratulations

1960 APR 20 PM 7 03

.NA530 PD=NEW YORK NY 20 553P=
PAULA STEWART=PLYMOUTH THEATRE=

IF JACK WASNT THERE YOU WOULD BE SINGING MY MEDLEY'LL
GET YOURS GOOD LUCK LOVE=
JULE STYNE=..

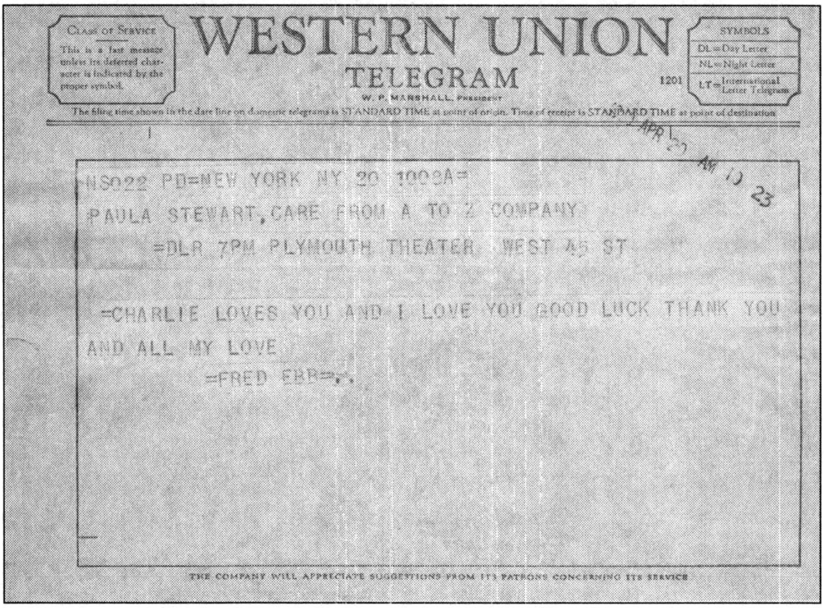

WESTERN UNION
TELEGRAM
W. P. MARSHALL, PRESIDENT

CLASS OF SERVICE
This is a fast message unless its deferred character is indicated by the proper symbol.

SYMBOLS
DL=Day Letter
NL=Night Letter
LT=International Letter Telegram

1201

The filing time shown in the date line on domestic telegrams is STANDARD TIME at point of origin. Time of receipt is STANDARD TIME at point of destination

NS022 PD=NEW YORK NY 20 1003A=
PAULA STEWART,CARE FROM A TO Z COMPANY
=DLR 7PM PLYMOUTH THEATER WEST 45 ST

=CHARLIE LOVES YOU AND I LOVE YOU GOOD LUCK THANK YOU
AND ALL MY LOVE
=FRED EBB=..

THE COMPANY WILL APPRECIATE SUGGESTIONS FROM ITS PATRONS CONCERNING ITS SERVICE

telegrams from Woody Allen, Fred Ebb and Jule Styne himself for my show-stopping dance number! So, I dismissed it.

Wildcat and Miss Ball were entirely forgotten by dinner that evening. I had other priorities going on in my life such as putting the finishing touches on my nightclub act. Plus, I had just made my recording debut on the album *The Gershwin Years* for Decca

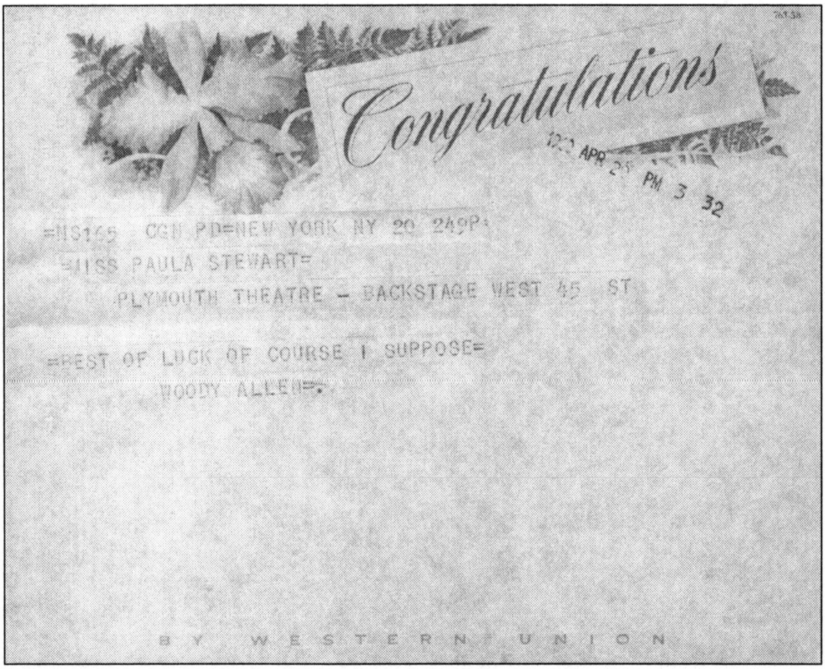

Congratulations

APR PM 3 32

=NS165 CGN PD=NEW YORK NY 20 249P=

=MISS PAULA STEWART=

PLYMOUTH THEATRE – BACKSTAGE WEST 45 ST

=BEST OF LUCK OF COURSE I SUPPOSE=

WOODY ALLEN=.

BY WESTERN UNION

Woody wrote one of the hysterical sketches I did in A To Z in which I played the Harpo Marx character doing the "gookie" face.

Records that was conducted and arranged by George Bassman. Billboard gushed, "*The definite Gershwin Album of this year or any other! . . . 58 Gershwin songs thrillingly performed by . . . superb soloists ...*"

I was on my way to being the hottest thing on Broadway and I was engaged to comedian Jack Carter. My life was truly fine. What more could I ask for?

Two days later when Jack returned from his performance in Las Vegas, I told him what had happened.

"Paula, I gotta tell you, in my opinion, as far as your career goes, that's too bad," he said. "It certainly couldn't hurt to play second banana to Lucille Ball." Early in Jack's career he had hosted a television variety program called *Cavalcade of Stars* and then later his own program entitled *The Jack Carter Show.* I did respect his opinion.

It just so happened that Jack's agent, Danny Welkes, was squiring Lucy around New York. She told Danny she wasn't thrilled with Michael Kidd's choice to play her sister, Kidd's then-girl-

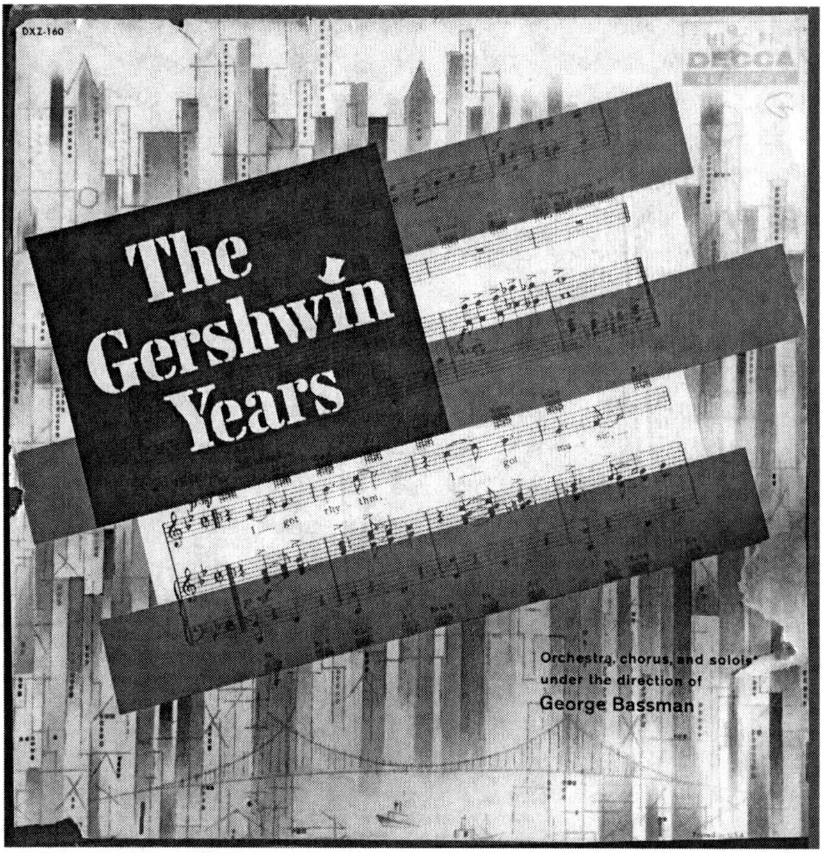

1959. A multi-disk record set and highly acclaimed. I was recording this during the day and performing The Most Happy Fella *at the New York City Center at night. It was brutal, challenging and still amazes me that I was able to do both at the same time*

friend, Jill Corey. Danny told Lucy about me and asked her why I wasn't cast in the role. Lucy hadn't heard about me, but when she inquired, Michael Kidd told her he had seen me, but felt I was too much like her.

"What's wrong with that?" Lucy snapped back. "She's supposed to be my sister!" Another audition was scheduled, only this time, Lucy would make the final decision.

Meanwhile, I had no idea that Jack and Danny quickly plotted for me to meet Lucy the night before my callback. Danny was with Lucy at the El Morocco, a legendary nightclub in the heart of Manhattan. But moments before entering the place I got wind that Lucy was aware that Jack was bringing me in order to meet her. I refused to go inside, not out of fear, just indignation. In my book, that wasn't the way to get hired. Like sleeping with someone to get the job, which was a no-no in my book.

Lucy and Danny were waiting for me to come in, while Jill Corey, who also coincidentally happened to be in the club, approached Lucy and introduced herself to Lucy as her "sister."

"The hell you are," Lucy laughed. "The girl who's playing my sister is outside the club and is afraid to come in!"

The next day when I arrived at the theater for the audition, Lucy was seated in the very last row. I hadn't sung two bars when I heard her yell, "That's it!" For all I knew, she was calling for "the hook"—you know—get her off! I started to get my music and leave when Michael Kidd came down to the edge of the stage and said, "Have your agent call me."

I got the part. Gus was thrilled. I thought, "Shit, another ingénue..." Most of my friends thought it was the opportunity of a lifetime. It was, but not in a career sense. It was the beginning of a thirty-year friendship unlike any other in my life.

★ ★ ★

Lucy financed *Wildcat* through Desilu, the company she owned with her now ex-husband Desi Arnaz, ultimately investing $360,000 in the show for 36 percent of the profits and the rights to the original cast recording. She also got to pick her leading man. Kirk Douglas was her first choice, but salary demands and a heavy film schedule eliminated him. Gordon MacRae, who had just starred in the movie versions of *Oklahoma!* and *Carousel*, was also considered before she selected Keith Andes, a rugged blonde with a beautiful voice...and the rest of him wasn't too bad either.

Nash had envisioned the lead character in her late twenties. He rewrote it for Lucy who'd just turned forty-nine. The story centered on Wildcat "Wildy" Jackson who arrives in Centavo City in 1912 with dreams of striking oil so that she can get her crippled sister medical help. All she lacks is the money and the know-how.

She sets her sights on "Joe Dynamite," the most successful crew foreman in the territory. He agrees to work with her, but is certain the property is dry.

Wildy tries to lure him with her feminine charms. When that fails, she has him falsely arrested, then released into her custody. Grateful, Joe agrees to work on the project but quits when he discovers it was Wildy who had him jailed. Left high and literally dry by her partner and crew, Wildy resorts to desperate measures to strike a gusher.

I didn't meet Lucy until rehearsals began. Jack and the rest of the world had finally drilled into me what a BIG star she was, but naturally I was eager to hear her sing. Rehearsals were usually held at one of the many dance studios on 6th Avenue. The whole cast was there, most dressed in dance leotards. I remember Lucy looked elegant in a black dress with black hose, a pearl necklace and a handsome red wig. She had regal stature.

Lucy was gracious and very friendly. I could see she was nervous. She shook everyone's hand and then sat at a long table for the "first read-through" of the script. It was in her delivery of the dialogue that I could tell this woman not only understood comedy, she had the great expansiveness necessary for the theater. She filled the room and had us all laughing. You could see the kids relax and settle in for a nice long run on the Great White Way.

When it came time for her to sing one of the songs, I could see sweat pouring down from the side of her wig, down her neck and continuing down to the dark spot accumulating under her armpits and down her black nylon stockings. Lucy was literally drowning in flop sweat. I felt so sorry for her. Then she sang. Her singing did indeed sound like Jimmy Durante as quoted many times by Cy Coleman. I couldn't help but notice the startled look on everyone's face. She was really bad. She didn't know how to breathe, how to phrase, let alone how to stay on pitch.

The "gypsies," a term used to describe the chorus and dancers, looked the other way and there was a thundering silence. I am sure they must have known that Lucy was embarrassed beyond belief having to expose her utter lack of musicality. I could feel her pain. Nobody said anything. Nobody would dare say anything.

While her celebrity status held the rest of the cast at bay, I could see the poor woman needed some help. It never occurred to me not to offer any.

Without thinking, during a break, I ran over to her before she could light her cigarette and asked, "Would you like me to help you with the songs?"

She grabbed my hands, pulled me into her, threw her arms around me and said, "Would you please??!!" She knew I meant it in the kindest way.

At the following rehearsal, I suggested that Swen Swenson, the lead male dancer in the show and good friend of mine since our days in summer stock theater in the early fifties, help Lucy with her dancing. He was a strict taskmaster, as was I. Between the two of us, we got her through the nightmare of rehearsals and the out-of-town tryout.

Lucy was now fifty. Although she was in great shape, she would be carrying the whole show for eight performances a week. She was in almost every scene dancing, talking or singing. The first thing that had to go was the cigarettes. I explained to her that I, too, was a smoker, but that during the entire run of any show, I also had to give it up.

"Lucy, it's extremely damaging to the vocal cords, it deprives your body of oxygen and you don't have as much energy for the show, and believe me, you'll need it."

"Whaaat? Well, who told you that?"

"My father. He's a doctor."

"Oh. Well, okay."

Lucy knew in her heart she couldn't smoke so I got no argument from her. She quit and that increased her overall energy and the dynamics of her performance. I taught her my singing method, which I learned from Mary Martin's teacher, a yoga-type method of breathing and muscle control of the ribcage. When I showed Lucy these relaxation techniques, she loved them because they were so ridiculous.

In one, I had her panting like a dog to work her diaphragm. This was called an "Ooom." In another—Lucy's favorite—she filled her mouth with crackers and chewed and talked at the same time.

The exercise gets your tongue moving freely and eases up the throat, but bits of crackers spill out of your mouth like a real slob. Eventually, the crackers are eliminated and the chewing is minimized. Has anyone ever watched Johnny Mathis chew up a song?

Anyway, Lucy thought that was hilarious. During the run of the show, she loved to stand in the wings and try to break me up by mimicking the chewing routine. What a great student she was, with phenomenal concentration and attention to detail. She worked hard and improved at a remarkable rate. By the time of the cast album recording, she was in control and very pleased with herself... and with me.

Lucy returned the favor and saved my job later when we took *Wildcat* to Philadelphia for the out of town tryout, before we hit Broadway. I was a "method" actress, always searching for the truth in an emotion or a scene. Michael Kidd had no patience with method actors. After all, the part wasn't that involved; it was a musical, not Shakespeare. Most of the dialogue was a set up for a song anyway, but as a pro I was always prepared.

I was underplaying the disabled ingénue being introspective. Lucy came over to me in a break and said, "You're going to get replaced if you don't show them a performance right now. Do it and forget that actor shit!" I understood. So, using the acting technique of "indicating," like pretending to cry when there are no tears, I kept my job which is really what Lucy wanted. She liked having me around. Lucy made me feel like her real sister. She was protecting me. I had been there for her and she was now there for me, foreshadowing the tone of our friendship over the years to come.

Quid pro quo.

★ ★ ★

If anyone wants to know what it was like working with Lucy on stage, just ask the cast members, future stars Valerie Harper and Hal Linden who were among the chorus. Lucy had a way of making everyone feel important and loved, and the cast was so sup-

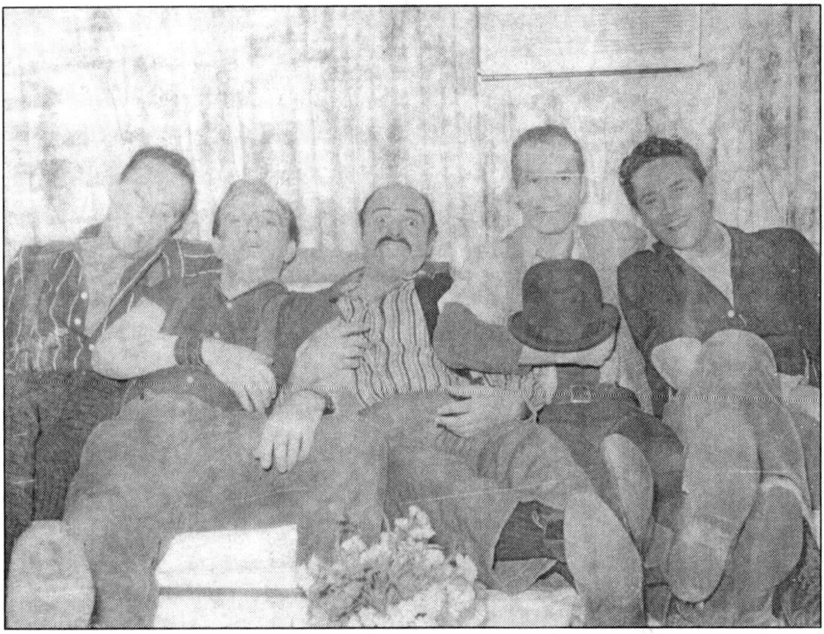

Backstage in Lucy's dressing room on Wildcat. *Swen Swenson and Hal Linden on the right. Hal was in the chorus then.*

portive and proud of their star that didn't act like a "star." I was impressed by her humanity and genuine care for everyone.

Lucy loved hanging out with the gypsies. This was a person I knew I could be good friends with. Her dressing room had a small anteroom with a large sofa where the cast members, especially the male chorus members would come by and hang out between acts. It was like one big happy family, with her kibitzing and joking with everyone. Even the stagehands adored her because she came across like a regular person. It was a very relaxed atmosphere and she was glad to have them around. We all got along like a house on fire. I was beginning to see that it was just what she needed after her devastating public divorce.

Even though the news media were not the piranhas they are today, (i.e., Brad and Jen and even pre-Dick and Liz) most celebrities were not accustomed to having every detail of their break-up publicized, but Lucy's divorce was different. America's favorite couple split and the demand to know why was enormous. Everybody had an opinion about it...everybody, seemingly, except me, that is. In hindsight, maybe that was part of the attraction for Lucy. I didn't have any preconceived notions or judgments.

I hadn't seen her show, hadn't read the stories, and hadn't slept with Desi, which made me an instant candidate since I was a very rare thing to be sure. We were just two gals getting to know each other, sharing our secrets, becoming pals. After the divorce, she was isolated and distrustful of people and rightfully so. Lucy poured her heart out to me about Desi.

"The worst part," she confessed, "I'm still in love with the sonofabitch." At this point, I was still enough of an optimist to hope that she could overcome this painful hurdle in her life.

"Paula, I wrestled long and hard with my decision to leave him and still have this terrible guilt because of the kids. I just couldn't put up with his drinking and womanizing anymore. His office 'casting couch' was worn out during our show! The public humiliation was just too much."

I thought she was amazing. Can you imagine, at the critical age of forty-nine, Lucy had the guts to walk away from both her marriage and Hollywood to try something entirely different: Broadway. Wow! At 31 my own worst problems were yet to come. My "big sister" was an inspiring role model. When those problems hit, Lucy was a true friend, ready to do battle with anyone who challenged me.

★ ★ ★

After a month of rehearsals in New York, we were ready for the out of town tryouts in Philadelphia. We had just started when Harry Millard came to cheer me on. Of course, I introduced him to Lucy after the show and went out for drinks. I could tell Lucy was as charmed by him as I was. Harry sported rugged, movie star handsome and was an actor also.

Harry Millard Williams was a wealthy socialite, very much in favor with the upper crust ladies of the day and in demand for his good looks, bizarre ways, and lavish parties. Where *Gatsby* had a need to impress, people were impressed by Harry. As wild as he was, he had an earthiness to him that decried all the bullshit.

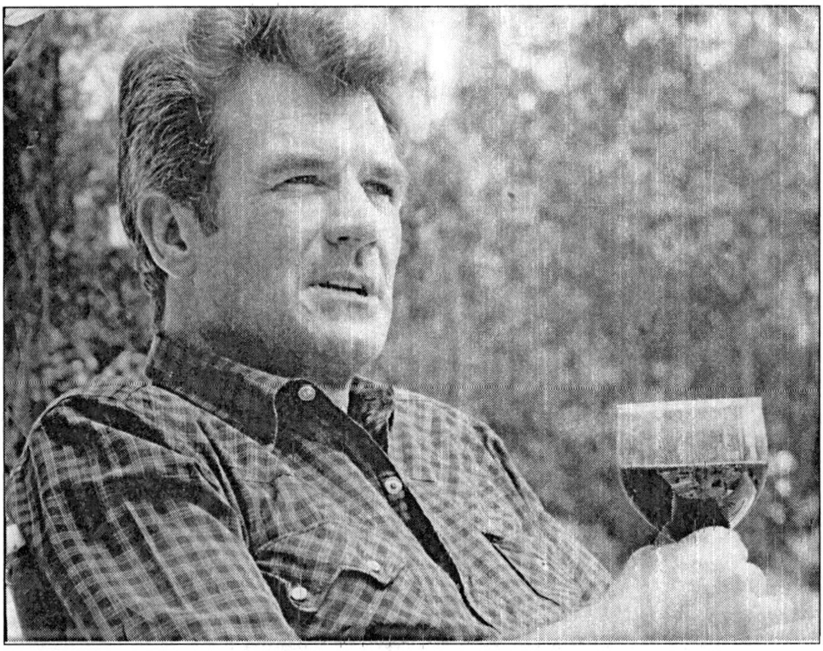

Harry Millard. What can I say?

He saw beyond the phonies, pomp and puffery. Nothing kept him from his own eccentricities. He was off-beat—for example, he drove a hearse. Harry had a rugged demeanor that dispelled his obvious breeding and class. And he was Captain of the American Polo Team. How cosmopolitan can you get? He also studied acting under the tutelage of Sanford Meisner at the Neighborhood Playhouse, which is where we first met.

After our evening and before the next night's show, Lucy called me into her dressing room. I couldn't imagine what she wanted. She sat me down and said, "Are you kidding? What's up with you and Harry? I have to know. There's obvious chemistry between you two? I know you love Jack, but what goes on here?"

I explained we were acting partners and in the beginning, as it was with Burt, it was not love at first sight. There is an intimate interaction that happens in scenes when the chemistry clicks. I can understand why actors working in movies often have affairs. And ours began like that.

"It's simple, Lucy, he just doesn't want to get married. We really have something, but it was going nowhere. I want a family. I had to move on."

"Oh, dear," Lucy sighed, "we all have our crossroads to contend with." It wasn't a judgment, but I stuffed that information somewhere into the back of my mind.

In Philly, Lucy really let loose, being less reclusive and more alive. She started inviting everyone in the cast to some of the local pubs. A new dance was being introduced around town—the twist—and Lucy loved it and was good at it.

★ ★ ★

During her vocal and physical sessions with Swen and me, Lucy became intrigued listening to us talk about Bucks County. A stone's throw from Philadelphia, it housed the Bucks County Playhouse in New Hope where big stars like Don Murray, Efrem Zimbalist, Jr., Jack Cassidy, Colleen Dewhurst, E.G. Marshall, and Lois Smith would go and perform shows there. Swen and I were big antique aficionados and had both worked many summer stock shows at the Playhouse. We knew where all the hidden treasures were in the old roadside barns and antique stores. Lucy overheard us planning an excursion for our one day off from the show and interrupted.

"I'm coming along," she stated.

"Well, you'll need grubby clothes and some really sturdy shoes," Swen told her.

"What do you think my rehearsal clothes are? Let's go!" So, on a Sunday we jumped into Lucy's limo.

"Bucks County!" she ordered.

It was a beautiful drive in autumn and the air was brisk and energizing. We drove past St. John Terrell's Music Circus in Lambertville where Swen and I had performed many musicals. "Remember when Bob Goulet was in the chorus of *Kismet*, Paula?" Swen asked me.

"Oh yeah! He had a small part, but the featured role was in his pants," I laughed.

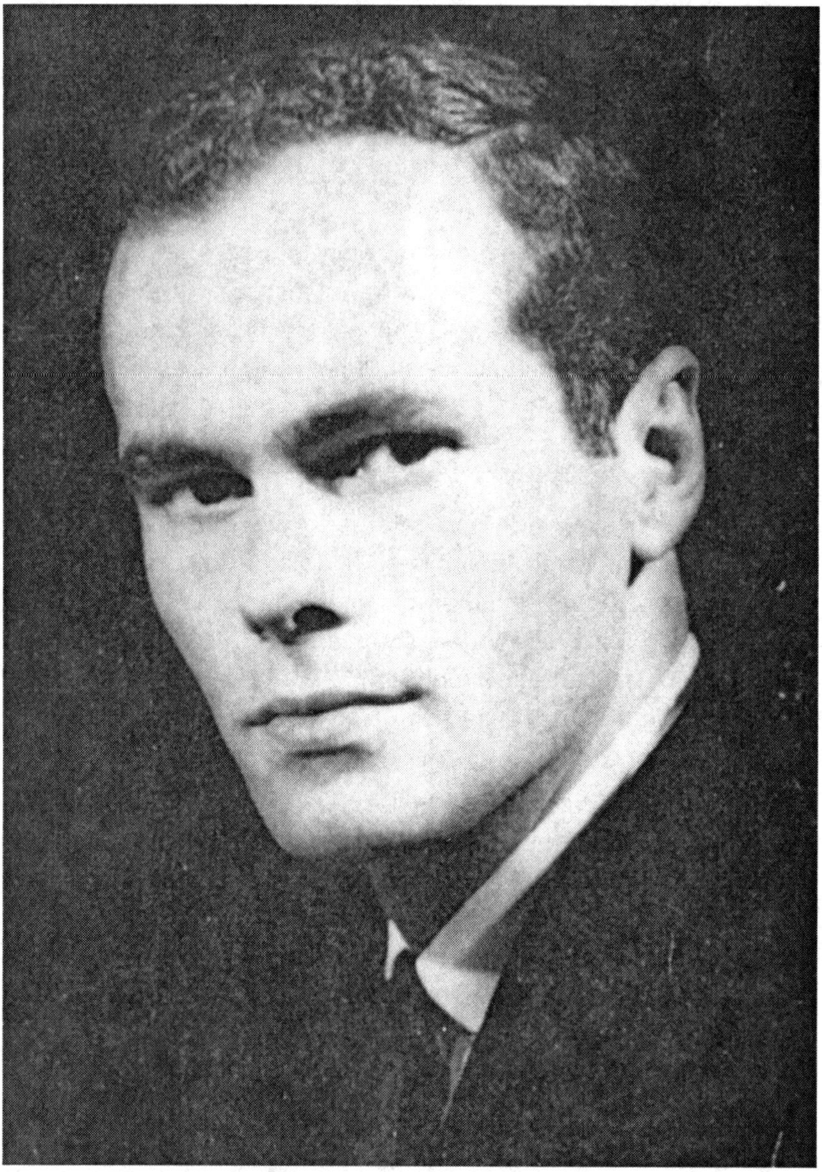

Swen Swenson.

Lucy remarked, "Of course. You know right now he's starring in *Camelot* with Burton."

"Oh, we always knew he was going to be a BIG star, Lucy," I added as Swen and I chuckled. Lucy had to know more.

"So who else was in that chorus?" Lucy quizzically asked. Swen and I entertained Lucy with our wild stories, which she just ate right up.

When we got to Bucks County, naturally we visited all the "in" spots and I pointed out to Lucy the tiny house Burt and I rented while we were married. It had been our summer getaway from the big city. Lucy loved Bucks County. We drove up to The Bucks County Playhouse and had lunch at the Playhouse Inn run by Odette Myrtil, a once-famous French chanteuse. Then I looked up Bob Scoble, another friend of mine who owned one of the most fabulous little antique shops. I had known Bob since my days of *Brigadoon*. He was gay and lived there with his lover. Interestingly, I remember that he was one of a set of identical twins, however his other brother was straight. Go figure.

Lucy, ever the relentless inquisitor, hearing that I'd toured in the National Company with Bob was all ears to find out more about me, and here was someone I'd actually started my show biz career alongside when I was nineteen years old and fresh out of Northwestern University. Bob told her how we'd travel all the major cities, living out of our steamer trunks that held a basic hot plate to cook our meals on. It was my introduction to a life of gourmet inventiveness. Little by little, I kept adding more spices and fancier culinary equipment to my trunk. We hardly made enough money for the expenses or luxury of the local restaurants. In those days, I was in the chorus of *Brigadoon* and Virginia Oswald was the star. Her benefactor was none other than Fritz Loewe, the show's composer. Lucy remarked, "Isn't she the Virginia in our chorus?"

"Yes."

"And now you're playing a lead and she's in the chorus...life certainly is strange."

Lucy was the perfect person to go antiquing with. She loved a bargain. She'd pick something up and say, "What do you think of this, Paula?"

I'd say, "It's a piece of shit! If you like it buy it. It's certainly cheap enough." Most of the time she'd listen to me. Then we'd go out driving on the country roads. In those days, there were the most

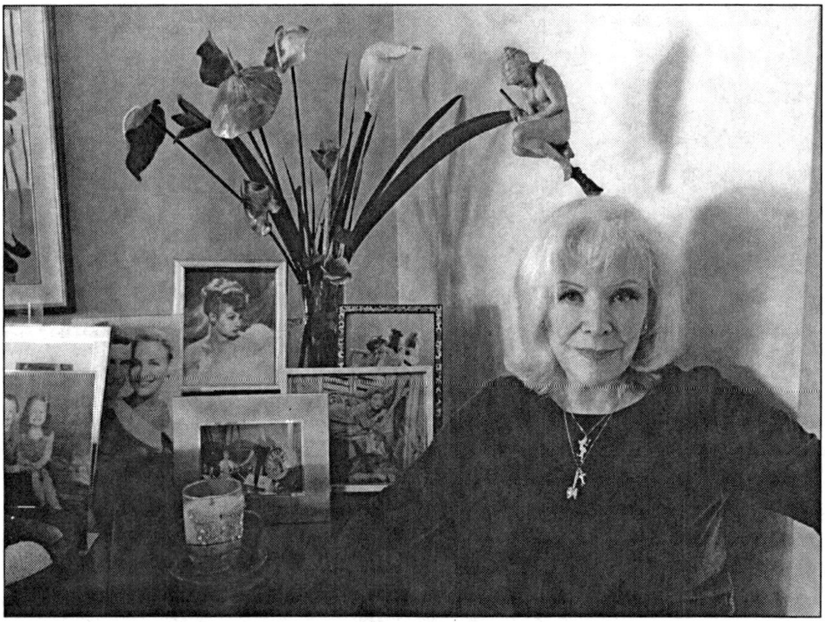

Above my head hangs the little witch on a broom that Lucy and I both wanted, but she insisted I keep.

incredible little barns where you could stop and poke around. They had wonderful assortments of all kinds of weird stuff.

In one of these places, Lucy and I were wandering through the different rooms; most of the stuff was covered with dust. You had to really scrounge around. Sometimes a treasure would pop out at you. And sure enough, we spotted this little item at the same time. It was a darling ceramic nude witch on a broom. She was about a foot long from beginning to end. We both wanted it. I said, "I got it first!" Lucy said, "No, I saw it."

"Alright Lucy, you want it, it's yours."

"Oh no, Paula, you take it."

"Lucy, listen, you know I'm always here in Bucks County. I can find this stuff any time."

"No, I want you to have this."

That's how generous she was. I still have this unusual little doll, and it hangs over Lucy's photo on my baby grand piano.

★ ★ ★

The opening of *Wildcat* took place in Philadelphia on October 29, 1960 to a glowing review from *Variety*. However, we hit a sour note with local reviewers. *Wildcat* was poorly received, and Lucy was shaken. She was the producer; it was her money at stake. Truth is, the music itself was good but the script was bad.

When Lucy wasn't onstage, it fell flat and went nowhere. The public only wanted to see her. Sensing something had to be done, the powers-that-be pushed her on stage every minute of the show to keep the audience amused. She called the person she relied on the most regarding her career, Desi.

He had an instinct of what was best for her and she had the highest respect for his opinion. He'd never let her fail and she knew that. She always credited the success of *I Love Lucy* to Desi. When he showed up, nursing a hangover, he pinpointed the problem at once after he saw the show. The public was coming to see Lucy, but instead they saw "Wildy," this strange new character and they just couldn't accept it. They wanted THE Lucy they knew and loved. Desi's solution was to inject "Lucyisms" into the show—much to the horror of Nash and Kidd. So, she gave them the Lucy "wail and wackiness" they expected from their TV idol. Lo and behold, the house would go crazy and I got to experience it first hand; the energy, the magic.

I remember one performance where she said to one of the male characters in the show, "Are you sure you don't know Fred Mertz?" which caused the audience to scream with laughter. Another night, the small Yorkshire Terrier in the show, Miss Mouse, had an accident on stage. With the next scene a big dance number, it was potentially a dangerous situation. Lucy ran off and came back with a mop and bucket. She ad-libbed to the audience, "I forgot to read the small print in my contract." The patrons couldn't get enough of her. Screw the critics, but never the audience. Michale Kidd and the writers were aghast, but they saw the difference in the audience response and I did too. They fought but she prevailed. Lucy did whatever had to be done to make the show a success. The public couldn't get enough of her. We were suddenly SRO—standing room only—nightly.

After that performance, we all had plans for dinner, but Lucy and Michael needed to meet about dialogue changes. She asked me to go ahead with Desi and she would meet us shortly. In hindsight, not a good idea. Desi was bombed. No sooner were we in the limo than he was on top of me. I had been warned about his wild lechery, but it never occurred to me that he would be so insensitive and attack me. I had to fight like hell. Thank god the restaurant was only a few blocks away.

When the car pulled close to the curb, I leaped out, flew into the restaurant and went directly to the ladies room with Lucy following close behind. My clothes were all twisted around and my makeup was smeared. I was furious. I bit my tongue, but she could see something wasn't right. She took a good guess, ran out and confronted Desi screaming, "You sonofabitch, how dare you!?" She knew he attacked me. Desi, by then, was melting into the leather booth in a drunken stupor. I witnessed first-hand why Lucy left him. He was gone long ago. Ever since then, Lucy could tell when I was stressed out.

Finally, we were ready for Broadway. After two previews, the show opened on December 16th at the Alvin. Local reviews were lukewarm, but audiences were red hot. Once again we played to SRO houses every night for the entire run. Even on heavy snowy nights, the lines at the stage door were long with fans hoping for a chance to see their idol and perhaps get an autograph. One thing about Lucy I witnessed over the many years of our friendship was that she never refused an autograph. Even during a blizzard she would sign as many as possible with her limo nearby ready to whisk her off.

One bitter, cold night in New York after the opening, we were to go to a special late party with her good friend Radie Harris, an elderly columnist, who incidentally had lost her leg and wore a prosthetic. Radie was patiently standing in the snow over a grate, when her wooden foot got caught somehow. We were already late for the event and it became increasingly clear that Radie was stuck. Lucy wouldn't think of abandoning her old friend who was freezing and panicky. We knew that getting an emergency wagon in that weather was going to take a while.

The fans had no idea what was happening, so Lucy just kept signing autographs as her fingers got so cold she couldn't hold a pen anymore. Lucy was shivering and starting to hyperventilate. Eventually the emergency wagon arrived and finally had to relieve Radie of her removable limb and cart her off to her home. They remained friends but rarely spoke of the incident. Lucy and I ended up at the party, snow-caked, wet and in no mood for frivolity. In later years, when I reminded Lucy of Radie and the grate, we shared a guilty laugh.

★ ★ ★

It was during the New York run, that my friendship with Lucy truly blossomed. Lucy had taken an apartment at the Imperial House on 150 East 69th Street.

Her kids, Little Lucie, eleven and Desi, Jr., seven, were also there for what was hoped to be a long run. On matinee days, I would join Lucy and her brood at a nearby restaurant. Lucy would play imaginary games with them. The favorite being fantasy trips

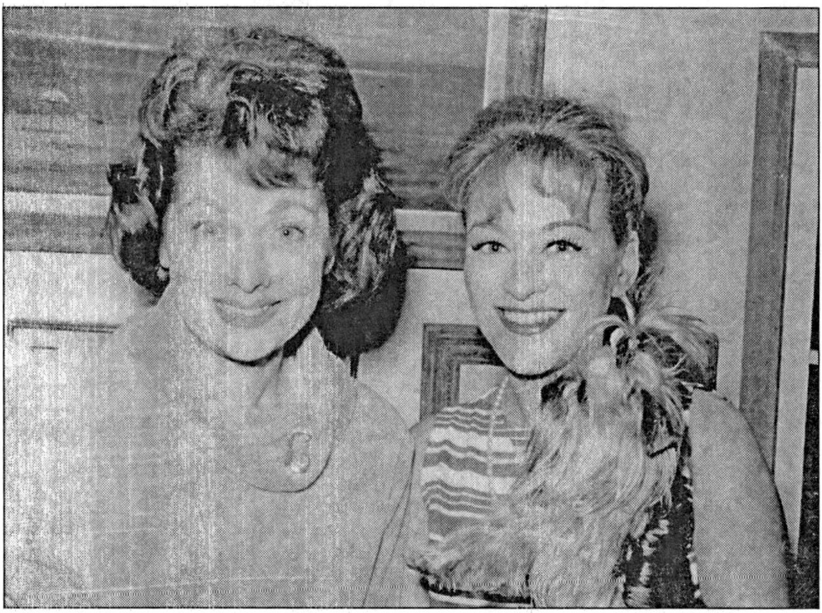

Jack took this photo of Lucy and me with my dog, Wildy, during rehearsals of Wildcat.

to foreign lands. She was a most caring and loving mother in my opinion. She spoke to me about being torn by the fact that she couldn't spend more time with her children, but when she did, it was meaningful.

One never gets a second chance to make a first impression, and so it is even with children. At an early age their personalities are very evident. My impression of the kids remained the same as they grew up. My most clear recollection was that Little Lucie was withdrawn and not eager to participate in her mother's games. She rarely smiled and was slumped down in her seat with a pout on her face. Lucy confided in me that she felt so badly because she had taken the kids away from their comfortable California home to the cold sterile environment of apartment living in New York.

Lucy could see Little Lucie's disenchantment with her preoccupation with the show. I could understand Lucy's dilemma, but when she asked, "What am I going to do, Paula?" I had no good answer.

"That's life, isn't it?"

On the other hand, Desi, Jr. was gung-ho to participate with Lucy's fantasy trips as he was always cheerful and smiling.

★ ★ ★

Lucy wasn't snobbish and there was nothing phony about her. I truly admired this. She was down to earth and friendly and never played the diva card. Just a regular gal that was so comfortable to be around. Her motherly concern for me made it easy for me to trust her.

Lucy loved my sense of humor. She also liked that I was educated and well-versed in areas such as art and decorating. She felt she could ask me about anything and I could explain things to her that were beyond her knowledge and she enjoyed that about me. We were becoming confidants.

As girlfriends are prone to become involved in each other's lives, she professed her concern about the fact that I was engaged to Jack Carter. Aside from hosting his own variety show on television and having starred on Broadway with Sammy Davis, Jr. in *Mr. Wonderful*, Jack was one of the top comedians of the time.

"Paula, you know I like Jack a lot. He's funny and amusing but is he is the right person for you?" Lucy queried.

To tell the truth, she hit a nerve with that one because I was silently conflicted myself. I knew she was just being a mentor. Even after my failed marriage to Burt, I was still an emotional novice. And by this point, Lucy was very aware of the other man in my personal closet—Harry Millard. I had known him since my days at The Neighborhood Playhouse when we had been scene partners. She had witnessed how close we still were. I called him my best friend.

Throughout my life, my father, Dr. Walter Zürndorfer, had been pressuring me to get married. "Poppy" was a highly regarded doctor in Chicago and came from a prominent family in Germany. I can't make any presumptions, but Poppy's impeccable records and extensive photographs indicate that his great grandfather was actually named Levi Strauss and the Zürndorfers owned an early version of a retail department store. Who knows if there's a "jean" (gene) connection somewhere in Poppy's family tree.

Poppy was elegant with a charming German accent and demeanor. He spoke seven languages fluently, was an accomplished concert pianist, and was the president of the Flying Physicians of

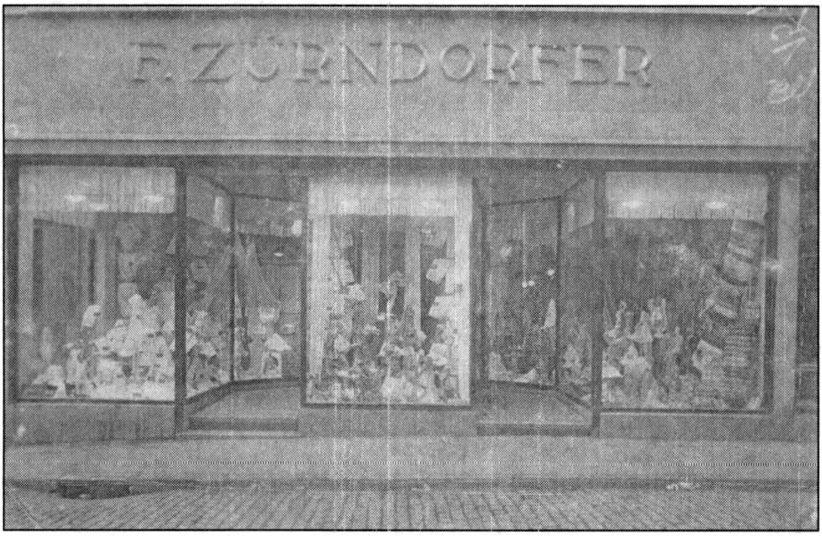

My family's retail store in Dortmund, Germany from the late 1800s.

America. (In 1973 he was the recipient of the FPA Distinguished Service Award and was featured on the January 1974 cover of FPA's magazine with Adarine, his best and last wife, who was also a pilot. All the women, including me, in Poppy's life had to be pilots.) He was a hard man to say "no" to. I told Lucy what my father constantly nagged when I first moved to New York. "What am I going to tell my patients—I have an unmarried daughter in show business?" I shut him up for a while when I married Burt. But when Burt and I divorced, my disappointed father said, "What am I going to tell my patients—I have a divorced daughter in show business?"

"I have to meet your father," Lucy said.

On December 16, 1960 Poppy came to the opening of *Wildcat* in New York. Lucy told me to bring him backstage immediately after the show. He complimented Lucy on her energy to which she confessed she was exhausted! He asked politely if he could feel her pulse.

"It's slightly rapid. Maybe you should relax a little bit." Lucy was taken by my father's instinctive concern for her well-being, and

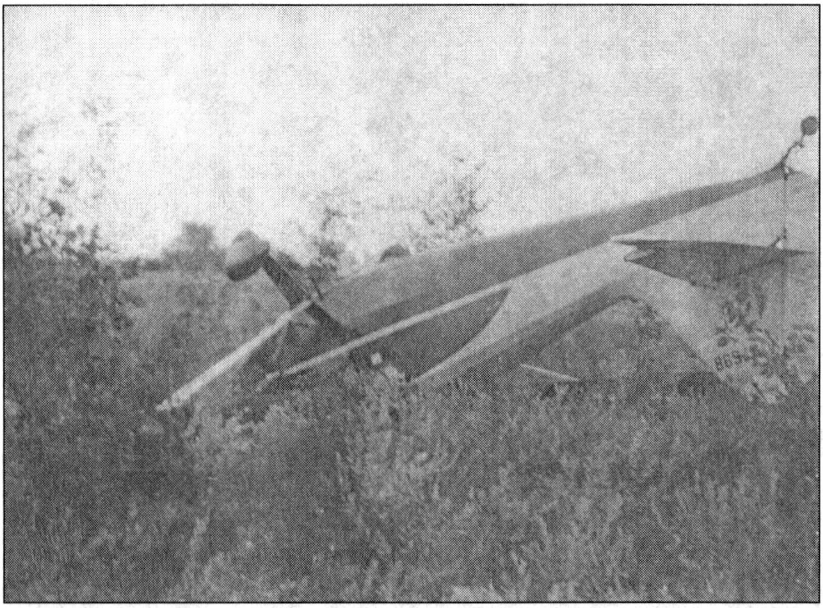

My Cessna after landing in a field and hitting an overgrown ditch. My handsome passenger was glad to be alive and immediately lost my number.

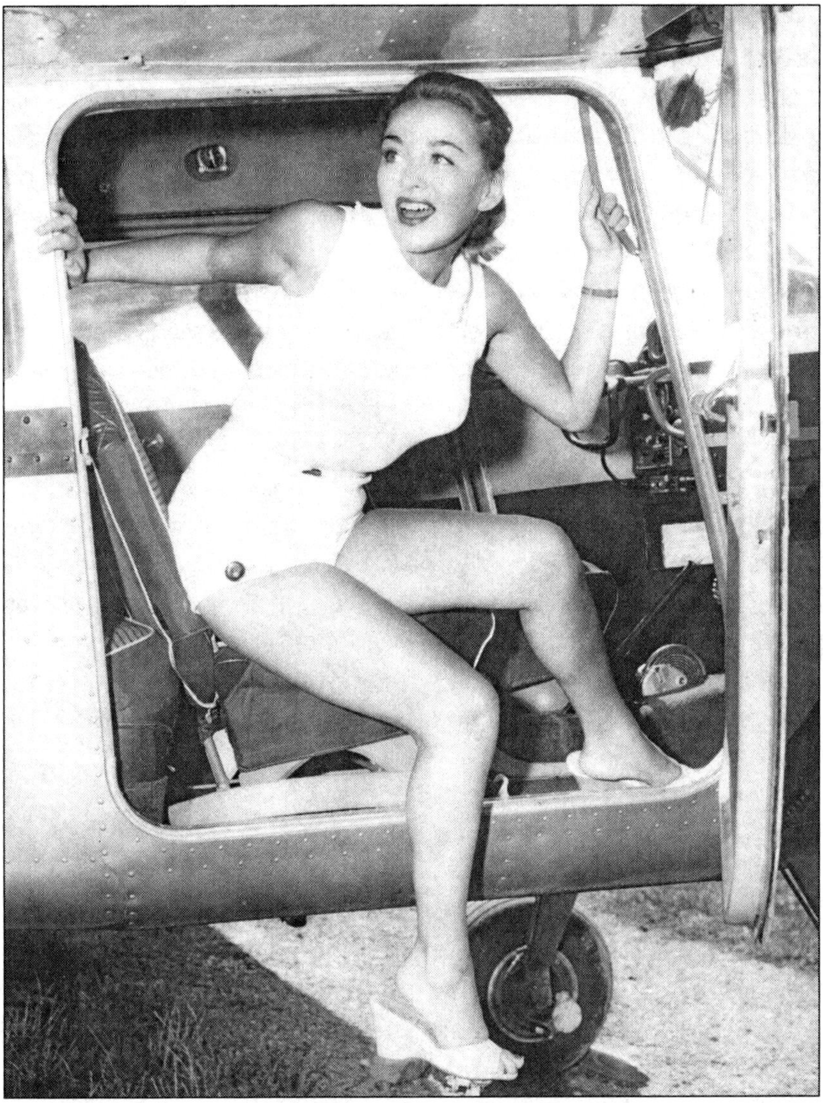

Deplaning at Santa Monica Airport after a few spins. Note the heels which I always wore. - Photo credit Herman Seid

she insisted he join us for dinner. He did and proceeded to tell Lucy about the time I crashed my Cessna when I was eighteen.

"Whaaat!!!" Lucy was wide-eyed. How could I keep that one from her? Yes, I had my own plane as Poppy insisted all his wives and children learn to fly. At the time of the accident, I was attending Northwestern University in Chicago.

"Well, she was still in one piece but the plane was *kaput*," my father told Lucy. Lucy asked him if he had been angry to which he replied, "How could I be? It wasn't Paula's fault. She made a miraculous landing after engine failure on the take off. She is lucky to be alive and here working with you." It's true. At a thousand feet, the engine cut out but I was able to land in a field, where the wheels hit an overgrown ditch and flipped the plane over. *The Chicago Tribune* reported "Co-ed Lands Disabled Plane" and declared my landing "masterful" with a photo of me in a chic suit and shamelessly wearing platform heels, no less. My vanity was showing.

On the many occasions through the years when my father came to California, Lucy always insisted on having him over for dinner. She enjoyed listening to his stories mainly about me. Lucy made me feel that I was the real superstar at the table. She was also genuinely thrilled that the spotlight was off of her. My father was an amusing and excellent conversationalist and Lucy just loved listening to him talk especially with such admiration for his daughter. She was enthralled by his knowledge, style and, of course, his "charming German accent."

★ ★ ★

After my dad left New York, Lucy became ever more aware how conflicted I was between Harry and Jack. She had already listened for hours how I came to love both of them and which one would be best for me. Lucy knew about and didn't like Jack's reputation as a lady-killer.

"Paula, you know he's compulsive, don't you?" she said.

"Oh, I've seen his roving eye, because when I first met him he was going with this really attractive brunette. I even said to him at the time, 'Why are you flirting with me?' He was so persistent, that I finally acquiesced and jokingly told him to take my mother out to dinner first. If she likes you, I'll give you a chance."

"Did he take your mother out?"

"Yes! She even called me backstage when I was performing in *The Threepenny Opera* to tell me what a good time she had."

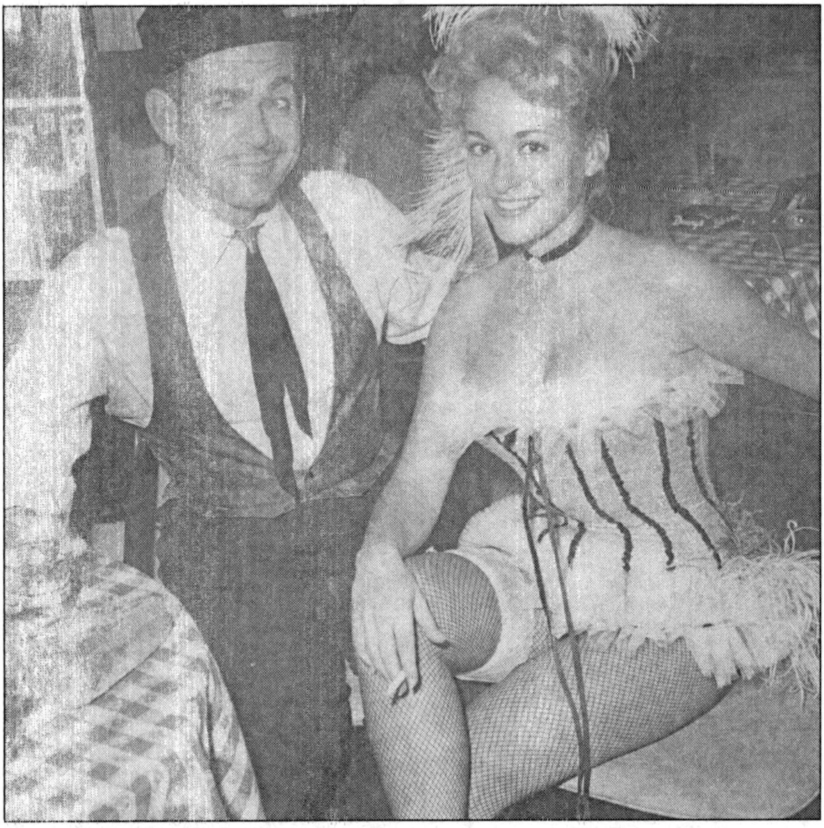

Jack as Clark Gable and I as Belle Starr at a Wild West party at Danny's Hideaway, a popular celebrity spot.

Truth was, there was an attractive quality about Jack. His passion and energy was so infectious and compelling. Aside from that, I was flattered that he wasn't jealous of my career. In fact, Jack took such an interest that he wanted to promote an act together.

Lucy really understood because Desi had been so helpful in her career. She made the connection of how I depended on Jack because she depended on Desi, but still, kept questioning my relationship with Jack. An interesting comment she made to me once during rehearsals was, "You know, Paula, I met Desi in *Too Many Girls* and it ended with too many girls."

★ ★ ★

From the conversations with Lucy about what was going on with my love life, I was beginning to realize what was lacking in hers. I mentioned to Jack many times that I thought she was missing something—a man. Lucy was still a beautiful woman and looked much younger than her years—had the body of a thirty-five-year-old. Lucy still owned Desilu. She was a hot prize and Hollywood moguls were making a play for her but Lucy suspected their intentions weren't necessarily sincere.

"Paula, they all want the same thing and it isn't motivated by love," she said.

Herb Segal was a perfect example. Herb was thirty-two, nice looking, suave, and ran General Artists Group, a big entertainment organization. He later would become CEO of Chris-Craft Industries, a premier luxury boat company. Herb had convinced his beautiful wife, Anne, to divorce him so he could woo Lucy and make a stab at the empire she controlled. Anne was so devastated that she confided this information to Lucy's mother, DeDe, who immediately told Lucy. Such deception left Lucy feeling depressed and even lonelier.

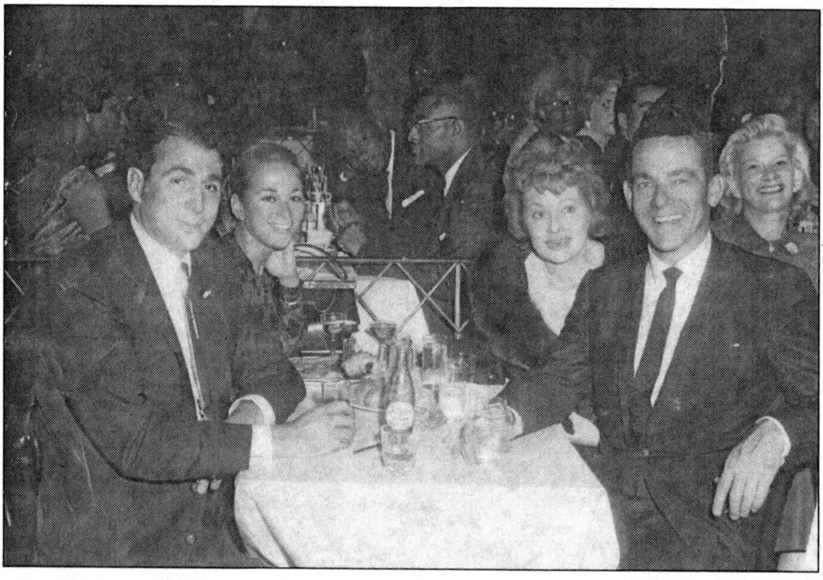

In our early days, Lucy could relax with Jack and me and we enjoyed each other's company. Here with Jack's and Lucy's agent, Danny Welkes before I introduced her to Gary Morton.

Without her knowledge, I began thinking about a suitable companion for her. I kept asking Jack to think about someone who wouldn't just be interested in Lucy's net worth or empire. Aside from being a stunner, Lucy also happened to be a warm, loving person with a great sense of humor. Surely there had to be someone who would be attracted to these stellar qualities. For godsake, the world loved her. There had to be one man out there who could see beyond her fame and fortune.

When Jack first introduced me to Gary Morton, "née" Morty Goldaper, he was an out-of-work comic who worked occasionally as an opening act for Johnnie Ray. When he did work, he commanded the low-rent sum of $200-a-week and was widely known to use discarded material from Jack's act and anyone else's he could borrow a joke from. That said, he had a few assets but none of them were financial. He was tall, nice-looking with an engaging laugh, but his real claim to fame was in his pants. He packed a wallop and that was no joke. He was quite the ladies' man.

In December of 1960 Gary was on the bill at Radio City and coincidentally, my mother, Esther Morris, was also working there as a wardrobe mistress to the Rockettes. My mother liked Gary but she couldn't wait to tell me how he was going through the Rockettes like a dose of salts.

"I can always tell which one he's gotten to," she joked, "when she can't make the high kicks the next day."

I talked it over with Jack and suggested he and Gary meet us one night after the show for a late night bite provided I could get Lucy to agree. "Lucy likes to laugh. She might find him fun. She isn't looking for a business partner; she just wants to have a couple drinks and a few laughs. Besides, he's harmless."

"Are you kidding? Gary isn't anywhere near her league. He can't afford her."

"That's not the point, Jack. She needs a little romance, not someone to support her. And Lucy can handle him."

So, Jack told Gary what I had in mind. After that, every time I saw him, poor Gary pleaded with me, "Please introduce me and I'll always be grateful. Please make it happen, Paula!!" Well, it didn't happen right away. Lucy just kept saying "no." But I was relentless. She finally agreed to go just to shut me up. One night after the show, we all met at a little cafe around the corner from the theater. Gary finally got his wish. By the way, I've read it erroneously reported by others that our meeting was at a pizza parlor. Wrong. It was Chinese food and it was at the Blue Moon Café.

From the outset, I could see the sparks fly between them. Gary was really "on," giggling through his teeth like a naughty schoolboy. Lucy however, was playing aloof, but flirtatious. She kept throwing cigarettes at him telling him to light them like a queen to her lackey. And like the mischievous knave, he threw them right back. I hadn't seen this side of Lucy. Yes, she kibitzed with the cast, but this was more youthful and coquettish. Even Jack was surprised by her behavior. They acted like a couple of teenagers. Lucy liked his sense of humor; he did make her laugh and his self-effacing attitude made her feel comfortable. Jack and I joined in, laughing and acting silly. It was just what she needed. After that, the four of us went out on a regular basis. Lucy and I grew closer than ever, and she became more confiding in me.

I also saw a change in Lucy. Her performances were brighter, more energized, her moods lighter. It wasn't just me, the rest of the cast noticed, too. Lucy would ask me about Gary, his family and what I knew about him.

"Paula, is there anything about Gary you haven't told me?" I knew she was getting serious and I had a hard time with that question.

Really, I only knew Gary through Jack and what I did know wasn't that bad. He had a penchant for pot—marijuana—like a lot of nightclub performers and musicians. Weed wasn't a big deal in those circles, but it was to his neighbors. They complained that the smell of it filled the hallway and you could get high just walking past his apartment.

Dating and bedding women is typical for any bachelor. The fact that he wore a rug seemed obvious, though Lucy later told me she didn't find out until they were making love. Gary had a good sense of humor, especially for a guy who was a lousy comic.

I remember Buddy Hackett's story about a club date of Gary's where he was doing a pantomime and the audience kept yelling, "Louder!" There are many tales of Gary's failures as a standup.

His greatest talent far and away was pleasing Lucy. I weighed whether or not these things were important enough to put the kibosh on Lucy's budding romance. I was so happy to see her laughing and enjoying herself, I was afraid of ruining it. I decided to say nothing "major" and left it at that. My decision to withhold these few possible negatives bothers me to this day. In the final analysis, he gave her many happy years. And, to my credit, I never thought she'd marry him; I just wanted to get her laid.

★ ★ ★

In the early part of 1961, despite the lukewarm reviews, Lucy triumphed as the new "Queen of Broadway."

Try to name a star that hadn't seen the show: Lansbury, Sinatra, Davis, Jr., Newhart, Hackett, Caesar, Sullivan, Hope; they all came to see their beloved Lucy on Broadway. For Lucy, the personal highlight was when Marlene Dietrich came to pay tribute.

A fact about Lucy that I don't think that anyone has ever mentioned was that Lucy idolized Marlene Dietrich, who personified her idea of a sexual icon. She even emulated her looks; the startled high eyebrows, the sunken cheeks, and her haughty sophisticated demeanor in most of her publicity photographs. Lucy often spoke to me of her infatuation with Marlene. One night Lucy excitedly pulled me aside off stage to tell me some news.

"Marlene is here, Paula. I want you to come back after the show to meet her." I had never told Lucy that I had already met Marlene, in Vegas when Burt was conducting her nightclub act. Marlene had paired up with Burt to retune the performance to maximize her limited musical range. The result was a spectacular show that was the hit of the Strip. In the show, she was ravishing, dressed in a seemingly see-through gown that had audiences gasping -- and me, too, when I first met her.

At the time, I was staying at Burt's suite at some small hotel on my way to Los Angeles for an audition in the upcoming Elvis Presley film, *King Creole*. At the time, Burt and I had been divorced for about one year, but remained friendly. We were no longer intimate. He was just being accommodating to me for a couple of days.

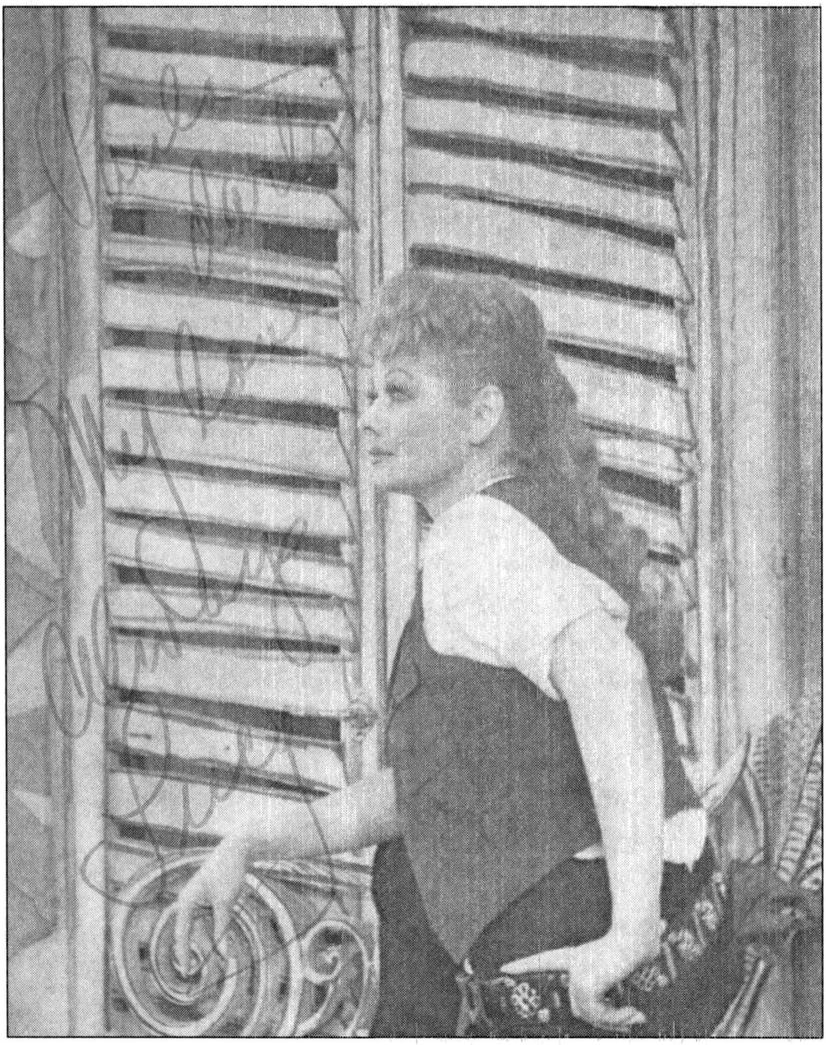

Wildcat *publicity. Working with Lucy, I, too, became an ardent fan.*

About mid-morning there was a knock on the door—the cleaning lady who had a kerchief around her head, a mop, a pail and rubber gloves. She pushed past me muttering in a German accent, "I vill be kvick!"

At first I didn't recognize her, but the accent clued me.

Oh my god! It's Marlene Dietrich!

A bit in shock, I pretended not to know who she was. She, in turn, must have thought I was some tootsie that Burt had left over from the night before. I held my breath and watched her go about cleaning like a pro, oblivious to my complete amazement. When she was finished she gathered up her equipment and left as quickly as she came.

I couldn't wait to ask Burt what the *hell* was that all about? What he said floored me. "She does it all the time, you know, like Joan Crawford."

Come to think of it, I have this same strange urge to some degree myself. My father called it the *Putzfrau complex*, a cleaning woman's compulsion to clean.

My answer to Lucy was, "Of course I'll meet her."

Marlene arrived with a flourish, resplendent in a stunning white satin moiré pantsuit with rhinestone epaulets on her shoulders and a magnificent white mink stole over her arm. Lucy was all a-twitter like a fawning fan. Marlene was effusive, congratulating her with kisses and hugs after which Lucy pointed toward me and said, "How about my sis here?"

I extended my hand as she looked at me quizzically. "Haven't ve met before?"

"I don't think so." Yeah, I lied.

"So, zis is who my Burt vas married to! Vhy vould he leave such a beauty?"

"*Ich weiss nicht,*" I replied. (I don't know)

"*Ach, Sie sprechen Deutsch*?" (Oh, you speak German?)

I winked at her and jokingly said, "*Niemand kann wissen, ob die Fische pissen.*" (Nobody knows if fish piss—a German non sequitur for "who knows").

Marlene heartily chuckled and said, "*Das stimmt.*" (That's true) She told Lucy, "I vil go sign *zum* autographs, vile you dress, *Liebchen.*" Meanwhile, Lucy was just staring at me dumbfounded.

"What did you just say to her?" So I told her.

"Whaaat!" Lucy exclaimed, "You just told Dietrich about fish piss? Well, I just give up. You're too much. Grab your things. You're coming with us to Danny's Hideaway."

"But, Lucy, I have plans with Jack."

"Bring him along. He can pick up the check!"

★ ★ ★

The critics, however, were not as supportive about *Wildcat* as Lucy's distinguished colleagues. She was constantly being pursued by the news media for interviews, which really were only interested in knowing whether she and Desi might get back together, much less about her taking on Broadway. Either that or they had it out for her.

Dorothy Kilgallen had a widely popular syndicated column *The Voice of Broadway* and was a regular on the game show *What's My Line*? For whatever reasons, Dorothy always made some sort of dig at Lucy and even Gary in her column. Lucy would tell me, "I don't understand why this woman has it in for me."

I thought perhaps it had something to do with the fact that Dorothy had tried to produce a musical on Broadway a few years earlier with her husband actor Richard Kollmar. It was a short-lived musical called *The Body Beautiful* that failed miserably. Ironically, back in the day, Richard had co-starred with Desi in *Too Many Girls*.

It was also well known that Dorothy was rumored to be having an "affair" with singer Johnnie Ray. Johnnie was a flamboyant performer who has been credited by Tony Bennett as the true father of rock and roll. He was also known to be a switch hitter, and as I mentioned before, the standup act occasionally on Johnnie's bill was none other than Gary Morton.

"Maybe she's just jealous that your show is sold out and you're going with a stud and she's stuck with a fairy," I would tell Lucy. She would pretend not to laugh but I could see her smile, "Anyway, who cares, it's certainly not changing the receipts at the box office!"

Earl Wilson, another famous columnist and a good friend of mine, begged me to get Lucy to agree to an interview. I told him the chances were slim; but if he promised **NO** Desi questions, she might talk to him. I explained to Lucy that he was harmless, a true professional with a good sense of humor. Furthermore, I trusted him.

"If you trust him, Paula, he's okay with me," Lucy said.

One afternoon, on a matinee day, between shows, Earl got his wish. Lucy insisted I come along as a safeguard and maybe some diversionary talk. We met at Sardi's, our favorite place where Vincent Sardi, Jr. would always make sure we weren't pestered and sat us in the "primo" section with our backs to the entrance. It was only 4:30 so the crowds had not arrived.

Lucy was looking forward to some little neck clams while my mouth was watering for that green turtle soup, frog legs and, of course, the "*piece de resistance*," a sinful desert called "*boccone dolce*," a combination of strawberries, whipped cream, crisp meringue drizzled with melted chocolate. Vincent gave me the recipe for it, which became a staple at all my future dinner parties.

Lucy and I were still in full make-up, but it was a leisurely meal. Soon after we were seated, another regular, Richard Burton arrived. At the time he was starring with Julie Andrews and Robert Goulet in *Camelot* at the Majestic Theater. I remember he wore a beige wool turtleneck sweater and a houndstooth jacket with leather patches at the elbows. He cut a very dashing figure. He had a script under his arm and though he was seated near us, he barely took any notice. The view was partially obstructed between us but I could see that he was engrossed in his reading.

Earl's line of questioning revolved around the show. How Lucy felt working on stage and her daily routine and so on. We had just recorded the show album for RCA. Lucy confided to Earl that she could never have gotten through it without my help, with all the singing scales, breathing techniques and the relaxing exercises that I had her practice every day. Especially the chewing one that she got a big kick out of demonstrating to everyone. Lucy thought it would be funny to show Earl.

When she did it, it astonished Earl, and caused Burton to jump out of his seat. He ran over to our table. "Are you all right, mum?!" He thought she was choking. They stared at each other and Lucy just burst out laughing, spitting crackers everywhere. I saw Richard's bewilderment and quickly explained that she was fine and was demonstrating a vocal technique for relaxation. I could see his embarrassment.

"Yes, of course, vocal exercise, how foolish of me..." He returned to his seat and picked up his script. But now, I could see him peering at us over the top. I knew he was thinking: "*They're crackers all right!*"

The interview was fun and the whole thing amused Earl no end. Lucy gave him a lot of small talk and charmed the socks off the guy. She knew how to do that, mostly about how she loved the audiences, being in New York with the kids and the snow, and so on.

Meanwhile, I was aware that Richard was actually observing *me* ever so subtly. Our eyes met briefly several times. They were a piercing shade of blue green that would make most girls feel all gooey inside and want to jump up out of their seats and go sit on his lap. I, however, was not that inclined.

Dessert finally arrived just as Richard was leaving and he stopped by our table on his way out and said, "I'd like to see that exercise with the *boccone dolce*." Huge laughter erupted, especially from Lucy. I, of course, took that as an invitation for more than eating and that I was the dessert. After the interview on the way back to the theater, Lucy just kind of casually said, "Listen Paula, watch out for that Burton. Even though he's married, you're just his type."

"What? Don't be silly. Besides I'm engaged to Jack!" I muttered. Lucy gave me a "sure you are" look. I have to admit, I was titillated. The next day when I arrived at the theater, the stage doorman handed me the most beautifully wrapped package.

"Richard Burton dropped this off for you." It was a box of saltines.

Lucy and I were scheduled to do "Hey Look Me Over" on *The Ed Sullivan Show* about the time Burton was also supposed to perform a solo from *Camelot*. I saw Richard at rehearsals, but Lucy was watching me like a mother hen, not letting me out of her sight. She had seen the sparks fly and was apprehensive. Robert Goulet was also on the show. He had the most glorious voice, but had a misguided penchant for giving me deep soul kisses whenever we met. I didn't have the heart to tell him I didn't find it appealing. It didn't go unnoticed by Richard.

During one of the breaks, Bob asked me in a puzzled manner, "Hey, Burton wants me to get your private number backstage at the Alvin. You want me to give it to him?" I said, "Sure, why not?" What's wrong with that? Privately I thought he didn't need vocal coaching. His voice was strange but his delivery was phenomenal. I admired the way Shakespearean actors could make you think they were singing by just intoning and modulating their voices. He really talked a great song. Besides, I've always felt singing is an extension of speech using controlled breath.

After *The Ed Sullivan Show* aired, more packages began being delivered backstage, always wrapped in the most exquisite fashion, with notes like "You're the prettiest cripple in the theater." "Where did you learn to limp?" "Have you considered a career in chewing?" "Why Jack Carter?" True, I was committed to marry Jack, but what girl isn't intrigued by this kind of attention from a theatrical giant? Jack was famous for his Burton imitation, now here was the real thing!

When he finally called me on my dressing room phone, I'd hesitated for a moment, not sure if it was Jack or Richard. I'd go along with the dialogue until I was certain it wasn't Jack. While I had no intention of being another feather in Richard's cap, I must admit I was highly tickled. I didn't dare tell Lucy, as she was adamant about messing around with married men. I had no one to tell and it was becoming an extraordinary fantasy.

I loved the verbal banter and the sexy innuendos. It was phone sex and it was fun. He'd call just before curtain time and ask what I had on. I'd reply that I was sitting in my bra and panties. He'd say, "Bugger, I knew I should have called sooner!"

The next time he'd call, I'd tell him I was naked.

"Don't lie to me. You'd never sit around naked. Besides, the Shuberts are too cheap with the heat backstage!"

The calls became so wild I started having dreams about having sex with Richard. I thought I would incorporate a current joke that was making the rounds.

"In one of my dreams you showed up with a tall blonde and a hunched-back midget. I asked, what's she doing here? You answered, she's a friend of mine and he's her date. Well, it's wrong to bring them into my dream."

Richard roared and played along. Clearly, he had heard the same joke.

"I had that exact dream too, except you were intrigued with this hunchback, and wanted to know if they had huge cocks. The hunchback said yes. You said, well, can I see it? The hunchback said yes, so you unzipped his fly. You said, can I suck it? The hunchback said yes, but don't blow on it, that's how I got the hump!!"

Little did I know that Lucy was well aware of all the packages and phone calls. There were no secrets backstage. It had always been my habit to arrive early at the theater to relax and leisurely put on my makeup and prepare for the performance. I hated to be rushed. One night I found Lucy waiting in my dressing room. I guess curiosity finally made her want to confront me for some explanations. "Do you mind my asking what's going on with all these boxes I see here?" (I really didn't think it was any of her business, but I knew I needed to hear this.)

"They're from an admirer. Just an assortment of crackers and biscuits from around the world," I casually replied. "You can't imagine all the varieties."

"Cut the crap, Paula. Who's the fan?"

"Richard Burton, but it's all really innocent, just his sense of humor. I guess he's got nothing else to do."

"Hmmmmm. Well, I hope that is all there is to this," she said, indicating the pile of boxes stacked around the room. "Burton, huh? I suppose you're flattered by it. Remember, I warned you about him. He is a big philanderer and you're only a small crumb to him." That hurt and she saw it in my eyes. "Oh Paula, I only want to protect you. What he'll do to you is more painful than you can imagine."

At that moment, there was a knock on the door and Richard Burton poked his head in. He had never showed up in person before. This brazen act shocked all of us.

"Come in!" Lucy smiled and gave me a sideway glance that said, "A-HA!"

Richard sheepishly opened the door wider, revealing another package under his arm.

"How nice to see you. But don't you have a curtain pretty soon?" Lucy quizzically asked.

"Yes, mum. But I don't appear in the first scene so I wanted to deliver this package personally as its very special and I didn't want it to get lost," Richard replied.

"Oh, I've heard all about the ***special*** packages over in *Camelot,*" Lucy said.

"I'm sorry, mum?"

"Oh, come on, Richard, I'm not that dumb. The package you want to deliver isn't in that box under your arm. Be a good boy and get over to your other performance before I let you know what I really think, sir!" Lucy said, like a patient school marm to her naughty pupil. Final Curtain. End of that play.

★ ★ ★

Clearly, Lucy was the draw for the show. The theatrical demands of a musical were too ambitious for her physical capacity, whereas on television they weren't as strenuous; she was mercilessly on stage every night for practically every minute of the two-and-a-half hours of each performance. She was on every night and twice on Wednesdays and Saturdays with only one day to rest. She carried the entire show. It was downright criminal. I'd call it star abuse.

As the months passed, the play was sapping all her reserve strength. It taxed her system and compromised her health. She became anemic. She lost a lot of weight. Visibly she looked strained and fragile. Her stamina began to fail. Everyone in the cast was aware of this and it was obvious that she desperately needed a rest.

One night, she fell off the onstage oil rig which scared Kidd and the show closed down for a week. "Hey Lucy, guess what? Jack's working at the Fontainebleau in Miami. Why don't we just go down there and join him?"

"Great idea, Paula! Who wants to sit around here in this cold weather anyway?" Lucy responded.

"Let's do it!"

So, Lucy, Gary and I jumped on a plane and met up with Jack for some badly needed R and R. By this point we had become a

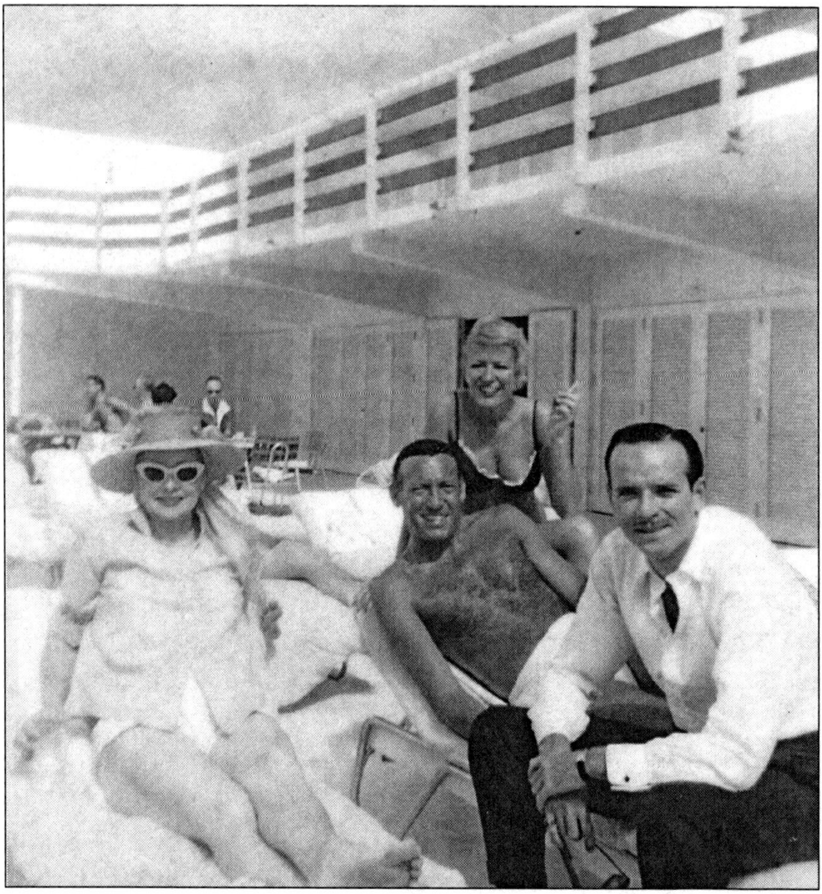

Lucy recuperating from her fall on Wildcat at the Fountainebleau pool in Miami. Here with me, Gary, and Freddie Fields. Jack and I were engaged and Lucy was thrilled we tagged along. No pressures of a nightly show for once.

foursome. I knew that Lucy and Gary still weren't intimate by this point but it was fun watching them pussyfoot around the issue. They were still in the courting period and it warmed my heart to see her have a good time. Gary, with all his charm, was allowing Lucy to move past the trauma with Desi. Jack, as always, lent his quick-witted humor to keep us all laughing.

★ ★ ★

The second time we closed the show was for a week around Easter in March, when Lucy fell off the oil rig again, badly injuring her leg, causing her to limp about. The doctors insisted she rest her leg for a week.

Jack and I took the opportunity to get married in Florida even though Lucy and Gary would not be able to attend.

"Paula," Lucy said, "there's nothing more in the world I want than to be at your side for this occasion but you know I've got doctor's orders to stay in bed. I promise to make it up to you and Jack when you're back home. I'm so happy for you!"

I must admit that I was sad that my best girlfriend wasn't going to be by my side. However, I understood it was physically impossible for Lucy to make the trip, and with our busy schedules, was the only time for Jack and I to get married.

Luckily, one of my other girlfriends, Sondra Lee served as my maid of honor. Sondra had played "Tiger Lily" in the original Broadway production of *Peter Pan* and had appeared in Federico

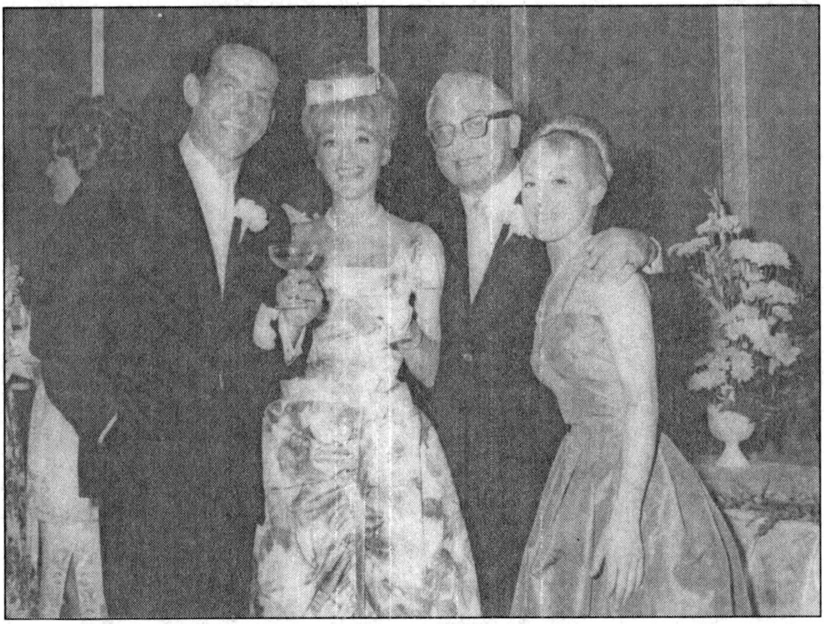

Best Man Mickey Hayes, and Matron of Honor Sondra Lee at my wedding to Jack. We married in Miami at Morris Lansburgh's home, March 30, 1961. - Photo credit Noel Lanham

Fellini's *La Dolce Vita*. So March 30th 1961, I became Mrs. Jack Carter, although my beloved Poppy would forever question, "Why him, Paula, why him?"

Morris Lansburgh, a prominent figure in the hotel industry, threw us a lovely Jewish wedding under a *huppah*. Joey Lewis,

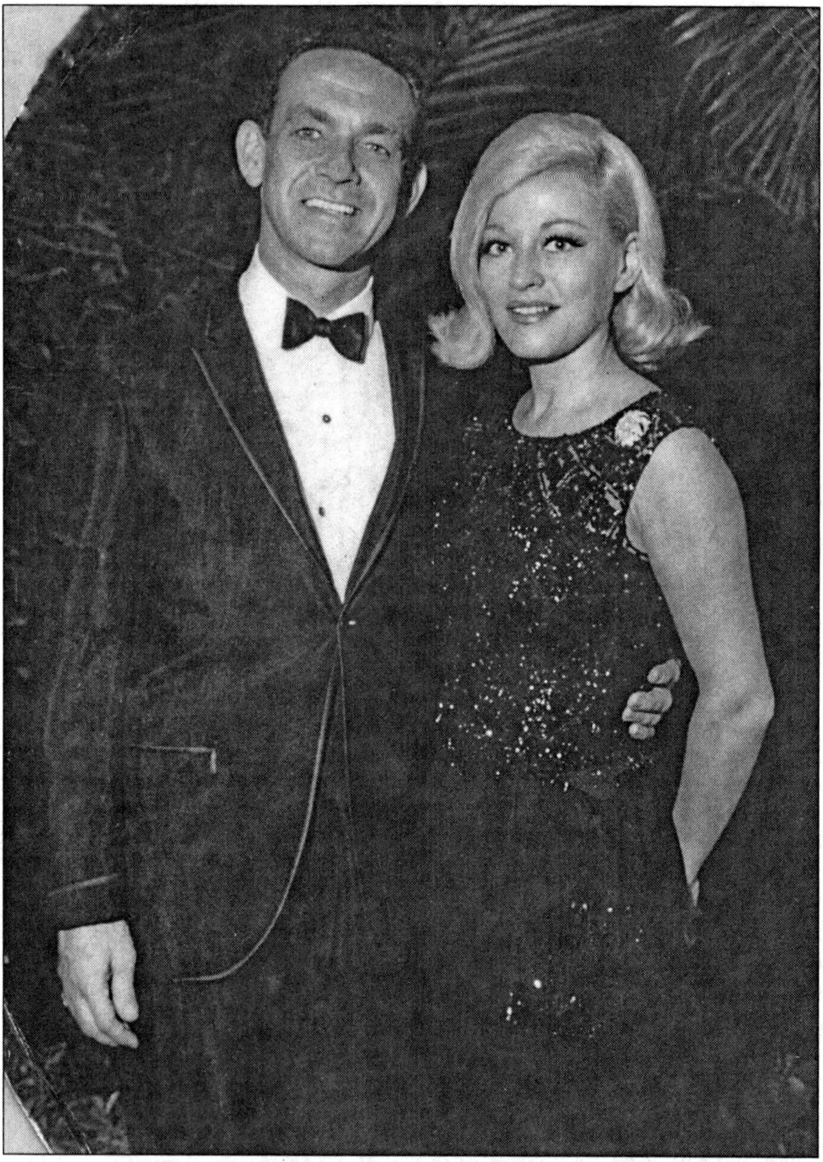

In the early fun days, Jack and I loved performing together when I was still the "angel bride."

well-known comedian, but probably more famous for losing fortunes at the track, had everyone throw spent horse race tickets in the air instead of rice. My father could now say to his patients, "I've got a married daughter in show business."

Just after our marriage and before a big wedding party photo spread in the *New York Daily News* would hit the stands (*Gathering heralds the marriage of Jack Carter and Paula Stewart*), Joan Mann Carter popped out of the woodwork claiming that their Nevada divorce in 1957 was invalid because neither she nor Jack had been Nevada residents (*She Sues to Nullify Carter's New Mrs.*) and therefore, she was still his wife, proclaiming Jack's "new role as husband of actress Paula Stewart is thereby void."

I know I hurt Harry's feelings when I chose to marry Jack. He did, however, get even by dating my maid of honor Sondra Lee, which in turn hurt my feelings. I got over it by passing it off as a spite fuck and we remained friends.

★ ★ ★

Lucy finally got back on her feet. However, it became obvious she was losing her stamina and she was physically unable to perform. On the few occasions that her understudy went on, the box office had to refund all the tickets. It wasn't possible to just shut down a Broadway show while the star rested. There were hundreds of people involved: musicians, stagehands, electricians, and performers.

Lucy at this point had to make a big decision. "Paula, I'm really conflicted. I don't know what to do. Should I bite the bullet and just close the show and write the whole thing off?" I knew in the back of her mind she desperately wanted to resume her life in California with her children and let this budding romance with Gary takes its course. She had empathy for the entire cast and crew but it was clear she needed some time off, so I came up with a solution.

"Lucy, would you be willing to put up some money for everyone while you rested? That way you can take a break and everyone still gets paid."

"That's a good idea, Paula, I'll do that!" She did, and every one of the unions from the actors to the stagehands agreed to accept minimum wage for a couple of weeks while Lucy recouped — everyone, that is, but the musicians' union. No doubt about it, the musicians themselves would have loved to concede, but the union wouldn't give in and demanded full salaries for their members. It was the most powerful union and couldn't care less that hundreds of people would be out of work or that its own members would be affected. The musicians' full salaries alone would cost too much for any reasonable consideration. The fate of the show depended on this one union. Musicals are such high-risk investments. The musicians' union didn't blink an eye and closed *Wildcat* for good. After nearly six months and 171 performances, Lucy officially closed *Wildcat* on June 3, 1961.

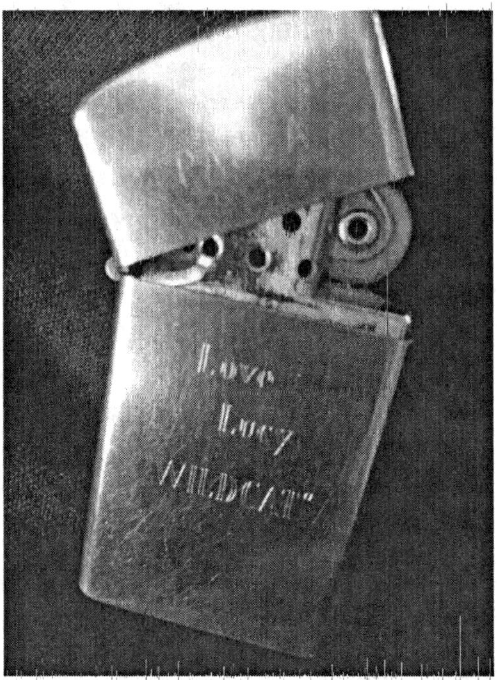

Lucy gave all the cast of Wildcat *a gold zippo lighter. Most of us still smoked in those days, however I never smoked during the run of a show.*

In gratitude for their support, Lucy gave the entire cast and crew (including the musicians) a gold Zippo lighter engraved with their name and "Love Lucy." I still have mine.

★ ★ ★

11
Paula East

I knew Lucy really liked Gary a lot, but she had been slow to commit. She'd barely extracted herself from her marriage to Desi. I was, however, shocked to find out that Gary let his buddies know of his success at bedding the great Lucille Ball. Jack couldn't wait to tell me that one of his closest friends Mickey Hayes, a celebrity Miami haberdasher, had called to say that Gary had bragged of his latest conquest. This was by far most distasteful and gross. It seems some men just can't keep their fucking mouths shut.

I wanted to see her have some fun and have a romance to ease her pain and memory of her failure with Desi, but this boasting was not befitting for this wonderful woman. I was so remorseful, I only prayed that things would turn out all right. I held my breath for thirty years, and, thank God, Gary never embarrassed Lucy by cheating on her. Lucy once told me, "I know Gary didn't love me in the beginning, but I think he's learned to after all these years."

After *Wildcat's* closing, Lucy gave up the apartment at the Imperial House and returned to Beverly Hills with the kids. Gary wasn't about to let her get away, so he borrowed money from his mother, Rose and sister, Helen. They had to hock some jewelry to raise the funds for plane fare and spending money.

Gary flew to LA and went straight to Lucy's magnificent home in Beverly Hills at 1000 North Roxbury Drive. Her neighbors were two of her oldest and dearest friends in Hollywood: Jack Benny to the north, and Jimmy Stewart to the south. Pals Rosie Clooney and Esther Williams were just up the street. Gary's jaw must have hit the pavement. He didn't tell his buddies how long it took him to get the balls to knock on the front door. Just as Lucy appeared, a tour bus drove past. As she stood in the doorway of her grand home, fans shouted and cheered. "Lucy! We love you!"

Cameras clicked as Gary dropped to one knee, grabbed her hand and said, "Lucy, let me take you away from all this." That was actually pretty clever for Gary, whom I considered a hack comedian.

Lucy took it slow. She was very moral. She wouldn't allow Gary to stay in her house or even in the guesthouse because of the children. Lucy wanted to get to know him and see how he was with the kids. She also knew he wasn't working and had limited funds so she rented him a little house in the hills above Sunset Boulevard.

Lucy's mother, DeDe, a devout Catholic, didn't care for Gary in the beginning, but she remained silent, just hoping he would go away. In fact, Dede would refer to Gary as "the Jew." Well, Lucy didn't want him to go away. Gary was amusing, charming, and easy-going. DeDe disapproved for reasons like the fact that Gary was easily fifteen years younger and there was his lack of a job...until she saw how happy he made her daughter. Lucy had been so lonely. This would give the kids some stability after the anguished last years with Desi. Eventually, DeDe relented and gave her blessing. How could she object to a man that was giving her daughter a new reason in life? I guess Lucy also felt the same way. She figured, how bad could it be?

★ ★ ★

The dust settled as we all settled into our respective homes: Lucy and Gary in Los Angeles, Jack and I, though married, to our still separate bachelor pads. Hence, Jack and I were now being referred to in the gossip columns as "Carter East" and "Carter West" with no immediate plans for cohabitation on the horizon. I was readily hired to play opposite George Gobel in a new musical *Let It Ride*, also featuring Sam Levine and Barbara Nichols.

George was a huge star in television, and Barbara was a Hollywood character actress in the vein of Marilyn Monroe or Jayne Mansfield: blonde, buxom and batty. She was perfect for the role,

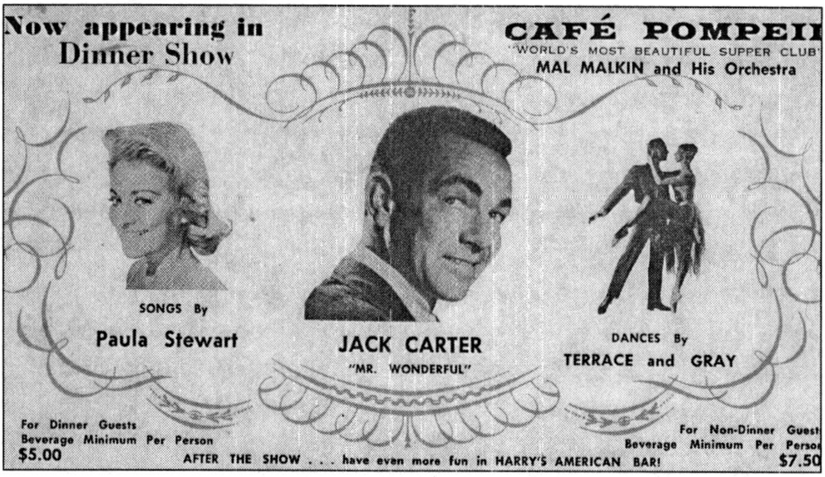

After we were married, Jack and I worked a lot. Even together. Couldn't find the time to move in together.

but sadly, her work habits were dulled by too much vodka. This became obvious to the producers and they approached me about playing her part, which meant she was going to be fired. I would have loved to do a ditsy sexpot for a change but I honestly felt sorry for Barbara. She really was a sweet person so unlike her image.

So, on the train ride to Philly for the out-of-town stint, I cornered her in her stateroom and gave it to her straight, "a la Lucy."

"You're going to get canned if you don't put a lid on it!" I said in a very straightforward manner. In her case it was cooling the booze and getting down to learning her lines and delivering what she was being paid for—a full-out performance! Personally, I hated the show even though I really enjoyed working with George. I thought the music was pedestrian and the script trite. But it was a paying job.

One night after the show opened in New York to mediocre reviews, I fell into a deep sleep and I was awakened at the unforgivable hour of 11 a.m. *Jesus*, I thought, my friends knew better when I was working on a show not to call this early. Someone must have died, again. Nope. It was an excited Lucy.

"Paula, we're getting married! I wanted you to be the first to know and be my matron of honor. Gary's calling Jack in Vegas right now to ask him to be best man. We've made arrangements with Dr. Vincent Peale. He's only got one day open so we took it.

It's next Monday. We have a week. So now I need you to help me get something special to wear for both of us." She then gave me a list of things she required.

"Congratulations, Lucy. Don't worry. I'll take care of it." I was flattered that she trusted my taste enough to plan something as important as her wedding. I realized there was not enough time for couture like Scassi or Pucci, so I called Pauline Hyman, the head of the couturier department at Bergdorf. Lucy had been a good customer so they would be very accommodating. Check. Remind Lucy to bring furs, it's cold. Check. Corsages, well, that would depend on the clothes. Check. Hotel would handle all the extras. Check. Lucy called me hourly with more requests until she got to New York.

Lucy also told me she wanted to see me in *Let It Ride*. George Gobel was huge at that time and Lucy liked him a lot. Since Gary didn't care about theater, Lucy came to the Wednesday matinee. I remember she was mobbed for autographs to which she, as usual, graciously signed till the curtain went up. Afterwards, she stopped backstage, kissed us all and went back to her limo to join Gary for dinner while I completed the evening performance.

Early afternoon the next day, Pauline had everything laid out for us in our sizes and color preferences when we arrived at Bergdorf and we had a vast collection to choose from. Lucy settled on a stunning turquoise suit and I on a lime green one that complimented each other. At the time, I was a red-head because Barbara was to be the only blonde in the show. Lucy and I really looked like sisters now. After Bergdorf's, we went to the Tavern on The Green in Central Park where we played catch up with small talk about the show.

"You know, I'm not fond of Barbara," Lucy said. "But I have to say, she was good in the show. I know you had something to do with that, Paula."

"Well, just a little," I said, winking at her. "As a matter of fact, she was so down in her cups I thought she needed a boost, so I called Burt. You know he's a big-boob lover, and, well, he got her out of her stupor and gave her a *shtupp* or two!" Lucy laughed long and hard at that one.

Lucy and I rarely talked show business except what was on the horizon. While nibbling on my *coq au vin* I mentioned that Jack had signed us to do *Critics Choice* at the prestigious Playhouse in the Park Theater in Philadelphia next year even though it hadn't been a hit on Broadway. Jack was always looking for shows in which we could work together and become a team like Nichols and May; Stiller and Meara; Steve Lawrence and Eydie Gormé. Couple acts were big at that time.

"*Critic's Choice*!" Lucy exclaimed. "Desilu just optioned it for Bob Hope and me to film next year. Wow, some coincidence." I told Lucy personally I wasn't too thrilled about it. I thought it was a weak show. But since Henry Fonda had starred in it, Jack okayed it with his agent. They thought Jack and I would be a good draw in it, and, of course Jack would love to be compared to Henry Fonda.

"Hmmmmm," Lucy bit her lip. "Wonder if you're right.... We'll it's too late now. Let's go drive around the park and enjoy the winter wonderland. Besides, there is an issue I need to discuss with you."

"Oh no," I thought, "what is it this time?"

Once in the limo, Lucy launched into the living arrangements between Jack and me. We still had our separate apartments.

"Really now, Paula—Carter East and Carter West?"

"I know it's strange, Lucy, but I think suddenly Jack's afraid to commit." Personally, I think now Jack was reluctant to give up our bachelor living arrangement. Nobody found it stranger than Lucy and she wasn't about to sit around and allow this to go on.

"Whaaat!!??? You're married! That's a commitment enough! Besides, I'm not giving you your wedding gift until you're both in one place." Lucy stopped and pointed to the San Remo Towers. "There. That's a good place to live!" Well, of course it was, it was one of the most desirable and expensive apartment buildings in New York.

"Jack will never go for it," I said.

"Driver! Take us to the San Remo," Lucy ordered. "We'll see if there's one available." I just sat there with my mouth agape.

Upon arriving there, Lucy rolled down the window as the doorman approached the limo.

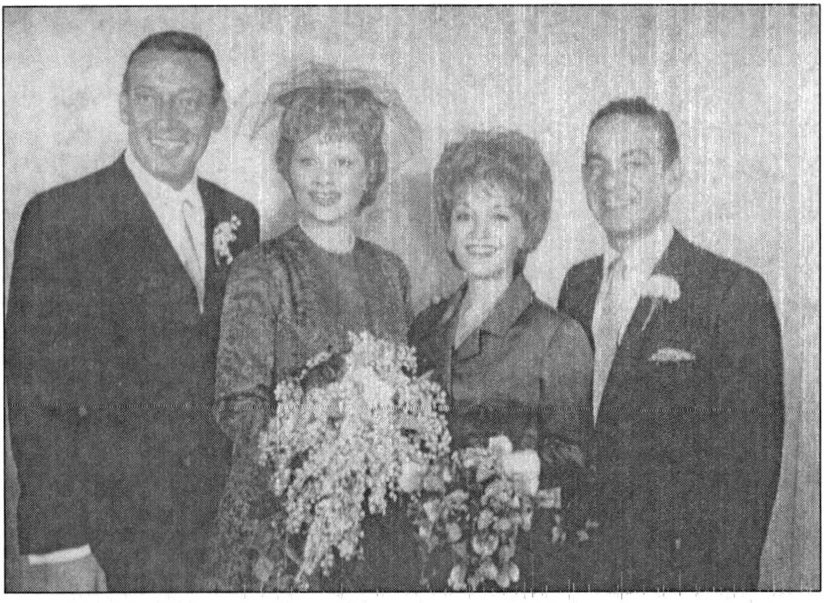

Lucy's and Gary's wedding, November 1961. Coincidentally, Jack and I were newlyweds too that year.

"Is there a manager on the premises?" Lucy asked. The doorman replied, "He happens to be here, madam. Who shall I say is calling?"

"Just tell him Lucille Ball wants to know if there's an apartment available."

I thought the doorman was going to keel over when he realized his faux pas. Stumbling to regain his composure and thinking this was for Lucy, he uttered, "Miss Ball, I happen to know that there's an apartment available right now." To which she replied, "Good, can I see it?" To which he continued to fumble in speech, "Well, um, er, the apartment is open because they are doing some repairs. Are you sure you want to see it in this condition?"

"Why not?" Lucy retorted. "Let's go."

Up to the nineteenth floor we went, stepping over old ripped up carpeting, into an empty apartment with a huge 360-degree view of the whole city.

"Wow," I said. "This is fabulous!" To myself I'm thinking, oh boy, would I love to live here, but there's no way I'll ever be able to talk Jack into this. "It's got to be a fortune, Lucy, he'll never go for it."

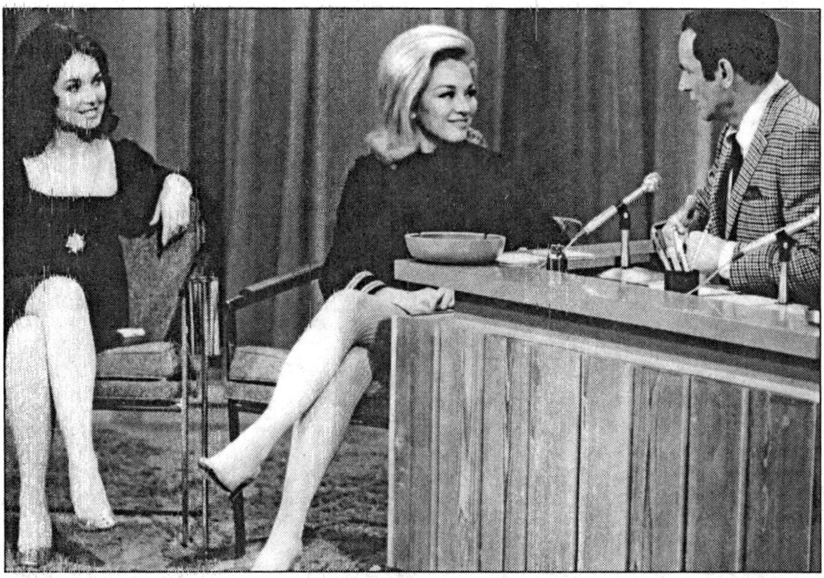

I did a wonderful sketch with Joey Bishop on his television show. Suzanne Pleshette was also a guest that day - nice gal.

"Don't you worry," Lucy said. "I'll talk him into it." And, amazingly, she did.

Lucy and Gary's wedding which was supposed to be a small and private affair, turned into a three-ring circus. Because of the time constraints, Lucy didn't want the press there making a big deal over it. It was her second marriage but the press got hold of it somehow, and the morning of the wedding there was such a mob scene that we could hardly get into Marble Collegiate Church. The crowd had to be restrained by a police barricade.

A few intimate friends and relatives, and an agent or two, attended the brief and spiritual ceremony. Lucy's bouquet was Lilies of the Valley and mine was baby orchids. I have had a love affair with them ever since. Lucy was so radiant; I choked up completely through it all. Everyone was buoyed by her gaiety and exuberance and obvious joy. I silently felt relieved and gratified. I was happy to have been responsible for her newfound love.

We went back to the Imperial House for a small reception. Then Lucy and Gary went off on their honeymoon while Jack and I settled into the glorious San Remo. Not long after, a pair of magnificent three-foot high candlesticks arrived with a note saying, "Try not to burn at both ends, Love, Lucy."

★ ★ ★

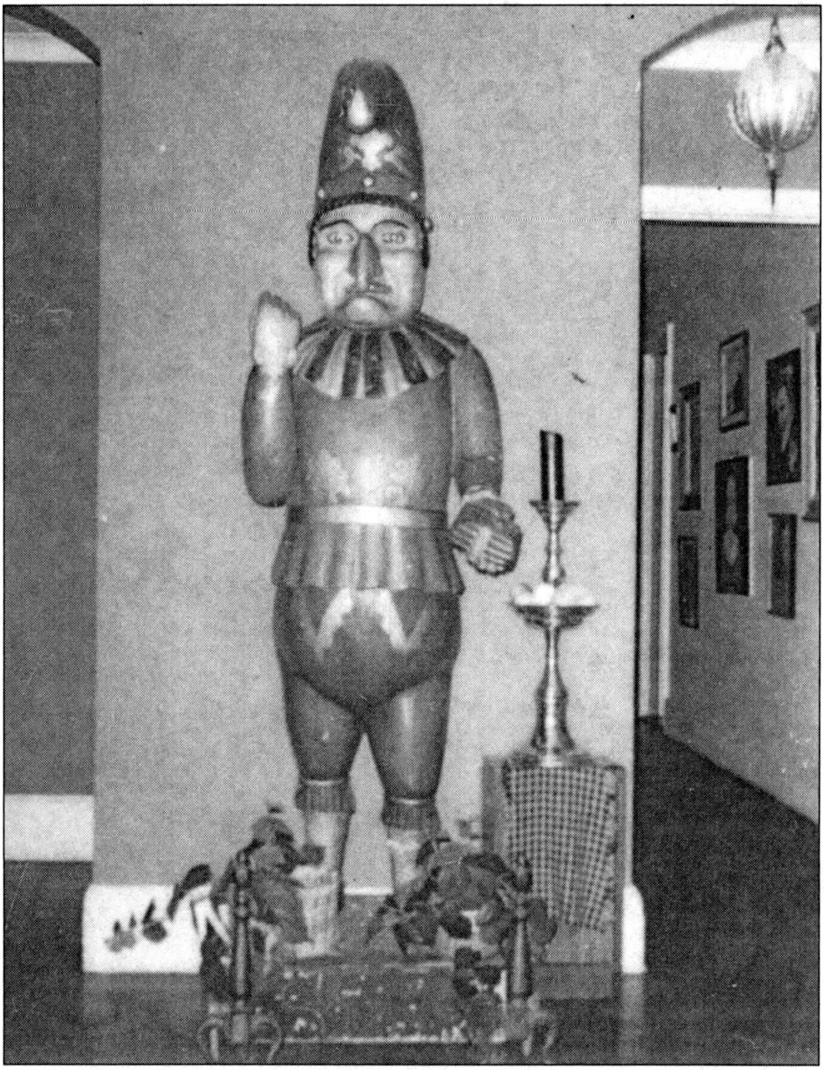

Jack hated my seven-foot-tall "Punch." Swen Swenson, who was well-known for his collection of outstanding carnival figures, helped me acquire him.

Jack and I were always working, either as a team or apart. We were on *The Ed Sullivan Show*, *The Joey Bishop Show* and a multitude of talk shows in between our theater and club dates.

Shortly after we moved into the San Remo, I was hired for a movie, *Diary of A Bachelor*, luckily shot in New York. I got the part because of my athleticism—horse riding, motorcycling skills, love of hiking, tennis, golfing; and also my culinary prowess in the kitchen. The only thing they didn't take advantage of was my flying a plane.

Jack was in Vegas or doing various club dates everywhere; I was also performing in one or two Broadway productions. In-between, I managed to squeeze in a quick trip to LA to visit Lucy. Because of our busy schedules, it became necessary to hire someone to decorate our new digs at the San Remo. We settled on Blaine and Booth, the current hot designers, to get things started, which they did quickly and fashionably until Jack tightened the purse strings.

"Hey, angel, you've got great taste. What do we need fucking designers for?" I questioned whether this was a compliment or an excuse to save money. However, I bought his line of argument because it gave me an opportunity to develop my sense of décor.

One of the first major purchases I made, with Swen Swenson's help of course, was a seven-foot tall-carved wooden figure, "Punch," inspired by the puppet pair Punch and Judy, who were always beating each other up. His stunning collection of carousel figures were featured in the book, *The Pictorial History of The Carousel* by Frederick Fried. Punch was beautifully grotesque, beckoning visitors to enter with an outstretched hand that seemed to say welcome or pay me. Either way, I thought it befittingly humorous for our entryway, the first thing a visitor would encounter, and I couldn't wait to send photos of Punch to Lucy and get her reaction.

Jack was not as taken with him as I was and it became a constant topic for his tirades.

"That ugly hooked-nosed monster at the gate belongs in a circus. But, oh no, it's 'Join us for some freaky fun here at crazy Chez Carter's kook house.'" Punch didn't stop the mass parade of our frequent parties with our close friends like Buddy Hackett, Milton Berle, Phil Silvers, Sammy Davis, Jr. and his wife May Britt, Allen King, Sid Caesar, Jan and Tony Murray, Angela Lansbury, Ed Sullivan, and Red Buttons with Alicia, his new bride (thanks to me introducing them) to name a few. Everyone wanted to have a birthday party at our place because Jack would do his famous "opening of the gifts" routine where he'd have everyone in hysterics reading the notes, commenting on the wrapping, the sizes and sometimes even tossing the whole package out the 19th floor window.

Comedy was king in the 1960s. Duos were hot. At every big party there was at least one celebrity comic. Comedians were a breed apart and liked to hang out together. They didn't necessarily share jokes, because they probably just paid a fortune for a routine or a current topic in the news.

Lucy's comedy was purely physical. Slapstick. But what made her exceptional was that Lucy's was downright zany. She would get into outrageous and off-the-wall situations and apply her sense of physical comedy to perfection. As gorgeous as she was, she was the clown, unafraid, uninhibited, caring less if people saw her as a dowdy housewife or a toothless hobo. It didn't matter, as long as the laughs were coming.

Lucy was an original. Her unique, crazy antics as an actress were like none other and there hasn't been anyone like her since. Lucy admired exceptional talent like Katherine Hepburn, Judy Garland, Dean Martin, Bob Hope, Bobby Darrin, and Sammy Davis, Jr. Lucy really liked Jack.

Jack's brand of comedy set him apart from his fellow comedians because he was an incredible mimic. And he was quick. Jack was a genius. He was almost like a savant in a sense. No one could ad lib hours on end like Jack. He could walk into a room and pick up the whole vibe and go off on a tangent, sometimes ignoring his usual routine and elaborating on something completely extraneous. We would be exhausted watching him. Jack would go on like the Energizer Bunny, leaving his audience limp with laughter.

Because of his exceptional talent, everybody wanted to be around Jack, including myself. He was the most innovative person I knew. That was part of Jack's charm. In those days most

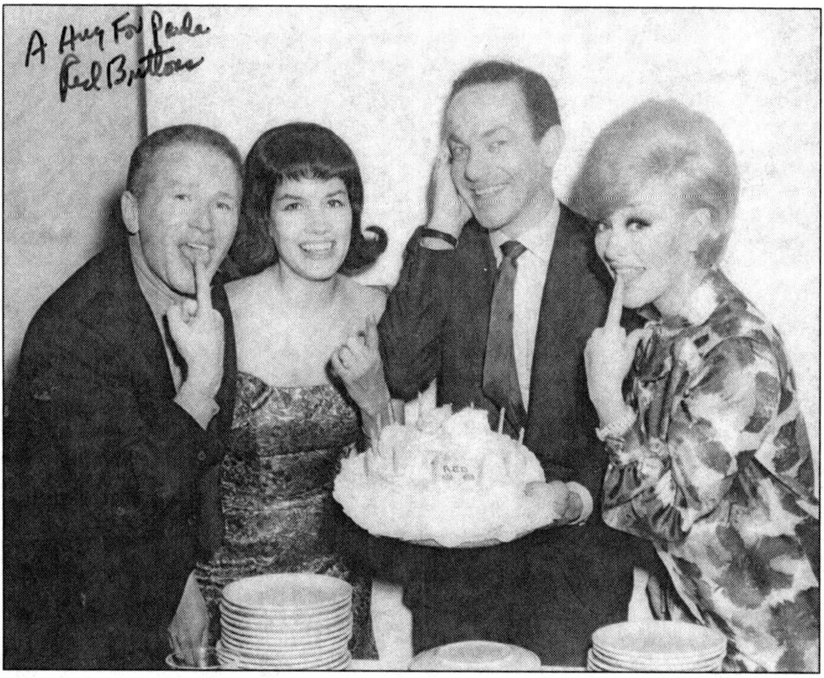

I also introduced Red Buttons to his wife, Alicia. I was a good matchmaker for everyone, but not for myself.

comedians also played an instrument or had some sort of other musical talent. Jack's instrument was his body, which seemed in perpetual motion, either moving or dancing to some crazy rhythm. Jack did it all.

★ ★ ★

Even though it was supposed to be our honeymoon, Jack's agent had him booked in London on a television special where we were put up in a posh hotel suite until the show date. I like to call this the first leg of my honeymoon tour. I wasn't really shocked when Jack had us moved to a cheaper room, unwilling to pay for all the bells and whistles. His excuse being we were never there except to sleep and change clothes. True, he was making a big salary, but after all, it was our honeymoon. Oh well. I not only lived with it but learned to be a quick-change artist to keep up with Jack. He

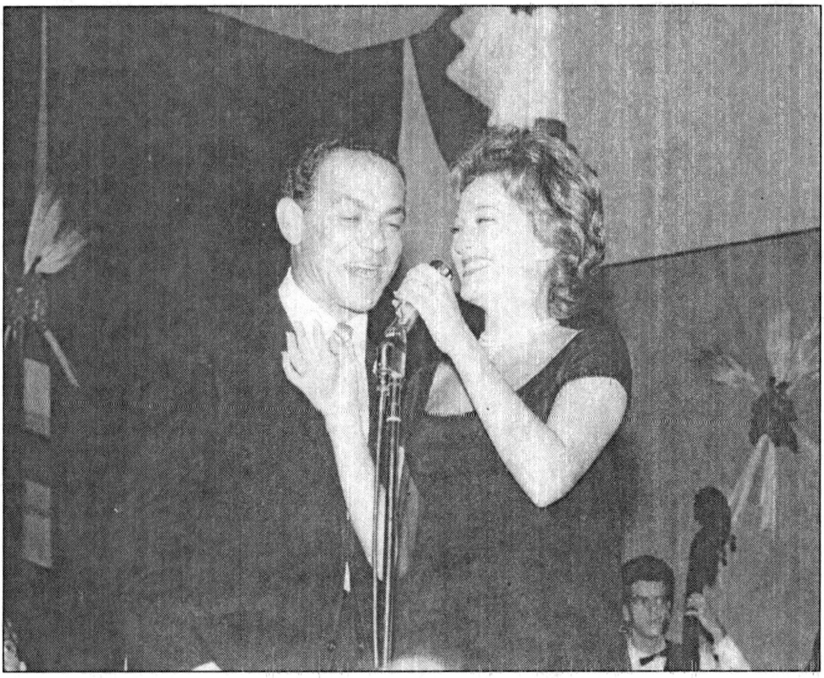

Jack and I on a USO tour in Europe doing our act together after Wildcat *- on our honeymoon yet!*

was "Flash Gordon" in the flesh. We hit all the infamous bars, bistros and landmarks, non-stop at a whirlwind pace. The man was a living typhoon. It makes my feet ache just to think about it. It's a good thing we took lots of pictures, as it still remains a blur. We saw Rome in a day, and I mean **all** of it.

Along the way we managed to join up with some fellow performers like Vic Damone who was between engagements and marriages. Then it was off to Germany where we were booked on a brief USO Tour where we could try out our new act together. Jack being a linguist, wanted to impress me with his German, which was actually much closer to Yiddish. So, one night at an upscale Ratskeller, serving the typical knockwurst and *bier*, he got his chance to show off his "deutche." We were seated at a cozy booth with an impressive ancient keg on the wall. The maitre d' who took our order looked suspiciously like an SS Officer with an air of superiority. Jack asked in his German, "So how old is this place?"

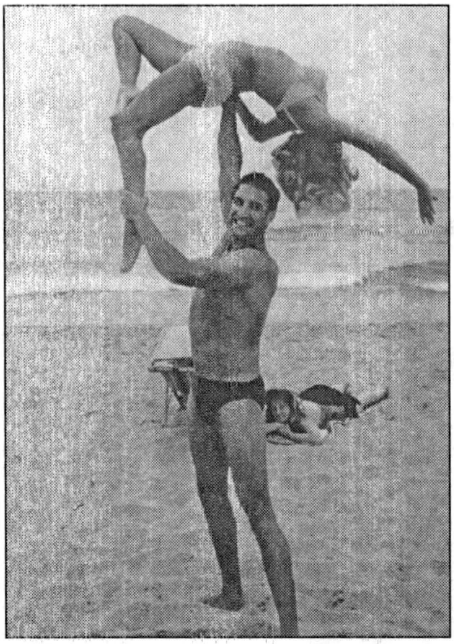

Life metaphor - as I wished it...

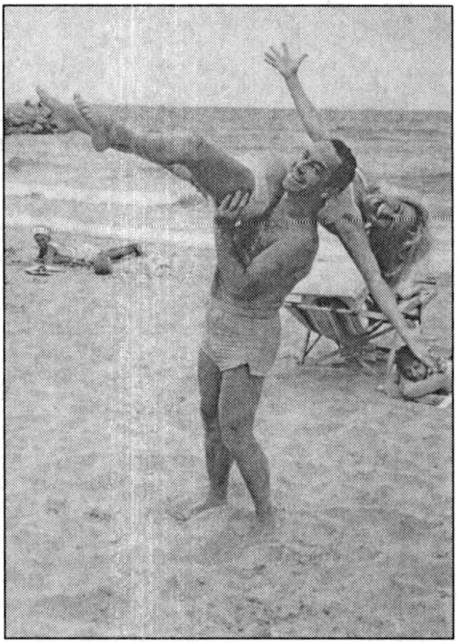

...and as it was.

"*Dreihundert Jahren*" (300 years), he replied. Jack, pointing to the keg asks, "*So, varum sag es trink* Coca Cola." (Why does it say drink Coca Cola?) The humor was not appreciated; as a result the food was cold and the beer was flat. So was the maitre d's chilly glare.

Happily we were off to a warmer climate in St. Tropez. I was surprised to see Jack's close buddies, Mickey Hayes and Danny Welkes greeting us upon our arrival at the spectacular Cap Ferrat. Now we were a crowd. There has to be something wrong when a newly married couple has an entourage of bachelors tagging along on their honeymoon trip.

By now I got the idea that Mickey and Danny were permanently attached to any itinerary of interest that we would embark on. *Mutt and Jeff* describes them both as Mickey was short and chubby, not unattractive, but almost, and Danny was tall, not handsome, but just missing it. There were always women on their arms, and you would never see the same broad twice.

Why they would figure our long overdue honeymoon would be a good pussy hunt is still a mystery to me as Lucy remarked later, "Yes, Paula, a mystery, I'd say." I even asked Jack, "Why?"

"They're here for the laughs."

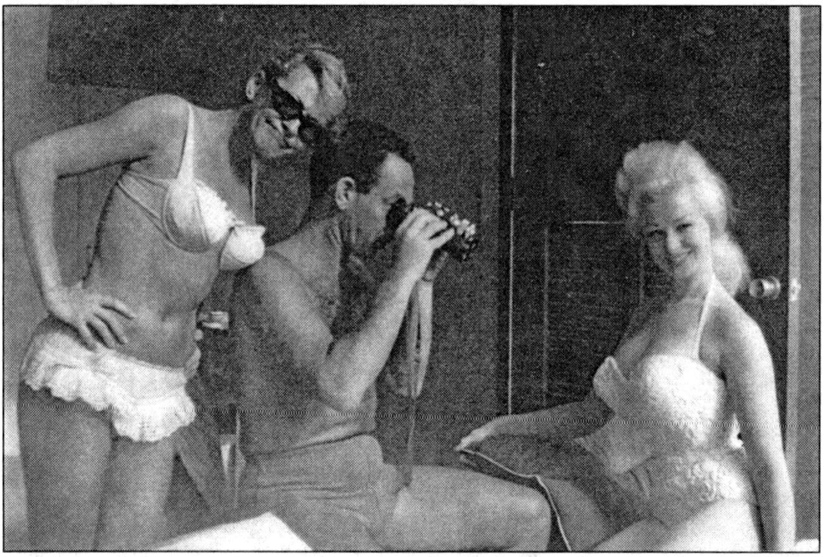

Jack doing the usual sightseeing.

"Oh...oh? God forbid if we were supposed to have some privacy!"

Every night we went to another hot disco. I listened to them speak their fractured French, which consisted of: "Sava the table! Bringa the drinks!" I watched teenage idiots shaking their asses while downing champagne and sniffing Amys (now known as Poppers), which were all the craze that hadn't yet crossed over to our country. My feet hurt from the stilettos du jour and I drank a lot to kill the pain.

While staggering back to the hotel, the street lamps flickered as warm Mediterranean breezes caressed our tired drunken bodies, I ventured jokingly, "Hey guys, why don't we go get our dicks sucked!" For a minute, they actually gave it a thought, forgetting that it was in jest by a broad. I was getting tired of being dragged along with these immature morons. In the end, Mickey and Danny never married and I don't think anyone but me even remembers them.

Jack and I attempted another go at an actual honeymoon, what I'd like to call the second leg of my honeymoon tour. We planned some fun in Paris after a brief sojourn at the Madrid bull fights to see Manolete, the legendary toreador of Spain in one of his magnificent bouts with the bulls.

This was years before his demise when he was gored by a horn.

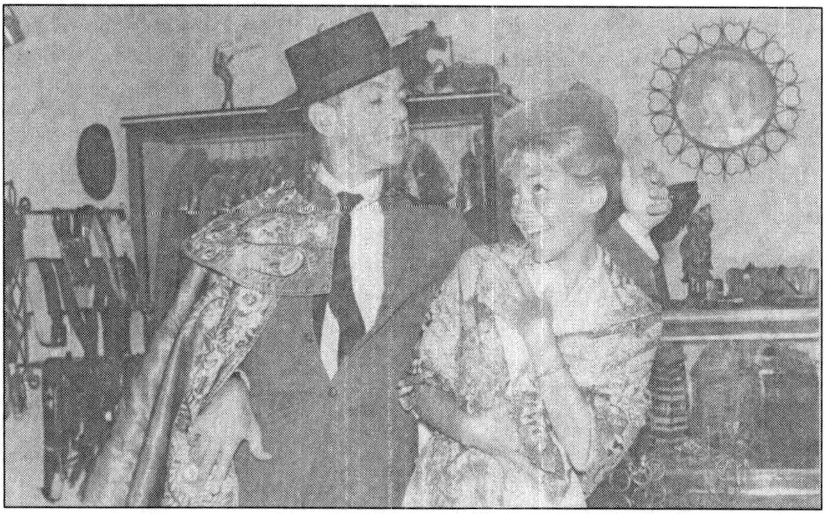

Jack and I posing for the press on our honeymoon in Madrid, Spain 1961.

Paris was exciting since there were several big films being shot there, one with Gene Kelly directing Jackie Gleason in *Gigot*. Lucy knew Jackie was working on *Gigot*, and asked Jack and me to stop by and convey her best wishes. Lucy adored Jackie and referred to him as "The Great One," a name bestowed upon him by Orson Wells. Of course we had to drop in and schmooze with Jackie and his live-in girlfriend, as I had promised Lucy.

With our entourage finally down to just Jack and me, we actually were now beginning to enjoy our time alone. New things were happening in France. All the rage was the *cause célèbre* of the moment: a spectacular blonde beauty had emerged on the continent, a transsexual extraordinaire with a much-anticipated vagina. Coccinelle was a renowned club singer and a national celebrity. Her name in French meant "ladybug," but in Hebrew it had an all-together derogatory meaning.

Gleason's girlfriend hinted to me that Bob Hope was "intrigued," knowing his obsession for conquering blondes. It just so happened that Coccinelle was appearing at Le Carrousel de Paris. I, for one, wasn't going to pass up what all the talk was about and convinced Jack we needed a "looksee."

Our butts barely hit our seats and there was Bob Hope being ushered to an inconspicuous corner table. Out of respect, Jack and I pretended we didn't see him. Lucy was sure to love this. I was anticipating the look on her face when I would be telling her this story. For the record, Coccinelle was certainly ravishing—everything and more than what she was touted to be. I'm pretty sure Bob Hope thought so, too.

★ ★ ★

Lucy detested the business side of Desilu. Previously, she always relied on Desi for that, but they were divorced and she hadn't promoted Gary to fill Desi's shoes as yet. A lot of decision making rested on her shoulders. She came to New York around the fall of 1963 for a big meeting with the Lever Brothers, a leading manufacturing company that was a sponsor on *The Lucy Show*.

The next day Lucy wanted to go to a show. Gary bowed out. The theater bored him and Jack had prior commitments. That left Lucy and me. There was one show I especially wanted her to see: *Barefoot in the Park* and I couldn't wait for her reaction to the actor whose name was on everybody's lips—the very young, but devastatingly handsome Robert Redford. Like every other member of the female species, I was really taken with Robert. He had gotten great reviews and I'm sure I must have sounded like his press agent to Lucy.

"He's electric, Lucy, sparks fly when he's on stage. I can't wait for you to see him."

"Coming from you, Paula, I can't miss it."

Lucy just loved the show, and we went backstage so she could compliment Robert. He was beside himself and so thrilled that the great Lucille Ball was there telling him how much she enjoyed his performance.

Later, during a late dinner at Sardi's, Lucy said to me, "You know, Paula, I meant what I said about Robert's performance. He really is wonderful, but he'll never make it in movies because he's a blonde."

"What do you mean? I've seen blondes before. What about Van Johnson?"

"Oh, no, he's a rarity."

"What about William Holden?"

"He's an exception. Look, this Redford is very good, but believe me he's just not going to make it. But enough about Redford. You haven't told me about your trip to Mexico."

Jack and I had just returned from a trip there. As usual, things didn't quite pan out as I had hoped.

"Jack was so cheap. He was fascinated with the *pesos*. Rather than spending them, he saved them and brought them home."

Lucy sensed there was something else and pushed me for more. "I suspect you're hiding something from me."

"Believe me, you don't want to know, Lucy."

After some more prodding, she pulled it out of me.

"Well, we were at the Jacaranda and ran into J. Lee Thompson and Brad Dexter." J. Lee Thompson was a well-known director and they were filming *Kings of the Sun* with Yul Brynner. Brad was a relatively unknown actor, but he would go on to be remembered for famously saving Frank Sinatra from drowning in the ocean during the filming of *None but the Brave* the following year.

"One day over lunch, Jack was sulking because J. Lee and Brad planned on going to a famous whorehouse that evening."

"In other words, you were his ball and chain?"

"Right. I was keeping him from having fun. I told Jack, it's okay if he wanted to go, but I wanted to come along."

"What!?? Why would you want to go?"

"Wouldn't you?"

"Oh, come on, Paula."

"I was really curious, Lucy. First of all, it was worth seeing the look on the madam's face when I showed up dangling on the guys' arms. Can you imagine me sitting at the bar, fending off advances from some of the patrons?" Lucy laughed.

"And then what happened?"

"J. Lee was cavorting around, drunk as a skunk, and at one point he appeared at the top of the stairs with a bed sheet and collapsed in a heap. Anyway, I got bored and told Jack I was leaving. He could stay but I made him promise 'no funny stuff.' Truly I wasn't seriously worried leaving Jack there alone—we were in a good place together at the time and I thought he was too cheap to pay for something he could get for free.

"Jack crept back to the hotel at 4 or 5 a.m. and there wasn't a peep out of him. The next morning Brad couldn't wait to tell me over *huevos rancheros* that Jack 'didn't do anything.' Supposedly, he cornered a real Liz Taylor look-alike with his 'what's-a-nice-girl-like-you-doing-in-a-place-like-this' line. I gave Brad the-finger-in-my-eye gesture, 'SURE! Tell me another one!'"

"And the moon is made of blue cheese. Christ, Paula, what did you expect?"

"It just confirmed, Lucy, that I married an immoral moron."

Lucy shook her head and added, "It seems most men see nothing wrong with cheating on their wives. They make up for it by buying them a fur coat, not to keep them warm but to keep them quiet."

I had to bear all the blame. Lucy had warned me from the beginning. I knew what I was getting into with Jack and now I decided to live with the absurdity of my life. Jack could be a prime sonofabitch...but he was my sonofabitch.

★ ★ ★

While international travel was rather special, flying from New York to Los Angeles was a lark. Flying was so easy back then. You could just walk up to the gate with your loved ones as they saw you off or they would be there waiting for you upon your return. Not like today. 9/11 changed everything.

Our social calendar was filled and whenever I was in Los Angeles visiting Lucy it was even busier. I remember one time Lucy brought me over to Judy Garland's home for cocktails. Lucy adored Judy. She was one of her favorite entertainers and loved watching her new series, *The Judy Garland Show.*

There was plenty of talk during that time of Judy's financial woes but Judy never let it show on her face. Lucy and I were chatting up Judy with some small talk and compliments. Judy's manager, David Begelman, was across the room surrounded by some of his other clients.

"What's David holding court about?" Lucy asked with a subtle dig. "He certainly has a big attitude about himself," she sniffed. She was very protective in her concern for Judy. Lucy lived through many of Judy's ordeals as her confidant over the years. Her instincts were racing and I couldn't help wondering what was going through her mind. Lucy formed snap opinions based on body language and—oh boy, Begelman had a rather strong aura about him that attracted men and women equally. Personally, I thought Lucy was going a little overboard in her assessment of David.

I had known David and his then-wife, Lee Reynolds, for a while socially in New York. David represented Jack for a period of time. He was a charmer besides being a major dealmaker. He had taken over Judy's business affairs after she divorced Sid Luft. Judy was quick to defend David. "Oh Lucy, he's harmless and so sweet. You know he's taking good care of my problems. Hey, the show's a hit! I have no complaints about anything, darling."

I could tell Lucy smelled something fishy despite Judy's assurances. "I don't know, Judy, I'd be careful." Sadly, Lucy was spot-on about David. He took Judy to the cleaners and left her penniless again.

Another party, thrown by Abe Lipsey, a prominent furrier and his wife Muriel, found Lucy and me head to head with a serpent. No, not a real snake, but one by the name of Jim Aubrey. He was thusly referred to in the industry as the "smiling cobra." I knew Jim casually and found him very attractive. Jim was currently president of CBS where he presided over hit shows like *Green Acres, The Beverly Hillbillies, Gilligan's Island* and Lucy's show.

Jim pulled me aside and wanted me to ask Lucy something that was very important. I didn't quite understand it at the time. A short time later, I conveyed his message to Lucy.

"Tell him to go fuck himself," she hissed, as she crunched down on her ice from her Jack Daniels. It was obvious that she had issues with Jim but I didn't know exactly what they were. Lucy would later tell me it was over a critical time slot change with her show that was not to her liking.

When I went back to Jim to inform him of her answer, I really didn't have to tell him. He had been watching the whole time and saw Lucy's reaction—she damn near blew her wig off. I didn't have to tell him how Lucy really felt.

"Jim, whatever it is you wanted, it isn't going to work," I said. He gave me a peck on the cheek and said, "Thanks, I owe you one."

★ ★ ★

Swen Swenson was unusually tall for a dancer, which gave him a unique angular flow to his movements. He was blonde, and very handsome in his Swedish looks. He carried himself like an athlete, very macho, yet friendly and engaging in his aloofness. Choreographers loved his style and he was always in demand. Besides being one of my dearest and best friends in show business, Swen and I eventually bred Yorkshire Terriers together.

We were also avid collectors of unusual antiquities. Swen's specialty was carved lifelike carousel figures, such as lions, peacocks, ostriches and other animals from the kingdom. His house on Minetta Lane in Greenwich Village was filled and jam-packed with oddities of all kinds. If you wanted to sit, it had to be on a set of four old side-by-side movie theater seats or on an animal's body.

I knew Lucy would get a kick out of his place so we visited his home on one of our days off during *Wildcat*. She would later describe it as a witch's den, too scary for her own kids to venture through. She loved to tell everyone about it.

"Can you imagine, living in a jungle? Swen, you are some weird cat," she giggled.

What Lucy didn't yet know was that Swen's boyfriend was a prominent plastic surgeon who was footing the bill for most of Swen's extravagant investments, including Swen's house. Dr. Manfred Graf von Linde was presumably of some Germanic titled ancestry, the equivalent of a count. I had already gone to see Manfred as a patient about removing a suspicious mole. His appearance was intimidating, very Aryan, tall and gorgeous. He literally looked like he stepped out of central casting as a German officer. One might expect him to click-click his heels and salute

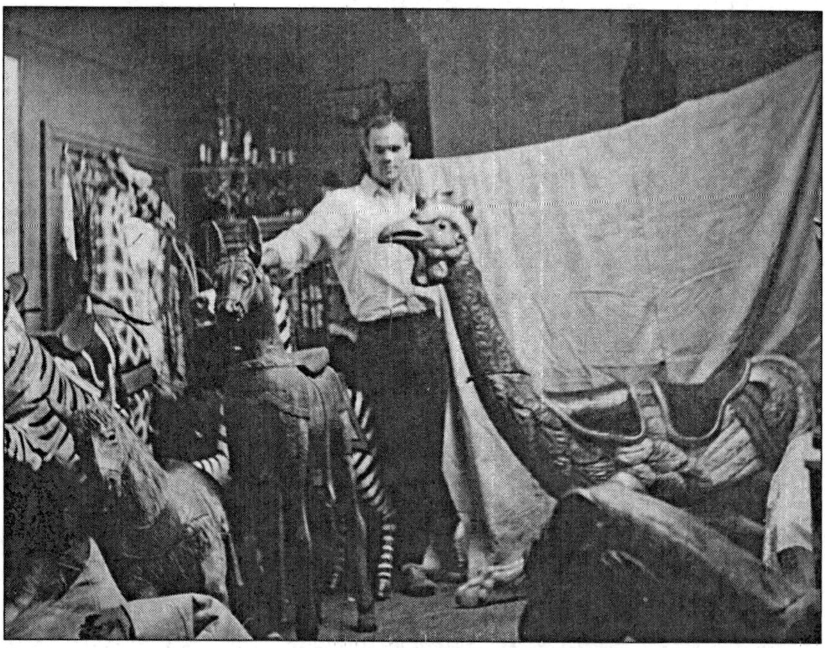

Lucy was surprised on her visit to Swen Swenson's place on Minetta Lane. Imagine these carousel figures as furniture. - Photo credit Frederick Fried

"*Sieg heil!*" upon being introduced. Turned out he was very polite, although his conversation was sparse and chilly. I didn't really "get" their relationship.

One memorable winter evening, while Lucy was in New York for some promotion and when Jack was appearing in Las Vegas, she called me to join her for dinner at her hotel.

"Better yet Lucy," I replied, "I'm cooking oso *bucco*, your favorite. Swen and his boyfriend are coming over for dinner."

"Is that an invitation?" she asked.

"Sure, Lucy. I'll have them pick you up and you can see what I've done with the apartment." I couldn't wait for her reaction and especially to Punch. I wasn't working at the time so I had the whole afternoon to prepare my entree. I rarely got a chance to cook for Jack because of all the openings and social parties that Jack insisted on attending. I went all out with candles, mood music and lighting. I loved giving intimate parties as opposed to all the phony baloney press shit that became part of my new life with Jack.

When they arrived, I could tell they were impressed with not only the spectacular views, but also the aromas coming from the kitchen, bombarding their senses. My little dog, Wildy, had recently whelped two pups to delight us with their cuteness. There is nothing more adorable than Yorkie puppies.

Dinner went as expected with small talk and after several attempts on my part to speak to Manfred in German, he acted like he didn't hear. Swen quickly changed the subject. I wasn't sure if Lucy noticed it or not. I certainly found it odd and couldn't wait to dish with Lucy. They left rather early, due to Manfred having an early scheduled surgery.

"Well, Miss Paula, you've done it again," Lucy said as she sunk into the down filled sofa. "It is so you. I love Punch, the puppies, where you placed my candlesticks, and especially you!" Lucy's approval and admiration always made me feel exceptional. "Now tell me what the hell is with that doctor? I'm even more surprised at Swen. Even I could tell that Manfred couldn't speak German. What a phony. Let's have some Jack Daniels, do the dishes and you can call me a cab later." She went on saying, "Have you seen that limo that they picked me up in?"

"You mean the one that looks like a touring *Reichstadt* car?" We laughed into the evening and I gave her a tour of the rest of the apartment.

Lucy asked me what I was doing for the weekend. I hadn't had much planned, just a few parties and dinner engagements.

"Cancel them," Lucy said. "Gary and I have to stop in Vegas on the way back. Frank is playing there. Come with us. Besides, you can surprise Jack!" Lucy was always fun to be with in Vegas. We both loved Frank Sinatra and I'd get to see Jack, so I had no complaints with her offer. I packed my bags and it was off to Silver City. I'll never forget that trip.

We had just seen Frank's show, which was absolutely amazing. Frank could command a stage like no one else. We had some time in between shows (we were seeing Jack's show next) so Lucy wanted to play a little craps. Boy, was she ever red hot. She made over twenty passes and people were crowding ten deep around the table shouting, "Go Lucy!" I will always remember those beautiful graceful hands with perfectly manicured nails and the way she threw the dice with a flourish. Her femininity was really reflected in those flowing motions. Lucy loved any game that involved throwing dice.

Frank was with us and was standing right next to me. Now I was always intrigued with Frank but not in a sexual way. Those blue eyes didn't hypnotize me the way they did other women. And as the crowd grew bigger, we were pushed closer together and Frank just started coming on to me.

Lucy, not missing a beat while making these incredible throws at the table, said, "Come on, Frank, you think the passes I'm throwing here are on fire? Yours are burning up the table. Can it, she's married!"

That didn't deter Frank. He was very sweet and had his arm playfully around my waist. But even Frank couldn't resist joining in, shouting and screaming with the crowd as Lucy was making an incredible delivery with the dice. She made so much money for people at the table it was unbelievable. It became a legendary night—an evening in which Lucy made twenty passes and I avoided all of Frank's.

Meanwhile back in New York, Manfred was making headlines, too. It turned out he was indeed a phony. His real name was Dick Glick from Puppen, Wisconsin, or Robert E. Dent of Birmingham, Alabama. While Swen and Manfred were together, Manfred had married a woman fourteen years his senior named Lucille Rogers. She was very wealthy and was mysteriously murdered in Cap-Haïtien, Haiti while they were on their honeymoon cruise.

Manfred was held in Haiti for questioning and released. I felt awful for Swen. I never believed Swen was in on the nefarious plot or that he would have known what Manfred was up to. Swen claimed he was not involved with Manfred, that he was just a "tenant" living in Manfred's house. But before the trial, Manfred committed suicide in the house he and Swen shared on Minetta Lane by drowning himself in the bathtub. Poor Swen! He had to be mortified. We never spoke about it again.

Unfortunately, Lucy wasn't so forgiving and was cautious of Swen after that scandal came to light. I knew Lucy believed Swen was innocent, but she was profoundly disturbed about Manfred, because the murdered woman's name was Lucille, and she had been a redhead to boot!

★ ★ ★

Jack Carter and Sammy Davis, Jr. had been buddies since co-starring on Broadway in *Mr. Wonderful*. Jack was known as the white Sammy Davis and had that same dynamic quality which attracted me to him, except a much taller version. It was through Jack that I got to know Sammy better and Sammy's wife, May. The four of us became good friends and spent quality time together. I especially enjoyed hanging out with May. She and Sammy had the most adorable children and they both doted on them. I loved photographing them all as a family.

Men envied Sammy because they saw the effect he had on their women which was an incredible sexual energy, all rolled into one small bundle. His audiences were equally exhausted when he performed. He had a wild sense of humor. Jack and Sammy were a strange pair of comedians and enjoyed the battle of wits for which they were both famous.

One night after Jack and I saw Sammy perform at a casino in Jersey, Sammy confided to us that he was approached by producer Hilliard "Hilly" Elkins to do the musical version of *Golden Boy*. More specifically, he wanted to know how would we feel about my playing opposite him as his girlfriend "Lorna." I was overwhelmed with joy, and Jack didn't have a problem with it either. The chance to play in Odets' famous classic was an actor's dream. I hugged and kissed Sammy—I couldn't contain myself, practically falling out of my chair.

Naturally the newspaper columns picked it up and although production was a year away, there was much talk about me doing the show from then on. I was floating on air in anticipation during all that time. Lucy got wind of it in Los Angeles and called to congratulate me. She understood my excitement, but eventually she had her own thoughts about it.

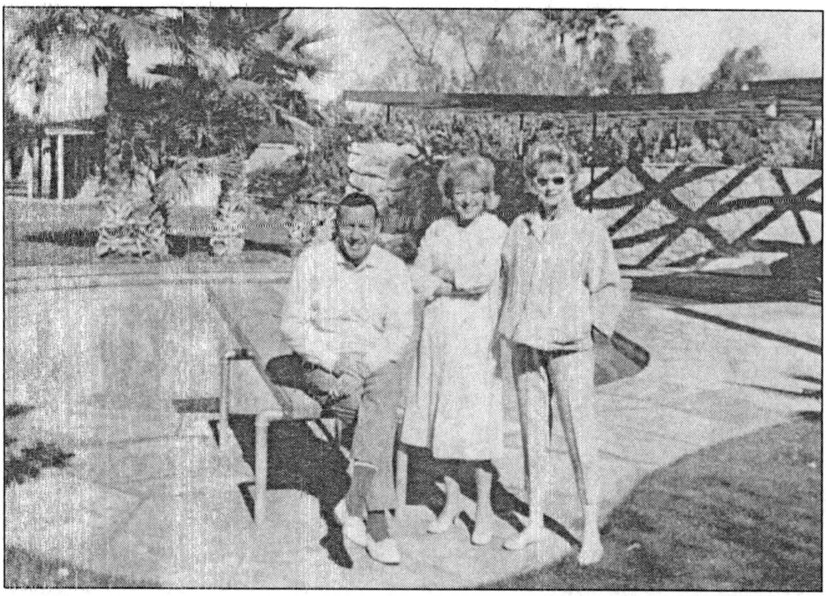

At Lucy's house, Thunderbird golf course, Palm Springs.

On one of our visits to Los Angeles, we stayed with Lucy and Gary at their Thunderbird Palm Springs house.

From there we drove down to the Hotel Del Coronado in San Diego for some sea air and golf because Jack and Gary couldn't play on the course at the Thunderbird because they were Jewish.

While the boys were off golfing, we girls had long brunches and sipped piña coladas at the famous bar. Lucy had said she needed to have a serious talk to me about something. I could tell it was bothering her. I prayed that it wasn't about her marriage to Gary, because she appeared to be really happy. I was anxiously waiting for her to open up and tell me. Savoring my eggs benedict, she surprised me with, "Paula, I'm concerned about *Golden Boy*."

"What about it?"

"Are you sure it's a good career choice?"

"Of course! It's a great chance for me to do something in a more serious vein. Plus, I can't wait to work with Sammy!"

"I understand that. We both love and admire him dearly. He's sure to be successful in the show, but it won't work that way for you, my dear!"

"How's that?"

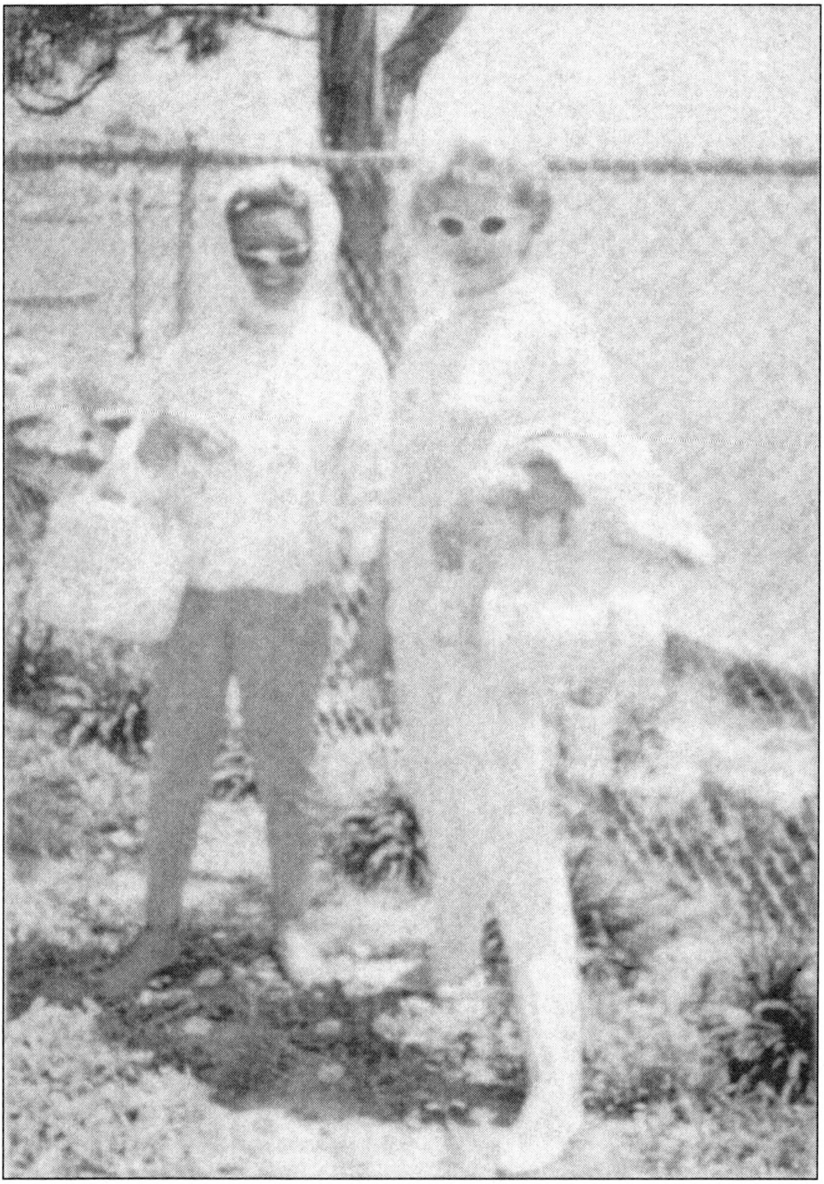

Lucy with me at the Del Coronado in San Diego

"How naïve can you be! Don't you know what's going on here? Half the country still has laws prohibiting interracial marriage or cohabitation. And you think the audiences are going to be comfortable witnessing love scenes on stage?"

"That's not my problem."

"Yes it is! Listen to me. You're on a hot roll right now. Why jeopardize it? You can't change the way people think. You've worked too long and hard to throw away your career."

"But, Lucy, Jack doesn't see anything wrong with it."

"Of course not. It's not his career that will be affected. Look what happened with Kim Novak. When was the last time you saw her in any big movies? When the press got hold of the fact that she was having an affair with Sammy all hell broke loose. Harry Cohen, head of Columbia Studios gave her an ultimatum, 'Cut it off or you'll never work here again!' There were even rumors the mob got involved and threatened to kill Sammy."

"Ah, well... Lucy..."

"Well, ***what***? Believe me, the timing isn't right. Someday, but not here, not yet."

"I can't quit now. I've committed myself to Sammy!"

"If I know you, you'll find away."

By now, my eggs benedict were cold and unappetizing in what looked like yellow gooey crap. It didn't dawn on me the potential ramifications this could have on my career. Sammy insisted on getting Jack's okay. Jack was very open minded, as were most performers. It wouldn't have dawned on him that this would have an adverse effect on my career. All of us were only thinking of the artistic elements involved—what's best for the show.

Lucy took on this mentor role as far as it would affect me and my future. This was a big decision but thanks to Lucy, I now knew the answer. I only didn't know how I could face Sammy without hurting him. In my mind, there was no way out. But as fate would have it, there was one. When it came time to talk contracts and the offer officially came in, it was surprisingly low. Luckily, I had established my going rate in previous shows.

I had known Hilly Elkins for years—back when he started off as a manager, and at one point he had Sammy as a client. He was upgrading his image now from "wheeler dealer" agent/manager to legitimate Broadway producer and felt his lowball offer to me was justified by Sammy's celebrity. I reminded him I had worked with big stars like Lucille Ball and George Gobel and I couldn't accept anything less than my established salaries on those shows. That's something that Sammy could easily understand.

As it turned out, Hilly hired an unknown actress Paula Wayne, for the part of "Lorna." She got lukewarm reviews, which just about ruined my movie career. Out in clueless Hollywood, when casting the movie *Bob and Carol and Ted and Alice*, my name was suggested for the role of "Alice Henderson." Director Paul Mazursky said, "Forget it. She got terrible reviews in *Golden Boy* on Broadway," mistaking Paula Wayne for Paula Stewart. Ironically, *Golden Boy* actually did end up hurting my movie career!

Many years later, when I ran into Mazursky, I reminded him of this and he just shrugged his shoulders and said, "Yeah, I guess I was wrong. Sorry about that." Dyan Cannon got the part and went on to marry Cary Grant. Humorously I thought to myself, "Gosh, I could have been Cary's fifth." Jack and I attended the *Golden Boy* preview and congratulated Sammy on a stellar performance.

"I know we couldn't have afforded you, Paula, and I wish we had," Sammy quipped.

"Oh, Sammy, Paula Wayne was just fine," I said.

"She isn't *you*, Paula!" Sammy was too kind...and a class act.

The show was a big success and Sammy went on to receive a Tony nomination for his performance. Hilly garnered a nomination for "Best Producer" and the show received a nomination for "Best Musical."

And I ended up getting the short end of the stick despite the fact I had nothing to do with the production.

★ ★ ★

"Dying is easy, comedy is hard," was a showbiz expression I'd heard more than once. Turned out it was absolutely true. Doing an act together with Jack was never my idea, and it wasn't easy. I was a soloist; I had already performed in supper clubs and other long-since vanished nighteries. I had music arrangements that Burt had scored for me while we were married, but my lasting love was always theater. In smoked-filled nightclubs you had to

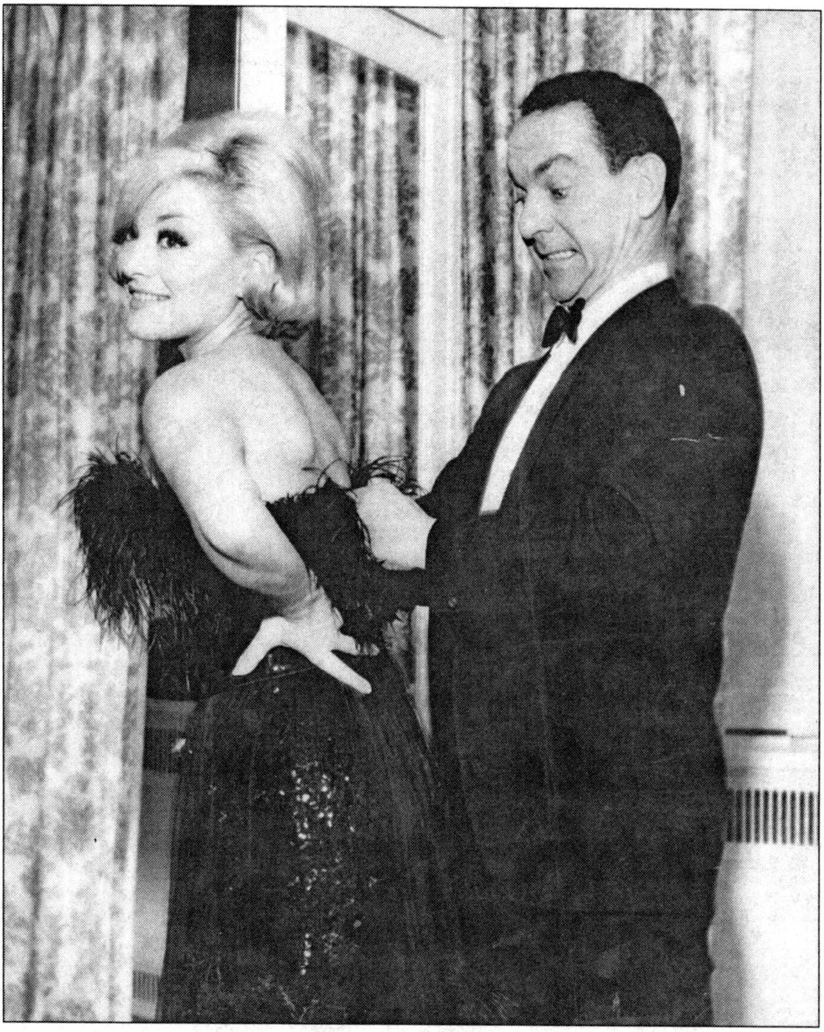

Jack and I backstage during our performance together at the Empire Room, Waldorf Astoria 1961. No patience for zippers or anything else! - Photo credit Bert Andrews

fight the booze, noisy patrons and waiters. In theater there were no distractions.

There is a formula from the earliest vaudeville till now, which is the comic versus the straight man. Comedy relies on opposites, timing, and rhythm. Jack initially just wanted to help me broaden my horizons by having me on the bill with him as an opening act. He would then follow me on stage and include me in some small

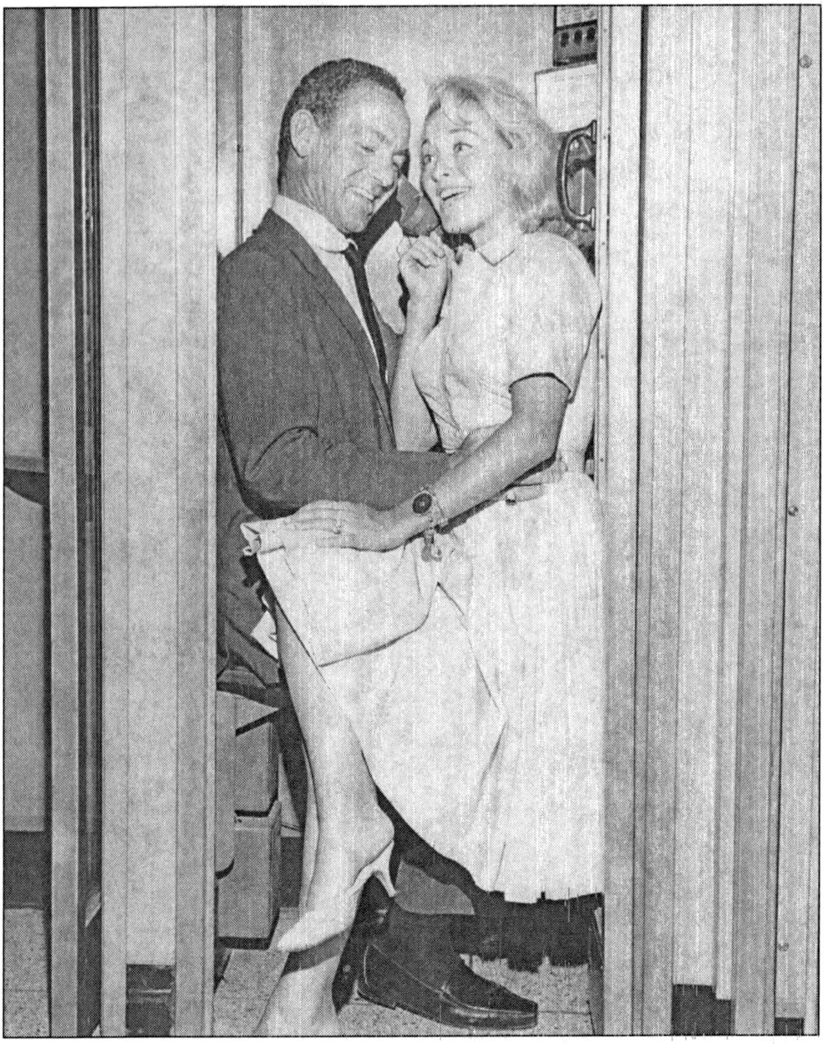

Remember phone booths? Just the two of us alone in a rare moment. Jack gave me the bracelet I'm wearing and a charm for each show I was in. Photo credit David Workman.

husband and wife banter usually about my obsession to constantly fix things around the house—how all day long I build, paint and fix things.

Jack: "Are you going to do the dishes?"

Paula: "Why are they broken?"

Jack: "I didn't lose a wife, I gained a carpenter."

Jack: "Boy, you kill me Paula."

Paula: "Ok, I'll build the coffin."

A reviewer once said about our act, "Jack Carter is brash, bouncy, full of fun—and more so with Paula Stewart added." The audiences loved it and Jack noted the latest teams like Stiller and Meara were really hot draws in the clubs. He got his writers to come up with some routines for us to do. At first they were cute repartees on current topics or spoofs on current Broadway shows from *South Pacific* to *My Fair Lady*. Over time we moved on from lightweight digs to put downs that were hurtful to me, despite the huge laughs. We were becoming the "Contentious Carters." We even made an album called *Battle Hymns for Married Lovers*. Bickering became an art with us—onstage and off. I was getting discouraged doing the act and felt demeaned as Jack's pawn. I suggested we do more theater.

Working with Jack in a play was intense but gratifying because he would have to stick to the script, play the scene and not ad lib all over the place. He was an amazingly good actor. Even later at ninety years old, before his death, he worked bare-assed on the hit cable show *Shameless*.

Jack and I performed in all the top resorts around the United States and Europe intermittently for two years. We played the Empire Room at the Waldorf Astoria Hotel in 1964 and were heralded as the new "*Peter Lind and Mary Healy team, coming across with zing and charm*."

There were always a myriad of stars twinkling in the audience. The following year we played the Royal Box at the Americana Hotel. It just happened that our opening night coincided with the premiere of *How to Murder Your Wife*, which catered a party for the stars in town at the El Morocco. Frank Farrell wrote in the New York World-Telegram and Sun that Jack and I "...complement each other" and we "are always fun to be with on or off stage..."

Since Jack and I had a late performance, everyone ended up at our show including Frank Sinatra, Lauren Bacall, Jason Robards, Buddy Hackett, Jack Lemon, Sammy Davis, Jr., Rudy Valle, Eddie Fisher, Gregory Peck, and my good friend Eva Gabor. First to congratulate me was Lucy in one of her famous early morning wake up calls to say even Frank told her, "That Carter's got some wife. She's a knock-out and boy can she sing." Then Lucy added, "You know, Paula, I'm convinced there's nothing you can't do." Well, unfortunately this was the one time Lucy was wrong. There was something I seemed I couldn't do and that was save my marriage to Jack. My hope that we would last long enough to read off our press notices to each other in our old age was becoming questionable.

★ ★ ★

Up until now, Jack had always referred to me in the press as well as in his act as his "Angel Bride." In the beginning it was a term of endearment. But overnight, I became the wife who turned an apartment into a house of horrors with creepy wallpaper, gargoyle furniture, and abstract art. He used me in his act like so many other comedians used their wives, to get a cheap laugh. I was becoming the brunt of his humor. It was Henny Youngman's "Take my wife, please!" on steroids. I was in shock, humiliated and devastated. I tried to laugh it off at first. It was funny, but then we would start squabbling in public and I took on a very defensive attitude, alien to my normally cheerful nature and echoing his contentious nature.

At this point, we were never home together. He was always playing the casinos and big clubs in Las Vegas and nightspots in Florida while I was working on Broadway. Over time, I became emotionally estranged from Jack. My resentment was seething under the surface.

Meanwhile, Harry Millard had bought a townhouse on Manhattan's Lower East Side. It needed a lot of work, so when Jack was out of town, I helped Harry turn it in into a fabulous bachelor's pad. He hosted legendary parties for which I was the grand hostess. I began living two different lives. Living with Harry as his celebrity paramour, and then deftly switching over as "Mrs. Carter" when Jack was in town back to the nightclub scene. Leading this dual lifestyle was very schizophrenic. That said, I was having a ball.

But people were beginning to talk about the Carters, not all of it good. They also didn't want to be around us because it was uncomfortable the way Jack would put me down. Lucy especially didn't

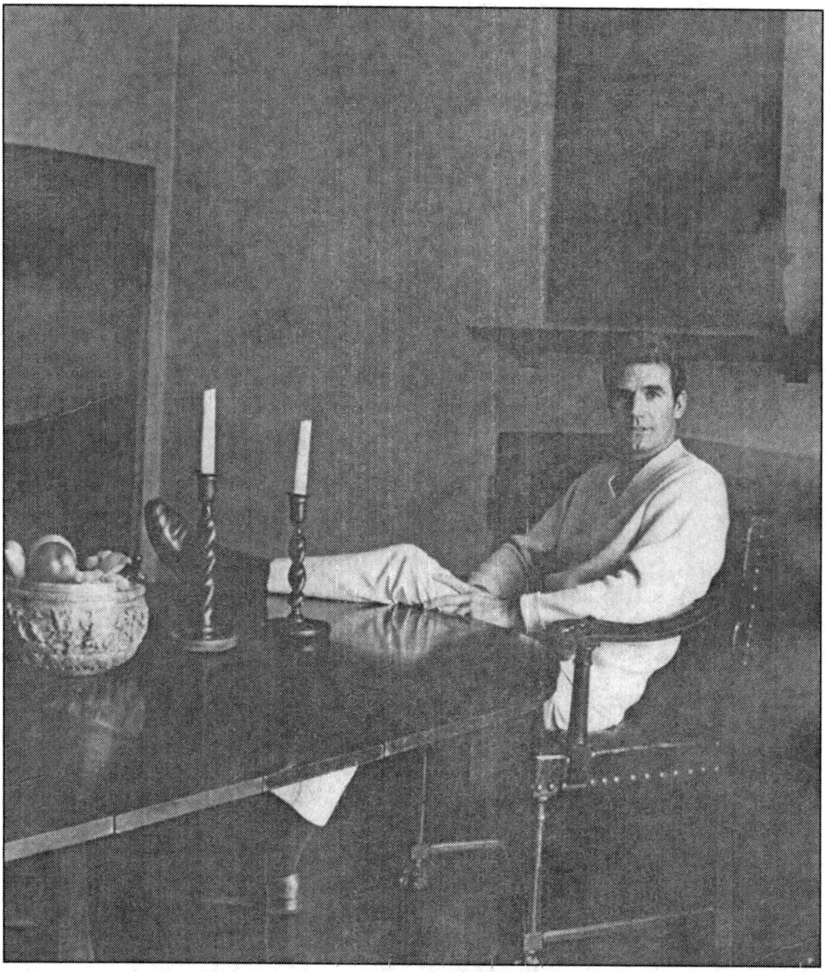

Harry at home. - Photo credit Millard Garas

like it—very turned off by what she saw and how it was affecting me. I called Lucy during one of my breakdowns and she said, "Paula, why don't you come out here. You need a change of air."

So I flew to LA and stayed with Lucy and Gary in the guesthouse. They took me to Palm Springs and then down to La Costa. Jack got wind through Gary and showed up like nothing was wrong. Instead of being on his best behavior in front of Lucy, Jack continued with his shabby treatment of me. It got so bad that Lucy would visibly cringe. She got so upset that she confronted

Jack: "What's wrong with you? Can't you see you're going to lose her if you continue your verbal abuse?"

"I can't help myself. I really love her, but it's no use. That's the way I am."

"Don't give me that crap, Jack, you can do something about it. You just have to learn to control your irresponsible mouth!"

Jack did try and went to a shrink for a while, but it didn't help. He was an angry person and he would take out his frustrations on whoever was closest to him and that person just so happened to be me. Although Jack was a difficult person to live with, he was a great workmate. I've always said, "I'd rather work with him than live with him!" His demons were so ingrained in his psyche, I don't think the best shrink in the world could have helped him. He was always sorry after his tirades, but the damage had been done. Strangely, I felt his pain, even though I bore the brunt of his outbursts.

There was no way to even sit in a car with him. He would fight traffic, scream at the other drivers, and carry on like a mad man, especially with cab drivers. Many times they would refuse to take him any further, stopping the car, telling him to get out. I gifted him once with a pair of gold cufflinks shaped like stop lights with

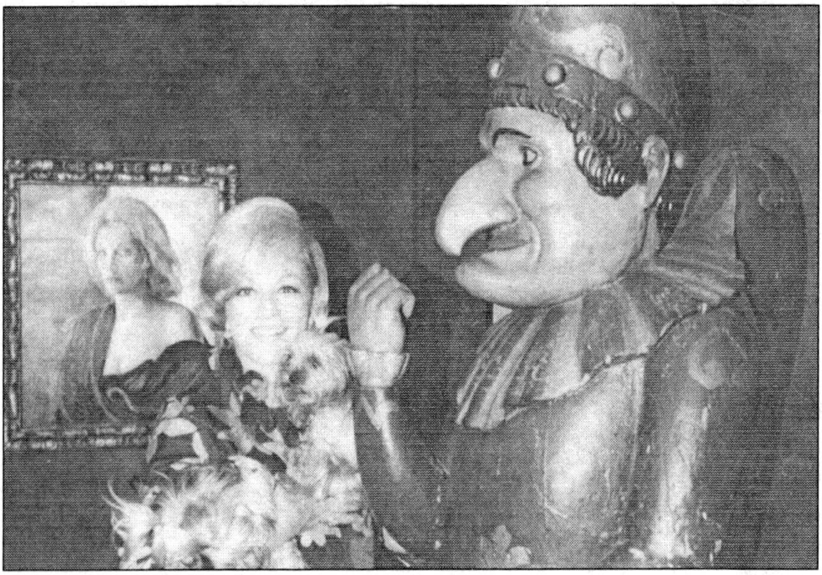

With my Yorkies and "Punch" in the San Remo apartment, New York City. Tom Keogh painted my portrait in the background.

emeralds and rubies for the lights as a reminder that he needed to work on his impatience. He regretfully told me years later they had been stolen. Jack admitted they were his favorite because they were a most insightful gift.

Jack was just never satisfied with anything. We ate out most of the time because no matter what I cooked for him, he'd criticize whatever I prepared. We would go to a restaurant and Jack was famous for his "send backs." It didn't matter what restaurant—from Danny's Hideaway to Toots Shorr or even Lutèce, Jack would send the food back—even before tasting it, just because it didn't look right to him. The owners would put up with it because he was a celebrity, but it was embarrassing because the man was a raving maniac. Plus, he had atrocious table manners.

My father found these things intolerable and never understood how I could live with such a crude person. I had every intention of leaving Jack and had packed my bags at least a dozen times only to break down laughing too hard to ever make it to the elevator. Jack would say, "Aren't you forgetting your boyfriend, Mr. Punch? How can I live without you and your broom flying around here?... Oh my god, what will I tell my friends, she left me because of a hunchback!" He would have me in stitches.

Still, I couldn't get him to ease up on his public verbal abuse. The magic was diminishing in our life at in increasing rate. This was not what I had dreamed of as blissful. It was marital blasphemy.

I also resented the fact that our sex life was practically nil. I really wanted to start a family but I couldn't seem to get pregnant and the hopes of motherhood were vanishing rapidly. A doctor once told Jack, "If you'd stop playing around and save a little for your wife once in a while, maybe you might have a family." Another crushing blow to my hopes of motherhood at the time was the scary result of the removal of a precancerous growth in my breast. I was warned not to get pregnant. Hormonal changes in a woman due to pregnancy can aggravate precancerous cells and the cancer would come back again. It seemed even fate was working against me in my hopes of becoming a mother. To add insult to injury, I got tired of reading in the papers who Jack was dating while he was married to me. Was this the wakeup call the

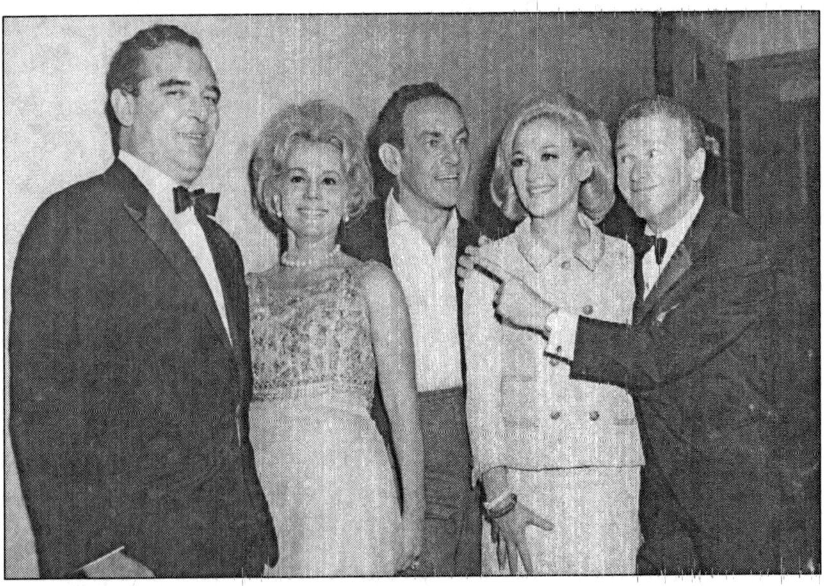

Jack and I with Dick Brown, Eva's husband at the time and Red Buttons. Eva and I are both wearing bargains from Loehmann's—mine was a silver Chanel! - Photo credit Will Weissberg.

marriage was over? Finished? *Kaput*? How much more bullshit was I willing to take?

★ ★ ★

As I mentioned, among our circle of friends were Eva Gabor and her husband, Dick Brown. Dick Brown was the son of a very, very wealthy man. Not a real surprise, the Gabors only married rich men, but Eva was really mad for this Dick Brown. I never understood what she saw in him because I thought his personality and appearance were unattractive.

Eva and I used to be very close. Being a Gabor meant she adored gorgeous dresses, gowns and jewelry. We had that in common plus loving a bargain. When I wasn't working she would pick me up in her chauffeured Rolls Royce and we would venture to Loehmann's Back Room, where you could get incredible deals on designer apparel.

One night, when Eva was in California doing *Green Acres* and Jack was in Canada working, Ray Katz, Eva and Jack's manager

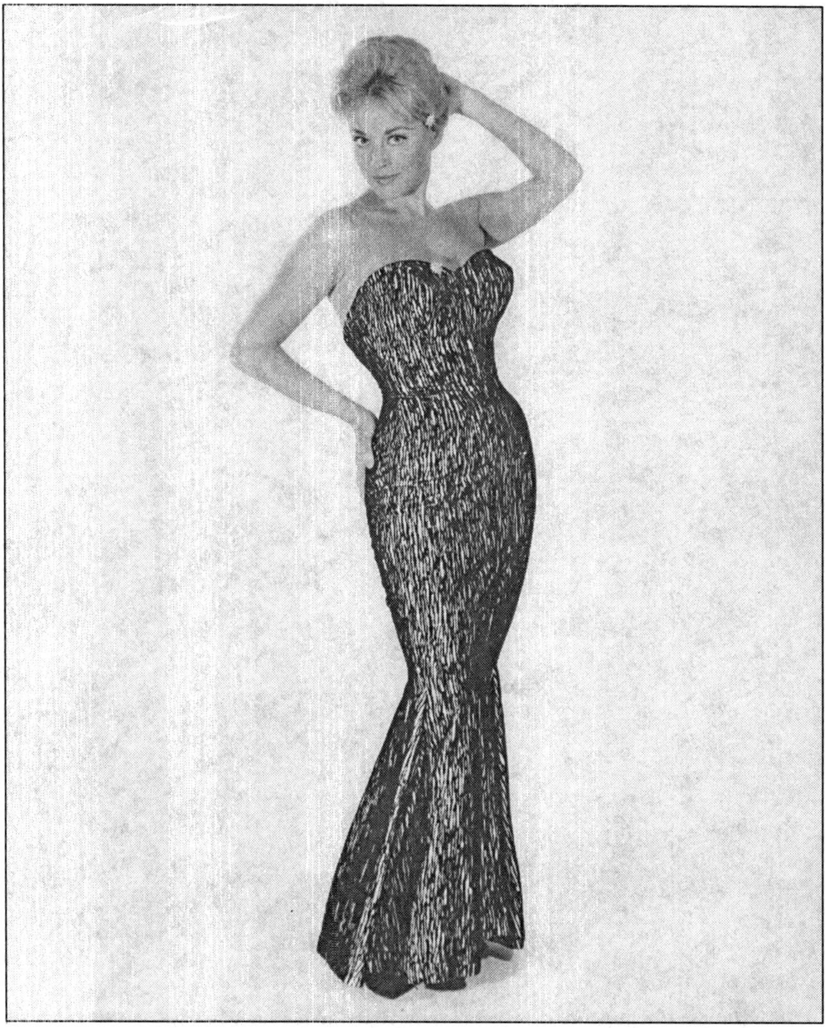

The cut-velvet Cosmo Sirchio dress—not one of my bargains! - Photo credit Friedman-Abeles

called me to come join him and Dick at P.J. Clark's to have hamburgers. We had an early dinner and then Ray wanted to leave. He was tired and had to get up early in the morning. Well, I didn't feel like going back to my empty apartment at the San Remo just yet and Dick said, "Hey listen, I'll take you home later. Why don't we go down to the Village to catch a couple of acts?"

Coming from a theater background, I was naturally a night person—9:00 p.m. was early evening for me. So we went downtown

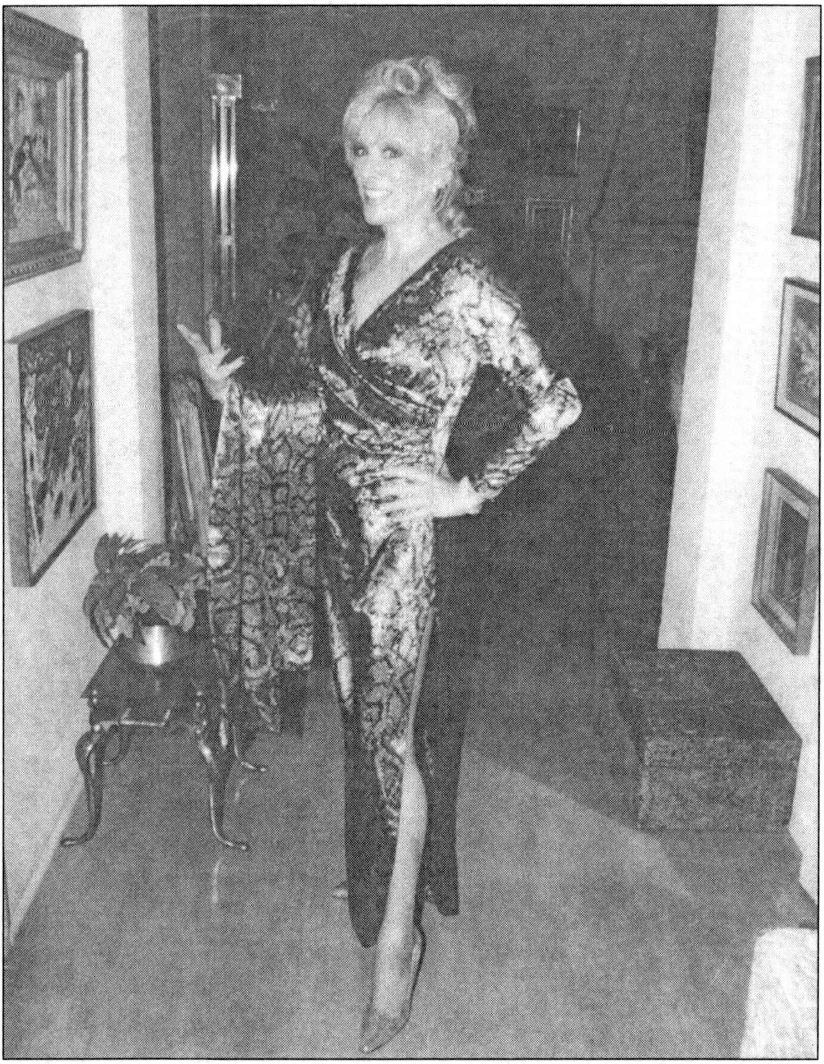

I loved this gold Oscar de la Renta given to me by Zsa Zsa Gabor. Of course, it needed major alterations.

and hit a couple of clubs, among them the Blue Angel, seeing Barbra Streisand who was unknown at the time, and whoever else happened to be playing in the area. Around 2:00 a.m. the clubs started closing so I said, "Well, I guess it's about time. You can take me home now." So he had his chauffeur drive me back to the San Remo and I went to bed.

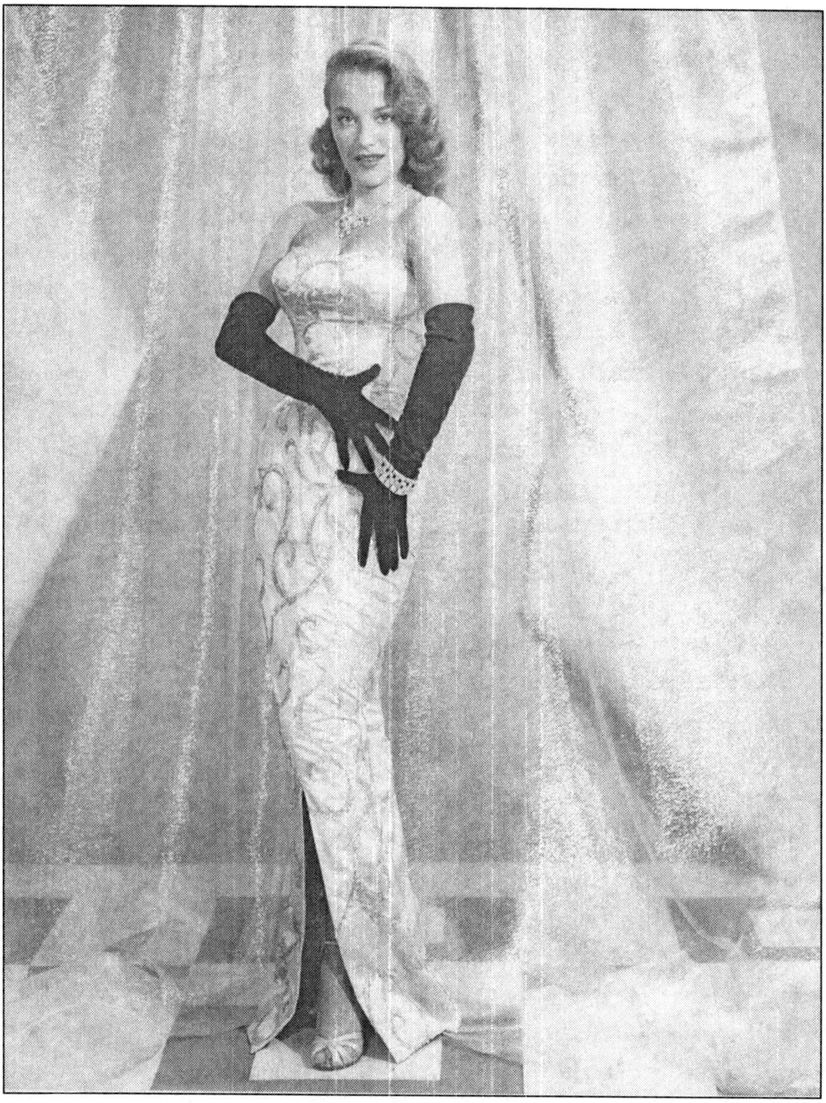

I wish I still owned this gorgeous gown. - Photo credit Irving Christenson Studios

At 8:00 a.m. I heard the phone ring. "Jesus Christ, if this isn't Lucy or another audition, somebody better have died this morning!" Close enough, it was Eva.

"Vere is Richard?" She screamed in an agitated Hungarian fit. "Vere is he? I know Richard is zere, I know you vas out vid him last night! Put him on ze phone!"

Still half asleep I replied, "Eva, are you crazy? Your husband is not here. Why don't you call him at home?"

"I haf called him at home and he is not zere!"

"Well, he sure as hell isn't here!"

"I know you vent out vid him last night and I know you are having problems with Jack. I know he is zer vid you!"

"Eva, this is ridiculous. I refuse to continue this conversation!" And I hung up on her. Years later Eva apologized to me. She said, "Paula, you vaz so right to hang up on me. If it vaz me, I vouldn't haf talked to me eezer."

By now, I was fully awake and confused, so I called Jack in Toronto and told him what happened. I asked him what did Eva mean about the inference that she knew "we" were having problems. Jack said, "Oh, don't pay any attention to it. You know how jealous she is of Dick. He's probably screwing around and why should you care?"

"Well, I do care because I would never play around with a friend's husband. I do have some ethics, you know! Our problems don't justify that."

Knowing Lucy would get a laugh out of this, I proceeded to call and tell her this one. Lucy said, "Come on, Paula, you know Eva. If Richard were poor she probably would have let you sleep with him!" Well, Lucy was right about that. Weirdest of all, I think Eva really loved him.

Years after her divorce from Brown and having played hostess for years to Merv Griffin, she hit on widowed Gary Morton three months after Lucy died. Eva appalled the help when she moved into Lucy's house and bed. But when she found out how cheap Gary was, she moved out just as fast.

Funny thing is, shortly after Gary and Lucy were married, it was obligatory to meet the Morton in-laws, one of them being Sid Gould. Sid was a cherubic comedic character actor who had a funny way of speaking and using his comedic mannerisms to get laughs from people, and one of them was Lucy. She loved his endearing brand of humor. Sid appeared regularly on her show throughout the '60s.

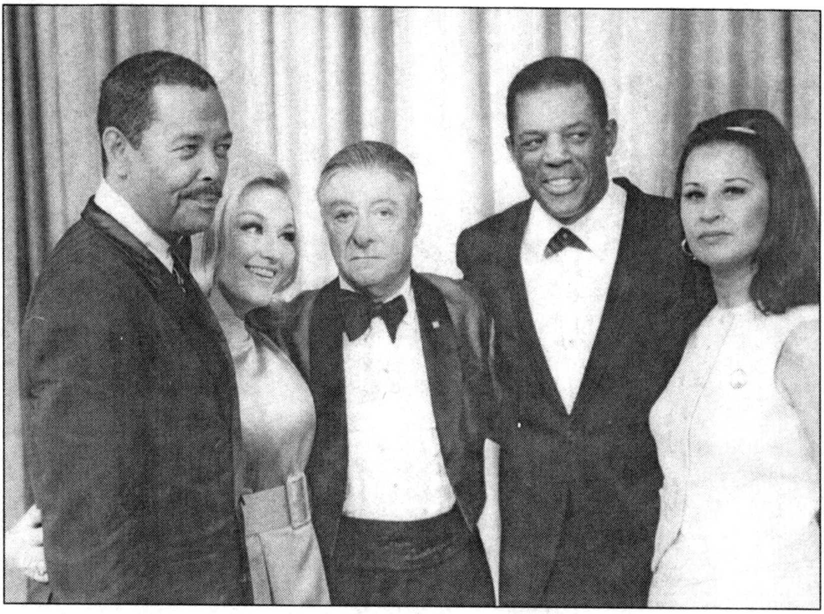

Billy Eckstein, George Jessel, Willie Mays, Mimi Weber and I at a celebrity function. One of so many I enthusiastically attended after my divorce from Jack.

One night over dinner at Lucy's when Sid was in attendance, he reminded Lucy about the skeletons in the Morton Family closet back in the Bronx. Sid, in his cute funny way warned Lucy, "Be careful when you leave town, some of Gary's cousins have moved here from the East and they might back up their truck to the house." Lucy roared with laughter while Gary slightly chuckled.

★ ★ ★

Confiding in Lucy was easy. She felt sorry for me because she obviously had gone through this herself. At this point in my career, I was flying back and forth quite often from New York to Los Angeles for auditions. I was thrilled Hollywood was noticing my work and I was eager to expand my work.

Sometimes I would stay with Lucy. Not always, because the guesthouse could be occupied. On one occasion while Jack was in Las Vegas at the Flamingo, I had flown out to Los Angeles and stayed with my manager, Mimi Weber, at the Beverly Hills Hotel.

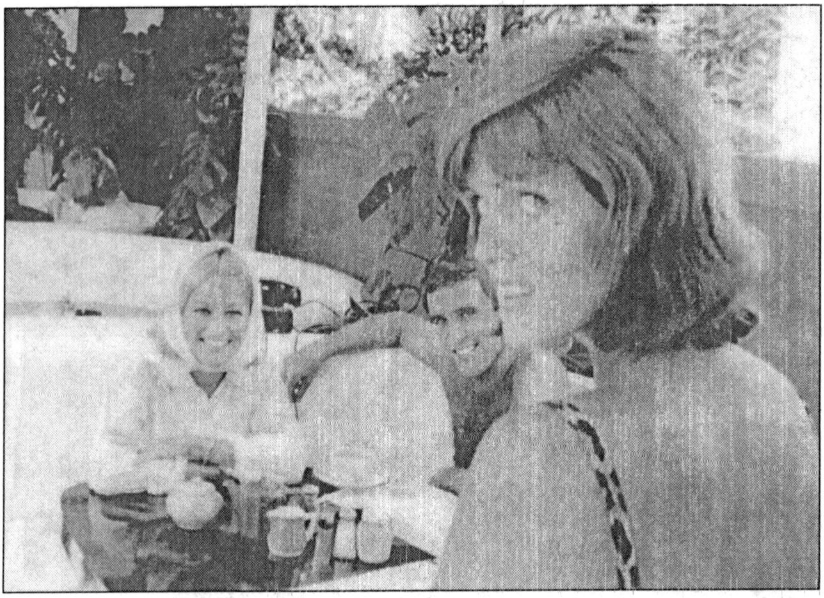

A chance meeting with Burt and his then-girlfriend, Slim Brandy at the Beverly Hills Hotel. Jack and I were just married.

Mimi had been a prominent agent representing clients like Bette Davis and Warren Beatty and was now a manager whose clients included Nick Nolte, Myrna Loy and me.

I believe I was up for a part on *Hogan's Heroes*. It just so happened that my ex-husband, Burt (Happy) Bacharach with whom I was still friendly, was also staying at the hotel with his then main squeeze and my future best friend Slim Brandy, a stunning beauty that always stopped traffic wherever she went.

We had a few cocktails and laughs before I joined Mimi for a late lunch by the pool. Munching on our burgers, we could overhear a woman at the next table, who was going on and on to her friends about how she was going to Las Vegas this weekend to be with...Jack Carter! Mimi's and my ears perked up right away. We just looked at each other through our sunglasses and kept quiet. She was a redhead and was married to someone else.

"Oh yes, it's all over between Jack and Paula," she told her girlfriends. She then went on about how Jack was begging her to come because Paula wasn't there.

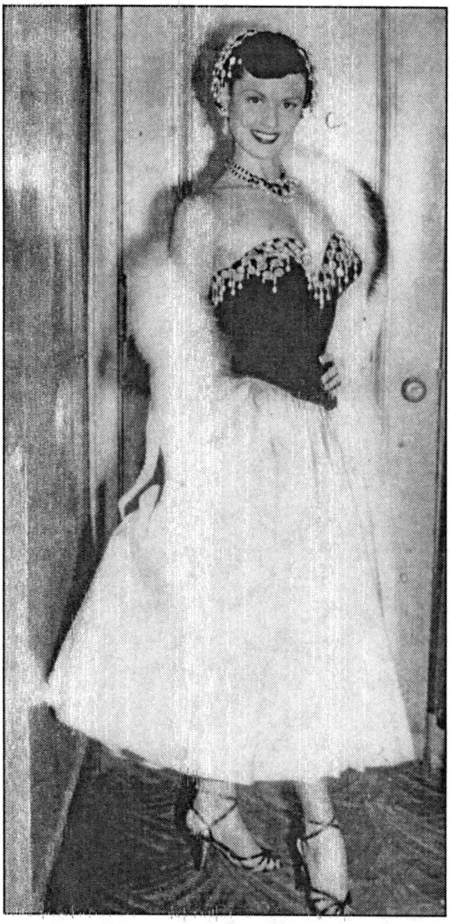

Slim Brandy was a long-time girlfriend of Burt's. She and I are still dear friends.

So I leaned over to Mimi and said, "Mimi, go page me on the intercom." Mimi quietly got up from our table and went over to the other side of the pool. In a couple of minutes, there was a voice booming over the intercom, "Paging Mrs. Jack Carter! Mrs. Jack Carter, you have a call."

Well, you could just see these women's bodies stiffening. They were frantically looking all around as I got up very slowly from my chair and walked calmly to the telephone sitting on the top side of their booth. I picked it up and said, "Hello, this is Mrs. Jack Carter. Yes, I'll hold." I was glaring at this woman as she looked at me with her mouth wide open. She had been running her mouth and she knew I had heard everything.

"Oh, hello, darling. Yes, Jack, I'm having a wonderful time with Mimi. Of course I'll be up to see you this weekend. Yes, sweetheart, bye-bye. I love you, too."

The phone barely hit the receiver and the woman said, "Oh, Paula, you remember me?" I looked at her and said, "Not with your clothes on, honey!"

That's just an example of Jack's infidelity; the man just couldn't keep his pants zipped up. Of course I didn't go to see him that time because I was so furious. I called Jack and told him what had happened and put him down for it. Naturally he said, "That's ridiculous. I don't even know who you're talking about!" I said, "Oh really? She obviously knew all about us."

That night I was invited over to dinner at Lucy's, and I told her what had happened earlier.

"So what else is new, Paula?" she said, instead of, "I told you so." We sat there in silence watching *What's My Line*? The worst part about that story was hearing the woman acknowledge it was over between Jack and me. Carterville was headed towards splitsville.

★ ★ ★

III
Paula West

I had just closed in What Makes Sammy Run with Steve Lawrence on Broadway. Burt's father, Bert Bacharach, always made a point of coming to my shows, and Sammy, was no exception. He was there for me closing night, though this was years after my divorce from Burt. Big Bert continued to remain one of my biggest fans and I dearly loved him.

I had replaced Bernice Massi for the last six months of the show's run. Harry had decided to move out to California to pursue his acting career. He was renting a house off Benedict Canyon while negotiating the purchase of a baronial mansion across the street from the Beverly Hills Hotel. With Lucy on the West Coast and now with Harry gone, I was feeling very lonely and reclusive.

Jack, sensing a widening rift in our relationship, booked us in Garson Kanin's *Born Yesterday* in an attempt to rekindle what was left of our marriage. It was rocky between Jack and me and with the gossip columns reporting both fact and fiction, our producers were nervous about our personal situation—how it would affect the show. But Jack and I were true professionals. He played the millionaire junk dealer and I played the dumb broad. And to everyone's relief, reviews were great, we were a "winning hit." The reviews reflected his comedic brilliance and, to boot, highlighted me as "an accomplished actress" beyond my musical talents, glowing that I had "too much personal allure ever to be mistaken for anyone else" in the part of "Billie Dawn." Then after Jack and I were a hit in *Critic's Choice*, we were in demand for other husband and wife roles and the great reviews kept rolling in.

Unfortunately, our personal relationship wasn't up to our professional prowess. I missed Harry. I missed Lucy. One night after a performance I told Jack, "I'm sorry, honey, it's over. I'm taking

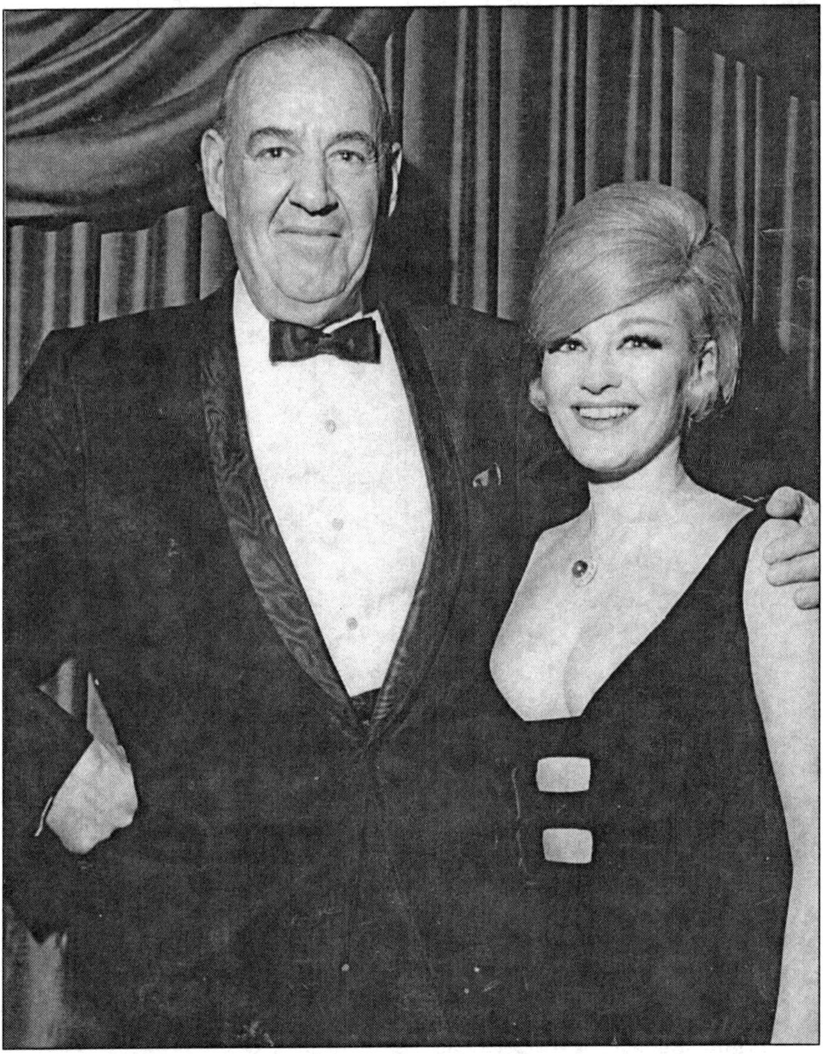

"Big" Bert Bacharach (Burt's dad) backstage of What Makes Sammy Run. *He always championed me and I loved him. He was such a dear. The star sapphire necklace–a gift from Jack. Another one of my fave gowns, a velvet sensation I designed with Cosmo Sirchio who made many of my outfits. - Photo credit Bill Mark*

the Yorkies, and heading west." I just needed to get away and do some serious contemplation. Jack never took my threats seriously, but this time I told him I got an apartment and mentioned it was next door to Barbara Nichols.

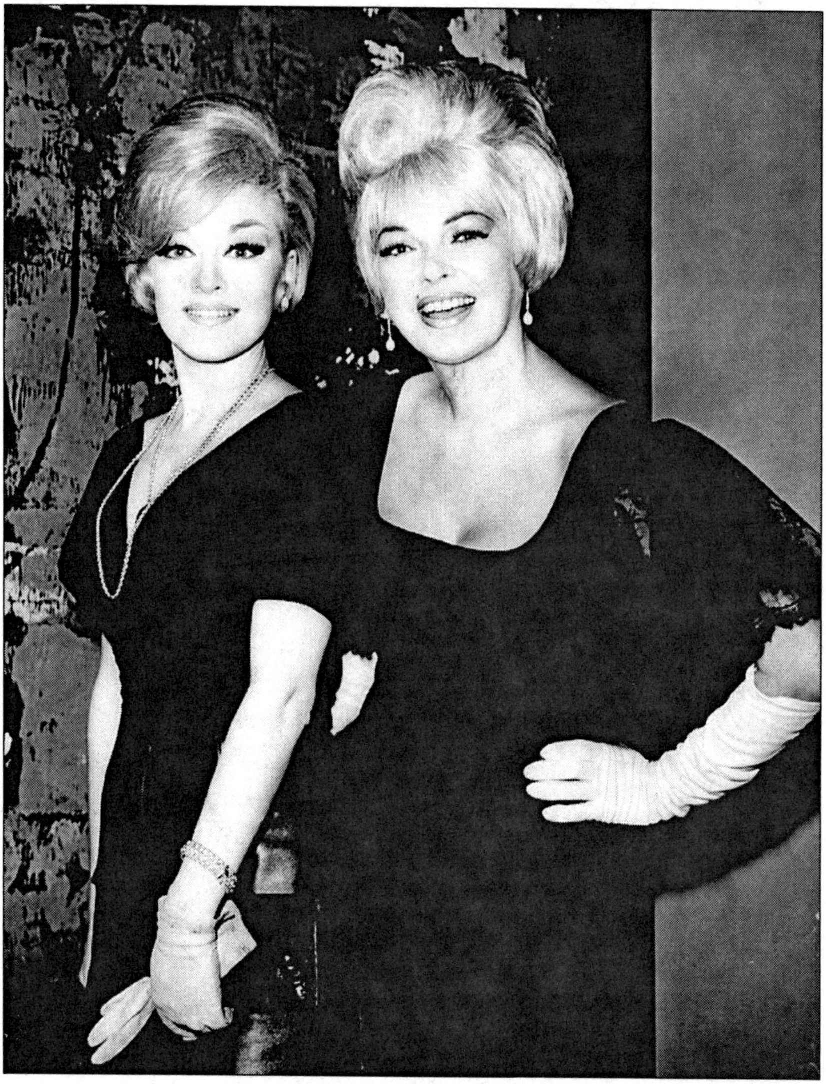

Barbara Nichols, my friend, L.A. neighbor and co-star in Let It Ride. *At the* What's New Pussycat *premiere.*

"Oh, so now you're leaving me for your 'girlfriend' huh?" There were rumors about Barbara having been gay and a "switch hitter." We had been photographed together at the premiere of *What's New Pussycat?* which raised a few eyebrows.

"So you're a lesbian now?"

"No, Jack. You know better."

Jack's comic genius failed to deter me this time. So I packed my bags and headed to California. Jack would continue to live at the San Remo, and in his mind, I was only taking a short vacation.

Lucy knew how unhappy I was and welcomed me with open arms. She did question why I would ever choose to live next door to Barbara Nichols.

"I don't like the fact that you're moving next to Barbara." Lucy suspected everyone of having slept with Desi.

"But, Lucy, she swore Desi was too much of a drunk, even for her."

"Ha! That's the pot calling the kettle black."

We both laughed, Barbara was known for her overindulgences. In the end, Lucy understood my point, there just simply happened to be a neat duplex available in Barbara Nichols' great building.

Even though I was terribly depressed because of my disastrous relationship with Jack, I was very happy for Lucy's current success with her new series, *Here's Lucy,* which was a top ten hit in the ratings. She was back where she belonged, on television. Despite that, she found time to be my sounding board, my angel. Lucy knew that our breakup at some point was inevitable. And to top it off, my darling Yorkshire Terrier, Wildy, died. She had licked some ant spray poison that was carelessly left around by a tennis pro. Swen had bred her, and I had named her after Lucy's character from *Wildcat.* Wildy had been with me from the beginning of our marriage, and her death was almost symbolic of the end of my relationship with Jack.

Lucy listened to me for hours on end struggling about my feelings toward Harry and my deteriorating situation with Jack. She finally suggested I call her lawyer Milton "Mickey" Rudin. Mickey was a highly respected entertainment lawyer who represented stars like Marilyn Monroe and Frank Sinatra. Mickey was a star in his own right.

★ ★ ★

Jack was playing somewhere in Las Vegas and I planned a trip out there to let him know I was filing for divorce. I told Mickey I would have a conversation with Jack to ensure this was going to be uncomplicated. Harry supported me—he was now seeing a future for us and Lucy was there every step of the way, too.

When I met up with Jack in Vegas, we talked and not only did it end agreeably, but we also had one last roll in the hay. A little farewell fuck as I remember it. Goodbye, sweetheart. See you in the next life. I got back and told Lucy immediately.

"So you left him with no *hard* feelings, huh?" Lucy asked. We laughed.

Mickey and Jack's lawyer kept going back and forth for a couple of weeks because Jack would balk at any mention of money to be paid to me. He wasn't about to part with a nickel, particularly since I was leaving him, something women didn't do. He said, "Why should I give her two hundred dollars a week? Paula still works and besides, we don't have any children."

When he said that my ears perked up. No, we didn't have any children, however, it occurred to me I was late with my period. I began counting on my fingers. I seemed to be two or three weeks late, which was very unusual for me. So after this particular session with the lawyers, I asked Lucy if she had a gynecologist I could see—I still couldn't believe it was even possible that I was pregnant. Sure enough, I was pregnant.

"Do I want to keep it?" I remembered the warning I received about the potential threat of precancerous cells recurring as a result of getting pregnant. I told Harry about my dilemma.

"Of course you're going to abort!"

"No. I don't want to do that. I know I'm taking a big chance. I'd rather risk a cancer scare."

"All the more reason, Paula. You could die!"

"I just can't do it, Harry. I can't lose this baby! I made that mistake once when I was with Burt and I won't do it again! Besides, I'm pushing forty. Who knows if I'll ever get pregnant again?" Harry was furious and took off to Europe because I wouldn't have the abortion.

When I told Jack, he was completely stunned and in perfect jackass-fashion denied my pregnancy, "Oh no! No way, no, that's not possible!"

Lucy, however, was beside herself and over the moon for me. She also understood my frustration at not knowing what to do with my situation between Jack and Harry.

"Do you want to go back to Jack?" Lucy asked me.

"He's saying that's it's not his, Lucy. He was even quoted in the press saying Barbara Nichols is the father of my child!"

"Is it Harry's?" Lucy had to ask, although she already knew.

"No, Harry and I haven't been sexual at all as of late. I'm gonna go ahead with the pregnancy." Even with the risk of cancer, Lucy understood the reasons for my commitment.

After a couple of weeks I started spotting and I went back to the doctor who said, "I don't think you're going to carry this baby full term." He gave me a shot to stop the bleeding but cautioned me, "Now look, if you really want to have this baby, you're going to have to go to bed with your feet up for the whole nine months."

"My god," I thought, but I was determined to have this baby. It was a fluke that I got pregnant at all, but I knew in my heart this was my last chance because of my age.

I didn't give a damn what Jack thought. I believed I could make it on my own and I told him so. The whole entertainment community knew about it and was condemning Jack. Not everyone knew about my relationship with Harry, however, which meant I had a pretty spotless reputation in our showbiz circle of friends. Jack would grouse, "It's Harry Millard's baby!" I kept arguing, "No it isn't. It's your baby. Just forget about it. You never have to see it!"

★ ★ ★

Lucy was extremely supportive during this whole process. When I was in about my sixth month she tried talking Jack into being reasonable and to come back to me, at least to see me through the birth. I said, "No, I don't want anything to do with him. You remember that time in Mexico?"

"Yes, the whorehouse. But come on, Paula; let's be smart about this. At least he's not a drunk." I knew she meant Desi.

Because Jack had great respect for Lucy, he weighed his options: the public, his fans, and his own friends were all solidly against him. Everyone thought he should stand by me—that it was the only decent thing to do. But Jack was hesitant, doubting his paternity. I wasn't too happy about the prospect of living with him again either. However, he did rent me a little house in Coldwater Canyon on Cedarbrook Drive.

Lucy also urged Jack to bring my mother to Los Angeles to help me out. Interestingly, all of my husbands adored my mother and lavished attention and gifts upon her. In New York I couldn't have a party without her. But what neither Jack nor Lucy knew was that my relationship with my mother had always been somewhat strained as my father had actually raised my brother and me.

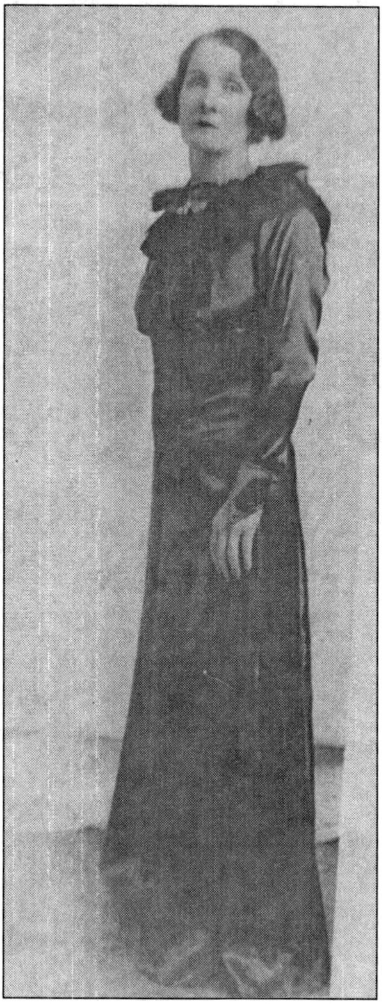

Grandma Leah Morris was a theatrical costumer in New York City and credited for making Milton Berle's first Buster Brown outfit. I have her original Singer sewing machine—it still works!

"Would this be a good idea?" I pondered, struggling inwardly. My mother and I had showbusiness in common, but our personalities constantly clashed, and we often fought over petty things. But I did need help. So, considering my doctor's orders that I stay in bed for the entire pregnancy, and the fact that Jack would not be around because of out-of-town commitments, I half-heartedly agreed. With Jack's full support, it wasn't long before mom was moved in.

It was then that I observed Esther Morris Zürndorfer, not as my mother, but as a woman. I slowly began to understand that my poor distraught mom simply

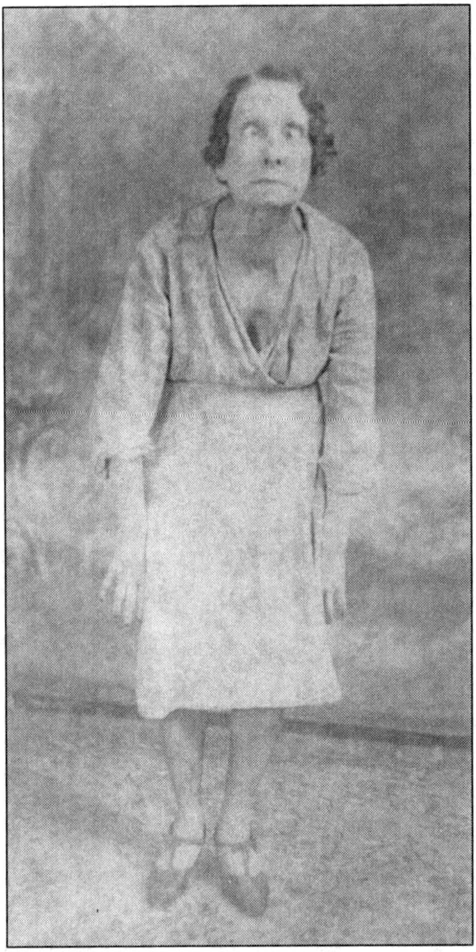

Grandma Leah campy. A sense of humor was a Morris trait.

hadn't been able to cope with her marriage or her children. She was an artist and a performer as were her sisters, and her mother, Grandma Leah, before her. Esther couldn't be confined in any mundane way—she had no desire nor talent for domesticity. And she didn't have to worry about these things being married to my father. He provided servants.

While we lived together on Cedarbrook, she told me about the time she first met my father. It was the 1920s and Esther Morris was a young beauty, a star on the stage with Fred Astaire among others. Back in those early career days when she was in the Ziegfield Follies she was considered a "pony" —that is, a petite beauty with talent who could dance—as opposed to "showgirl" who just pranced around in luscious outfits, extravagant headgear, looking beautiful and once in a while, kicked up a leg without losing her balance.

My handsome, proper German father was simply captivated by her winsome ways. Esther spoke no German and he barely spoke English having just immigrated from Germany. They were young, in love, and in lust. When they finally learned to communicate, they were married with more than a few surprises and two children. My father's Germanic, ordered manner conflicted with her

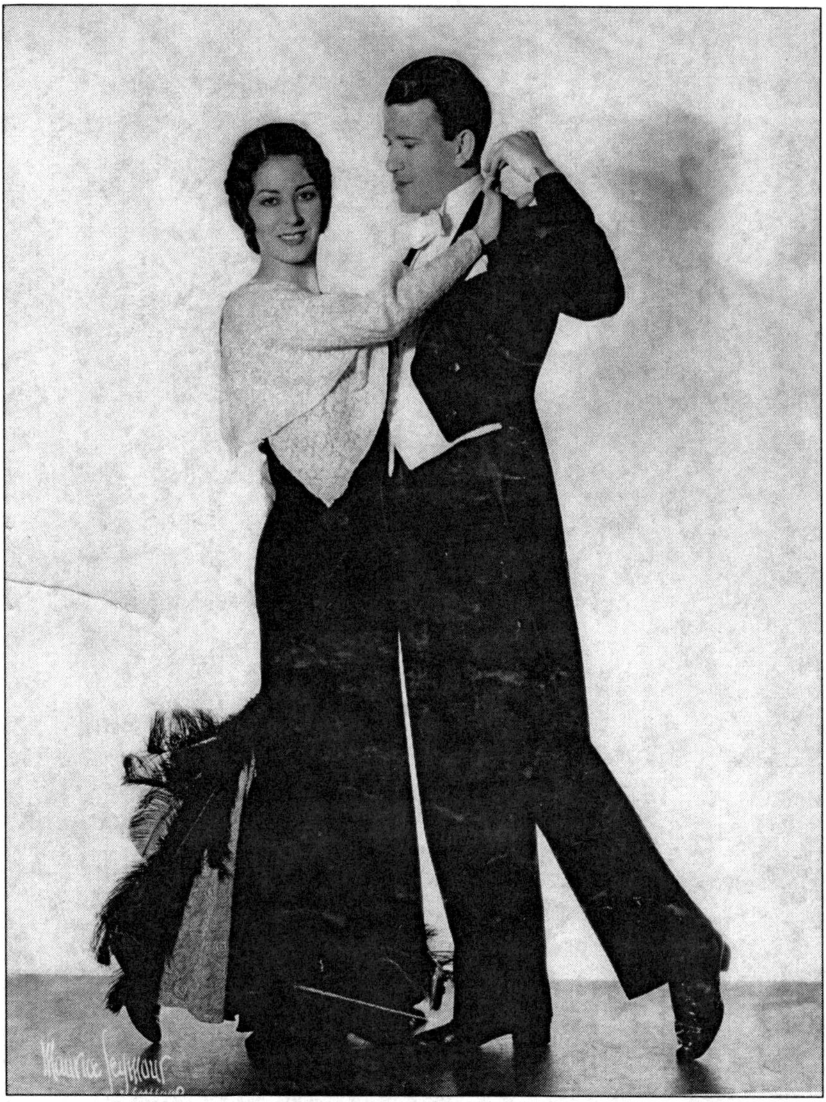

My mother's sister, my Aunt Beade Morris, in her act billed as DeLoge & Russell. - Photo credit Maurice Seymour, a noted photographer of the day.

free-spirited ways. Esther could barely take care of herself, much less mother two children. Divorce was imminent and when it happened, my mother, being a Catholic, did what to her was the "right thing." She sent my younger brother, Fred, and me to a convent somewhere in the Chicago suburbs where we lived for a period of time. I was about five years old and Fred was about three.

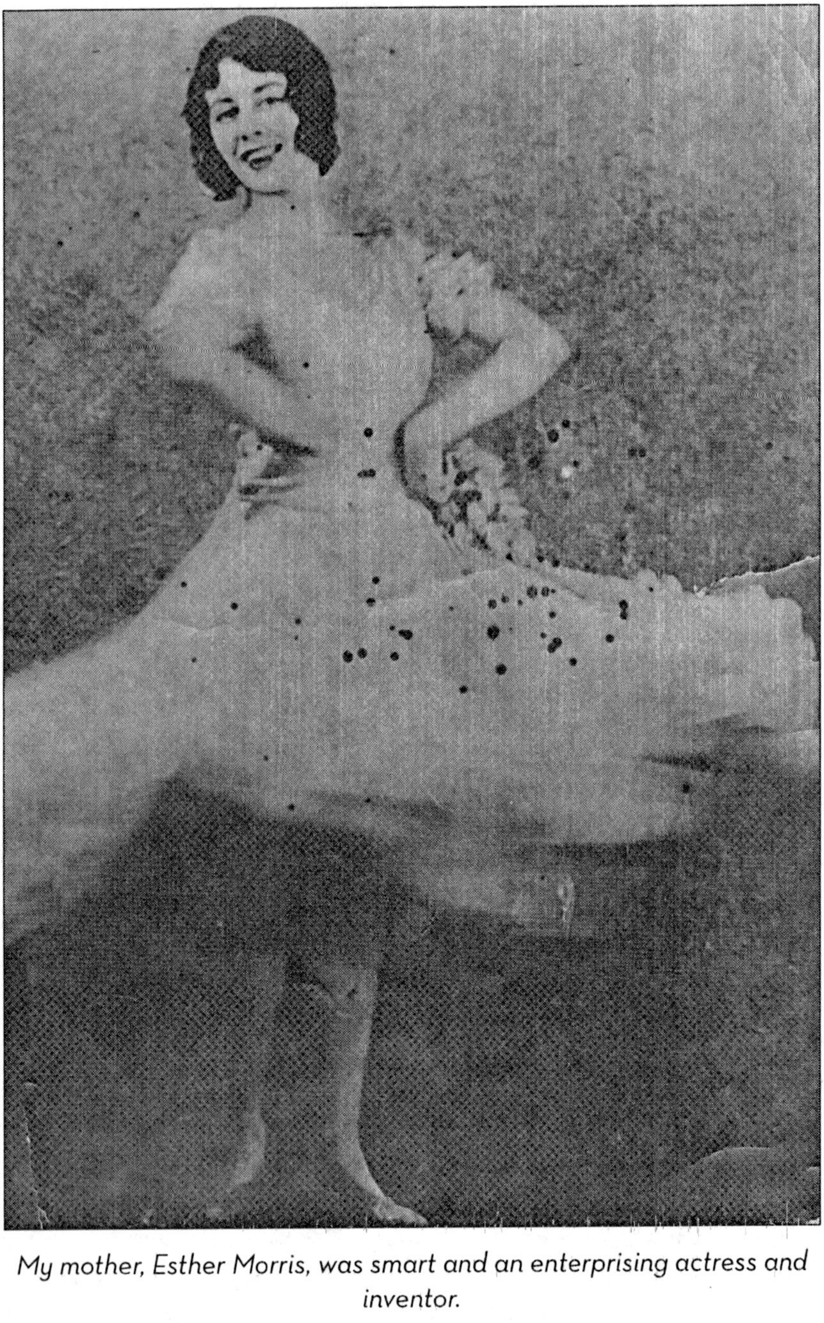

My mother, Esther Morris, was smart and an enterprising actress and inventor.

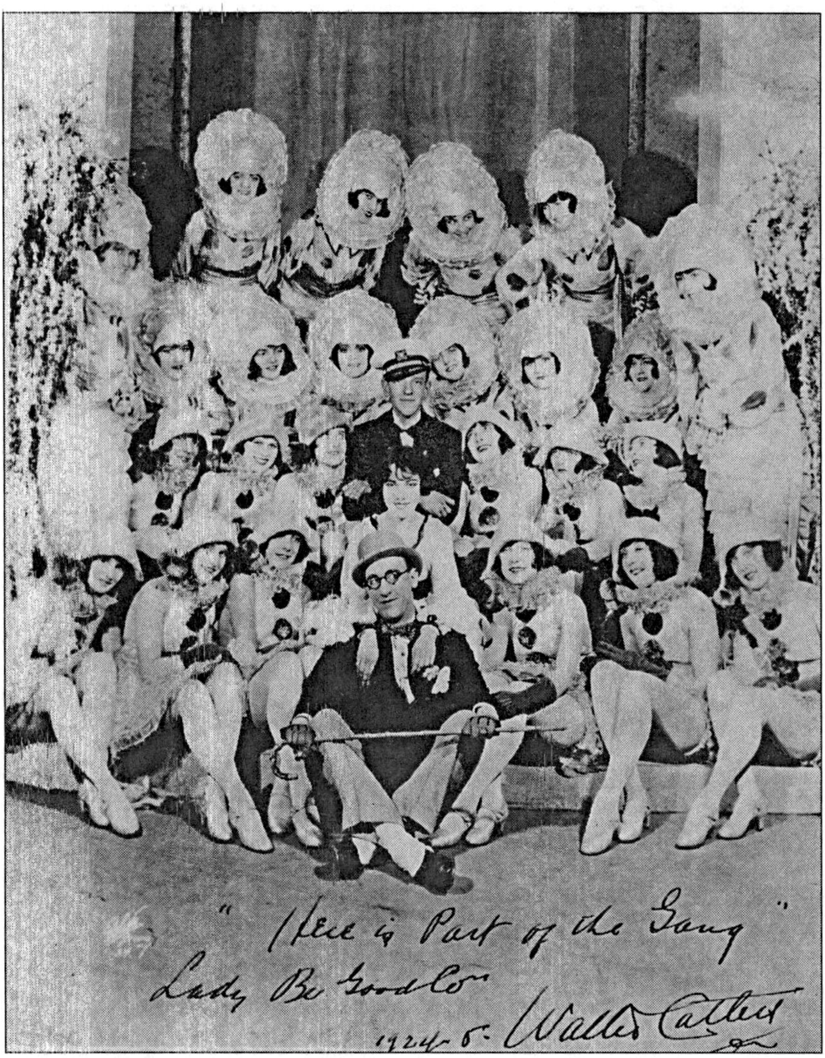

My mom, (at Fred Astaire's left side) in Lady Be Good starring Walter Catlett. 1924

My paternal grandmother, "*Grossmutti*" Zürndorfer, would show up in her chauffeured limousine every week, delivering homemade *sauerbraten*, always tearfully appalled at the general state of affairs and how thin we appeared. I'm sure it was she who insisted my father take custody of my brother and me. To his credit, Poppy did and the two of us kids moved happily back into his house. However, this idyll was relatively short-lived. When

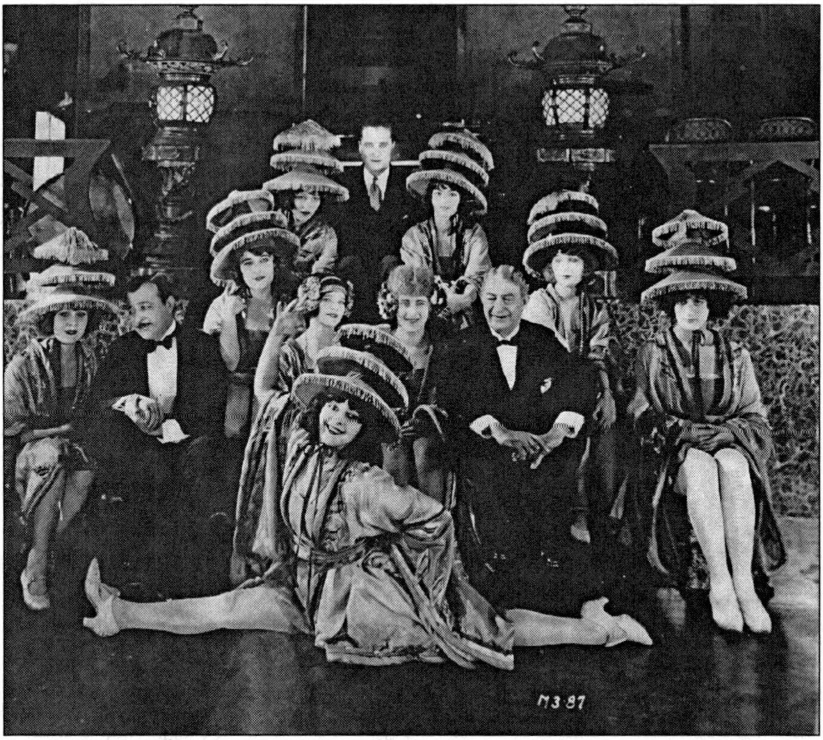

Mom does the splits which she was able to do even in old age!

Poppy eventually remarried and discovered his bride was an alcoholic, I was thirteen and once again shipped off, this time to the Francis Shimer Academy, a posh girls' school, and my brother to a military academy while he sorted out his second divorce.

Meanwhile after my parents had divorced my mom returned to what she knew and loved and eventually took a job at the Roxy Theater in New York as a dresser to the Rockettes. She loved being around young girls—it reminded her of her youth. And that's where she first met Gary Morton.

In truth, mom and I did manage much better than I ever thought possible. Maybe it was maturity or my imminent motherhood which kicked in. She was funny—a "teetotaler" despite her occasional "toking" because, as she told it, in her youth, marijuana was widely accepted. We laughed a lot and in the end, when I became ever more bed-ridden, mom was there doing the best she could helping me out. Her culinary arts, however, were disastrous and

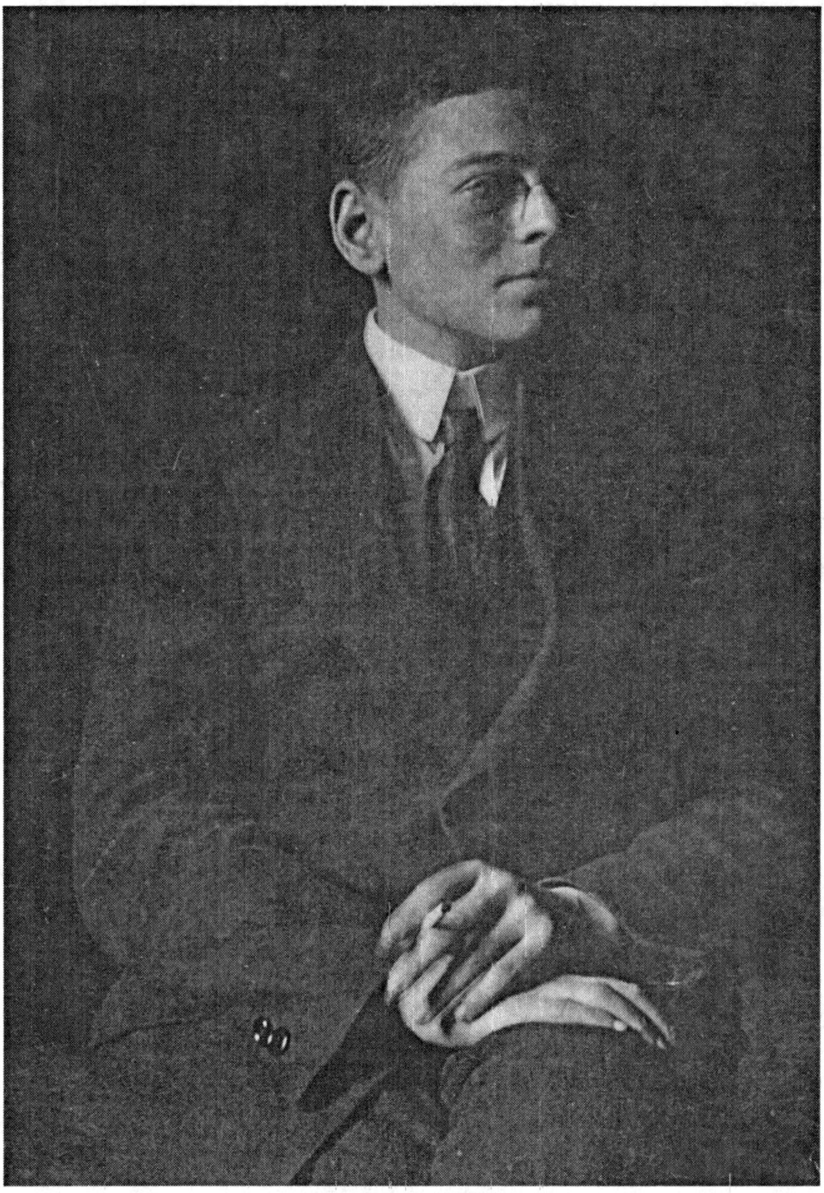

My elegant father, Dr. Walter Zürndorfer, about the time he met my mother.

there were many take-out dinners, but in my condition, I appreciated them nevertheless.

Cedarbrook was a charming, secluded little house and Lucy would come over almost every day. She would sit there and knit

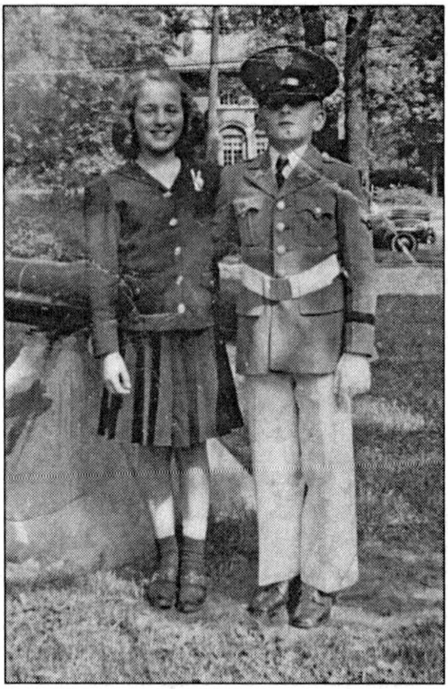

Visiting Fred, my brother, at his military academy. It was the most disciplined time of Fred's life. Both Lucy and I had a brother named Fred.

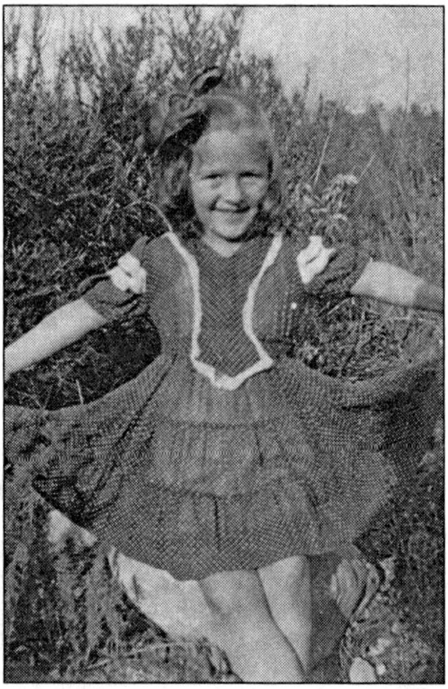

Showing off my pretty dresses even then.

baby blankets in the only stitch she knew, knit one, pearl one. She made so many her fingers were bruised from the needles. Lucy was really excited for me. She just loved the whole thing.

Jack eventually moved back in with me. All of a sudden, he started getting a kick out of the idea of being a father. There was a new glow about him, while I had nothing else to do but lie in bed, eat chocolates all day as compensation, and add on another fifty pounds.

★ ★ ★

Most baby showers are girly affairs that include lunch or afternoon tea, minus the husbands. Somehow, Lucy wanted the one she gave me and Jack to be a celebrity happening like no other with all the female guests instructed to wear pillows under their clothes, to make me feel more comfortable about my exploding size. No one dared to do otherwise and it became a running

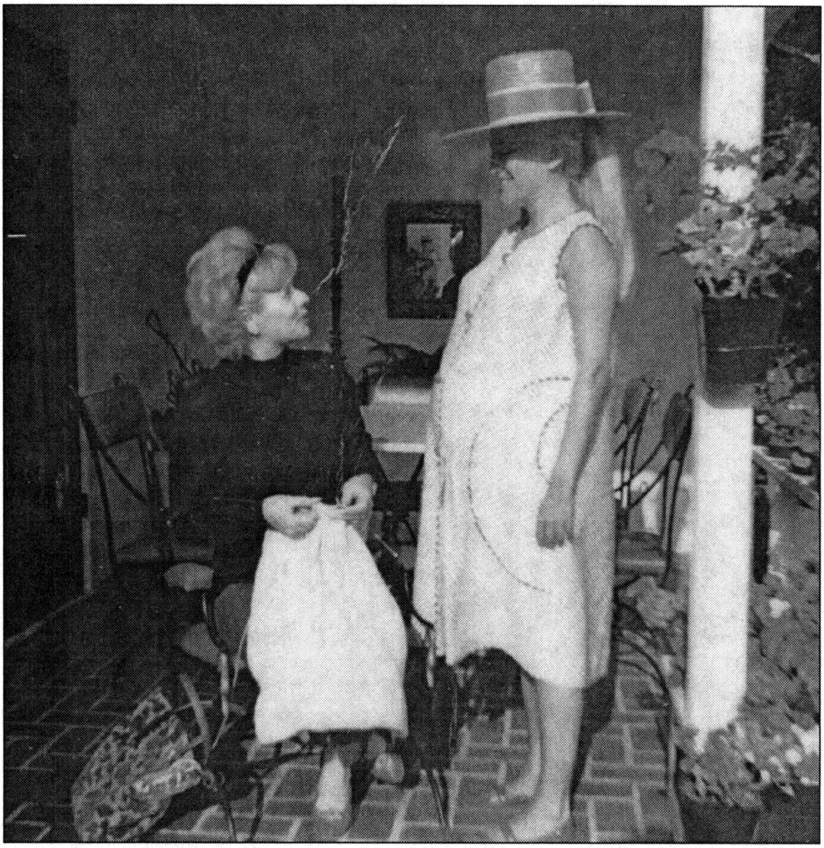

Lucy knitted a lot of little blankets for baby Mike. She really loved my being pregnant.

source of fun with everyone bulging and bumping into one another. The list of stars was most impressive: Bob Hope, Milton Berle, Tony Newley, Yvie and Leslie Bricusse, Donald and Gloria O'Connor, Toni and Jan Murray, Bob and Ginny Newhart.

I was truly overwhelmed. Everyone was so gracious. Lucy even had a flowered throne for me to sit on to rest my heavy load. I had never seen her this excited and I suspect she enjoyed it more than anyone.

The food and drinks were lavishly served. The big hit, of course, was the "opening of the gifts." Jack was in especially rare form, with an outlandish rattle stuck to his forehead and hurling insults about the contents of each gift which were mostly expensive and

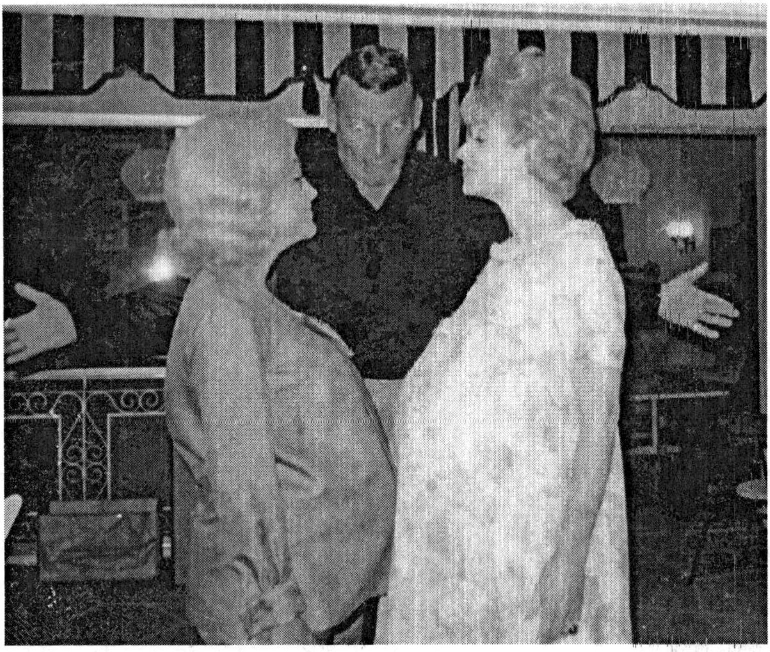

Gary between Lucy and me at the baby shower she threw for me. She had all the women wear pillows so they appeared pregnant, too.

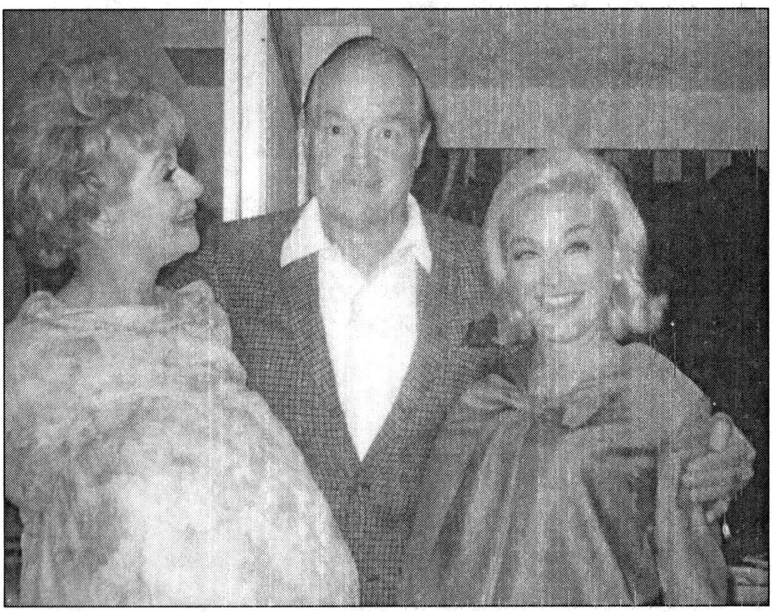

Bob Hope between Lucy and me.

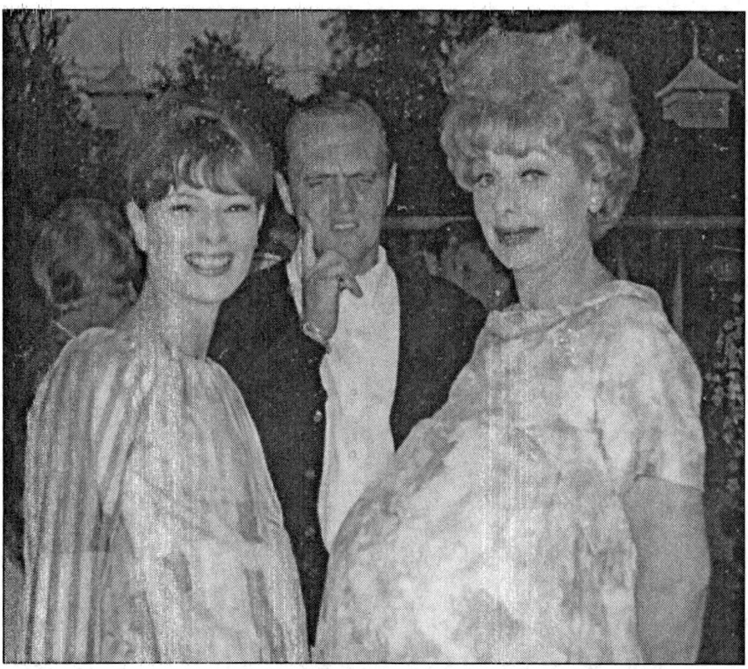

Ginny and Bob Newhart with Lucy.

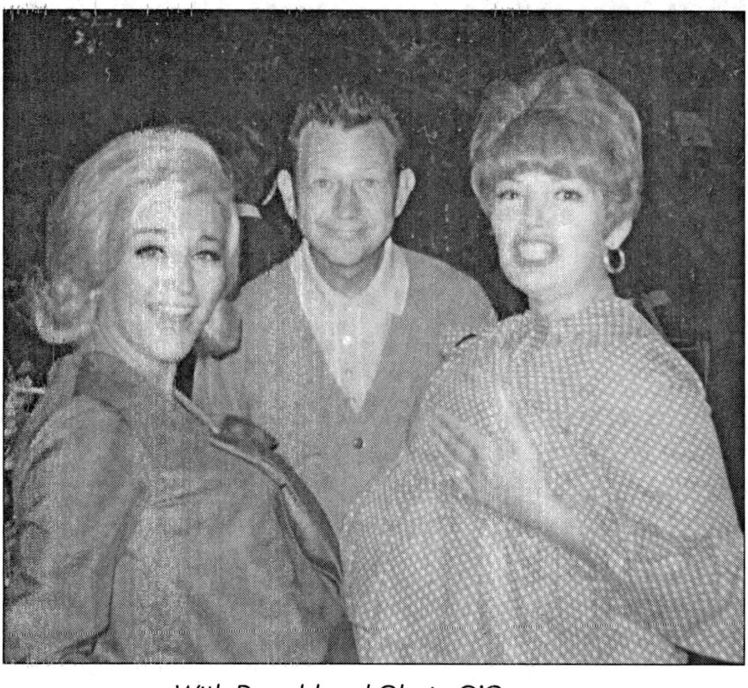

With Donald and Gloria O'Connor.

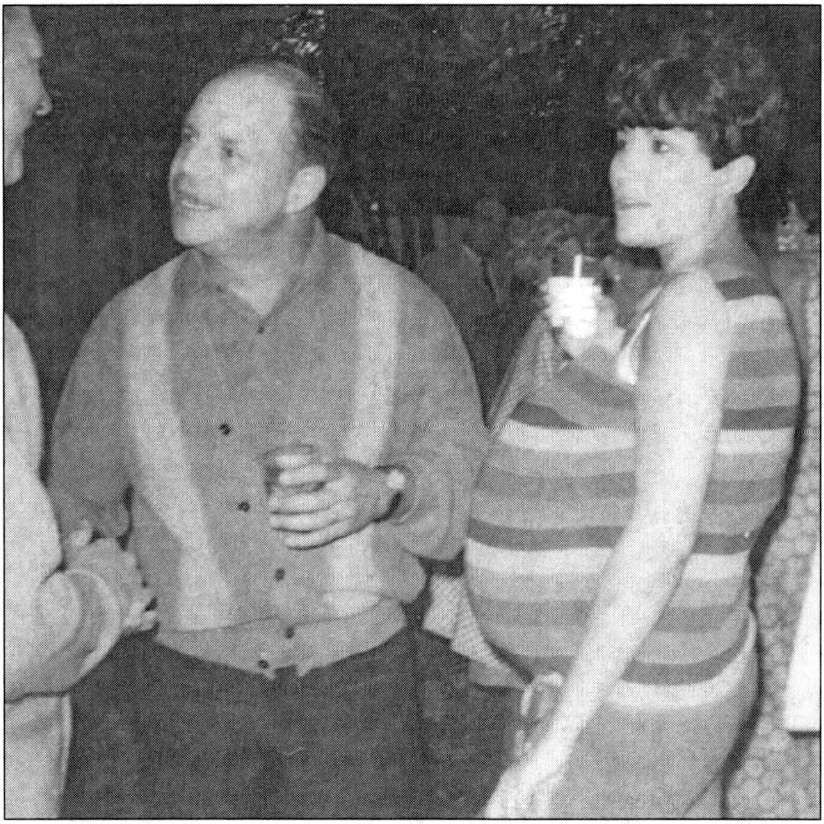

Don and Barbara Rickles.

unique baby clothes or toys. He couldn't repress an occasional dig like, "Harry's baby is gonna love this one," which Lucy and I heard but most likely flew over everyone's laughter and hysteria. Even though I was silently hurt by these remarks, I couldn't fault his brilliance.

Lucy had it all on tape but unfortunately it got lost over the years. It's possible it wound up in one of her home recordings. What a shame, because it was so dazzling with Lucy conducting it all in front of the crowd. A year later Lucy threw Carol Burnett a baby shower for her second child. Though I wasn't there, I quickly learned through mutual friends, that Gary had copied Jack's "opening of the gifts" routine at her shower. That's Gary for you, always using another comedian's shtick.

My time for delivery was edging near, and even though he was cutting it close, Jack had accepted a job doing *Little Me* at Melodyland, a fifty-minute drive away. After nine months of bed confinement and mountains of chocolate, I panicked that Sunday evening when my water burst and Jack insisted he first had to go to the closing night cast party. Of course, Lucy being the take-charge person encouraged me to hold on while she got a car to take me to Cedars, where I would go through seven hours of labor until Michael made his debut into this world. I remembered seeing him in the delivery room and thinking, "What a nice person." How true was my first impression of his sweet nature.

Meanwhile Lucy and Jack arrived at what became a comedy of confusion. By some twist of fate, my first husband Burt and his wife Angie Dickinson were also having their first child at the same time, at the same hospital, across the hall from me. Although their baby girl was a preemie and born a day later, the coincidence was still pretty weird. Had Michael been a girl his name would have been Leah (after my grandmother), which was the legal name Angie and Burt gave their child. However, their baby was referred to as Nikki by the nurses. To add to the pandemonium, Jack and Burt were running back and forth from Angie's and my rooms, making the nurses query, "Well whose husband is whose?" Lucy sat by, amused by everyone's confusion.

In perfect Jack fashion, the first thing he did, due to his suspicious nature, was have a blood test run on Michael. And surprise, surprise, Michael had the same rare blood type as Jack's. Well, that glow came shining back for Jack as he went all out with publicity and the press, now fully assured of his paternity.

Michael was a beautiful baby. Jack was behaving himself. He was just so unbelievably crazy about Michael. He even looked forward to diapering. I don't know any other man that would do that, especially in those days. Jack was so attentive and thrilled to have this little baby boy.

Lucy was over at our house everyday cooing over Michael. She insisted on being known as Michael's godmother.

★ ★ ★

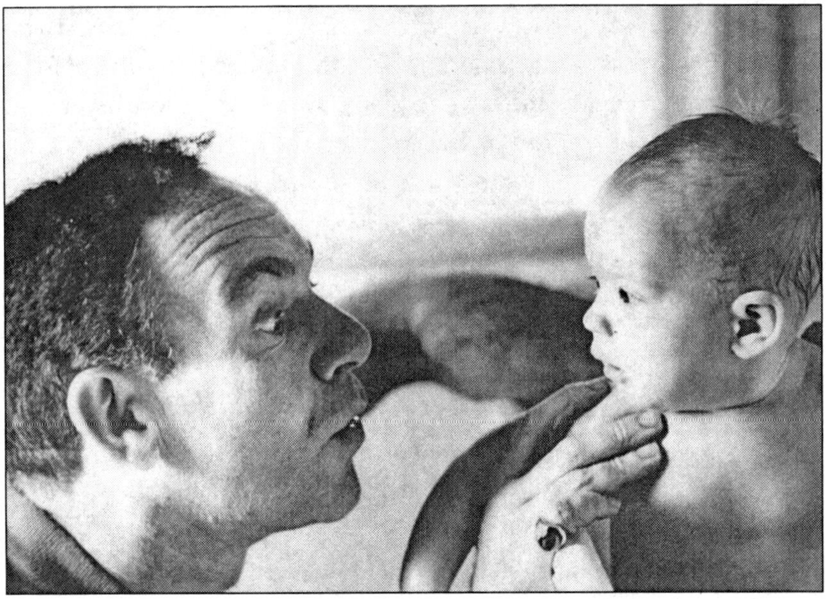

From day one, bonded forever.

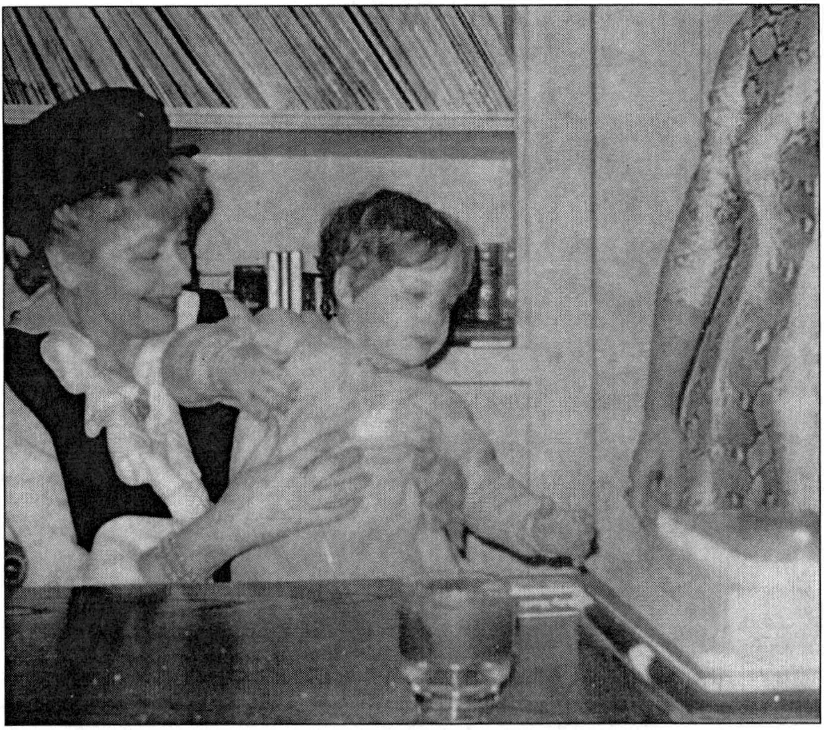

Michael with his godmother.

Our rental was up on Cedarbrook, and it was clear we needed a bigger house and once again, Lucy was dead set on helping Jack and me find a place before she had to go off and film *Yours, Mine and Ours* that summer (July 4, 1967). In between her busy schedule with *The Lucy Show*, we were Lucy's first priority. She drove around with us from place to place. I was relieved with her taking over this burden.

At one point, I had found one spectacular property that I was absolutely in love with off Benedict Canyon. It had high-beamed ceilings that I always adored, a separate guesthouse, and a wonderful long secluded driveway up to the property. The view was unbelievable. I couldn't wait for Lucy and Jack to see it. When they did, I was shocked by their reactions. They shuddered. For some unexplainable reason they both were adamantly against the place.

"No way," Jack said.

"Why not?" I protested like a child.

"Paula, this is not the place," Lucy chimed in.

I was really very upset and out-voted. As it turned out, just a couple of years later, this stunning home on Cielo Drive became infamous, the site of the horrific Manson murders. Lucy and Jack had gotten bad vibes. Somehow, I didn't.

We eventually bought a lovely, charming Spanish house on Foothill Road. It had an expansive lawn that led up to tall overhanging trees. At the entrance was a beautiful old iron gate leading to an enclosed bubbling fountain on the left and a stone patio on the right, which was overgrown with lush ferns. It had a tropical enchanted feeling. Then going forward under an archway was a huge carved Spanish style door with a quaint peephole in it.

As you entered the house, you walked down two steps into a huge living room with immense beamed high ceilings, which were bleached and pickled as were the oak floors. The huge brick fireplace was bookended by enormous French doors leading out to a fairytale garden covered in a sea of bougainvillea in the center of which was a kidney shaped pool and a pool house behind that.

"This is the place, Paula. I know you're going to do wonders with it!" Lucy said. And boy was she right. It was my dream house—our

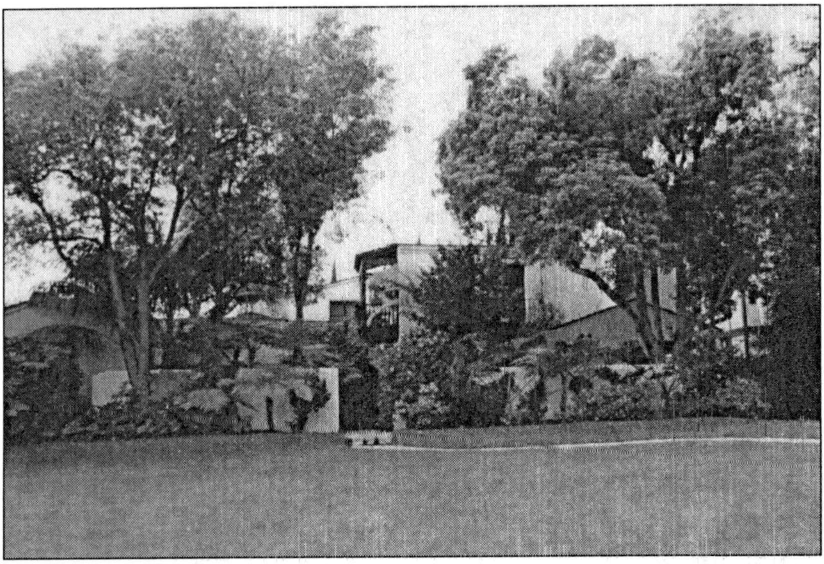

My house on Foothill in Beverly Hills. I grew a few MJ plants off my bedroom's private terrace while married to Chuck who approved most heartily.

house—and it would eventually also become a great source of income for me.

Things were looking up for me at this point. I loved our life at Foothill and with Jack behaving himself, at last I had my family

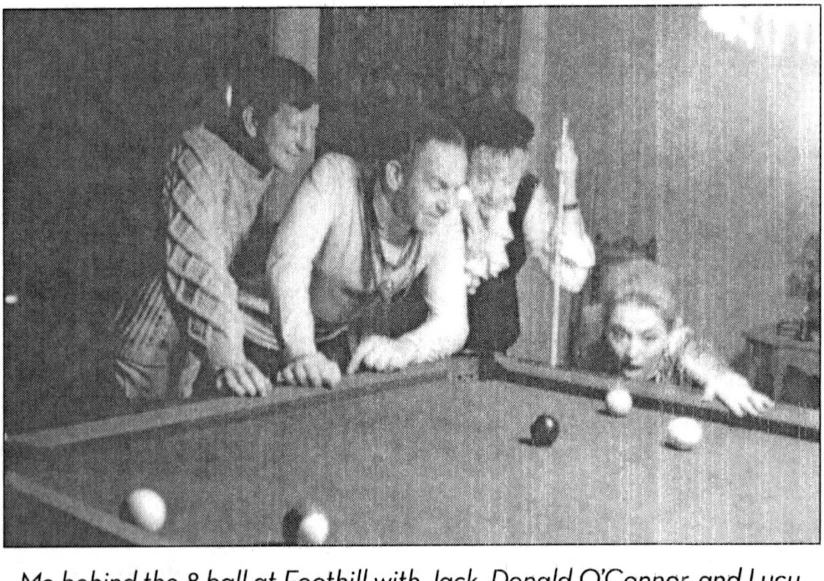

Me behind the 8 ball at Foothill with Jack, Donald O'Connor, and Lucy.

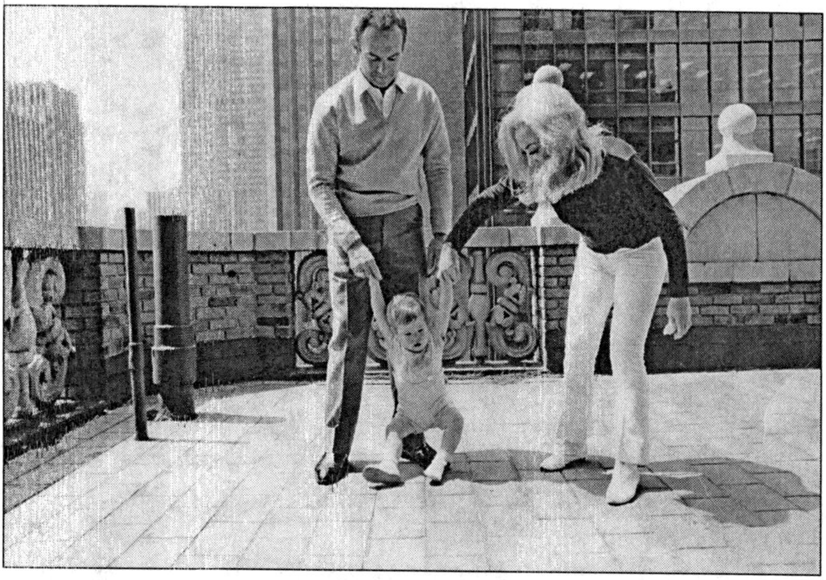

Jack, Michael and me - some of our happiest times. Here on the terrace in New York City.

—mom, Jack and Michael. My mom had rented a small apartment nearby in West Hollywood. Our home was perfect for entertaining our friends. I had a kitchen I loved cooking in. With the occasional trips back to New York, it seemed to be the best of times for us.

★ ★ ★

Now all that was missing was a job. Michael was two and I missed the theater; I yearned for that feeling of being on stage. I had to get back to work. As luck would have it, I booked a reprise of *Little Me* with Donald O'Connor.

The most important thing I needed to do was hire a nurse to take care of darling Michael while I was gone. A highly recommended English nanny met with Jack's and my approval and I was off to Vegas, relieved and glad that Michael would be well-taken care of.

Little Me with Donald O'Connor was incredible. He was great to perform with—so creative and inventive. I always loved working with him. I was actually playing several characters against his multiple characters. We had a ball and the reviews were fantastic—from

The LA Times, "Miss Stewart...shines rightly...matching O'Connor in an exhibition of versatility." *Daily Variety* proclaimed me "vivacious and alluring while exhibiting high proficiency for vocalizing." Joy Hamann of the *Hollywood Reporter* gushed "...[Paula Stewart's] voice is just right for the Cy Coleman tunes...O'Connor is really fine...A performer with his strength is required to keep Miss Stewart, by virtue of her role and ability, from stealing the show." And from Ralph Pearl of the *Las Vegas Sun*: "We joined many in that jam-packed audience screaming for sheer delight at not only Donald O'Connor's...antics, but also his leading lady Paula Stewart who exudes sex in an extremely colorful wrapper..." Joe Delaney of The Las Vegas Sun crowed that "Donald O'Connor and *Little Me* are big winners for the Sahara...Paula Stewart is the 'hit' of the show."

Lucy came to watch the performance because there was a part coming up in an episode of *Here's Lucy* that I might be right for. That particular night, Donald and I were ad-libbing like mad and way off script. We were so wild, the scenery behind us was literally collapsing. I could hear Lucy's distinctive and infectious guffaw—a very elongated deep baritone "Haaaah." Lucy was excited for me and a lot was going on for her, too, especially professionally with *Yours, Mine and Ours* coming out in the spring. There was good buzz around that film.

While working in Vegas, I couldn't help but wax about the time when I was first engaged to Jack. In those heady times, I had accompanied him to Vegas where he was performing at the Thunderbird. It was New Year's Eve and we ran into Beldon Katleman who owned the El Rancho Hotel. I was wearing a clinging Jax dress that really caught Beldon's eye.

He asked me if I had an act. And Jack piped up with, "Of course she does! It's fabulous!" I didn't have one at the time, but Jack made sure I did, anything to get me hired. He was really so supportive. And Beldon did hire me. I was on the bill with Lili St. Cyr, the notorious stripper who stopped the show every night by taking a bubble bath onstage, and Joey Louis who would attend our wedding in Florida not long after.

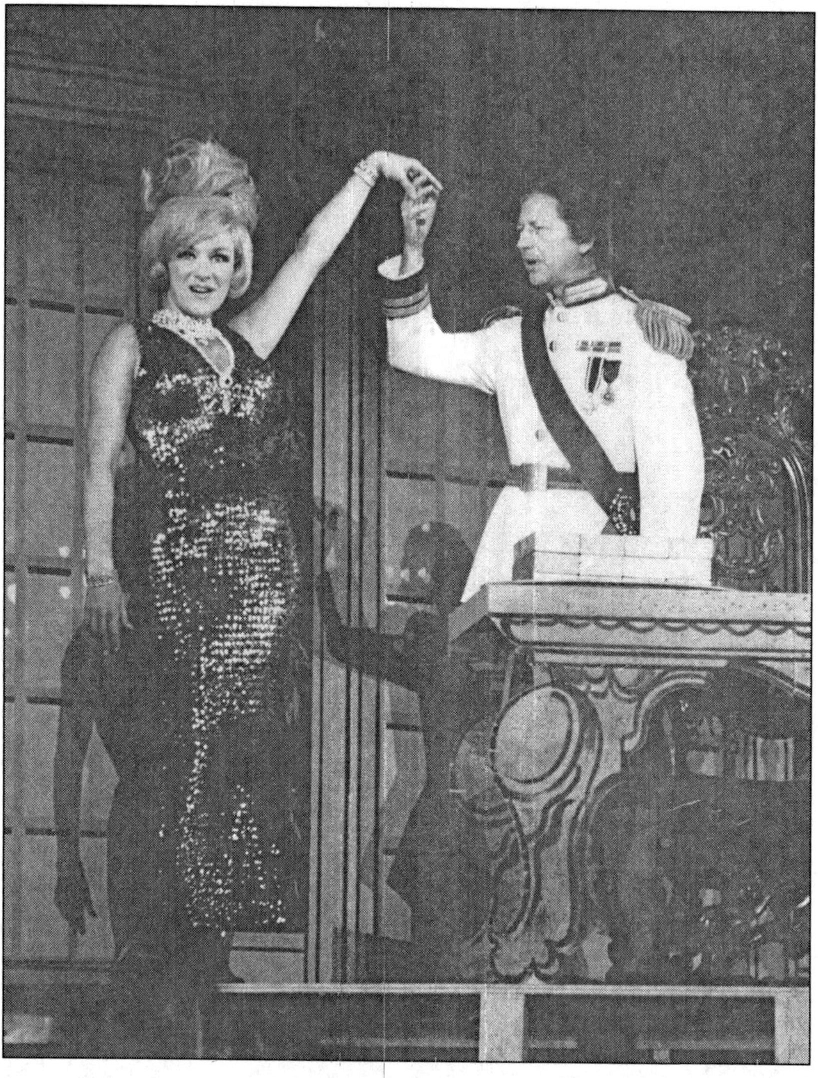

Donald O'Connor and I in Little Me, *Kansas City, Missouri State Fair. We were such a hit, we did it again in Vegas the following year where Lucy saw the show and hired me for the "Harry's Tonsils" episode on* Here's Lucy. *- Photo credit Alix Jeffry*

My reveries were shattered when my mother telephoned. She suspected that Jack was sleeping with the nanny —apparently she was just too attractive and well-endowed. I finally realized you couldn't change a dog's spots. It permanently turned me off Jack. I told him I couldn't take it anymore. Once again, he tried to atone

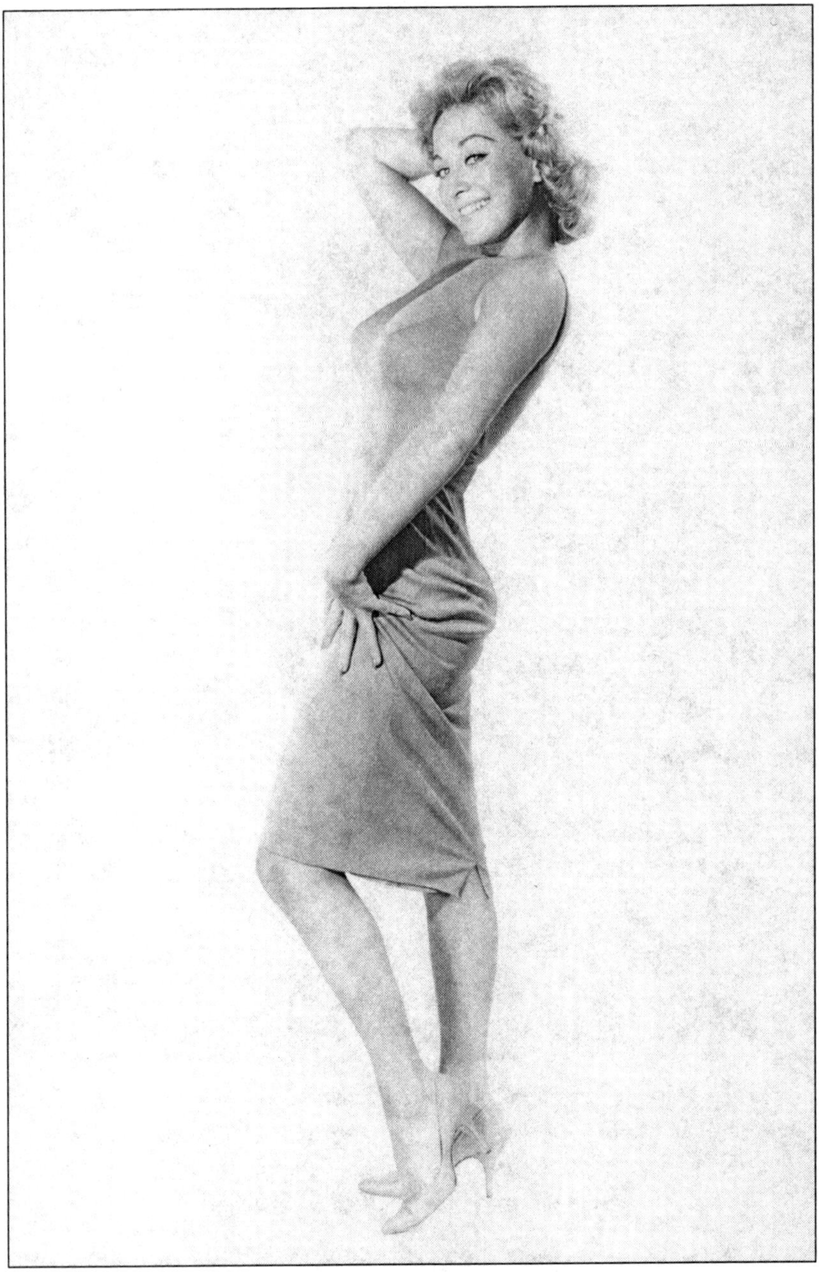

This Jax dress was a favorite. It was almost sure to get me the job when I wore it, thanks to Jack Hanson whose boutique in Beverly Hills was a top choice for all the gals.

with expensive gifts, an emerald bracelet and a Lincoln Continental. I was livid with Jack for announcing this as a "reconciliation gift" to the press. It soon became clear that ours was an impossible situation. I returned the bracelet but kept the car. Eventually, Jack moved out. And that was the end of my marriage to Jack.

★ ★ ★

With Jack gone, Harry returned and came over quite often. He got a kick out of holding Michael and bouncing him on his knee. After seeing how much Michael loved riding the ponies around Beverly Park, Harry was planning how he could teach Michael polo, of all things. I was overjoyed at Harry's reversal, he had been so adamant about an abortion. At this point, Harry was ready and eager to marry me. But, I still wanted to be sure he was really up to being a father before committing myself.

There was also the issue of my pending divorce. Harry reassured me there would be no messy scenes, as he wanted the divorce to be as smooth as possible. Jack couldn't complain because Harry was willing to take over my financial responsibilities, which I knew mattered greatly to Jack. Harry's love for Michael seemed to increase by the day, easing any doubts I had regarding his qualifications in that realm. Michael's well-being was foremost in my mind. My life was complicated enough without intrigues and jealousy. All the other men in my life would have to stand in line after that primal concern. My baby would always come first.

Harry would say, "After you leave Jack and we're married, I'll adopt Michael." Though this was music to my ears, I knew Jack would never go for that, but Harry was serious. "I'll get you a lawyer. You get divorced from Jack and we'll start working on the castle," which is what he now called his mansion. "We'll be a family."

Finally, my years of humiliation with Jack were over and my knight in shining armor, Harry, was miraculously ready to forgive me for my impatience with his reluctance to marry years ago. He was ready to forget the past and go forward with our life together. I loved his creative energy and positive attitude, so unlike Jack's.

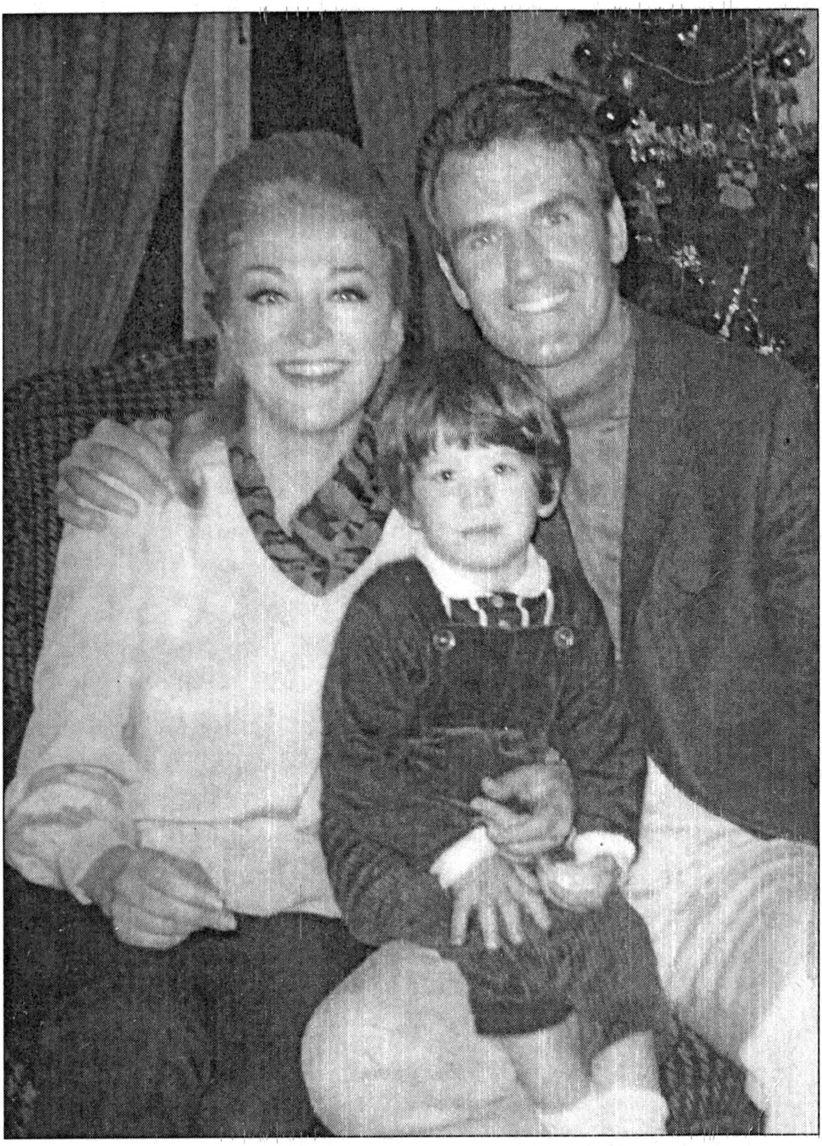

Michael and I with Harry.

What was I thinking back then when I chose Jack over Harry? That stubborn belief that I could change Jack's nature? We were nothing alike. Everything about us was different, from our backgrounds to our careers and lifestyles. It's so true, opposites do attract. I had been captivated by Jack's humorous negativity. It held me like a magnet. How else to explain it? Lucy tried.

That's what she meant when she cautioned me about Jack. She had been through the same thing herself and tried to warn me against the inevitable disillusionment I would suffer as she did. But now my future was turning from grim to glorious. How lucky I was to have Harry come to my rescue.

Harry and I had so much more in common; our privileged upbringings, culture, love of art, entertaining, remodeling, sense of humor, and yet a need to be avant-garde, free-spirited and have an out-of-the-box disregard for social restraints. How perfect a union. We started planning redoing the castle. I wasn't sure what to do with my lovely Foothill home. Somehow that would have to be addressed, but for now it could wait.

I realized through all of this turmoil with the divorce, that I hadn't even told Poppy, who was not one to read Hollywood gossip columns. In fact, I didn't want to worry him as he was now retired in Florida and getting on in years.

Meanwhile, Jack had started seeing Roxanne Wander, a divorcee with two young daughters. Believe it or not, everything was friendly between Jack and me due to the fact he knew he wasn't going to get clobbered financially because I was going to marry Harry. With Lucy's help and moral support, I began the divorce proceedings.

Jack had a powerful lawyer, Arthur Crowley, who was famous for getting the best deals for his clients because there were rampant rumors that "he had every top judge in his back pocket." Unfortunately, Jack got to Arthur before I could, and sadly the lawyer Harry got me was ultimately really inept.

Jack would tell the judge, "Oh Paula's a big star on Broadway and can continue working and living without my help." Besides the stint in *Little Me*, I hadn't worked in almost three years. Not to mention stars on Broadway still weren't making a lot of money in those days; the salaries were certainly nowhere near what Jack was making in clubs and on television. Jack was a huge earner. He was the "big star" and worth millions at the time. I wasn't earning anything. Jack's side would try to convince the judge that Jack didn't need to give me that much.

Beldon Katleman was by now a close friend of mine, and he also happened to be Arthur Crowley's neighbor. Besides not being fond of Jack, Beldon told me in the strictest confidence that Arthur Crowley had "gotten to the judge," hinting he might have made it possible for Jack to be favored in the divorce. This was a difficult time in my life and without my best friend Lucy to lean on, I don't know how I would have gotten through it. To make my life even more challenging, Harry received some news that hit me like a sucker punch in the gut.

★ ★ ★

One evening Harry and I went to the movies, and while eating popcorn he had these terrible pains in his stomach. We had to leave the theater immediately. The next morning he called me from the hospital.

"Harry, what's the matter? Why are you at the hospital?"

"They just opened me up, Paula, and they discovered I have cancer." I was in shock. I couldn't believe it.

"Please tell me it's not true, it can't be true," I said desperately.

"I wish it wasn't, Paula."

I raced to the hospital. When I got there Harry said, "Listen Paula, you can't go through this divorce with Jack because the prognosis for me isn't very good. I have colon cancer. Its metastasized and they don't hold out much hope for my survival. I may not live. I can't let you go through with the divorce."

"I don't care, Harry. I don't care how long you have to live, whatever time you have left on this earth I want to spend with you."

Harry finally got out of the hospital and he had a bag on the side of his abdomen. He wore special jumpsuits which didn't constrict him around the waist with a zipper down the front to access the bag. Harry was going to continue to live his life as planned. He had an original movie that he wanted to make with his own money to be shot in Positano, Italy. David Hedison, star of the television show *Voyage to the Bottom of the Sea*, was to be the lead along with Alexandra Stewart (a European actress). Harry had written a part in it for me because he wanted me by his side.

My lawyer and Lucy were very concerned how my trip with Harry would be perceived since I was still going through the divorce with Jack. Lucy said, "Paula look, you have to get something in writing that absolves you of looking like you're deserting your child." Michael at the time was three.

My lawyer crafted a document indicating that I was going to Europe to work as an actress, ensuring it wouldn't be perceived that I was going over there to be with my lover. At the time Harry and I weren't having any sexual relationships, not with this cancer hanging out of his gut. And Lucy reasoned with Jack, "Now look Jack, I think it would be a good idea for you to move back into the house while Paula's gone working." I agreed and was glad that Jack said "yes" because he wanted to be near Michael. Great. Jack was a good father and very attentive to Michael.

Positano was idyllic. Harry had rented us the most romantic villa on the side of a mountain overlooking the magnificent Mediterranean. Among our friends that had been included in the cast besides David and Alexandra was Robert Wolders who later went on to marry Merle Oberon, the exotic movie star twenty-five years his senior, and after she died, married Audrey Hepburn. He had a charm about him that I'm sure captivated his subsequent famous wives.

During the days, on our long lunch breaks, we would all get together in the scenic outdoor cafés overlooking the glistening sea, trying to be cheerful. All the time knowing the fateful end would be in Harry's demise.

Harry had hired one of the local chefs to delight us with exotic dinners after long days of shooting the film. David and Rob would join us for many a candle and moonlit dinners with the warm breezes kissing our tanned bodies as Harry tried to valiantly hide his obvious pain.

Then on other nights, Harry would join us at the local discos. His loving eyes watched me dance with David and Rob, imagining I'm sure, that I was dancing with him. How that memory haunts me still. I wrote in my journal, "What kind of god snuffs out a bright budding life in its bloom?"

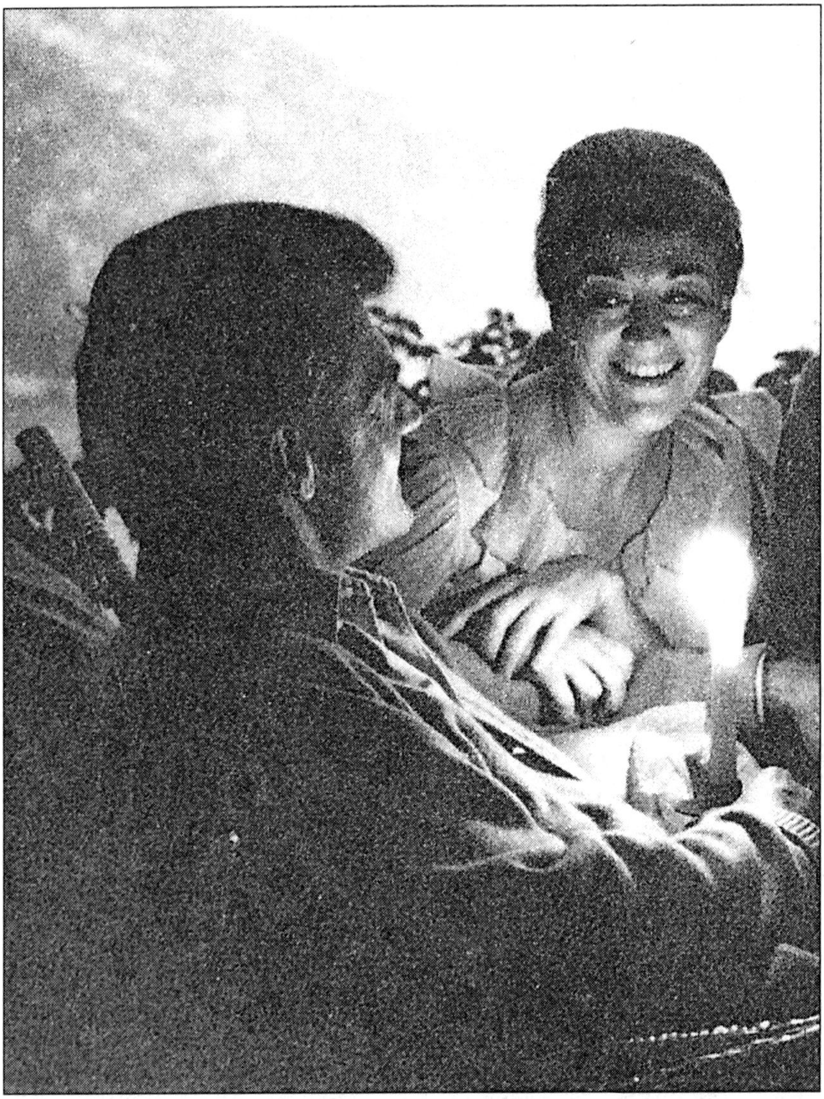

A fleeting moment of bliss with Harry in Positano.

On top of that, Lucy called frequently and I would update her on everything. On one occasion, Lucy called in the middle of the night. "Paula, Jack is threatening suicide."

"What!" I said. I was frightened at first with this news. Oh my god, another imminent death? The two men in my life were now both on the edge. Shockingly, Jack was heartbroken and very distraught that I was really leaving him for a man that had no future.

"Paula, I think Jack is hopeful that when this is all over, you'll come back to him," Lucy told me.

I don't know how he planned to kill himself, but I knew in my heart this was bullshit. Jack was just milking this situation to get Lucy's sympathy. He would never commit suicide, believe me. This from a man who fainted at his own son's bris.

When I got back from Italy, Jack moved out again since I was determined to go through with the divorce even though it looked like Harry was not going to make it. If you want to know the truth, I don't think Jack ever forgave me for leaving him for a dying man.

Harry got sicker every day, but he held his head high. We would have huge dinner parties at the castle that we were still planning on redoing.

Things were getting so bad, Harry decided to go back to New York to see the top cancer specialists hoping against hope there was something they could do. I begged to come, to be with him, and he said, "No, Paula, I don't want you to come yet. Don't come yet, please, I will tell you when you can come." Well, when he finally relented, I got on the plane but by the time I got there, Harry had passed away.

The funeral was held at the family estate in Pennsylvania where I commiserated with his mother and relatives. I couldn't stop crying the whole time I was there. I was devastated and again, I was adrift at sea. I had no career at that point in Los Angeles, I was going through with a divorce and the love of my life had just died.

★ ★ ★

Shortly after Harry's death, Lucy called me. "Paula, I'm hiring you for an episode on the show." Now I had completely forgotten about the conversation Lucy had with me earlier that year about getting me a regular role on her new show, *Here's Lucy*. With everything I had just been through, that was the last thing on my mind. I wasn't sure if this was not just for her to get producers to see my talent to be a regular on the series. I knew Lucy was no longer Madame President of Desilu, which she had sold to Gulf and Western, and was renamed Paramount Television, but it was most thoughtful of her. I was just appreciative to be back at work, throw myself into a character and move on with my life.

I was to play the ditsy nurse in the segment entitled "Harry's Tonsils" ministering unto Gale Gordon. Mary Wicks was in the show along with Little Lucie and Desi, Jr. Ironically, Lucy's character on the show was "Lucy Carter." Carter was still my married name. It was great fun and a much-needed break for me. I loved working with Lucy again. I enjoyed watching her work. I went to every taping possible. She particularly liked having DeDe and me at the rehearsals. Lucy and I had very similar laughs, a big bellow when we found something funny. She knew a joke would play well with the audience if she could hear me laugh.

Watching Lucy work in television was not the Lucy I had known on Broadway. In the theater, she took direction. Maybe it was because she was working in a somewhat unfamiliar medium, and she felt she needed all the help she could get. Whereas in television Lucy was the one who gave direction. She was in complete control.

At this point, I would now like to dispel a lot of the rumors about how tough she was to work with. Bottom line, she took responsibility for everything from the script to the cast performances down to the lighting, even though there were directors, producers, and technicians there. The shows had to go on every week. Lucy knew she had to use all of her accumulated knowledge to keep it sharp and funny. Because Desi was no longer there with his critical eye, she had to assume his role. If a man showed this kind of control and force he was admired. If a woman did, she was called a bitch.

I've defended her actions when most people were quick to criticize her. It was her show and she had her say. It wouldn't go on without her stamp of approval. After all, how else can you explain Lucy's remarkable dominance in television for all those years?

When "Harry's Tonsils" aired on October 20th, there were great expectations surrounding the episode regarding awards. It felt good, like a winner. On the heels of this positive experience just four days later, more was forthcoming when *Butch Cassidy and The Sundance Kid* opened wide in theaters—and was a huge hit. Even though by now Burt had had many successes, I was especially pleased for him. It made Lucy extremely curious.

"How come you never talk about Burt?" Of course, she was referring about the personal details. Truth be told, I found it difficult to address even after so many years after our divorce. I promised to tell her more later privately. Gary was away on some golf tour so we could have an intimate girls' conversation without him around. That night over dinner, she couldn't wait to grill me further. "Okay, Paula, so what happened? You obviously were a perfect pair, the music, youth, beauty. The two of you were like the figures on a wedding cake."

"That's true, Lucy, it was all that young, romantic love and it was wonderful." And even now looking back at my relationship with Burt, Lucy's words struck a chord. It was like the movie, *LaLa Land*. I confessed to Lucy the whole story because I knew she would understand.

Burt's Father, Bert Bacharach, "Big Bert," was a syndicated columnist, and responsible for our meeting. At a press party, I mentioned to Bert that I was in need of an accompanist for my auditions, and he said: "Have I got a guy for you!" So Bert invited me to his and Irma's home for a small party, and there was their son, Burt, whom they called "Happy," at the piano, still living at home. In those early years before he became famous, Burt was known as "Happy." I was really overwhelmed by his playing, even though he was quite aloof and distantly cool to me. It definitely was not a love-at-first sight introduction.

However, Happy and I did plan to get together to go over my audition materials at my studio apartment. I paid Happy five dollars for each audition, a lot of money then—my rent was thirty dollars a month—I must have been in love! I should mention that Byron Janis, my former boyfriend, a Vladimir Horowitz protégé, who went on to become a world-famous concert pianist and later married Gary Cooper's daughter, Maria, had been the one responsible for having gotten me into my tiny East 40th Street studio apartment. At the time I was dating Byron, he too, was still living with his parents and needed a place for us to rendezvous.

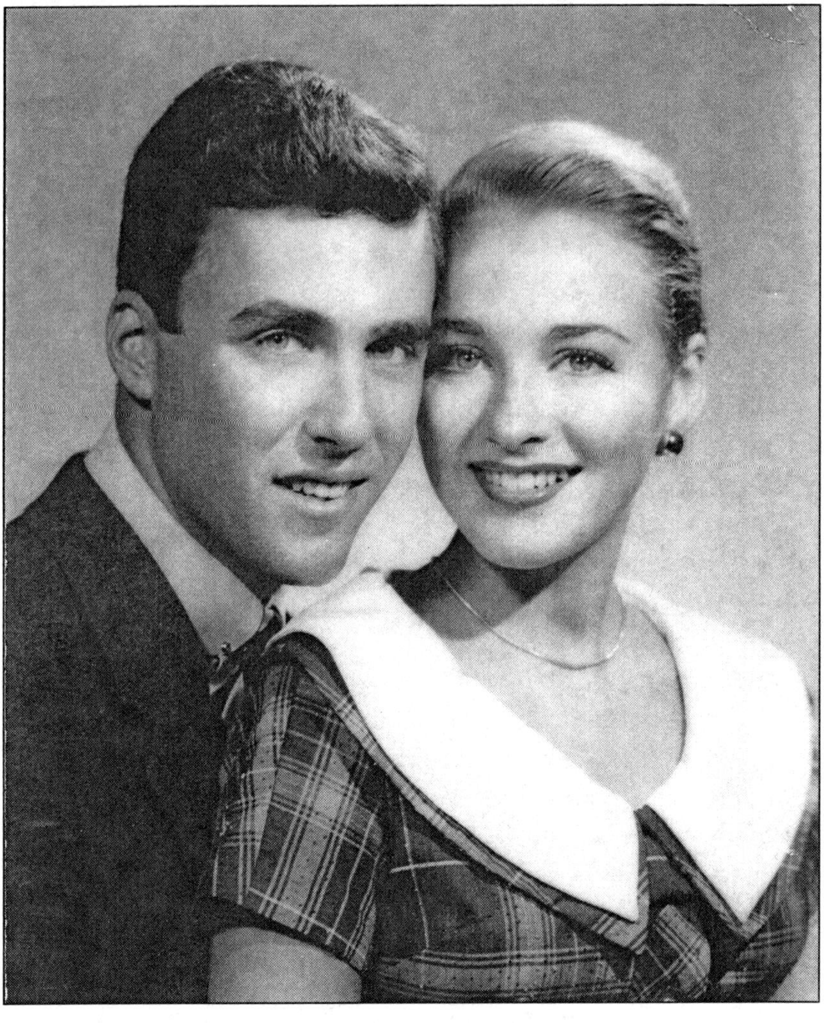

Burt (Happy) and I. Were we ever that adorable?

I had plenty of special memories even for the short period I had been renting the studio. I had painted the walls and ceiling completely black, except for the frenetic trail of white pawprints my crazy cat contributed after she got into a bucket of white water-based paint. It housed my pride and joy, the eighty-eight key Wurlitzer piano that Vladimir Horowitz had given me, upon which I had a framed photo of Byron.

As Happy and I got to know each other musically, we became friendlier and more relaxed. Love was abloom and he soon moved in.

I wasn't aware that he was a germaphobe until he proceeded to disinfect my tiny kitchen area. Of course I didn't object. I also thought it was charming that he always carried a bottle of Cepacol in his coat pocket. He asked me one day, "Hey, honey, how long do I have to stare at Byron's picture on the piano?" Oops, earth to Paula—apparently, reality hadn't quite set in yet. Not too long thereafter, I started sewing my wedding dress.

I was fortunately hired to sing as the ingenue lead in the new George White revue *Nice To See You* at the popular Versailles Club which got great critical acclaim, and *Billboard* touted, "...the longest run of any cafe package show in recent history is probably being set by George White's *Nice to See You.*"

George had once been a big-time theatrical producer and this was his comeback. As a coincidence, my mother, in her youth, had worked in one of *George White Scandals* shows in the 1920s. It was a great time. Happy and I were married during the show's run.

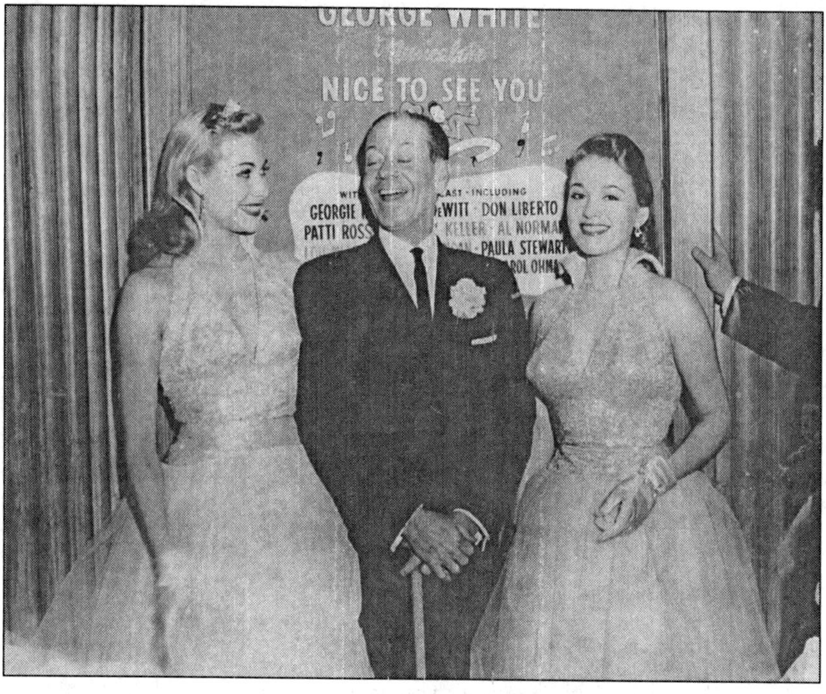

Patti Ross, Cole Porter and I at the Versailles Club in New York City during The George White Review, Nice to See You 1953. I was 24 and engaged to Burt.

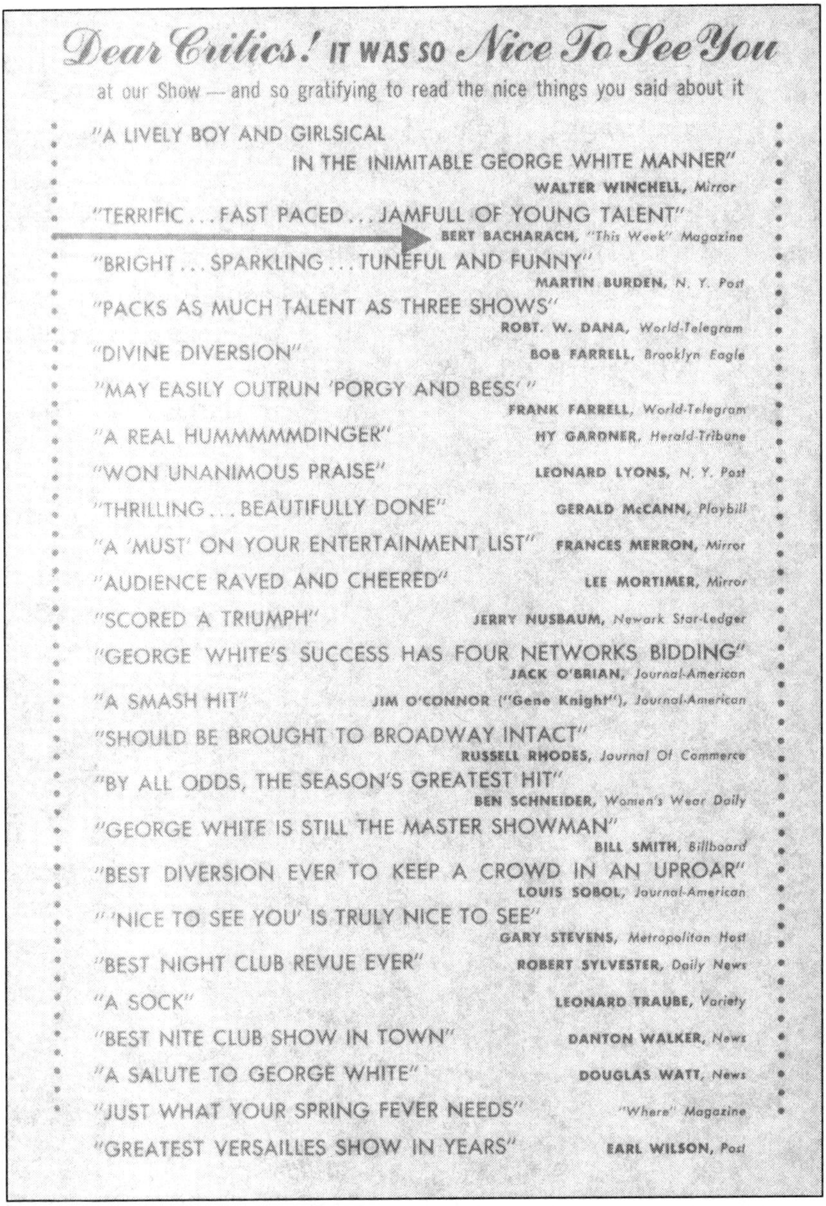

Burt's dad Bert Bacharach was a well-known syndicated newspaper columnist.

After the wedding, Big Bert found us a larger apartment closer to his and Irma's. We had a boxer puppy that we called "Stewba," a combination of our last names.

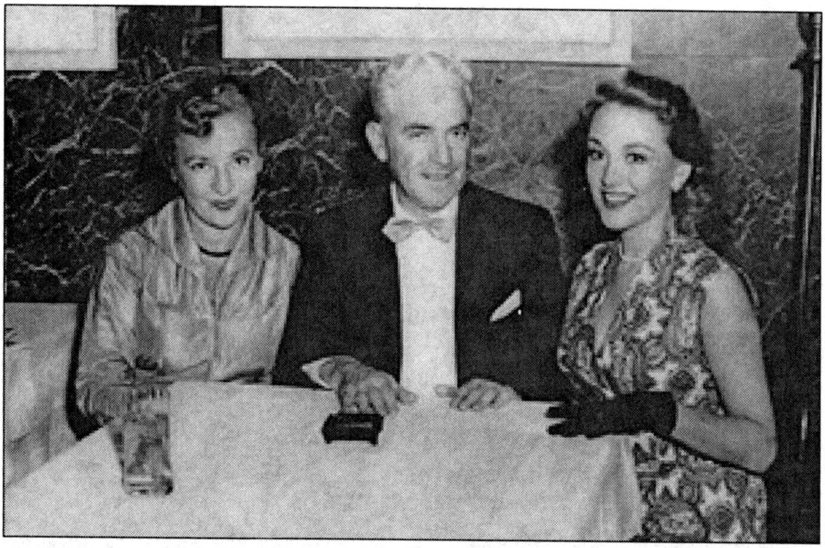

A reunion with my mom and George who had worked together in George White Scandals back in the 1920s.

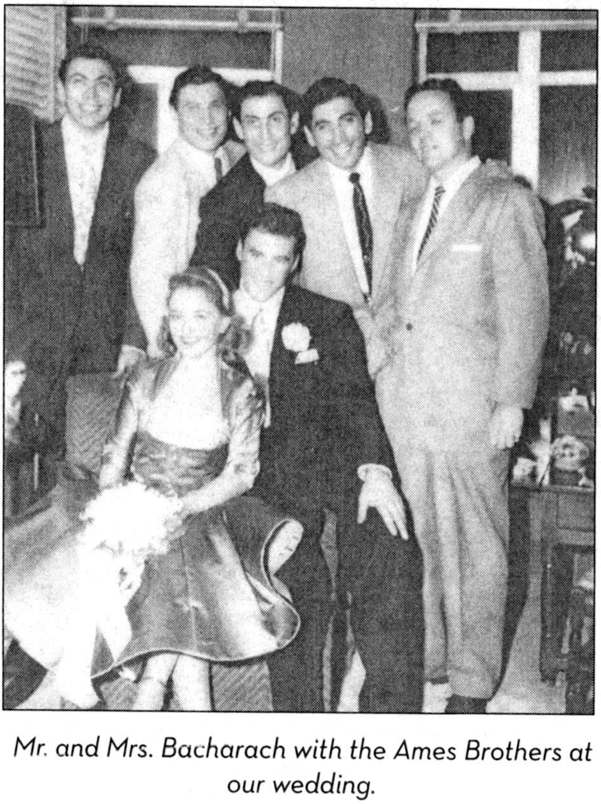

Mr. and Mrs. Bacharach with the Ames Brothers at our wedding.

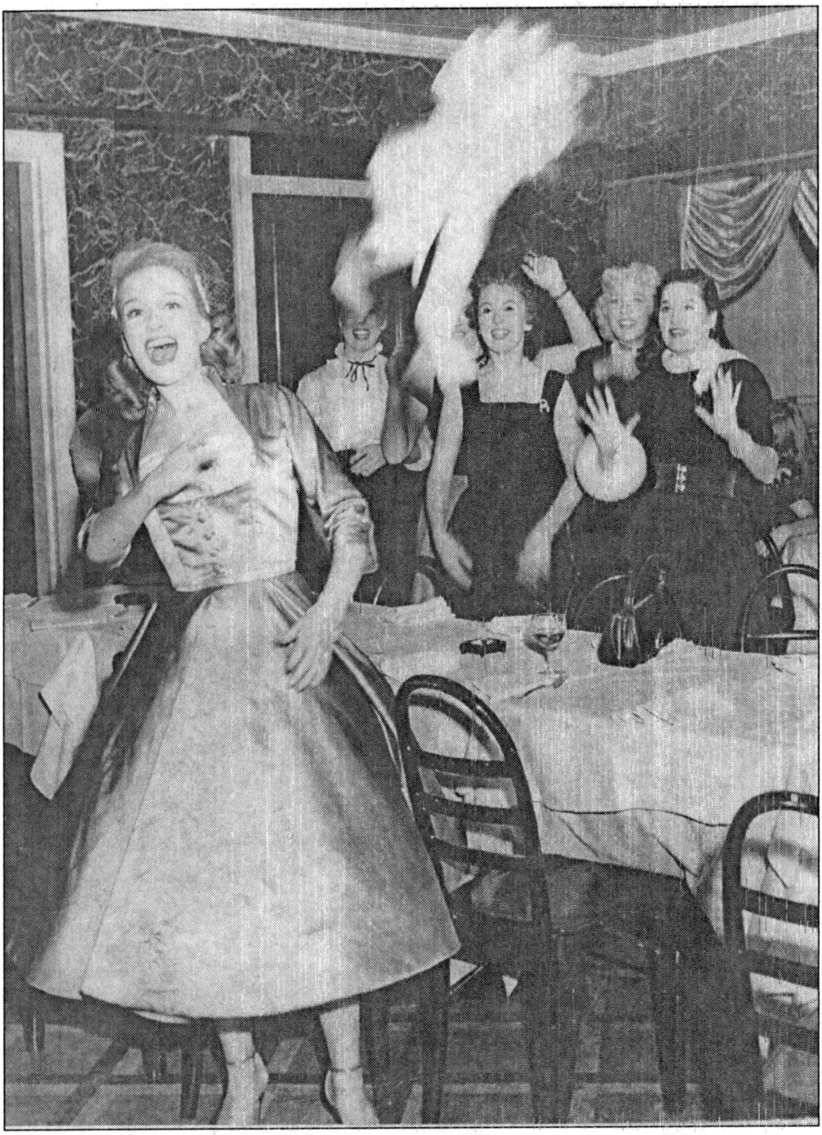

My good friends to this day, (from left to right) Margie Duncan, comedienne Fay DeWitt and Linda Lombard. All of us were cast in Nice to See You.

We were a darling family. Although we were often separated due to Happy being on tour with the Ames Brothers or me being away doing summer stock and commercial work, we were still madly in love and had an idyllic life together.

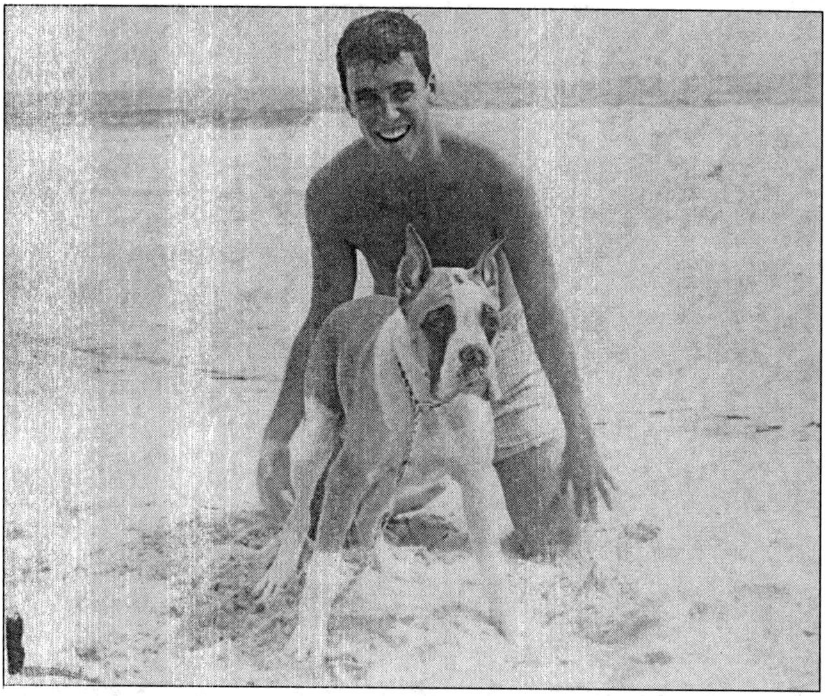

Burt (Happy) with our boxer Stewba - handsome pair.

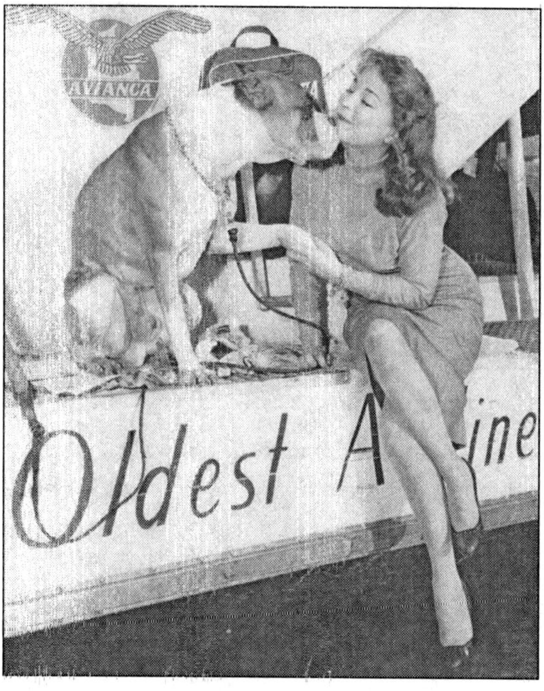

Stewba kissing me off to Hollywood for a screen test. He was sweet and huge.

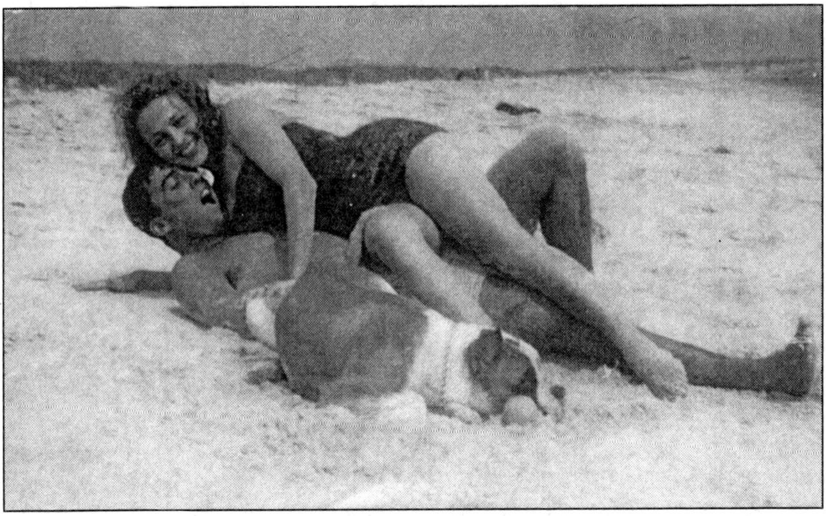

We were so sexy. Stewba put up with our antics.

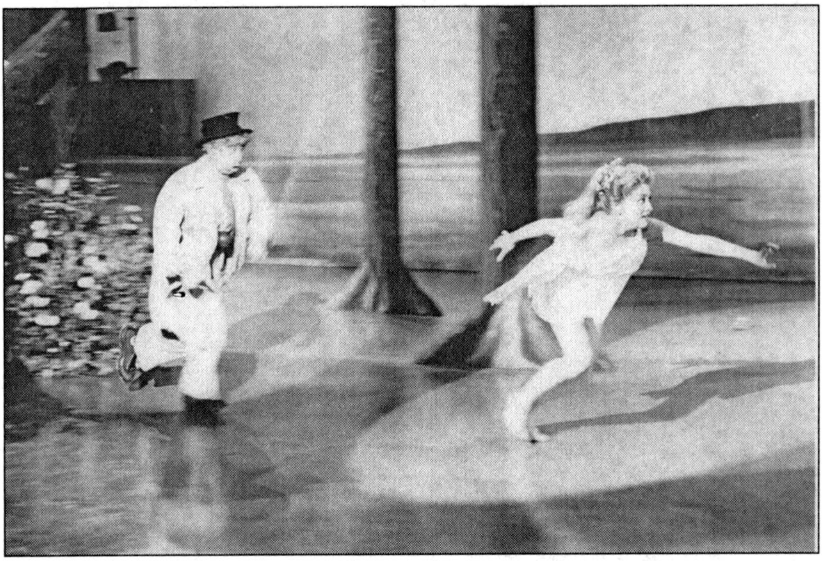

A long forgotten commercial with Harpo Marx.

As a popular duo, Happy and I were hired to perform for various society parties and dignitaries, such as the Duke and Duchess of Windsor who often invited us to join them for dinner.

The Duchess, formerly Wallis Simpson, was particularly fond of Happy, as the Duke was of me. In fact, the Duchess gave me a lovely art-deco jade and gold bracelet as a token of gratitude.

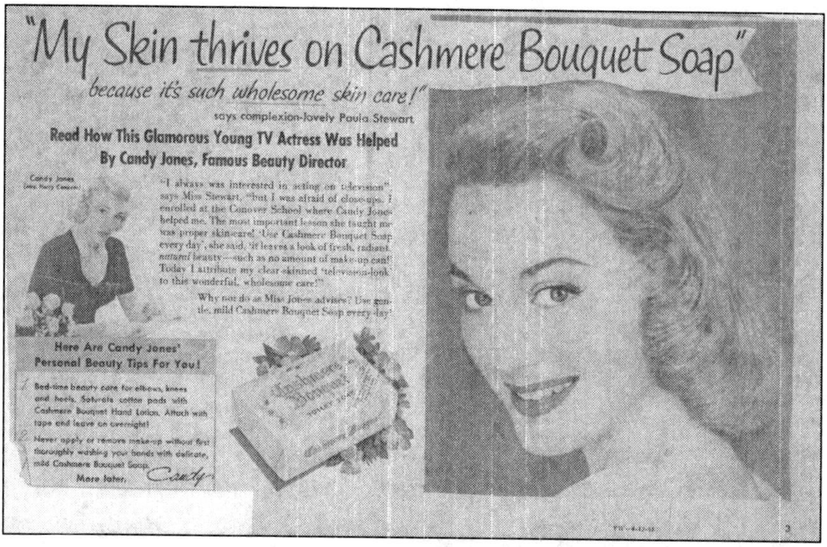

One of the many ads I did in the 50s and 60s.

Up to this point, Happy hadn't yet found a lyricist to team up with. The Ames Brothers were unresponsive to his music even though they loved his conducting and brilliance at the piano. Therefore, I introduced Happy to my good friend, composer and lyricist, Wilson Stone. I had sung one of Wilson's songs fea-

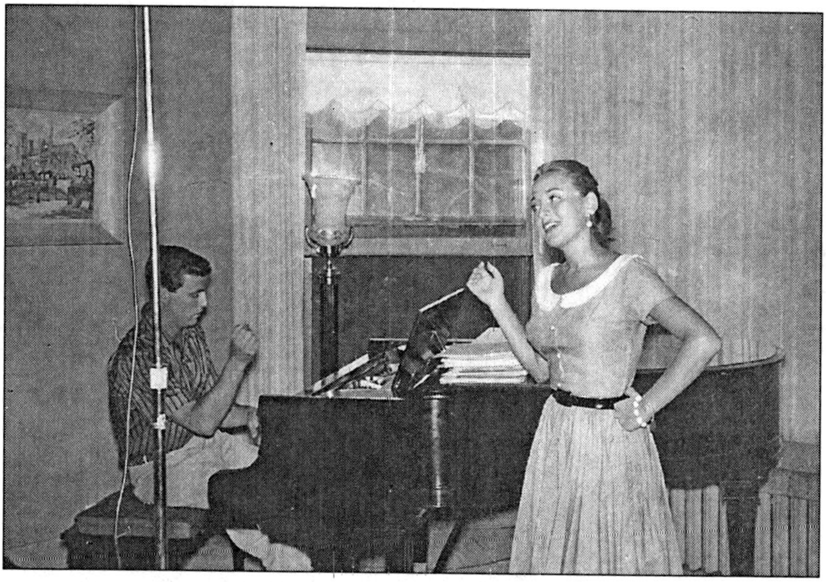

Burt and I rehearsing at Poppy's in Chicago.

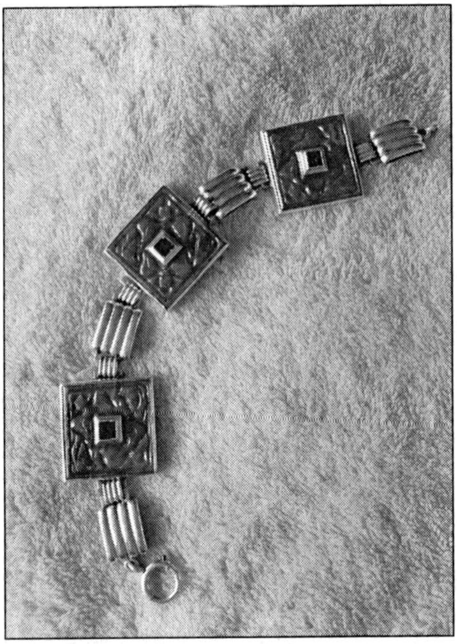

The gold deco-jade and sapphire bracelet given to me by the Duchess of Windsor. Burt and I spent many evenings performing for the Duke and Wallis

tured in the Waa-Mu Show when I was attending Northwestern. Wilson and Happy wrote a couple of songs together. Wilson, who was already signed with Paramount Famous Music took Happy over to the Brill Building where Happy met Eddie Wolpin, and, consequently, Famous Music signed Happy.

Living in our building on 55th Street were also some established and future celebrities such as Hermione Gingold, Ben Gazzara, Janis Rule, Shirley Jones and Jack Cassidy.

And we had some terrific friends in the city, among them Steve McQueen whom I had met at Sanford Meisner's Neighborhood Playhouse where he was often my scene partner. We became friends. Happy and I were delighted when he decided to marry Neile Adams, a talented performer who bedazzled him. They were a great couple and sports buffs. We had much in common and had a lot of fun together. Like many of my earliest meaningful friendships, Neile and I are still in touch to this day. Show biz bonds are somehow unique, often an enduring special connection. There are so few who can actually relate to the experiences, trials, and tribulations of a life in show business.

Jack Cassidy was a real flirt and would annoy me when he knew Happy was out of town with the Ames Brothers. Of course, Shirley hadn't a clue to this, and I didn't want to be the one to tell her. I remember one evening we all went down to the Village to hear a new, young singer, Johnny Mathis, who was causing a mild sensation. Jack was very well connected in the music industry, had pri-

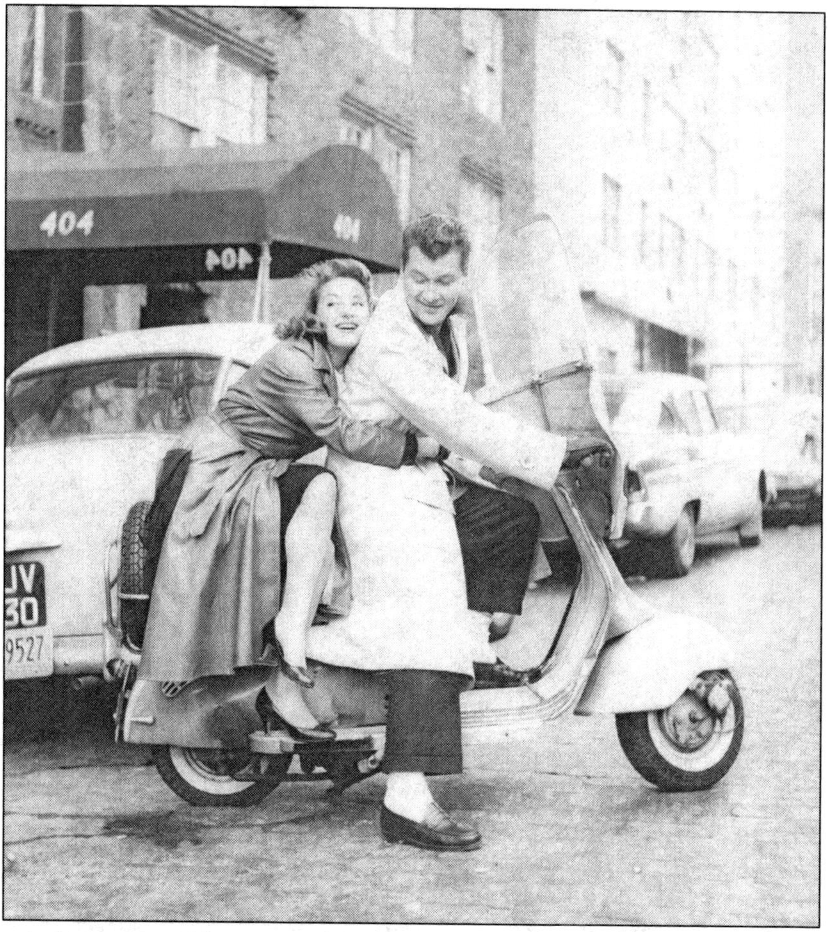

A publicity shot in front of Burt's and my apartment on my Lambretta. (Note heels again) The only way to get across town in those days! Or to the Village for The Threepenny Opera.

vate and home phone numbers, so he called Goddard Lieberson, head of Columbia Records, to tell him about Johnny Mathis. Lieberson subsequently signed Johnny up. Besides having a unique style and sound, Johnny Mathis was equally fresh and handsome, destined to become extremely famous with many great hits.

Now came the hard part—explaining something I found so deeply troubling to talk about, even to my best friend in the world, Lucy—about the time I was sent out to Hollywood by one of the New York movie studio scouts to audition for a movie. One evening, while out with some friends, I met an actor. He wasn't

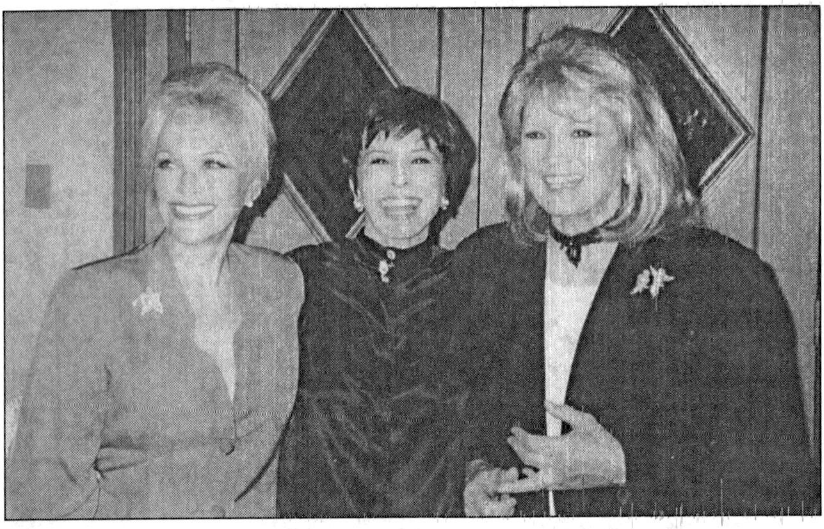

Ex wives on the town. Me after my divorce from Chuck Collins, Neille Adams after Steve McQueen and Angie Dickinson after Burt Bacharach.

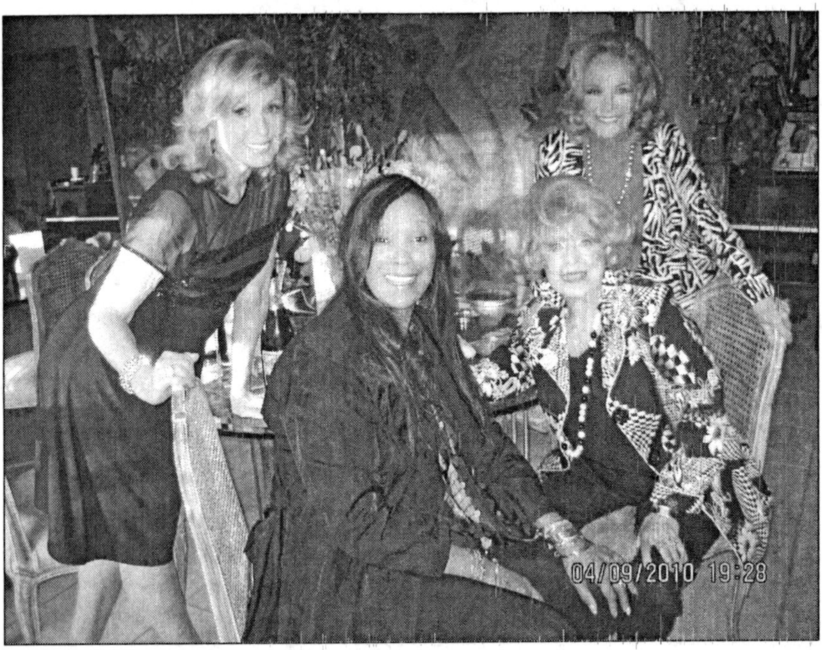

My 80th birthday with (from left to right) three of my BFFs: Slim Brandy, Anita Pointer, Sherye Woodley.

handsome but had a tremendous magnetism. I was immediately intrigued and subsequently became obsessed with him.

Only later did I discover that he was a serial seducer and had a number of girlfriends. I ended up going to a psychiatrist. I couldn't even explain my obsession with this actor. Needless to say, my relationship with Happy was destroyed. I was a mess and, of course, I couldn't tell Happy what was wrong. Subsequently this actor became a close friend of Happy's and I'm not sure Happy ever knew that this person was responsible for our break up. I suffered in silence and told Happy I wanted to divorce. I could never go back to the way I felt about him. What we had together was forever lost. I knew I hurt him deeply and to this day I can't help but feel ashamed of myself. It was my fault.

With her arms around me Lucy said, "Oh, Paula, if anyone knows about obsession it's me. I was obsessed with Desi. I do understand, baby." At this point I was in tears and could hardly continue.

So when Happy was in Las Vegas with the Ames Brothers, I agreed to let him file divorce papers there to make it easier for us both. We settled on him receiving half of my dowery from my father which was $5,000, each of us ending up with $2,500. Happy got Stewba, whom he renamed and he graciously agreed to play my future auditions. I'm pleased to say we've remained friends all these years, he even helping me much later during my terrible financial crisis.

I was completely overwhelmed with my life at the end of 1969. In that two-month period, the *Harry's Tonsils* episode aired, Harry passed away, my divorce from Jack was nearly finalized, and Burt was nominated for two Oscars. Three of the most important men in my life were impacting me all at one time. Wow!

★ ★ ★

IV
Producer

1970

Not quite free again, but close. Divorced, career on hold, life in limbo, big cultural changes, Lucy to the rescue again.

I was no stranger to the slopes, having skied for years, starting with early attempts in the New York Catskills and then many weekends at Mammoth Lakes in California after moving out West. Aspen was always my favorite with its abundance of après ski bars and fabulous eateries. It was the place to just relax, forget and feast, and of course shop for all the latest trends in "must-have" ski equipment and attire.

Lucy had not bought her condominiums in Colorado yet. She invited me to go along with the family to Snowmass to stay at a spectacular private lodge which had been offered to her for a couple of weeks by one of her wealthy corporate fans, Bud Bouse. Little Lucie was of some concern to her mother. Lucy told me, "I really don't like the people she's seeing lately. I have to get her away from those hippies and bra burners."

"Come on, Lucy. Didn't we all have our peccadilloes when we were her age? She has to have a chance to test the waters on her own. Maybe you should go a little easy on her." I knew Lucy was a little uptight about these new cultural changes happening with the youth, especially because now it was impacting her children. In these last ten years, I had come to realize that Lucy really didn't like change. I comforted her by adding, "Besides, Little Lucie's too smart for this. I'm sure she'll outgrow it." For myself, I was thrilled to be away from the depressing events happening in my own life in Los Angeles and couldn't wait to lose myself on the snowy ski moguls with their enticing challenges.

As luck would have it, after my first run, I happily ran into a former snow buddy by the name of Dick Melon, a young gorgeous stud who was there with his family, the prestigious Melons and his other friends, the hunky Wilson twins. The Wilson twins owned the famed Wilson's House of Suede on the corner of Wilshire and Santa Monica, a trendy place to hang out and hook up back in Los Angeles. Those boys were something else and doubled to boot.

I suggested to Lucy we invite the Melons over for cocktails and hors d'oeuvres. Lucy got my drift and quite liked the idea that I was trying to find someone appropriate for her daughter. Little Lucie was in a funk and resented being dragged away from her friends back home. I noticed she would stay in her room and mope around. Lucy would roll her eyes at me and lifted her hands in the air as if to say, "I give up." I felt sorry for Little Lucie and thought this might help get her out of her shell. The Melons were eager to come over and meet with the famous Lucille Ball and her daughter. Sadly, there were no sparks flying between Little Lucie and Dick.

The Melons were highly impressed with the place. It really was something. Picture a Playboy Alpine-orgy movie set with ten-foot high ceilings, deep red upholstered suede walls that were mounted with huge animal horns and a view like I've never seen before in my life. They begged for a tour of the place that revealed bedrooms with fur-covered mattresses, mirrored ceiling over the beds, his-and-her bejeweled bidets and showers with spigots for every conceivable bodily opening. Their eyes were popping out of their heads. I wondered to this day if they somehow thought this was Lucy's taste. It was also bizarre with Lucy not explaining that the place didn't belong to her. I'm sure she never even thought about it. It must have made great conversations when the Melons returned to their country club friends in Illinois. Lucy and I would share many laughs about this story over the years.

We had flown to Snowmass in a private plane. Lucy had planned to stay longer, but there was an imminent storm looming that would have had us snowed in for days. She couldn't miss filming episodes of *Here's Lucy*, so Lucy returned to LA. One morning shortly after arriving, Lucy and I were having breakfast, gazing out at the blinding light reflecting off the shimmering snow belying the soon-approaching storm that would cut her stay short. Although the chalet came completely staffed, Lucy had brought her houseman, Eddie Golab along to do any lifting and extra help with skis and luggage and stuff. He was bringing us some fresh coffee as we sat reminiscing the past traumatic few months.

Losing Harry and my divorce from Jack was weighing me down. She asked me something I myself had pondered over endlessly. Shoving aside her eggs, she came out with. "How did you ever choose such divergent men?"

"That's just it, Lucy, they were totally different," I said.

One was brash and funny; the other sophisticated and wry. Both were outrageous in their own ways. Jack poked fun at peoples' foibles. Harry dismissed their snobbery and social pretenses. They both liked to shock the world—Jack with words, Harry with his flamboyancy and lifestyle. Jack came from a poor Jewish background whose parents ran a candy store—had clawed his way up the show business ladder. Harry came from wealthy landed gentry, an heir to a steel dynasty, and had easily climbed up the debutant and Polo playing ranks of Philadelphia and New York society. Gratefully, I'd already explained my relationship with Burt, as painful as that revelation was, and hoped she would never bring it up again.

When it came to wooing me, their style was different, too. If Jack gave me a gold pearl, pin, or bauble, Harry had to top it with one with diamonds. Jack frequented the 47th Street wholesale jewelry market, whereas Harry preferred Tiffany's. Of course I was delighted wherever the jewels came from. Both were extremely generous but non-committal. Of course, Poppy still sounded like a broken record with, "What am I going to tell my patients? I've got a divorced daughter in show business?" Not that I cared so much about being married so soon again, but it was a thorn in my psyche nevertheless. Lucy urged on.

"I understand being torn between two very unusual men," I know she meant weird. "I hoped you had picked Harry. But now, you've got to think about the future for yourself and Michael. I only wish you the happiness you've helped me find with Gary. But I worry about your choices, Paula. From now on, just stick to your career for a while. I truly believe you can accomplish anything if you set your mind to it. But I've always believed in being good to yourself first. You know my philosophy is contained in *The Art of Selfishness*."

Lucy criticizing my apparent habit of putting others ahead of myself, with the implication that was my fatal flaw.

"Lucy, I chose Jack because he was more exciting, energetic and yet somehow more needy." What the hell was I thinking!

"Yes, but it was also more destructive and hurtful in the long run. But you couldn't see it until it dragged you down. Jack's neediness was a bottomless pit that no one could fill."

"I know, I know," I replied with tears streaming down my face. "I feel like such a failure."

She grabbed my hands in hers. "Stop it now, Paula. I know you have great strength in you. Just believe it." I wiped my tears and we were off to the slopes. The weather was beautiful, but prudence dictated Lucy leave immediately. She said, "You stay here and have some fun. There's no need for you to leave too. You need to relax after what you have been through with the divorce. I demand you have a good time, just don't surprise me with another husband!"

It wasn't hard to convince me to stay because Jack was back in Los Angeles looking after Michael and Lucy assured me she would check in to make sure everything was going fine. I was left alone to forget the past harrowing ordeals of the divorce. The expected snowstorm started covering the surrounding mountains and soon the view became a blur of twinkling lights through the blinding whiteness and gradual darkening sky.

I barely made it into Aspen, only to find my favorite bar was crowded with frustrated skiers jamming the tables. I could hardly find a place to squeeze into. When I did, I was having a hard time hailing a waiter, when an attractive man sat next to me. He couldn't help but notice my pink fur hat and pink skin-tight ski suit which I was literally busting out of. I looked like a vision in carnival cotton candy.

As he hailed a waiter for me, I couldn't help but notice how handsome he was. He asked, "Are you waiting for somebody?" I made up a story that my friends were trapped and couldn't get to Aspen because of the storm and I was all alone. Being a good enough actress, he saw my sad face, felt sorry for me and jumped at the opportunity to assist a "lady in distress." We introduced ourselves and made small talk. Then, after several Pink Ladies (my favorite drink), he offered to take me home. By now the snow made the drive back really difficult. You could imagine his surprise when he got a load of where I was staying. Needless to say, we made use of the ceiling mirrors.

The next morning the phone rang off the hook and when I answered, it was Lucy. I said, "I can't talk now."

"What do you mean you can't talk now!!?" (long pause) "Oh I get it, make sure you call me later," and she hung up the phone. Luckily the phone lines were down for the next couple of days due to the storm and there was no need for explanations at that moment. Upon my return to Beverly Hills, the phone at Foothill wouldn't stop ringing. Lucy pestered me for days, and I finally had to come clean about my latest escapades with John Dean, the handsome and unattached fellow that would turn into a delightful, long distance romance.

"I'm happy for you," Lucy said. "Just don't marry him yet!"

★ ★ ★

After Harry died, I was in an emotional limbo, with no career in Hollywood, Broadway a distant memory, and my divorce from Jack final. The settlement offer I received was insulting and I set an appeal in motion. The one shining star in my life was Michael but I was officially a single mother and had to get back to work. After many consistent years of performing in the theater, I had to occupy myself with something creative. Harry's attempt at producing stirred an interest in me. I'd been exposed to the intricacies of production through him. Naturally I was intrigued with the whole process. I wasn't poor at this point, and, therefore, a good target for some of the writers and promoters abounding in the hills of Beverly.

A press agent friend asked me to meet a successful songwriter, Gene Nash, who might be able to expand on a provocative rumor prevalent at that time; namely, the true sex of Mae West, a common query in some demented circles. It was somewhat of a guessing game. "Was she or wasn't she?" It was agreed that Gene Nash would come up with a story about a famous sex goddess and write a scenario that might be the basis for a movie.

Overnight, literally, he wrote a screenplay that knocked me out. The title: *Dinah East* (as opposed to Mae West) tells the story of a young male actor who can't get a part at a studio open call due to the fact the only openings are for girls. He comes back the next day dressed as a woman and gets hired. I loved the script, and even though Mae was a friend of mine, I saw the possibilities.

First thing I did was ask Lucy what she knew about Mae. I told her the premise, which she was not really clear about. I asked her point blank: "Lucy, do you know for sure that Mae is a woman?"

"How the hell would I know, I never saw her privates! But I know it's been a joke for years, Paula." Mae was known to like musclemen, but then so did a lot of the glamour queens. Mae's shoulders were often a subject of discussion, not exactly soft and rounded but somewhat stiff. Her waistline was almost non-existent. Her brazen innuendos were more of a tease for males than gals. Any wonder why the unveiling of a legend intrigued me?

I remember Lucy trying to talk me out of it. "Paula, you know how hard it is to raise any kind of money in this town. And for god's sake, you're a woman. Why do you want to take on this hurdle?" I was disappointed in her reaction. How could Lucy tell me there wasn't anything I couldn't do and now she was actually suggesting there was something I shouldn't attempt?

Unlike Lucy, I wasn't afraid to embrace the cultural changes happening around the world. It was no longer the "Camelot" of the 1960s. It was the "Sex, Drugs and Rock n' Roll" of the 1970s, and I for one was willing to take the bull by the horns. Women were beginning to take the blinders off men's view of them. Pioneers like Jane Fonda and Janice Joplin were challenging the established mores with Fonda winning an Academy Award for playing a prostitute in *Klute*, and Joplin openly embracing drugs while captivating a generation with her vocal originality. In a sense, I was taking on a double-edged sword by competing in the male dominated world of movie producing and by tackling a taboo subject. It never occurred to me that I couldn't.

I believed that I had a vehicle that addressed the changes head on. It was intriguing and sexually forward enough to cause attention and controversy. Just what the public was craving at the moment. Lucy in her sheltered life, security, and stardom didn't need to be concerned about these things. Naturally, I wouldn't say all that to her, what I did say however, was, "Remember when you and Desi bucked the system when the networks didn't believe that a Latino and a white woman could be accepted as a married couple on national television? You went out on a limb using your own money for the pilot and against all odds, were victorious in your belief. How is what I'm doing so different from that? I'm not doing anything more now than what you did then."

"Well, Paula, if you're gonna put it that way, I guess you're right."

Jokingly I added, "Lucy, there's a reason why women are burning their bras. We want to be known for more than just our tits! Besides, I'm not going to raise the money here, I'm going to New York."

"What!!?? When?"

"But before I do, I have a meeting with Jim Aubrey today at 2:00 o'clock."

"What!!! How do you know him?"

"Don't you remember at Lipsey's party when you told me to tell him to go fuck himself?"

"Oh yeah, oh yeah, right!!"

"I see Jim all the time at the Santa Monica Airport when I go out to do 'touch and go's' for practice. He has a plane out there."

Recently, I had landed a Cessna 172 when Jim had approached me with a big grin on his face. "I don't often see too many hot pilots out here. Don't I know you from somewhere?" Not wanting to remind him of the favor he owed me, I simply introduced myself and mentioned I was producing a movie.

"Paula," Lucy said, "You amaze me." Then what happened?"

"Nothing. He just gave me his card and said to call him if I needed something. It was as simple as that, so I called him."

"Oh my god. Just be careful. You know he's a snake. He's no Burton. He's much worse."

"Oh Lucy, here we go again. Do you know how many couches I've avoided in my life?"

"Probably as many as I have, but I'm dying to know what kind of bullshit he'll feed you. Call me the minute you leave his office. If you ever do."

Well, I took the meeting and of course, reported back to Lucy. Jim and I had a lot in common. We were both from Illinois and we shared the same pilot instructors. He loved talking aviation, especially about doing *chandelles* and *immelmanns* (aircraft acrobatic maneuvers). When I asked him about financing he was blunt. Although he was promoting titillating films at his studio, they weren't about to venture into the subject matter of my film which he felt was going to end up X rated anyway. He told me he really liked the premise and wished me luck with a wink and a kiss on the cheek.

"So how about that for Mr. Cobra, Lucy? No bites in any direction."

"Consider yourself lucky, honey. As far as New York goes, go with my blessing. Hurry back. I'll miss you."

★ ★ ★

The flight to New York gave me time to reflect on the past couple of years and my meager attempts at adapting to television and film, which still eluded me, perhaps because my heart and soul had always been committed to theater. Despite its many demands, generally musical roles didn't require too much character development. Most of the dialogue is mainly an introduction to a song. The few shows I relished for their content were few and far between – titles such as *The Threepenny Opera, The Most Happy Fella* and even *Carousel.* Not much to ponder about in *Let It Ride, Kismet* and *Little Me* except the rewarding applause which ends with the curtain call. I know it sounds crass, but what Patrick Pacheco of the *Daily News* would quote later on held true: "I like money more than applause." Fame can't buy you the taxi fare

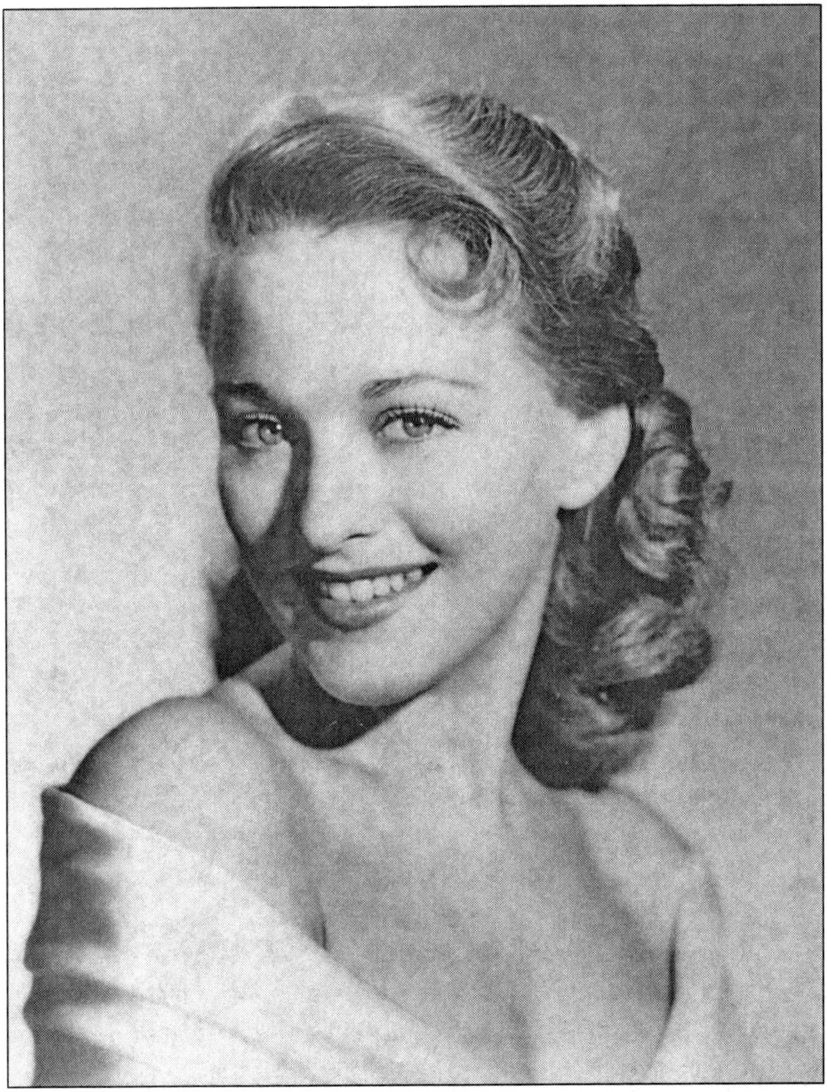

Frank Aston wrote that I brought "admirable vocal equipment to the role of Rosabella" in The Most Happy Fella.

to the unemployment office. For instance, my salary as one of the stars in *The Threepenny Opera* was $50 a week—by the way, standard salary for off-Broadway at that time—hardly enough to live on even then.

And then there are always those bizarre quirks of fate. For example, during my stint on *The Threepenny Opera*, I made a desperate decision—to take leave of the show and pursue the lucrative well-paid roles offered in summer stock. I needed to pay my accumulating bills. Unfortunately, during the summer, Frank Loesser had seen Jo Sullivan as Polly in the show, and it was Jo who landed the starring Broadway role of Rosabella in *The Most Happy Fella*. And subsequently, she also married him. However, later when it was revived at the City Center, Loesser chose me for Jo's role. I knew the challenges of entertainment—earning money and raising money and especially the luck you have to have. I had certainly lived it all.

But, I knew my *Dinah East* venture into the world of film did not sit well with Lucy for all those reasons. Mainly, she wasn't enthused for me, because personally she didn't understand why I wanted to put myself through the agonizing ordeal of producing. She didn't want me to take on those challenges with a project that was so controversial. Lucy was frustrated that even she couldn't give my career a real push at this time. She could get someone fired but not hired. She could get her daughter on her show but not into the film version of *Grease*. Lucy even told me that she had said to casting, "I once owned Paramount. Little Lucie doesn't have to screen test for one of the leads!"

At this point, while sipping on my martini and gazing out at the world below, I realized I was flying by the seat of my pants. I was not flush with money after the trouncing I took from the judicial system and Jack's extolling my mythical stature in the industry as a big star.

Even though I had done *The Big Valley*, *Hogan's Heroes*, *Love American Style*, *The Lucy Show*, *Perry Mason*, *The Joey Bishop Show*, *My Favorite Martian* along with various game shows, they were all for minimum salary, none of which would total up to pay one month's mortgage on Foothill. But here I was off to get financing for a movie that I couldn't even star in myself.

So what if it was a taboo subject. I was no stranger to alternative lifestyles, having lived in the theater for over fifteen years. Also, I was not raised in a judgmental atmosphere. My father was open-minded. He dated a biracial Asian woman, for whom I cared deeply. I never thought twice about one's sexual orientation. The theater was just as open and accepting back then as it is now. However, Tinseltown, then as it does now, still had its issues. It is a shame the backlash one encounters when deciding to publicly and openly be oneself.

The other challenge in my film was the sexual content, although this area was still gray in Hollywood. It would be another year before the landmark adult film *Deep Throat* would ignite the phrase "porn chic." I was a little ahead of the times but not by much.

Gay themes and heavy sexual content were enough for people to view my project as controversial. But hey, so was the *Kama Sutra* and look how that survived over the centuries, including a modern translation by my pal Richard Burton in 1962. But *Dinah East* wasn't just an X-rated sexploitation film; it was about the right to assert one's sexual identity with a love story at its heart. So here I was with a suitcase full of gorgeous clothes, a list of friends to call on, and a lot of chutzpah.

★ ★ ★

I was no stranger to Broadway investors. Unlike Hollywood, which functions more as an elite gentleman's club with the perversely few and snobbish studios, Broadway was an entirely different playing field. You could go to independent backers that were usually interested in theater and different trends and ideas. This more lucrative social group would have their finger on the offbeat genres, whereas Hollywood would follow three acts later and always safely with known stars.

Having a history with most of them, I chatted up Jim Nederlander, Joe Cates, Charlie Strouse, and David Susskind. Broadway was more accepting at that time to female producers like Ethel Linder Reiner who produced *The Rainmaker* starring Geraldine Page and written by my old pal Richard Nash. Cheryl Crawford, who started The Group Theater with Harold Clurman and Lee Strasberg, was also very helpful. Cheryl had produced numerous shows including *The Rose Tattoo*, *Paint Your Wagon*, *Golden Boy* and the original production of *Brigadoon*. I also reached out to another female producer, Lynn Loesser.

Lynn had produced *The Most Happy Fella* starring Jo Sullivan based on the book by her then-husband, Frank Loesser, who also had written the music and lyrics. I had taken over Jo's role in *The Threepenny Opera*. Lynn caught my performance and thought I was a better choice for *The Most Happy Fella*. She had convinced Frank to cast me in the revival at the City Center in New York. I'm certain Lynn was happy that Jo was out because Frank had divorced her to marry Jo.

Lynn was resourceful and kind, and hinted at looking outside the inner circle and more towards personal friends for help with *Dinah East*. Although having enough clout to have the right people listen to me and the "Mae West" intrigue, there were also those who were put off by the bizarre content. However, nobody wrote or knew better about taboo and risqué than my garrulous, gorgeous friend Jackie Susann.

I contacted her and she couldn't possibly have done more than she did to help me. What a gem! She was hot off her roaring success with *Valley of the Dolls* and her most recent tome, *The Love Machine*, depicting the "Smiling Cobra" himself. Jackie and I would spend hours getting our hair and nails done at Larry Matthews, the New York version of Gene Shacove in Beverly Hills. Larry was also most helpful with his client list.

While at Larry's salon I had to question Jackie endlessly about Aubrey. She couldn't believe that I was unscathed after my encounter with him. Maybe I wasn't his type? She also loved the idea of *Dinah East*.

"Let me make a few calls for you, Paula," she said.

I also reached out to my good friend Rex Reed. As luck would have it, Rex had just starred in *Myra Breckinridge* with none other than Mae West. The film's subject matter was also right alongside *Dinah East*, dealing with LGBT themes. The film was trashed by the critics, many calling it the worst film ever made. Rex just flipped for the idea. Even though his experience with *Myra* was dismal, he championed me as a trailblazing female producer.

"Keep at it, girl," Rex said. "More power to you." He suggested I call Dick Brooks, the press agent for *Myra* to give me some help.

When I called Lucy to give her an update she surprised me.

"Paula, I do owe you an apology," she said. "I know I was a little discouraging before you left, but I was only trying to protect you from another disappointment."

"I know Lucy, but I believe in this 100 percent."

I stayed for a week at The Hampshire House, thanks to the manager being an old beau. Luckily my old friend Dorothy Strelsin, a wealthy socialite, insisted that I stay with at her sumptuous Fifth Avenue penthouse. She helped me throw some backers auditions where I could do my sales spiel amidst the cacophony of popping champagne corks and the sounds of the Bee Gees on the Hi Fi system, all the while viewing the sparkling lights in the night sky shining down on Central Park. Directly across from her penthouse, I could see the silhouette of my former nineteenth floor apartment at The San Remo.

Jack and I had given up The San Remo apartment years ago, but against my wishes. I had wanted to continue leasing it. The rent was $495 a month and hardly a burden.

Actually, Jack's business managers were the problem. I used to walk up and down the streets when Jack and I lived at The San Remo—there were so many brownstones for sale in the neighborhood of thirty to forty-thousand dollars. I would say to Jack, "Why don't we buy one of these?" Even then I knew they were a good investment.

Jack's business managers would ultimately talk him out of it. They thought I was a blonde showbiz bimbo and I didn't know anything. "Dumb *shicksa*" is what they would call me. Dumb, huh? Properties in and around the Central Park West area today are worth millions.

Dorothy convinced her husband, Al, to invest in my film along with some of their friends. Likewise, my restaurant friends Billy Rosen, Toots Shoor, and Joe Kipness were most helpful with their generous parties for me as were some old flames like Denny Slater. Particularly helpful were investors like Murray Candib, Mal Malvin, Bob Magaziner, and Jack Meany. Happily, I got to see all my friends while encouraging them to invest in a fun venture. What did a few thousand mean to those guys anyway? They wagered more on the weekend sports games.

My old friend newspaper columnist Earl Wilson was there touting my new venture. I even got pals Hugh Downs and Joe Garagiola to give me exposure on *The Today Show*. I got good press out of that. The experience made me think I should have been a producer all those years instead of acting. Instead of beating the boards, I should have been beating the drum.

Actually, I was really good and enjoying the experience. It helps to believe in something and be able to sell it well, even if you were that rare animal, a female producer in the early 1970s.

★ ★ ★

The fund-raising portion of my project was finished in record time but there was one more hurdle before going back to sunny Los Angeles and that would be the crucial casting of the lead role, the part of lead character Dinah East. Gene Nash, my co-producer and director, was along for the trip. He and I couldn't have been farther apart in our ideas of who was to play the female lead in our movie.

My dear friend Sondra Lee kept touting a frail boy who just had starred on Broadway in *Fortune and Men's Eyes* which was a smash hit. Jeremy Stockwell was only five-two, about my height, blonde, slight and could easily look like a girl. Gene wanted an inexperienced brunette with a big Adams apple. I prevailed after threatening to walk away from the whole thing. Consequently, Jeremy who looked exactly like Marilyn Monroe when made up was able to wear all my clothes in the film. Phew! By the way, Lucy contributed one or two of her alligator purses to the production of *Dinah East* as I fondly recalled when seeing the movie in reruns.

While raising money for *Dinah East* in New York, I met a woman whom I knew had to be in the film. Isabelle Collin Dufresne (aka Ultra Violet) was a staple in the alluring world of "The Factory" where she was a Warhol superstar and muse. She was beautiful, French, and a gifted artist having studied under Salvador Dalí. I sparked immediately to her personality and cast her as "Daniela," the studio costumer who becomes Dinah's confidant.

I raved about Isabelle to Lucy who just had to meet this compelling woman. She agreed to stop by the set one day. I remember, because we were shooting the love scene with Ultra Violet and another actress. Because there was nudity involved, any non-crew members including Lucy, had to watch from behind a darkened mirror so as not to inhibit the actors' performances.

I was running around the set before Gene yelled "action." As usual, there were last minute approvals that needed my attention, from the staging of the props, to wardrobe, to Ultra's hair style. Doing a lesbian scene was not a big deal to the actresses and they were both extremely relaxed; a bright spot in what seemed to be a much-cluttered day.

I made last minute touch ups on the set, a quick opinion to our talented cinematographer Ross Kelsay on Ultra's lighting, and then I joined Lucy. She stood in awe.

"Wow, Paula," Lucy said.

"I know, isn't Ultra just gorgeous?" I replied.

"Of course she's a beautiful woman, but I was referring to your multi-tasking. Christ, Paula, you might as well be directing!"

Funny Lucy should have said that. I hadn't wanted to say it out loud, but I did not like the way Gene was handling things. Unfortunately, there wasn't anything I could do about it at this point. I didn't want to cause any friction between us, so I bit my tongue.

"Where did you learn all of this?" Lucy asked.

"Simple. I watched talented people over the years but I really got my basics at Northwestern."

Although singing garnered me attention, my great love has always been science. I wanted to be a doctor like my father. By the time I applied to Northwestern University I was told their quota for female applicants had been reached. How times have changed. Some of the best doctors in the world are women, and it's a shame I was told I couldn't pursue my passion.

My father, however, was persisting that I still attend the prestigious university, so I thought, why not the school of dramatic arts? I could sing after all. It was in Northwestern's theater department where I learned everything about set decorating, period furniture, costumes, lighting, props and scenery. I paid attention and that paid

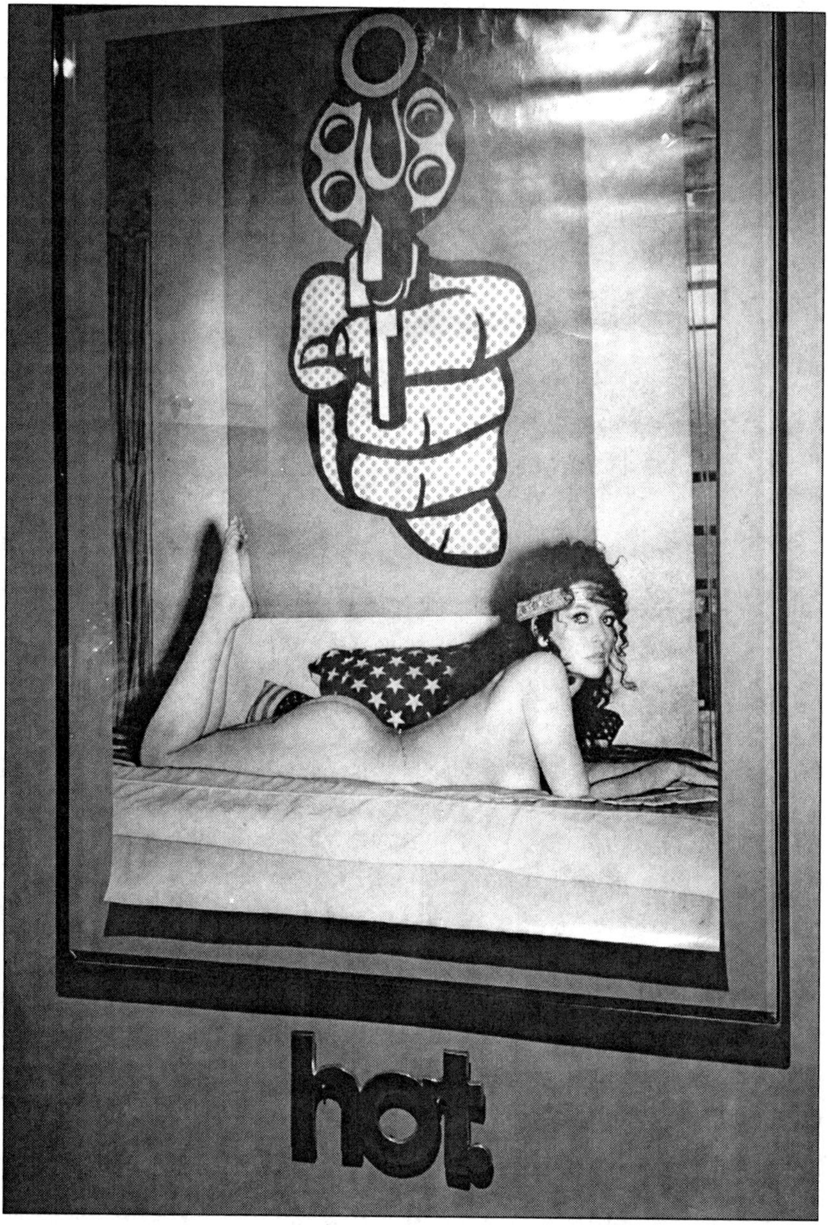

Does this say, "Stay out of my kitchen, while I'm cooking!?" Ultra Violet gave me this signed poster after she starred in my movie, Dinah East.

dividends in my future. When I later recounted all this to Lucy she said, "And here I thought casting you in *Wildcat* made me a *good* producer!" I always enjoyed a much-needed laugh with Lucy.

During the wrap of *Dinah East*, Lucy called me to come to her set on *Here's Lucy*.

"Paula, you'll never believe this," Lucy said. "Your old boyfriend, Richard Burton, and Liz are going to guest star on the season premiere of my show. Anyway, I thought you would get a kick out of coming. But no funny business!"

"Are you kidding? I wouldn't miss it for the world!"

So Dede, Lucy's mom and I showed up and were the only ones allowed on set. It was one of Lucy's funniest shows, the episode where Lucy tries on the famous Taylor-Burton Diamond Ring Richard had just given her. It was huge—69 carats and she couldn't get it off. I wasn't sure if Richard was still upset with Lucy for interrupting our tryst years ago, but I noticed she had to take him backstage during rehearsals. She told me later what she said to him.

"You know you missed twelve jokes with your mumbling? We can't stage the show or the jokes unless we can hear them. If we don't hear the joke, we can't anticipate the length of the laughter which impacts the overall timing of the show. We're playing to a live audience; treat it like it's the theater. You can't just give a mumbo jumbo performance in rehearsals!"

At the next run through Richard got serious laughs. She was thrilled and I think he was, too. I wasn't surprised Lucy couldn't pass up the chance to give Richard "notes" on his comedic performance after she had the guts to tell him to get out of my dressing room all those years ago. I know Richard didn't have nice things to say about Lucy in his memoir, but I was there. She was a professional and it was *her* show. When Lucy was performing, you were lucky enough to be a part of it, or watch in amazement. Meanwhile, Richard didn't dare let his eyes stray from Liz, but he gave me a surreptitious wink when she wasn't looking.

★ ★ ★

Dinah East opened February 25, 1971 at the New View Theater in Hollywood on a shoestring budget of just $180,000. Kevin Thomas of the *LA Times* called it, "An outrageous satire on Hollywood." As predicted by Jim Aubrey, it received an X-rating due

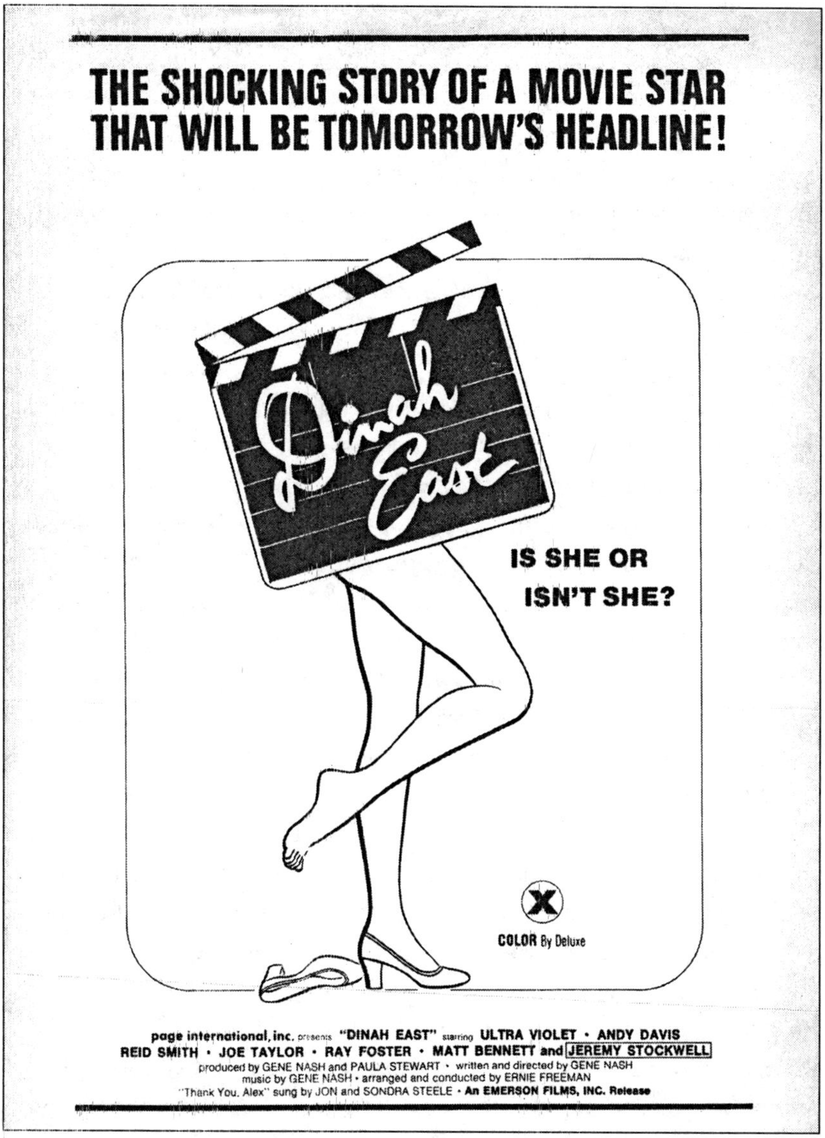

to the full frontal male nudity. Thomas' review continued, "The actors playing the men in Dinah's life have obviously been chosen for their looks and various physical endowments, displaying as much acting ability as they do skin. Sort of a male nudie that transcends the genre." A far cry from the negative reviews that *Myra Breckinridge* received.

Dinah East's premiere needed someone to host. It was very common in those days to hire an emcee to introduce cast members and other VIPs as they stepped out of their limos. We needed someone outrageous. Most of the current comedians were busy working club dates, but there was a new and far out comic on the scene by the name of Richard Pryor. I later learned that he was recently on the rebound from a drug bust and in need of some better publicity. However, nobody found this important enough to convey to me. The only thing I was told was that he was controversial and would be perfect for the occasion.

Richard and his manager, who was called "George," as I recall, agreed to meet with me and my associate producer, Marty Romley at his hotel at the Sunset Towers West. I was to call Marty once I was there, and he would join me and we would consummate our deal. I arrived dressed in bright purple, including my shoes.

When I knocked on the door, George let me in. The lights were very low. Richard and two blonde bimbos were seated around a coffee table with long straws attached to their noses. They stuck it into a mound of what looked to me like flour. I didn't like the feeling I was getting, so I nervously explained that I needed to call Marty.

At that instant and out of nowhere, Richard got up and socked me in the ear. He hit me so hard that I fell back onto the couch and saw stars. He screamed at the girls to get the hell out of there. Then he grabbed my beautiful new shoes and threw them out the open window onto Sunset Boulevard. He dragged me by my hair into the bedroom, pulled at my clothes, wrestling furiously. George did not interfere. It all happened so fast. I can only assume, he was equally shocked by Richard's crazy behavior. Maybe he had never seen it before. Or feared for his own safety.

Even though Richard was taller than I was, he was skinny and frail. Something was fueling his rage—that magical white dust. I was screaming at the top of my lungs and he put his hand over my mouth to silence me. I bit his finger to the bone which caused him to let me go. I got up and sprinted into the living room. At that very moment there was a knock at the door.

George frantically opened it and standing there was a sweet young boy delivering some beer they had ordered. By this time, Richard and I were struggling again on the couch. I screamed, "Get the police. They're trying to kill me!" The boy was in shock. Richard was tearing at my sleeve and telling him not to believe me, that I was high on drugs. Bewildered, the poor boy ran away in fear.

I was still yelling. I have a really loud voice and George and Richard were trying to get me to stop. I broke free once again and ran into the bathroom and locked the door. I tried to pull myself together. Not long after, there was heavy pounding on the door.

"It's the police. Open this door now!"

I could hear Richard and George noisily scraping away whatever was on top of that table. I was so happy the cops were there to save me, but flashed on how this would look in print.

"X-rated film producer Paula Stewart, recently divorced from actor Jack Carter, involved in a drug bust with comedian Richard Pryor, she being strangely barefoot."

The police demanded, "We hear there's a woman in trouble here. Where is she?" In that moment, I knew what I had to do.

Mustering all my years of improvisation, I came out of the bathroom very calmly with a big smile on my face. They wanted to know if I was all right and what was all the shouting about.

"Oh, that? Must have been the music we were listening to. You know how it sounds like screaming sometimes," I said dismissing the matter.

I convinced them, but before leaving they said, "Well, we need to take your names, anyway." I knew that should I have mysteriously been found to have fallen out of the window, Richard and George would be implicated. I felt a wave of power surge through me.

After the cops left, Richard collapsed on the couch in complete amazement. This must have sobered him up pretty fast.

"You just saved my ass, you're unreal. How can I ever thank you?"

Then I let him have it. Through clenched teeth, I snarled every foul word I knew at him. I threatened to tell the world what a disgrace he was.

"You better watch out for me, buster. I don't ever want to see your face again. And you'll be getting a bill for my shoes!"

I was still staggering and unsteady as I hailed a cab on Sunset and continued fuming all the way back home to Foothill. My head was pounding and my vision seemed blurred. The next morning I was still dizzy. I called Lucy for a doctor, spilling my guts to her about my entanglement with Pryor. She was aghast.

"Call Doctor Ed Cantor, the best ENT in Beverly Hills. You need to have your ears and balance checked. You may have serious injury—that bastard," she said, taking control. "Thank God you're not disfigured.

"That was quick thinking on your part, Paula, now let's hope that sonofabitch Richard wises up and gets help or he'll be dead in the water if this ever gets out." As a memento from that encounter, I still have hearing loss to this day.

One night after the opening of *Dinah East*, we sat around after dinner and Lucy hosted a special screening of the film in her lanai. She thought it was a tender love story but Gary felt differently. He said it was the worst piece of shit he'd ever seen.

Actually, the worst was yet to come. Shortly after the opening, *Dinah East* was removed from theaters. Instead of paying the IRS the withholding tax, Seymour Romley, Marty's father, who was in charge of the movie's financial matters, put the money on the ponies. The IRS slammed a lien on the film and I lost control of my baby. Many years later, a subsidiary of Fox snapped up the rights. I could have bought it back for $2,500—nearly $16,000 in today's market. A big stretch for me. But I asked the wrong person for help. At this point Lucy had moved her production company over to 20th Century Fox, so I went to Gary, who was in charge of her business affairs.

"Do me a favor," I said. "Talk to these people. I need you to help me because I can buy the movie back."

This was on a Friday and Gary seemed put out. He asked, "Can't it wait till next week?"

"No, it's going up for sale today."

"I've got a golf game with Marvin Davis. It'll have to wait."

I lost it again. Gary really could have helped me out of a jam. I was numb from his lack of concern. I was really begging. I remembered when the situation was reversed, when Gary, practically on bended knee, pleaded with me years ago, in the beginning, to "make it happen with Lucy." But my plea fell on deaf ears.

Having him intervene on my behalf could have been a lifesaving change for me.

★ ★ ★

After *Dinah East* was dead and buried, I met a nice guy through Beldon Katleman. His name was Ron Pruessing and he was in the paint manufacturing business. He lived in Newport Beach, was divorced, and had two little girls that were about Michael's age, about six at this time. Ron had a beautiful house and he was very friendly with his ex-wife. He was tall, blonde, rugged but slender, with a dancer's body, and a great lover. He was a gourmet cook, sailor, outdoors sportsman with a great sense of humor and adored me. He was almost too good to be true.

We would get together on the weekends when I would drive down to Newport with Michael and that was the best part. He had a fabulous boat and was wonderful with the kids. We took lots of camping, fishing, skiing and hunting trips, often bringing our kids along when they weren't in school.

One afternoon, Lucy invited me over to have lunch. I hadn't seen her in a couple of months because of my involvement with Ron. I could tell over the phone when she invited me, that I would be questioned about my new romance.

She was recuperating from a recent accident. A few months back, a skier hit Lucy while she was on a family vacation in Snowmass. And the lead in *Mame* was on the horizon for Lucy. We just had to play catch up.

When I arrived, I thought she looked tired and drawn. I immediately attributed it to the accident and the stress from the tabloids ragging on Desi, Jr.

She gave me a hug and led me into the kitchen, hobbling with her cast. It was the domestic help's day off. So, she pulled out

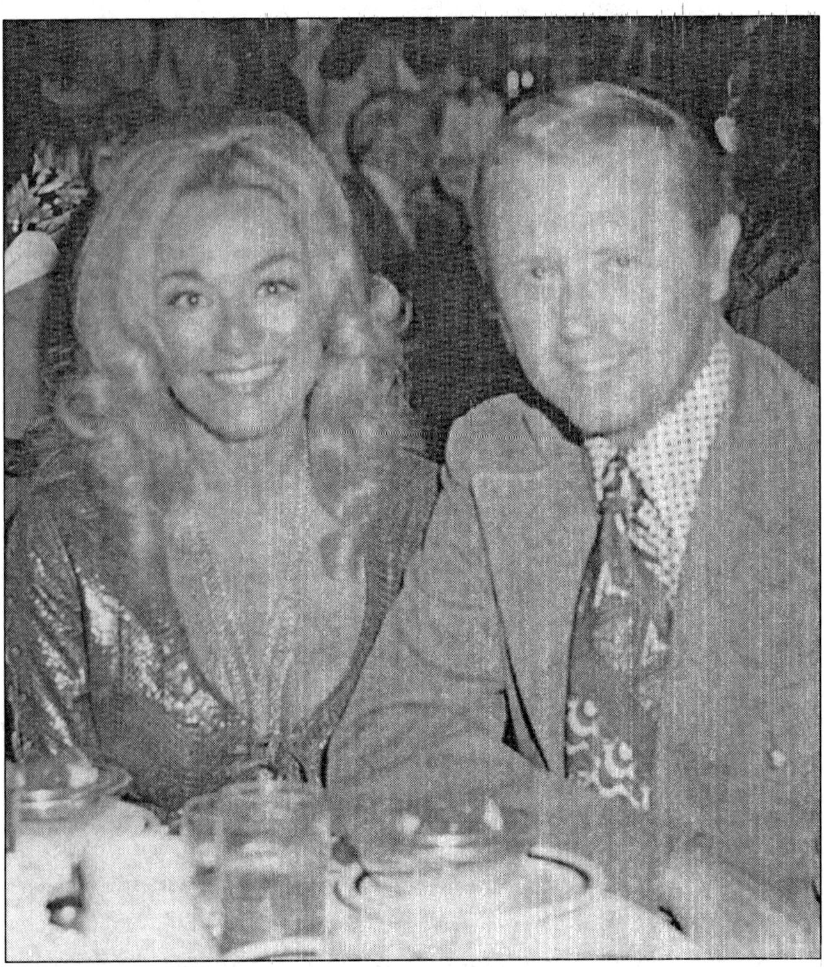

Ron Pruessing was a real "hunk," sportive, and a fun guy. Too bad I didn't marry him instead of...

some pre-made sandwiches, which were water crest and cream cheese, though I preferred Gary's lox and bagels. No sooner had she poured a glass of her famous throat-grabbing lemonade, which I doctored with heaps of remedial sugar, she came out with it.

"So, tell me about this Ron?"

"I'm not looking to marry him, Lucy, if that's what you're getting at." I knew she wanted me to tell her more, but the truth was, I really was just having a good time. It was a delightful distraction from all the recent showbiz craziness. I was just happy to get

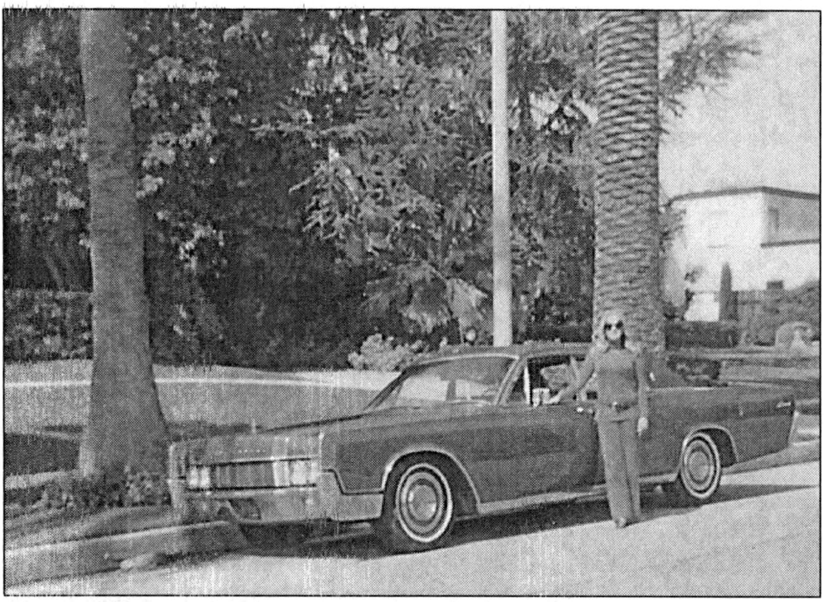

In front of my house on Foothill in my purple outfit and matching purple Lincoln. Ron Pruessing had it painted in my favorite color.

away from it all and have a seemingly "normal" relationship for the time being.

"Forget about me, Lucy, how are you feeling? When are you going to be out of your cast?"

"I can't wait to get this fucking thing off my leg...the truth is, I've got so much on my mind, and the cast is the least of my problems. I'm so worried about Desi, Jr. After he moved out because of that Patty Duke fiasco, I seem to have no control over him. I know he's doing drugs and it's anyone's guess where this thing with Liza (Minelli) is going."

I was really surprised at Lucy's sudden open candidness. Up until now, she had rarely discussed her issues with her children. I could sense her embarrassment and knew it pained her to even bring it up. It was enough that it was already plastered over the front pages of the major gossip magazines. As a mother, I wondered how I would feel if my own son was in the same situation at some future date. I could only sympathize with my friend and wouldn't want people sticking their nose in my business. I felt I had to say something.

"Lucy, Desi's a good kid. We both know that. I'm sure he'll get through this and straighten himself out eventually."

At this point, the air was getting a little heavy, so taking our sandwiches with us, we moved out to the pool area. I finally changed the subject when Lucy didn't respond.

"What kind of therapy are you doing, Lucy?" I asked.

"As a matter of fact, your old friend Onna White, who's doing the choreography on *Mame*, has agreed to come over and help me exercise my left leg." Lucy knew I had previously worked with Onna when I starred in *Let It Ride* on Broadway. Onna was tremendously helpful to me with my dance solos. It was greatly appreciated since I was not a natural hoofer and could never remember the routines. So when Onna would come back and give me notes on why I had adlibbed what she had choreographed, I reminded her I was a singer not a dancer.

"Well, just keep improvising. Nobody will notice the difference anyway," Onna would say.

Lucy guided the conversation to her ex.

"You know, Desi doesn't want me to do *Mame*..."

"What reason did he give you?" I asked.

"He reminded me how in *Wildcat* the audiences only wanted to see the 'Lucy' character and that 'Mame' was too much for them to accept. He also pointed out that Mame was in her forties and I'm now sixty. Christ, I played 'Wildy' as thirty when I was fifty."

"Lucy, you're ten years older now than you were in *Wildcat*. Also, there are no close-ups on Broadway. You could get away with it back then."

"Well, even Gary suggested I get a facelift, but when Little Lucie heard about it she said she'd never speak to me again." At first I thought it was inappropriate of Little Lucie to say that. Then I realized she had good reason, due to the fact that her mother didn't heal well because of her fair and thin skin. Lucy was also deathly afraid of the knife. There were no good options.

Despite all the naysayers, Lucy was dead set on playing the role originated by Rosalind Russell, for whom she had the highest regard. She planned on doing the role justice as our friend Angela Lansbury had done on Broadway in 1966.

When the release date for *Mame* was pushed back, it was a sign the studio knew there was a problem. When the reviews hit, they might as well have laid a coffin out for her. They were not kind. They cruelly pointed out how "old" Lucy looked. I felt terrible for my friend, knowing how painful it was for her. In my estimation, it wasn't her age so much as the fact that Lucy was miscast. Yes, she was innately a great actress but her image was not that of sophistication and hauteur. The long-cigarette-holding Mame belied the non-filtered-Philip Morris chain-smoking Lucy. Lucy was zany, off the wall and pratfall funny. The rapid-fire wordplay that was Russell's and Lansbury's forte didn't suit Lucy's brand of comedy. When she fell on her ass, it was sidesplittingly funny, not a faux pas as 'Mame's' character amusingly required. As usual, Desi was right.

This was Lucy's last feature film role, and years later she appeared in a made-for-television movie that was beneath her.

Before I left that day, Lucy remarked, "At least now you're on a nice plateau with Ron. I'm still in a quandary with all I have to go through. But for godsake, make yourself a little more available to me. You know how much I value our friendship. Please don't stay away for so long. I really miss it when you're not around."

"Of course, Lucy, I promise."

★ ★ ★

One of my friends Celeste "Cici" Shane was married to John Huston at the time. She hailed from a wealthy family. Besides being a very beautiful woman, she was also quite interesting. I know today she breeds champion winning Gypsy horses, which are extremely gorgeous. Before John, Cici's first husband was the acclaimed Walon Green who won an Oscar for *The Hellstrom Chronicle* and wrote *The Wild Bunch* among many others. Their son, Collin, was friends with my son, Michael. After Jack and I were divorced, he would pick up Michael from Cici's house. Cici recalls that, "Jack was the most vile insulting prick I had ever come across in that world at that time, and actually ever since. Filthy-mouthed and just mean." Lucy wasn't my only friend who pointed out that I had overlooked a lot. But by then, I wasn't in

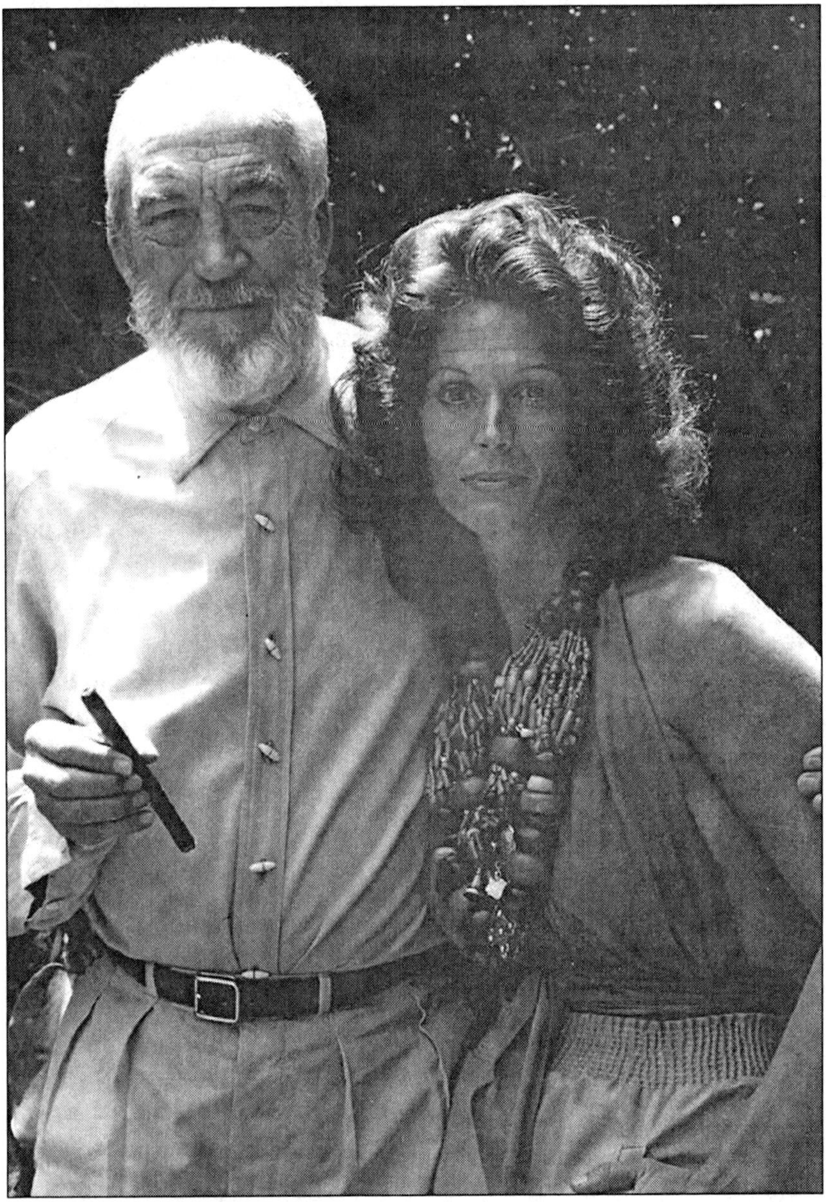

John and Cici Huston.

love with Jack anymore. It was Michael who had briefly brought us together. Cici was also married for a short time to celebrity hairstylist Gene Shacove who was the inspiration for the Warren Beatty character in *Shampoo*.

Cici invited me to a soirée she was throwing at her ranch-style house she owned in the Pacific Palisades. John had recently moved in and was making major improvements to her property. This particular occasion was the launching of an exotic elaborate hot tub which lecherous John had designed. No doubt, he had envisioned some wild and risqué times. Cici was much his junior but even so, John's celebrity, talent, and crazy wild-side could still attract a young woman like Cici.

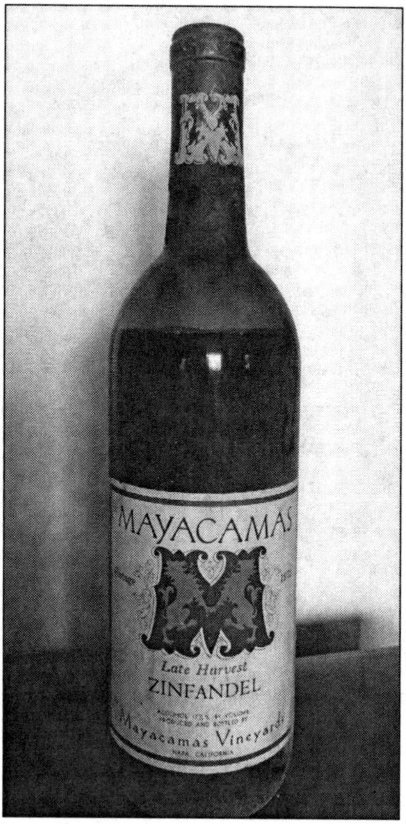

John Huston sent me a case of this Mayacamas wine as an apology for the hot tub incident. Today each bottle is worth more than $400.

John was a little long in the tooth at this stage. He liked me and openly flirted with all of Cici's young girlfriends, something he got a big kick out of. I extended the invitation for the soirée to Lucy who had heard about Cici from me as I spoke about her on numerous occasions. Lucy already knew of John's lecherous leanings. However, the most intimate dealings John and I ever had were over our love of pre-Columbian art and exotic wines, having bought several rare cases together.

Lucy wasn't feeling well as her leg was still healing and begged off with a promise from me to fill in all the details. She hated to miss meeting John and Cici, and was curious about their recent wedding. So I drove to the event myself.

That night the wine flowed abundantly. It got late, and after all the celebrities had gone. I was in my cups and Cici asked me to join her, John and his pal, former jockey turned-art dealer Billy Pearson in the hot tub.

Feeling no pain, I thought this might sober me up. I stripped down *au naturel* and joined them in the inviting, steaming water. John was smoking his usual cigar. I began to close my eyes relaxing in the bubbling water when everyone started giggling. I had no idea what was so funny. I lifted my heavy eyelids and I saw this long brown shape float right by my face. I thought John had dropped his cigar in the water.

Thinking no more of it, I continued to relax. By now they were laughing hysterically. I opened my eyes again only to see John was actually still puffing on his cigar. So what was that long brown shape that floated by my face? It sure as hell wasn't a stogie!

In my mental state, was it possible that John or the odious Billy had taken a big crap in the hot tub? That sobered me up pretty quickly. I jumped out of the tub, threw on my clothes and made a mad dash for my car.

When I called Lucy to tell her about it she screamed.

"Paula! I can't believe I missed the chance to meet that piece of shit!" We both laughed.

Cici called me the next morning, "Paula, darling, I was splashing at that floating piece of orchid bark to keep it from parking between your tits." John knew I had mistaken it for a turd and apologized to please forgive him for finding it so amusing.

Later Lucy finally met Cici and John at one of my dinner parties I hosted. It was fun watching John and Gary, these two imposing, over six feet tall men size each other up with glances. John pulled me aside later and asked me about Gary.

"What's up with that asshole? I don't understand Lucy's attraction to him."

For all John's crassness, he did have a lot of class. After he apologized for the hot tub incident, the next day he sent me a case of Mayacamas Zinfandel with a nice note. I still have one of the bottles today as a souvenir of the occasion.

★ ★ ★

Little did I know my idyllic sojourn with Ron was about to come to a screeching halt. Lucy would prove to be my all-time savior and champion again.

Roxanne Wander put the bug in Jack's ear that maybe he should try and get Michael away from me with a custody battle. I knew it was just a ploy to persuade Jack to marry her. I guess it wasn't that hard for Roxanne to persuade Jack to get hitched because married, they could prove they would be a better influence on Michael than me—unmarried and dating a divorced man with two children. The inference was that I was an immoral woman screwing Ron in front of Michael when we stayed at Ron's house. As outrageous as it was, they took me to court.

Lucy stood behind me through it all, which turned out to be a battle of the celebrities, each of us having a list of stars vouching for either side to contest my fitness as a mother. What could be the most grievous sin that I had committed? Well, it was no lie that in those days everybody was smoking marijuana and it was no big deal then.

Attorney Arthur Crowley put me up on the stand and asked me point blank, "When was the last time you smoked marijuana?" I had to get the sonofabitch right where he lived.

"Don't you remember, Arthur?" I said sweetly. "It was at one of your parties. No, I'm sorry...it was at one of Beldon's parties and you passed me a joint and I took a hit." That got his goat.

"I've never smoked marijuana!" Arthur snapped back.

Jack had Dick Martin of *Rowan and Martin* testify as one of his witnesses. I'm sure Jack leaned on Dick hard. Dick, funny as he was, in my mind was weak-willed and none too bright. He didn't know how to stand up for himself and didn't have the balls to look me in the eye. I was dumbfounded and confronted him in the hallway.

"What are you doing here?" I asked him. "Don't you realize you're helping Jack steal my son away from me?"

"Oh well, I'm Jack's friend. My wife and I are going through a divorce and—"

"—Dick, your problems with your wife have nothing to do with me. You know I am a good mother! You know I'm not a drug addict.

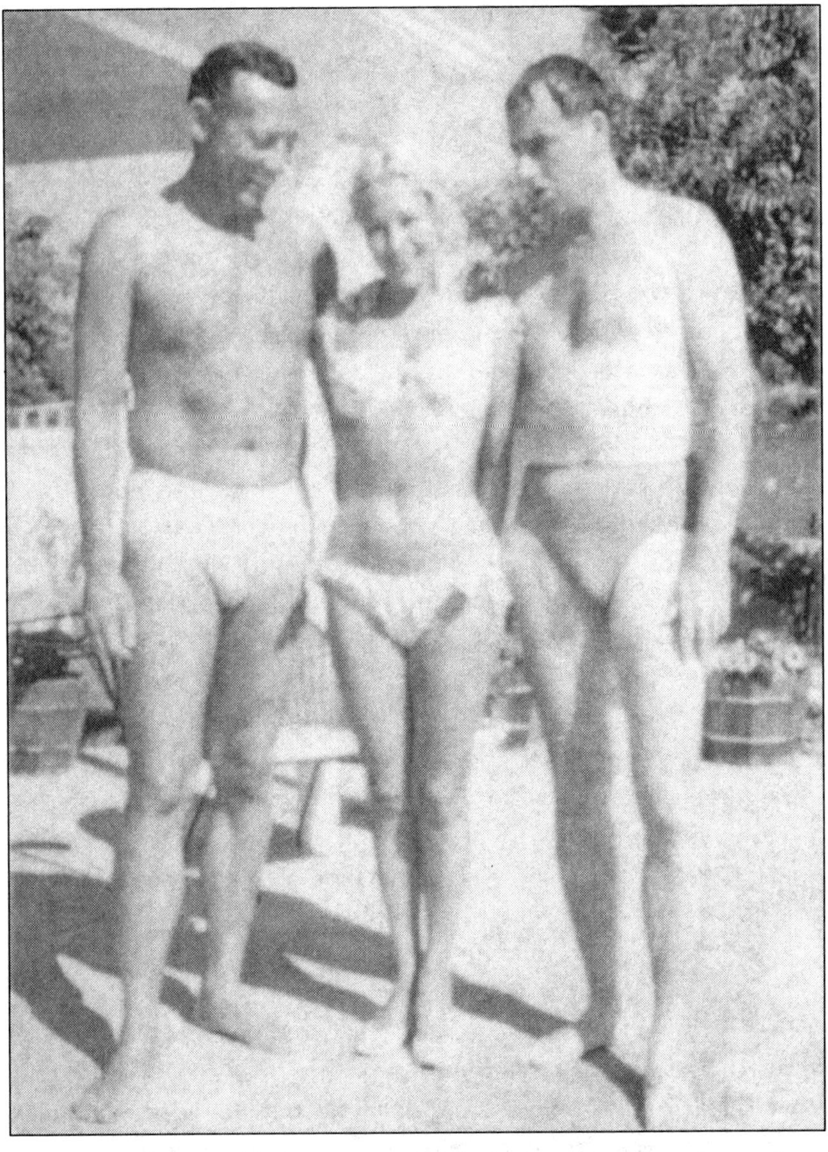

Me between Gary and Dick Martin (on right) who was a regular on Lucy's show.

We've smoked marijuana together for years! Christ, you were just over at my house two weeks ago for a dinner party."

The courtroom came to a halt when it was time for Lucy to testify. It was unheard of for a celebrity of her caliber to play an advocacy role in a private matter. Lucy had never gone to court for anyone, and Gary had furiously tried to talk her out of it.

"Lucy, it's none of your business!" he shouted. That didn't sit too well with her.

"Of course it's my business...Paula's my friend, goddammit. I'm not going to let her lose her kid because I didn't show up!"

He could insist all he wanted. Nothing would change her mind. Over the years, Lucy never listened to Gary when it came to personal matters about her friends, the kids, or me in particular. She did however, listen to him about business matters—and that would end up biting her in the ass later. It was a habit Lucy had carried over from her relationship with Desi, who, in contrast to Gary, was brilliant.

As Arthur Crowley approached her in the witness box, it was obvious to everyone that our judge was simply star struck with all these celebrities in his courtroom—far worse than Lance Ito. By the way, the judge wasn't even really a judge at all, he was only a commissioner. He gasped when Arthur called Lucy's name. His eyes glazed over and I was sure he was about to have a heart attack. He was sitting there with a pen and paper, looking like a fanboy who couldn't wait for an autograph. His knuckles were white trying to steady himself in his seat. Beads of sweat were literally pouring down his face.

When Lucy got to the stand she was fully aware of her presence. I'm certain this judge half-expected a "Lucy Ricardo" performance. On the contrary, she was very calm and relaxed. Crowley wasted no time getting to the point.

"Miss Ball, do you realize Miss Stewart smokes marijuana?"

Lucy, with a vague look on her face, shrugged her shoulders and said, "I don't think smoking marijuana makes a person a bad mother."

I don't think anyone expected that from America's Sweetheart, and the way she delivered the line, it made anyone feel stupid for thinking otherwise.

By now the judge was hanging over the side of his podium, ready to strike with all the intent of a fanatic's one chance to get the signature of his captive witness. If he didn't get it now, WHEN would he have another chance? He couldn't have cared less about her testimony.

At this point Lucy had the judge in the palm of her hand. She then winked at him and added, "I am certain she didn't smoke it in front of her son. I know Paula, and she would never do that."

The irony here is that Lucy was married to one of the biggest potheads in the world, Gary Morton. She knew he smoked and felt it harmless. She also knew that it was not a reason to take a child away from its loving mother. As far as Lucy was concerned, marijuana was not a nefarious drug. It simply took the edge off—no more, no less.

The end result: I retained custody of my son. However, just to give Jack a little something for his lost effort, the judge reduced my alimony payments, for which there was no justifiable reason. Perhaps it was to punish me for smoking dope and, maybe because in the end, he never did get Lucy's autograph.

To add insult to injury, he stated for the record that if he got wind that a man I wasn't married to was sleeping over at my house, he would take my child away from me.

Throughout this ordeal, my relationship with Ron was tested severely. As nice and sweet a guy as he was, I wasn't madly in love with him and not about to marry him, so we broke up. We couldn't continue on with our relationship—not with the threat of losing my son hanging over my head.

This was truly an eye opener. I guess I never thought Jack would stoop that low. Hell, I wouldn't be surprised if he was the one who came up with the puritanical ruling. I was beaten down. Lucy was outraged.

"So what does that mean, Jack can have sex in front of Michael?"

"Oh Lucy, don't make me laugh."

Her comment hit home. I was ostracized for being a woman who had a normal sex life. It was ugly and unfair and sexism at its worst. I was so lucky to have Lucy in my corner and I truly believe I would have lost Michael.

What a friend I had in Lucy, and this experience only tightened our bond.

★ ★ ★

V
Real Estate Mogul

1972

So here I was in Hollywood, stuck at Foothill and could hardly make ends meet with my now reduced settlement. I was in a jam because I couldn't make the mortgage payments. I certainly didn't want to sell my beautiful home. First my alimony appeal was recently denied and now this.

Every big real estate agent in town was approaching me about selling my house. My financial woes were no secret to the community as Jack made sure my situation was splashed in all the papers. Among those who contacted me was an agent named Carol Lembeck, who had another proposition in mind. She was married to comedian Harvey Lembeck and asked me if I would like to rent my house completely furnished to actor Rex Harrison for a very attractive sum. It was an interesting proposition, but I wondered aloud where I was going to live.

"You could buy a little house up on Coldwater," she suggested. "I know of a listing on Gloaming Way for $50,000. All you have to do is put down ten percent."

I called Lucy and explained the situation. She agreed to my decision to buy the house, but now what to do about furnishing it? Lucy said, "Paula, you know where all the bargains are at the auction houses. That shouldn't be a problem."

I called Carol and told her I was game. I leased Foothill for about $2,500 a month. With the first, last, and a security payment totaling around $7,500, it not only allowed me to put the down payment on the house up on Gloaming Way, but covered my moving

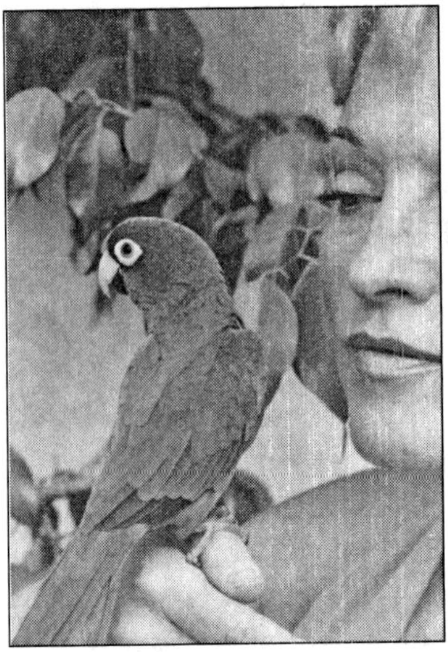

Moonie my half-moon parrot gave me kisses.

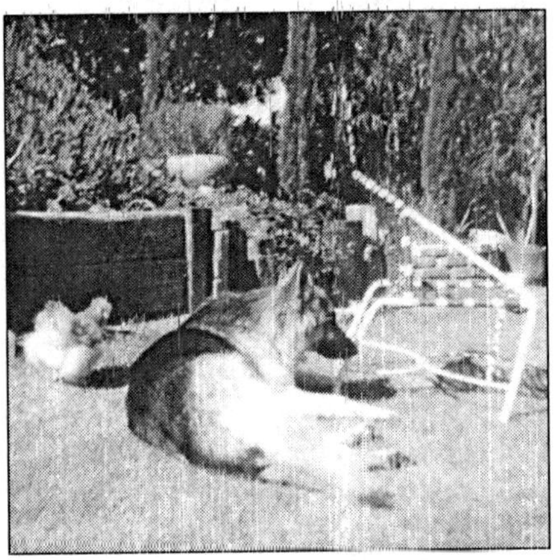

Peep, our Japanese Silkie Hen reminded me of Zsa Zsa in a fur coat. She was glamorous and smart. Here with Lulu our German Shepherd on Gloaming Way in Beverly Hills.

expenses, too. I was getting an income from the lease and paying off the house on Gloaming to boot.

Gloaming Way was a wonderful home for Michael and me. I loved animals—I could never have enough of them. Here we could open our doors to Priscilla the peahen (female "peacock"), Peep our Japanese Silky hen, Lulu the German Shepherd, Paolo the Doberman, (I called him Bitey around strangers because he was so friendly); Red and Blue, our Yorkies; and Winky, our one-eyed black cat. Everyone got along—if only my relationships fared as well.

The Foothill house turned out to be a great source of income because after Rex Harrison left, I increased the rent. With its luxurious décor, the house was a most desirable short-term rental for the constant flow of famous visiting out of town stars. Over the years I rented it out to Gene Wilder, The Bee Gees, Roger Moore, Michael Douglas, Telly Savalas and Woody Allen. Foothill was usually bringing in $5,000 and up a month. Turnover was no problem with first, last and a security yielding around $15,000.

With this increased cash flow, I saw a way to buy another house on Gloaming Way just a few houses up from the one I had just

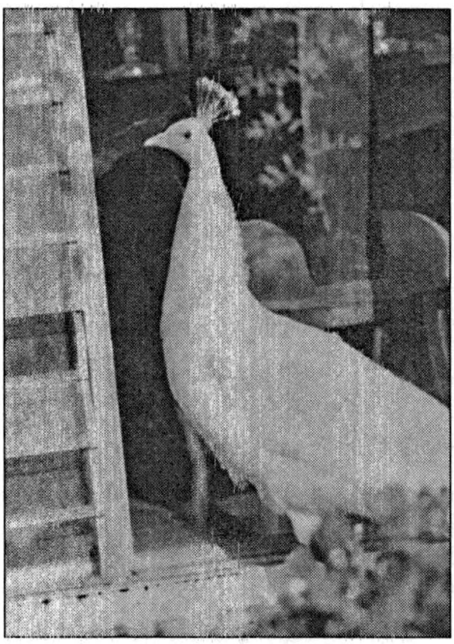

Priscilla our peahen loved showing off, strutting around our backyard to the delight of our friends.

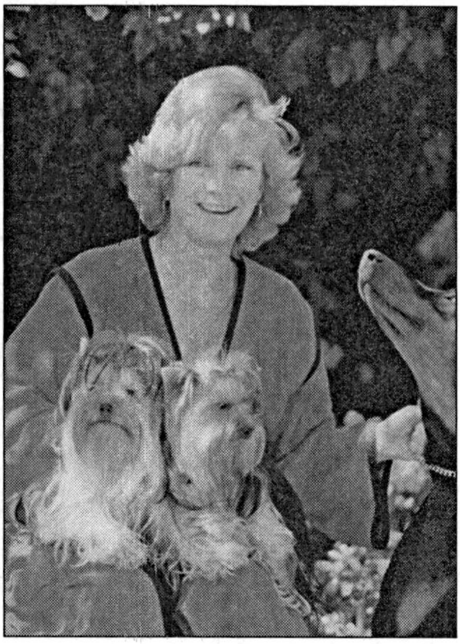

I'm holding Red and Blue. That's Paolo, my Doberman, gazing lovingly up at me. There was a lot of competition for my attention and happily everyone got along.

purchased. It was listed for $60,000. After I bought it, I fixed it up, furnished it and rented it to Alice Cooper, Dennis Edwards and Ruth Pointer. I now had three houses, was bringing in a good income and amassing some nice real estate for myself.

Lucy was more than impressed and was in awe that I could make the transition from entertainment to realty. She loved how I fixed up the houses. If one house became unavailable, I would move back into Foothill and lease the one I had just moved from. I was playing musical chairs with the homes and increasing my net worth. The timing was fortunate because this was a period of tremendous inflation. A house that I bought for fifty or sixty grand, a year later doubled in value.

Renting to celebrities, however, wasn't always without risk. There were a few headaches along the way. Like when Gene Wilder's girlfriend blew up my kitchen or when Woody Allen wanted out of his lease because the birds kept him awake. But Michael Douglas who rented the house with his new bride, Diandra Luker, caused the biggest damage. The day after they moved in, they abruptly left for their honeymoon. I was supposed to go over the inventory with Diandra that day as was the custom.

When I arrived, I was shocked to find all the furniture had disappeared and been replaced with dozens of huge overstuffed pillows scattered all over the floors. Keep in mind they had rented an entirely furnished house. I was hysterical. No one had a clue where the lovebirds had gone to reach them for an explanation. As it turned out, they had crammed everything into the basement. California houses don't have eastern type cellars. They're more like large closets that hold heaters, water meters and that's about all.

How they managed to put a 5,000 square-foot house full of antiques and accessories into that tiny room was a mystery. Everything was bent or scratched to the extent that it had to be refinished, recovered, or re-glued. It was a nightmare as I recounted the story over dinner one night with Lucy after the dust settled and the Douglas's were removed from their lease.

"Sounds like those two should have starred in the *Cuckoo's Nest,*" Lucy quipped.

Lucy also loved the story that I was renting to some Russian dignitaries because it recalled a party thrown by Kirk Douglas and his wife Anne in October of 1969. Kirk was hosting for Gregory Beregovoy, the Russian astronaut who had just orbited the earth. I went with Lucy and one of the first things that impressed me was the Douglas's incredible art collection. It was the most impressive one I had ever seen outside of a museum.

Gregory and his Russian companions were all standing around because nobody spoke their language. The interpreter wasn't much help since he seemed to be moping around right along with them. No one knew what to do with the Russian guests except me. I motioned Lucy to follow me over to where they were grouped together.

"Oh, really?" she queried with her eyes open. I whispered, "Just pretend like you know what I'm saying to them." I cheerfully said a few Russian phrases to each one like, "Your eyes are a lovely shade of blue and the mirror of your soul," to which they all responded like we must have been long lost relatives, shaking our hands and causing a big stir.

I didn't think twice as I kept repeating snippets of nursery rhymes and what little Russian I could remember. All the while, Lucy just smiled and shook her head like she, too, knew what I was saying.

"My little rabbit, oh my dear little rabbit...Your legs are like no dancer I've ever seen," . . .and more of the same. I think Lucy enjoyed it as much as the Russians did. And certainly all the other guests were just as dumbfounded. It was reminiscent of a "Lucy" sketch.

Lucy later said to me, "Paula, first German, now Russian? I have to know where you picked that up."

"From Vladimir Horowitz. But you should know what I told them wasn't simply common chit chat."

"Ha!" Lucy laughed and her eyes went wide. "You mean you actually learned from *the* Vladimir Horowitz?"

Vladimir happened to be good friends with my pal Byron Janis. Byron was only one of the few students that Vladimir ever acknowledged mentoring. I met Byron through his manager Alfred Katz and world-famous choreographer and dancer Anton Dolin while in Switzerland in early 1950. After the national tour for *Brigadoon* was over, my father had taken me there. This is where he began his tirade about my single marital status and introduced me to people as his "unmarried daughter in show business." When he mentioned this to Alfred, Anton then replied, "Have we got the guy for you!"

When I got back from Switzerland I briefly stayed at New York's famous Rehearsal Club, a boarding house for young showbiz girls who were cash-compromised and in-between jobs. The 1937 RKO movie, *Stage Door,* was based on the comings and goings of the Rehearsal Club starring Lucy, Ginger Rogers and Katherine Hepburn among others. That the Rehearsal Club figured in both of our early careers was a coincidence which amused Lucy.

Alfred called to let me know that Byron Janis would be contacting me shortly. I can only imagine what Alfred told him: "Byron, Anton and I met a very wealthy young girl in Switzerland. Her father was buying her jewelry at Gubelin. She's staying at the

Rehearsal Club because she wants to be an actress. You should meet her right away." They must have thought Byron needed a rich girlfriend to pay for his piano tuner.

Byron and I became fast "friends." He recommended I get my own apartment, which I did because there was no way we could "get together" while he was living at his prudish mother's apartment on 57th Street. It was a few steps from Steinway Hall where he was soon to debut.

Byron also introduced me to a lot of people, including Vladimir, who took a quick liking to me. When Byron was out of town, Vladimir invited me to lunch at the Russian Tea Room on 57th Street, where I was exposed to his onslaught of Russian phrases that he would drill into me with great relish. Vladimir enjoyed being around me because I would frequently have him over to my new apartment when Byron and I hosted parties for the cast of *Seventeen*, my first Broadway musical. He enjoyed the company of all my good-looking male dancer friends. Byron was definitely not into that aspect of Vladimir's leanings and was relieved because I took the pressure off of him in that regard. Byron wound up breaking my heart by marrying a very rich English girl who no doubt made life easier than I was able to at that time.

But I digress...the joyful expressions on the Russian guests that night were enough to make Lucy and I chuckle in our Jack Daniels for the rest of that party.

★ ★ ★

I remember an interviewer once asked Tina Turner if she ever watched *What's Love Got to Do With It*. She replied, "Oh no. Why would I want to watch Ike beat me up all over again?" Which brings me to husband number three: Charles Collins. "Chuck" as he preferred to be called, was a tall, silent hunk. He walked into my life as a result of my listing one of my homes on Gloaming Way. He was very good-looking, a dead ringer for Gary Cooper, my secret idol over the years. He also had that nefarious Jim Aubrey "off-putting" quality. And he wanted to lease my house. I was instantly attracted to him and the feeling was mutual. We started dating.

I liked to have a man in my life. At forty I was still a young woman, sexually active and here was a man that appeared to have some substance about him. I also felt Michael needed a more constant and present masculine father figure. After a night on the town, we returned to my house on Gloaming Way and were surprised that my former boyfriend, Ron Pruessing, was hiding in the closet as we entered the bedroom. Ron was more shocked than we were. I don't know what any of us expected to happen but Chuck immediately confronted him.

"Who the hell are you!?" he demanded to know.

Chuck ordered Ron out of the house and started pushing him toward the front door. They ended up on the street and Chuck beat the shit out of Ron, knocking out his front teeth. Ron barely made it to his car and drove away with his tail between his legs. Chuck and I were both shook up. Chuck had severely bruised knuckles and Ron's ego was equally bruised. I had never seen two men fight before except in a professional boxing ring and it was terrifying that these two were fighting over me. I really felt bad for Ron. It never occurred to me that Chuck's temper might become a bigger problem than even this in the future.

Instead, Chuck represented strength at a time when I was feeling vulnerable and in danger of losing my son because of the ongoing custody battles with Jack. I needed a protector. I was desperate and not thinking clearly. Here was my "knight in shining armor," ready to fight for me. My mind was too distracted to see anything but that.

Chuck's cool standoffish demeanor was not well-regarded by my close friends, who suspected he was some kind of secret agent. Probably because they didn't understand his type of work, a forerunner of the Kinko's copying of medical and legal documents. I, on the other hand, was impressed and found him intriguing. He ran his own business and, more importantly, owned a large ten-seater, twin-engine Queenaire plane. We flew to all kinds of romantic places like Puerto Vallarta, where we spent weekends in cozy tree lofts under the tropic moon. What wasn't to like about

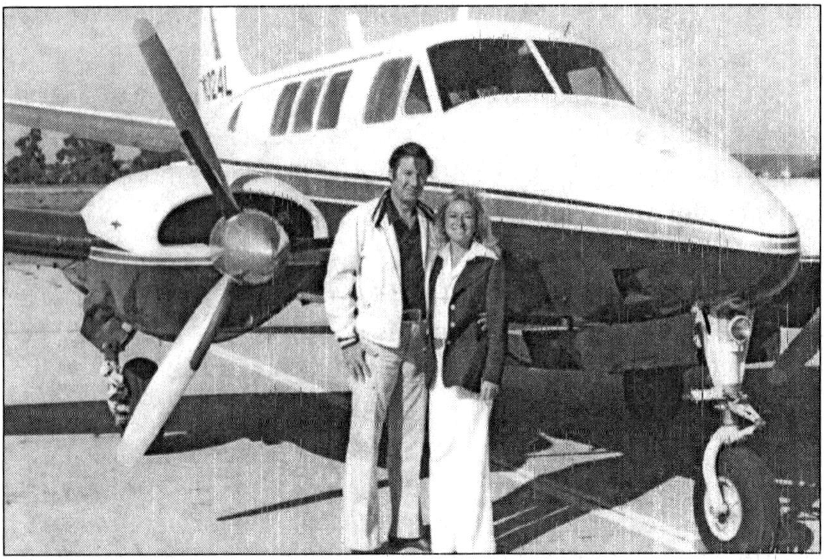

Love of flying, one of the few things Chuck Collins and I had in common. He owed me money, I took the plane.

that? Often, we would also bring along a few of my friends. We all smoked the local weed and drank endless margaritas. All this happened while Michael was spending time with Jack during summer vacation or other extended periods.

It wasn't long before I was totally enchanted. I was feeling secure with Chuck because he was business-oriented. He also took an interest in my real estate holdings, which were growing considerably due to the rampant inflation at that time. Gratefully, he got me to a management firm that took over the financial burden of running my properties. A real relief—as this was becoming quite an overpowering responsibility.

When Lucy got around to catching up with my new *amour*, the die was cast, so to speak. By then her cautionary advice would have been useless anyway. I was completely smitten with Chuck. He hadn't moved in yet because he had an apartment in Pasadena and would only spend weekends with me when Michael wasn't around—just to be on the safe side. There was no way I was going to jeopardize my child in any way.

Chuck surprised me by building a gazebo in my backyard along the steep hillside. Quite an achievement and amazed even the most critical of my astonished friends. He turned out to be a good carpenter. His business, however, was not in such good shape it seemed, because he was in need of a large cash loan. He asked for my help. Naturally, I was apprehensive, but my new business accountants made sure it was collateralized with the Queenaire. Meanwhile, he was most attentive and we continued flying off to many idyllic places.

★ ★ ★

When I was dating Chuck, I had been invited to a special birthday party for comedian Buddy Hackett given by his wife Sherry. It was held at the Friars Club in Beverly Hills. It was presented as an evening of mystics, clairvoyants and general bullshit. Everyone was invited. Chuck and I had smoked a joint before going because he was so ill at ease being with celebrities.

On the contrary, I was loose and happy in the ladies' room applying fresh lipstick when Dolly, Dick Martin's new wife, whom I had never met, approached me.

"You know, Dick feels really bad about his testimony in court."

"Well, it was kind of stupid, considering Dick and I had been pot pals for years."

"Are you calling my husband stupid!?" Dolly screamed.

"No, Dolly," I corrected her. "I said it—what he testified—was stupid."

I spoke my truth, even though it was fueled by weed.

With that, she lunged at me and we banged into the stall where poor Alicia Buttons fell into the toilet. Ginny Newhart became hysterical and ran from the restroom. I was calm throughout all of this, being pleasantly high and not giving a shit.

Dolly let everyone know at the party that I had been rude and had called Dick stupid. Sherry Hackett, hostess and decorator *du jour* of Dolly's and Steve Martin's new residence, came up and told me I was no longer welcome to stay at the party. Not a big deal. Chuck and I swiftly left and proceeded to roll another joint.

The next day everyone knew what had happened. The Hollywood rumor mill was as rapid as a wire service. Alicia called Sherry to tell her it was actually big-mouth Dolly who attacked me. I didn't even have to call Lucy. She phoned me right away (you want to guess what time of the day?) to tell me what she had heard. She loved a good catfight story and we shared some laughs. Then she said, "None of them are ever going to be invited to *my* house!"

Chuck had this karmic knack for attending parties that got out-of-hand and even the Ringling Brothers couldn't have topped this one. Which reminds me of another party. It was at Jack Rael's palatial spread in Beverly Hills. He managed Patti Page, Carmen McRae, The Everly Brothers and Steve Lawrence, my Broadway co-star in *What Makes Sammy Run*? Steve was The Great White Way's version of Sinatra with his smooth swagger and a voice to match. During one of our duets in the show, which was a suggestive number, he would annoy me by rubbing up against me at "full attention." To get back at him, I figured out a way to stop this. I surprised him the next performance by placing a pair of tennis balls under my skirt. Let's just say I successfully lobbed a match point back at him. That ended his game.

Jack Rael's parties were legendary. The mood was always festive with lots of booze, loud music and the usual nose candy being passed sumptuously around the food table. It was a birthday party and Lucy and Gary were present. Jim Aubrey, feeling no pain, walked in and abruptly injected himself between a woman whose back was turned to me.

"Well, well, well, Julia Phillips and Paula Stewart rubbing elbows no less," he said. "Taking over the town. Trying to rob us guys of our balls with your tits. Bravo, ladies. I'm all for you gals. Go to it. We need a kick in the ass."

He then staggered off, leaving us both facing each other in amazement, forcing an awkward introduction. Julia was someone I had actually longed to meet. I was a big fan of hers. After a brief exchange we laughed at the absurdity. Lucy approached and chimed in.

"What the hell was all that about?" she asked.

"Oh, just a typical Jim Aubrey asshole scenario," Julia said.

"Hah!" Lucy agreed. "I hate that son of a bitch. Obviously you do, too." Then before I could introduce them to each other, someone pulled Julia away, leaving Lucy to ask, "Who is she?"

"That's the woman who won the Academy Award for *The Sting*, starring your favorite movie star Robert Redford." And then I couldn't resist adding, "Remember, the *blonde actor* 'who would never make it in film'?"

"Alright, maybe I don't know everything," she chuckled. "So what's she up to now?"

"She's producing a movie for David Begelman over at Columbia."

"Well, that explains his presence here. Christ, Aubrey and Begelman at one party. I told you that Begelman was no good. Look what he did to Judy Garland. Well, I warned her."

"Lucy, you know she's producing a movie with that young director of *Jaws*."

"So what's that one about?" Lucy said somewhat irritated.

"Something to do with UFO's," I said.

"UFO's!" Lucy screamed. "Oh no, no, no no! No more goddamn UFO's." Under her breath over the blaring music she said, "Paula, can you believe I thought *Star Trek* was going to star Bob Hope on a USO tour in France?"

"Co-starring Coccinelle," I winked.

"Oh, Paula, you." Lucy jokingly poked me. Our conversation ended when Chuck came barreling over to us, constantly rubbing his nose. I could tell he was wired. He was also extremely annoying. Lucy decided it was time to leave. Chuck and I argued all the way back to my car. I was disappointed that my brief encounter with Julia didn't end with a lunch date. But I figured it just wasn't in the cards.

★ ★ ★

In December of 1974 Chuck insisted we go to Vegas and get married right away. I remember him being very disturbed about something. It made no sense and yet I went along with it. A super quickie! We were back the same day. Not the most romantic memory to have, for sure!

I don't know exactly when it started, but by degrees he seemed to become more critical of me. What I wore, how I cooked, my friends, just small things, but I was very sensitive to his negativity. Was it becoming Jack all over again, I wondered? He would stare at me during dinner, not saying a word, with a strange look in his eyes that caused me to turn away from him. What was that about? True, it was just on occasion, but mystifying, nonetheless. Or maybe I was imagining things. Because I was involved with overseeing my properties and renovating them as they changed tenants, I was distracted and therefore tried to minimize these happenings. I knew that Chuck had been married previously for a short time to a TV actress, Linda Cristal, an Argentinian beauty with two young sons. I'd seen pictures of them together and I saw sadness in her. They divorced after a brief while. He didn't like to talk about it.

After our marriage, we flew with Michael to visit Chuck's family in Wichita, Kansas at their summer home on a lake there. They were very welcoming, with the exception of Chuck's brother. The two men didn't seem to like each other and were distant. Sibling rivalry no doubt. I found his brother equally handsome and quite charming with me.

One day, everyone pitched in to build a brick cooker of sorts for a fish fry. So, naturally we went out in the family outboard motor boat. Michael was six and had loved boats since our days on Ron Pruessing's sailboat in Newport. He was eager to try his hand in this different boat with a fishing pole. We were cruising peacefully along, when suddenly the boat sped forward, knocking both Michael and I backwards—almost into the boat's rotor blades! I screamed: "Are you crazy? We could have been killed!!"

"It was an accident. I slipped and fell on the handle." I wasn't so sure. I thought long and hard about what might have happened to Michael, or both of us, for many a sleepless night. It might have been fatal. Our personal life was descending into something more ominous. From that moment on, I became more wary of Chuck Collins.

When we returned to LA, Chuck started pressuring me to buy the lot next to mine. This would become Gloaming Number 3. The asking price was low and the property could sustain a small, modest house, which would have fit in nicely with the feel of the neighborhood. But, no, he had something else in mind. He proposed his own plans that were out of proportion to the size of the lot and would overpower the neighboring houses. Plus, it required putting in pylons for support on the steep hillside. We had many fights over that one. I wanted a divorce, that's how bad it got. If I didn't agree to his demands about the construction of the property, Chuck threatened to tell Jack that I was a drug addict which would cause me to lose my beloved Michael. I was trapped. At this point, I was embarrassed and just couldn't burden Lucy one more time. She had her own issues to deal with.

The house turned out to be the biggest, ugliest piece of shit imaginable. I hated it from the beginning. Once again, I was in an unhappy, sexless marriage. At least my holdings belonged to me for now. I wasn't sure what the future held at this point. Still, it was good knowing even if I was miserable, at least I was rich.

★ ★ ★

I bought a mansion in Hancock Park for a song and leased it to the Spanish Ambassador for a nice return on the money.

Foothill became available and we moved back in, whereupon I resumed my former passion for entertaining my recently ignored and dear friends. Chuck, as I became aware over the past two years, had always had his nose in "The Stuff." What I didn't know was that he was also accommodating some of his friends with it. No doubt, some of his weird behavior was due to this fact. Cocaine. Even Lucy had her life upset by its invasiveness at the time with Desi, Jr. She suffered in many ways from that ordeal. Thankfully, she was able to get him the help he needed and today Desi is a crusader against it.

One night when I had Lucy and Gary over for dinner at Foothill with friends, I was concerned that Chuck was upstairs for too long a time. I went to insist that he join the rest of us, and he hauled off and actually slapped me in the face. When I returned to the party, Lucy saw my flaming cheek and the seething tears in

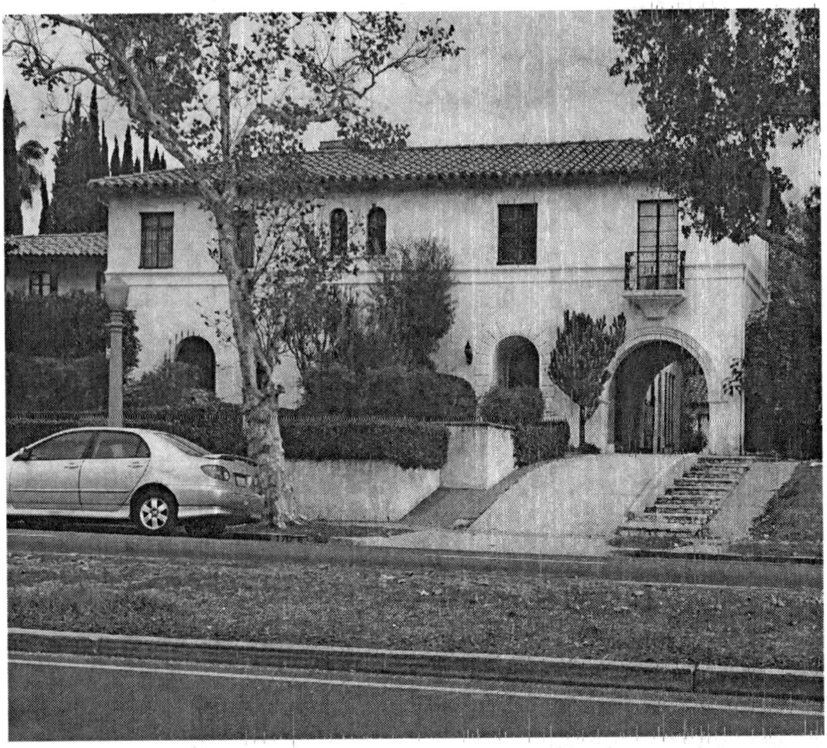

I rented my Highland Avenue house in Hancock Park to the Spanish Ambassador and later sold it to buy Vereda Sur in Palm Springs.

my eyes and instinctively knew that look. She couldn't believe it as she held me close.

"Paula, my god, you poor baby. You've gotten yourself into another fucking mess, right?" She saw that Chuck had gone into the bar and she went right over to him and said, "What the hell are you doing hitting a defenseless woman, you brute! She's half your size. Does it make you feel like a big shot striking a woman?"

"Lucy, I love Paula—"

"-Bullshit! I see how you act with her and this is not the way you treat somebody you love. I know what your problem is, so get off this fucking coke! I am sick and tired of you abusing this wonderful woman that saved your ass, and I know all about how she saved it!"

"I'll give it up, I promise!"

"You better, you motherfucker, or you'll answer to me!"

★ ★ ★

After Lucy's dressing Chuck down, things got a bit better. His attitude improved and, no doubt, it had something to do with his pushing another investment, this time in Palm Springs. On Vereda Sur, a luscious three-acre estate had come on the market. It had belonged to the Florsheim Shoe Company. With an Olympic-sized pool, sixty-five fruit trees, winding pathways and guest houses, it was stunning and in the middle of an exclusive part of old Palm Springs, where the rich and famous had played in years past. And to sweeten the deal, all the furniture, high-end Pratesi linens, cookware, you name it, were included in the sale. While it was fabulous, nothing could change the fact that Palm Springs real estate just didn't move. It was dead in the desert. And despite my reluctance to buy there, I fell for the charm of the place, knowing my enjoyment of it would be limited to only a few months out of the year because of my thermal problems—I go into heat shock when the temperature goes too high. But it would make Chuck very, very happy.

There was one minor problem. If I sold the Hancock Park property, I would still need a lump sum to close the Palm Springs deal. Reluctantly, I knew I could do it. There was still cash in my jewelry from Jack and Harry. I was confident; my jewelry from Jack alone could pay for Vereda Sur. Since Alicia Buttons had sold a lot of her other friends' items, and I had known her for many years—and had been responsible for her meeting Red—I approached her with the sale of my collection. Boy, was I disappointed with what I ended up with—shocked actually. I received so much less than I had expected. But at least I got enough to close the deal.

Lucy, of course, was thrilled. I would now have a place not far from her property in Thunderbird. I had acquired a couple of motorcycles which I would hop on to go visit her and tool around town on. Playing hostess on the weekends to my friends was a delight because I had room for their company with my guesthouses, and then there were all the wonderful restaurants and shopping available in Palm Springs as a plus.

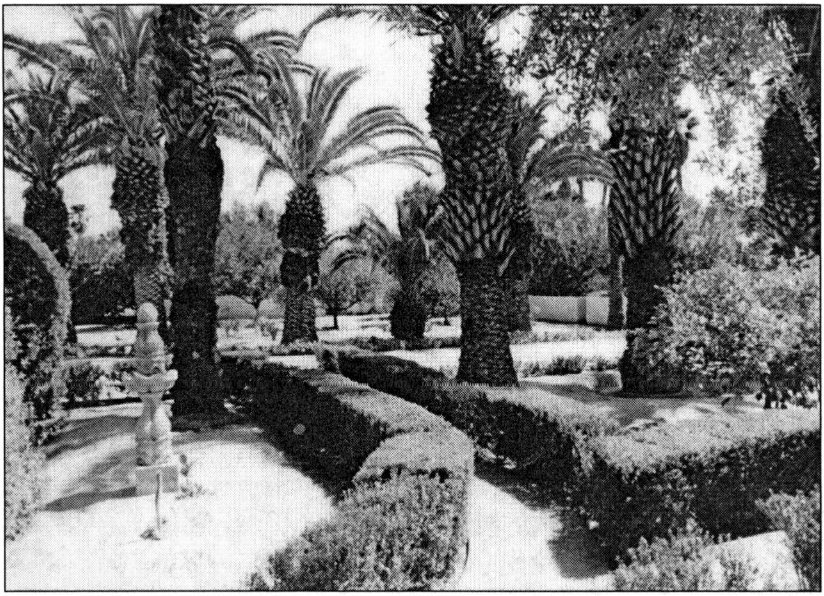

My home on Vereda Sur, Palm Springs - the entrance walkway from the gate.

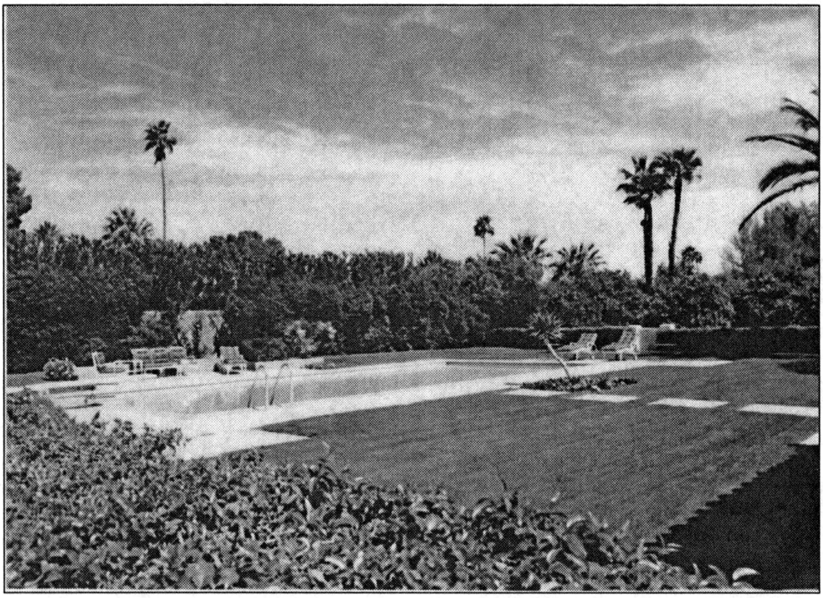

The huge pool at Vereda Sur. The three-acre property had 65 fruit trees. Beautiful, though I couldn't take the heat of summer or Chuck.

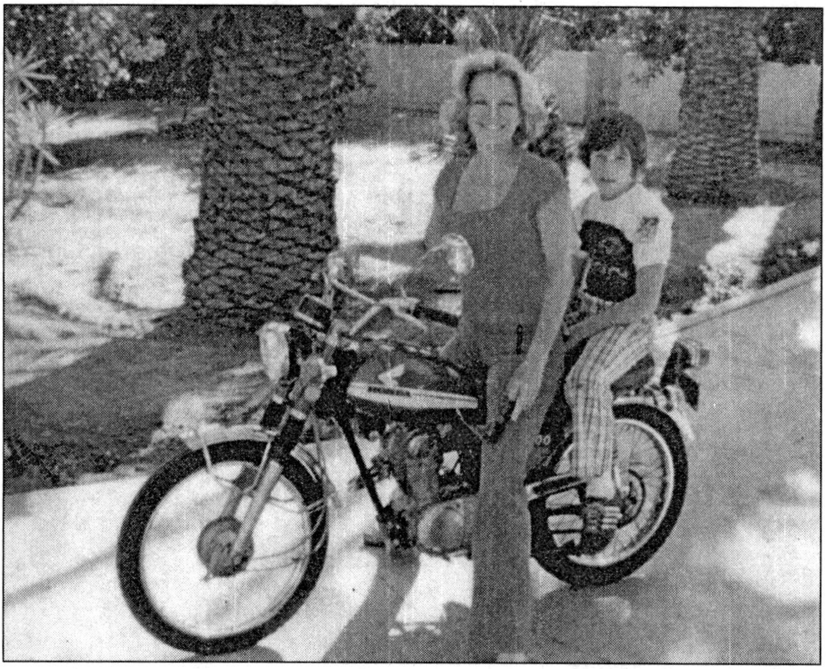

Michael and I back at Vereda Sur after zipping around Palm Springs.

Chuck and I had reached a living arrangement, where I would live alone during my preferred seasonal time (spring and fall) and he could have it the rest of the year. Several months of hundred-plus degree days did nothing for my well-being. Happily, my father was under the impression that his daughter was finally in a solid marriage. Hah!

My friends were sympathetic to my situation with Chuck and I threw quite a few parties at Vereda Sur sans Chuck. They often asked me to sing, and often I regaled them with *"Seven Beers With The Wrong Kind Of Man"* substituting "wine" for beers. Sadly, Chuck knew my passion for great wines and I really had no one to blame but myself. While it amused my pals, it was ridiculously true.

Meanwhile, I quietly picked up another smaller house I found on Rose in La Palmas. In my spare time, I remodeled the interior and sold it the following year turning a nice profit.

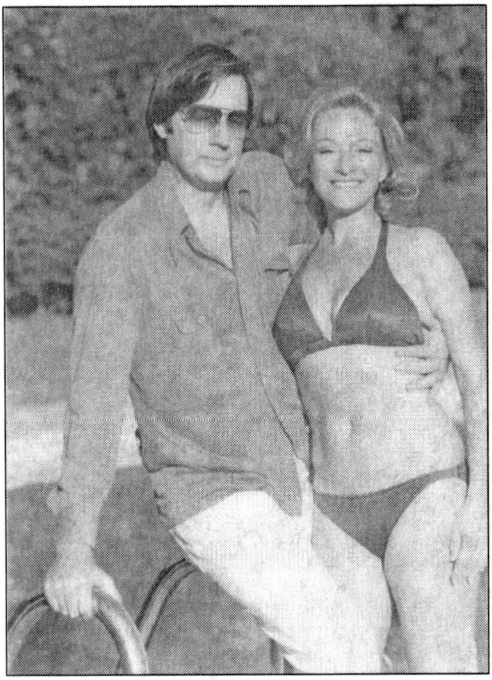

Pretend happiness at Vereda Sur with Chuck. Things going downhill and not only the real estate.

Chuck, by now, had insinuated himself into my real estate business and was giving me plenty of his own opinions as to how I should be running things. In the end, Chuck took over the management of all my real estate holdings, which turned out, were worth over six million dollars. There appeared to be no way to get rid of this monster.

During these years away from performing, I seem to have forgotten about my life in show business, the need for recognition, or to be appreciated for

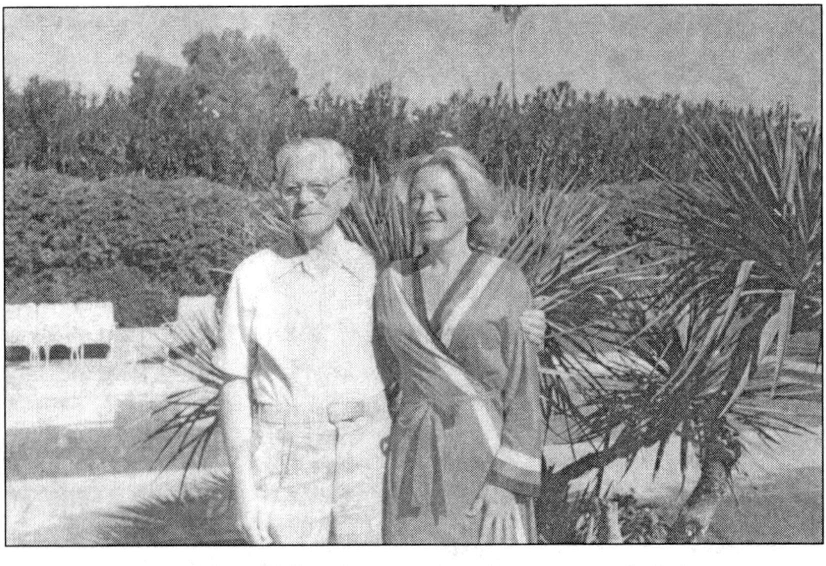

Poppy was relieved that I was married, unaware that there was trouble in paradise.

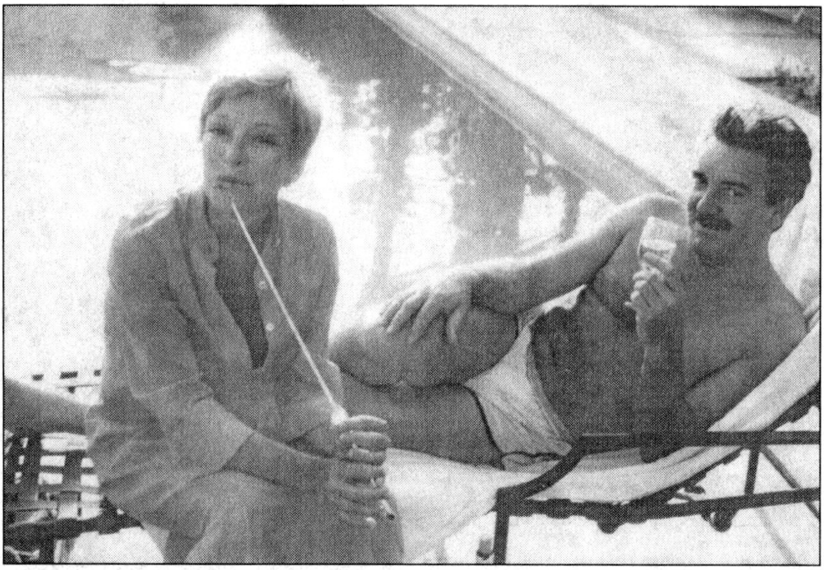

Poolside toke at Vereda Sur with Bill Gardner.

my talent. That didn't seem to exist in me anymore. But I loved playing the piano. Even though I was not very good at it, I admired anyone who could play an instrument. I was somewhat adept at the harmonica, still having my grandmother's tiny little one. Because Chuck played the guitar quite adequately, I talked him into showing me how to do the chord fingering. I was not a bad student, and soon was playing the song *"Feelings,"* by Morris Albert, popular at

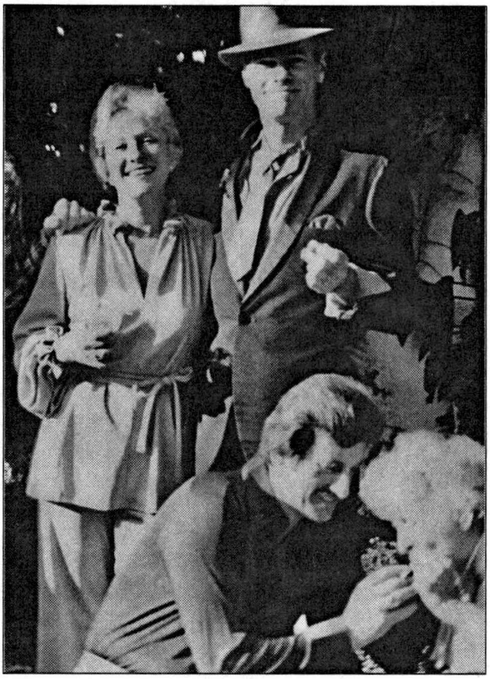

Swen is on my left and Steve Gerber is offering my mom a toke.

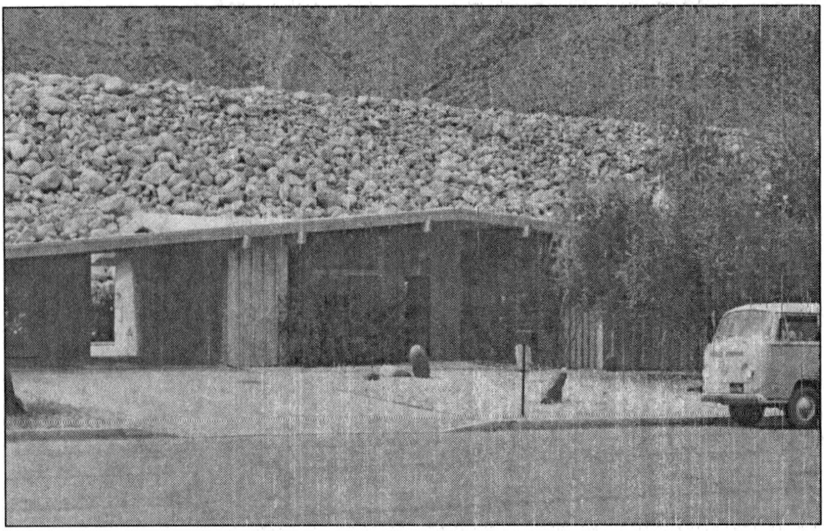

My mid-century modern Las Palmas house on Rose in Palm Springs backed up to a hill comprised of huge stones.

the time. It had very simple fingering. I loved the lyrics, so apt for my life: "*Trying to forget my feelings of love...I wish I'd never met you, boy...*" Little did I know how prophetic those words would become in just a short while.

During the winter months, Vereda Sur became a profitable holiday rental for producers like Robert Evans. There were always some headaches involved, but it paid off in the end. The fact that it was accessible to the airport made it even more desirable for the "in crowd." Life was good. The economy was still expanding. Inflation was high, but nothing to worry about—yet. I was progressing with the guitar and mastering the complications of fret technique.

Another holiday season was approaching and Chuck, Michael and I were packing up our things for the next rental. As usual, everyone was being hurried out by the impatience of Mr. Collins and his nasty temper. Chuck slammed the iron back door on my hand, almost severing the tip of my finger. We rushed to Eisenhower Hospital trying to save my dangling flesh. The pain was excruciating. I nearly passed out from nausea and the blood gushing from the wound. After an extended treatment and surgery, I was sedated and released without the assurance of an intact digit. Several weeks later when the bandage was removed, I had a shortened mid-finger on my left hand. Yes, the fret finger. My guitar playing was not to be.

★ ★ ★

While Lucy was away on location for *Mame*, Gary had the brilliant idea to surprise her by redecorating and updating their Palm Springs Thunderbird house as a birthday gift. He commissioned Val Arnold who was not only one of the top designers of the day but a legend. Gary had a habit of saying, "I know my wife." Oh yeah? Lucy did not like surprises and Val had not heard the stories about Lucy's aversion to change. I spoke to Val after the fiasco and he told me that Gary had assured him that all would be fine. Val Arnold could be faulted only for not researching Lucy's preferences for pastel colors and soft shapes. She hated squares. She didn't fancy browns and blacks or contemporary designs like lacquered finishes that were all the rage at that time.

So when I received a call from her insisting that I drop whatever I was doing and come over immediately, I sensed the urgency. I jumped onto one of my motorcycles and sped to her house, taking back roads that avoided any Palm Springs traffic. When I swooped into the driveway, she opened the door, and practically screamed.

"Look what Gary did to my house!" Before I could say wow—it looked fabulous to my designing eye—she added, "That sonofabitch has ruined it..."

At first I thought she was kidding, then I saw that crazed look in her eye. I knew she meant it. I quickly realized the problem—everything went contrary to her taste. Colors were off-whites with shades of tans, browns and blacks. Lucy hated it.

"And what's this big mirrored ball doing hanging from the ceiling?" she continued, "Is he going to have a disco party next? Over my dead body!" She continued to rage on, "I'm going to divorce that sonofabitch." Her reaction was a bit extreme, but I was able to calm her down.

"Come on, Lucy, this is silly," I said. "I'm sure Gary had good intentions." I could feel that lie come out of my mouth. Gary's biggest offense was ripping out a fountain Desi had built. Gary was still jealous of Desi, and this was a classic passive-aggressive act. He always believed she loved Desi more. She probably did.

"That piece of shit better change everything back," she said. And that Gary did. It was $200,000 worth of redecorating out the window and a million dollar's worth of humiliation. Poor Val Arnold was crushed and when he had to finally interface with Lucy at some point, was read the riot act.

"I like flowers, I like greens and yellows. Do you see any greens or yellows here?" Eventually, Lucy and Val made up over a couple of Jack Daniels and had a good laugh. But she never trusted Gary's choice in decorating ever again.

★ ★ ★

The Santa Barbara real estate market was getting hot in the mid-seventies. It had a much greater profit potential than Palm Springs. I would often take trips up there to see my good friend Bill Gardner, a real estate agent. He usually had some hot tips for me on current and future listings and, occasionally, some interior design work.

Seeing how I had amassed my real estate dynasty and how quickly I had achieved it, Lucy's interest was piqued. She was thinking of buying a house in Santa Barbara. So, I called Bill to let him know. He was thrilled at the prospect of selling a property to Lucille Ball, but even more importantly, wanted me to come up to meet a wealthy client whose huge home wasn't selling.

I picked Lucy up and we drove there one spring afternoon. We met with Bill, and on the way to lunch made a quick stop at a cliff-side lot overlooking the ocean. It was spectacular! We got out of the car and Lucy fell in love with it immediately.

"Bill!" Lucy nearly shrieked. "What a gorgeous place! I simply have to have it." Lucy was walking a little funny as she surveyed the place and finally she said, "Geez, I need to use the restroom."

"Go ahead Lucy, we'll turn our backs," I joked. Lucy couldn't wait until we got to the restaurant, so she relieved herself behind a tree.

"Now that you've marked it, Lucy," Bill said, "you have to buy it!" We all laughed as we got back to the car. We then met up with Bill's important client, Arthur Williams.

Arthur was very wealthy, dabbled in high-end real estate, and handsome. He was worldly, well-educated, and knew the business. He was not the usual reclusive Santa Barbara socialite.

Bill had the listing on a property that Arthur had personally built. It was a huge estate, high up on a mountain that overlooked all of Montecito. The view from the top was breathtaking. You could see the entire coastline on a clear day. It was a virtual palace, listed for $3.5 million dollars, a fortune in those days. It had been on the market for some time.

Bill told Arthur that buyers were hesitant because the place was unfurnished—the high ceilings and the immensity of the rooms made it hard to imagine the flow of the place. I realized Bill was subtly pitching Arthur for my help. But Arthur didn't seem to pick up on it.

Without anyone saying a word, Lucy chimed right in.

"Now Arthur, you've just got to hire Paula," she said. "I've seen what this woman can do with an empty house." I was flattered that Lucy spoke out on my behalf. Arthur was duly impressed and I got the job. Arthur agreed to give me $60,000 to furnish the place. Any other designer would have asked for twice as much, but being fair and wise with a dollar, I knew I could accomplish what he needed if I could score the right furniture at any of the main auctions in Los Angeles.

I just so happened to know about an incredible lot of high-end furniture coming up for sale at Abell's Auction House. Elton John was moving back to London and giving up his California digs. His furniture was colorful, stylish and well-made. The kind you would expect to see laid out in a photo spread in an issue of *Architectural Digest*. The pieces could not have been more perfect for Arthur's property, which gave it an elegant yet contemporary look. I was doing what is now known as "staging," meaning furnishing a place in order to sell it. Very common in today's real estate markets.

No sooner had I put the final touches in place, when I got a call from Bill—he had received an offer on the property. However, he was in a quandary because his listing was up and this could possibly affect his commission. He didn't know what to do. I rushed over to Bill's.

We called Arthur but he was out of town. So, we telephoned Arthur's son who thought he was going to pull a fast one on Bill. He told Bill the commission had to be reduced because Bill's listing was up. He then asked who the buyer was, at which point I frantically waved my arms and told Bill not to disclose the information. Furthermore, I told him to tell the son to go fuck himself, which Bill did. Not more than twenty minutes passed when the phone rang. It was Arthur, apologizing profusely for his son's faux pas. Arthur told Bill he would still honor his commission. As it turns out, the buyers were the Rockefellers, who bought everything lock, stock and barrel, including the furniture.

★ ★ ★

When I did spend time at my Palm Springs estate, I hosted many parties and lunches. Lucy attended when she was in town. I remember one time in particular when my friend Frederick Loewe came over for lunch. I invited Lucy over and Fritz was delighted to meet her. Lucy was immediately enchanted with Fritz's German accent. He sounded a lot like my father. We poured drinks and as the ice clinked in Lucy's Jack Daniels, she quizzed Frederick how we met.

Fritz was a brilliant composer who wrote the music for *Brigadoon*. He had teamed up with Alan Jay Lerner, a lyricist he met at the Lamb's Club in New York, a hangout spot for theater show biz people. Together they went on to write hit shows such as *My Fair Lady*, *Camelot* and *Gigi*.

While on the national tour of *Brigadoon*, I was 19 years old and rooming with Elizabeth Early, the understudy. She knew Virginia Oswald, who was not only the understudy in the original Broadway production, but was dating Fritz. Fritz dropped by every now and then during the tour to check in on his show and through Virginia, Fritz and I became fast friends. Virginia went on to star in two revivals of *Brigadoon*, and I later recommended her to Michael Kidd for *Wildcat*.

"She had a good voice, that Virginia," Lucy said to Fritz.

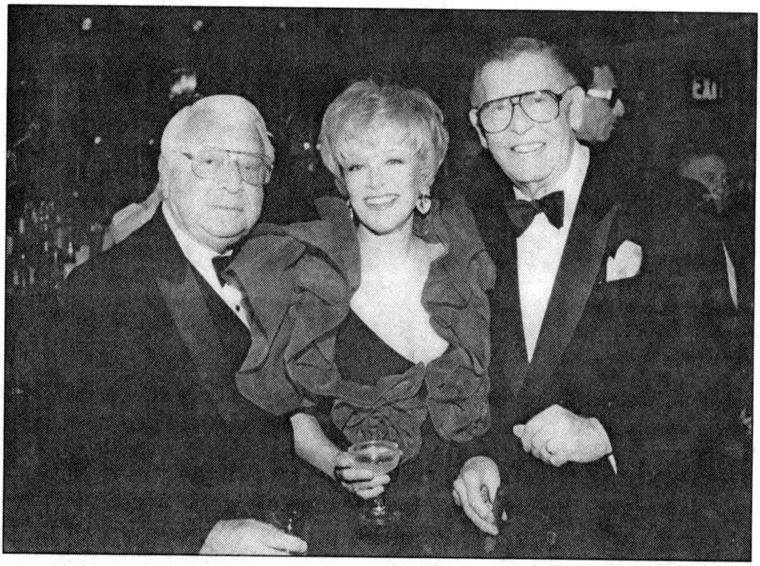

Mickey Hayes, Milton Berle and I. I had loved Milton since 1950. Mickey was also a long-time friend, best man at Jack's and my wedding, a sought after celebrity haberdasher in Miami. - Photo credit Irv Antler.

"Oh yes, I was very fond of her," he replied.

Fritz introduced me to a lot of people and when the show stopped in Detroit, Fritz set up a summit with the Nederlanders of the Nederlander Organization. Today they are the second largest theater owners on Broadway, right behind the Shubert Organization. David T. Nederlander founded the organization and I became very friendly with his son, Joseph, back then.

"Paula dated him," Fritz said.

"Whaaat! Christ, Paula," Lucy said.

"She should have married him," Fritz added.

When I got back to New York after the *Brigadoon* tour ended, Fritz introduced me to Dr. Sermi, of Warner/Chappell Music. He heard me sing and, knowing the producers of *Seventeen*, got me an audition. It was 1951. I was hired on the spot, which was where I met Milton Berle, who was one of the show's producers and with whom I would continue to have a lifelong friendship.

★ ★ ★

VI
Bankruptcy

Things were going from bad to worse with Chuck. I was making a lot money with all of my properties and had a nice cash flow, but his business was failing. What I didn't know about Charles Collins was that he was a major cocaine addict. I was fairly naïve about addiction because, unlike Lucy, I hadn't a clue how it controlled one's life. Aside from my experience with Richard Pryor, that was the closest I had come in contact with that particular drug. I didn't like it then, and grew to hate it even more.

Chuck was constantly high now, putting it up his nose and acting irrational. When I finally became aware, I was astounded and alarmed at how much he was spending on cocaine. He was forever borrowing money from me to loan to "friends." He had constantly verbally abused me, but lately he was becoming more physically abusive, pushing and shoving me around at his whim.

Now that I look back, I think if Chuck had had the chance to kill me, he would have. There was that time in Monaco...Chuck had questionable taste in friends, chief among them was Alan Chase, a royal bullshitter, impressed with himself and with Chuck's supposed real estate empire. Both men were social climbers with little or no talent for it. Chase worked for an international gourmet club called *Le Chaine des Rotisseurs*. Its members were wealthy hotel owners who loved cooking and traveled all over the world to learn the art first hand from famous chefs. They had somehow gotten us into this elite group. You had to be *very* rich to belong. I suspected they were up to something, but I went along for the trip to have some food and fun. We stayed at the Hotel de Paris in Monaco, did some sightseeing, and some gambling at the iconic Monte Carlo Casino. The main point of the trip was to get a few lessons with Roger Vergé at his restaurant/school in Mougins, a 45-minute drive from Monaco. We were each assigned our own separate cooking area. Roger gave us instruction and later critiqued our work. It was great fun for us gourmands. After our period of instruction, we returned to the hotel, changed into our finery and then headed back to the restaurant for a fabulous ten-course meal Roger had prepared for us. It was an exhausting but delicious experience.

I got on well with all the members. They were down to earth and likable. Not unsurprisingly, Chuck was his usual inappropriate self and I'm sure they were scratching their heads as to why I was with this jerk. He was embarrassingly gauche in his actions and speech, causing a lot of eye-rolling. Meanwhile, I was gaining weight, as he snorted up the stash he had carefully tucked in our suitcases. I was miserable. I wanted to leave immediately, but he hid my passport from me. He was watching my every move. I felt trapped, held hostage and blackmailed into staying in a relationship that seemed to become ever more toxic and disastrous.

One day after walking near a cliff, Chuck ran at me when I was looking out at the sea. Luckily, I turned just in time to see him ready to push me over the side and ran off. No shit. I was now fearful for my life. I didn't speak to him the rest of the trip and slept with one eye open. It was a nightmare. That story caused Lucy some real worry when I told it to her.

★ ★ ★

Chuck straightened up in the short term and rather than spending my money on coke, he switched gears towards real estate. He had his eye on 300 acres in Topanga Canyon. It was on the top of the crest of Topanga, and it was beautiful. It didn't have an ocean view, but there was a ranch house with goats, trails and a waterfall. It was not what I envisioned as being a really hot property and I wasn't into long-term development. I liked to buy and flip, earning a nice profit.

But Chuck had it bad for this place. He tried to persuade me again, over and over through pleading and threats. He wanted me to pledge all my properties to buy this sprawling land and develop it. I knew in my heart it wasn't right, just like Vereda Sur in Palm Springs. It would be a years-long project overcoming land use regulations, construction permits—there would be a myriad of obstacles down the road. But after months of pressuring me, despite my innate bullshit detector, I was tired, he wore me down and I relented.

By collateralizing all of my properties I bought Topanga and named it Summerhill. Immediately interest rates shot up to an all-time high, breaking 22 percent. I now had a bigger nut to crack in order to break even. The biggest problem was selling any property anywhere and especially in Palm Springs. I couldn't sell anything because nobody wanted to buy homes at those rates. I also couldn't rent if I needed to sell. I was in a tough, tough spot. My huge monthly debt was quickly draining my cash flow which was suddenly landlocked and sinking fast. There was no one to bail me out.

As much as Lucy wanted to help me, she was forbidden by her new business managers to reach for her checkbook. Gary, of course, could never be expected to help anybody in a pinch.

Chuck and I went separately. Even though, I was living at Foothill exclusively and Chuck was ensconced in Palm Springs at Vereda Sur, I was still obligated for the bills at both properties. He sold off everything that wasn't nailed down including my exquisite Pratesi linens, my prized zebra and tiger rugs, the gourmet pots and pans, fine cutlery and furniture.

I began bankruptcy proceedings in Los Angeles and Chuck filed for divorce in Palm Springs, forcing me to shuttle to and from both courthouses, hours apart with impossibly conflicting schedules. Nightmare time! The drain of bankruptcy was adding its toll on my psyche—I was a failure in life, love and business. I still wonder how I survived the humiliation and defeat.

Then one day, while I was out of my house at Foothill, Chuck came and kidnapped my three Yorkies and Doberman! I was furious! In a rage, I drove to Palm Springs with my .45 mm Smith & Wesson, fully intending to use it.

When I arrived, Chuck was off somewhere. A couple of his cronies and his part-time squeeze were lounging out at the pool. It was obvious he had already sold off the expensive Brown and Jordan lawn furniture through its conspicuous absence. The dogs came running and were jumping all over me while I scared the bejesus out of his friends by brandishing my gun like a crazy person.

"Get the hell away from here!" I screamed. Which they did, really fast. But I was only able to rescue one of my dogs, Red, by quickly hustling her into the car and getting the hell out of there just as Chuck was returning. I was beyond heartbroken but grateful I at least had her.

It was bad enough with the dogs and that Chuck was scavenging my properties, but now in addition, he was petitioning the Palm Springs court to give him my Mercedes, too. His actions fueled pure hatred—and a touch of inspiration, some of which was derived from my divorce from Jack.

Jack had used my successful career and my looks to work against me in court, so I changed my tactics. On the day of the hearing, I showed up looking like a ninety-year-old woman in a grey wig, an old housedress and stockings rolled down around my ankles. Chuck was stunned. He was in his finest Gucci wardrobe and looked every ounce the gigolo.

All eyes were glaring at him as I told the judge, "My husband has drained me dry and now he wants my only car that I need to drive myself to the doctor's office. He wants to give me the beat-up truck with the rusty clutch that hurts my crippled hands." It was the best bit of acting I'd done in years, and I should have received some kind of award.

"Your Honor, that's not my wife." Chuck was starring daggers at me. "She's a beautiful young woman!"

The judge looked kindly and sympathetically at me and said sweetly, "Of course she is." He banged on the podium, "Request denied!"

I still have my 1977 Mercedes. She is growing old with me gracefully. I can still hear Lucy screaming in disbelief, "You didn't, Paula!"

"Oh, yes I did!"

★ ★ ★

With bankruptcy and divorce consuming me, adding insult to injury was inevitable. That came in the form of Linda Tallen. Linda was a one-time aspiring model. It would only be much later on in life that she reached any kind of success when she became a philanthropist and started a charitable non-profit foundation with David Paul Kane but that's easy to do when it's other people's money you're donating.

Linda worked with David in the late 1970s and early 1980s when he produced and hosted a weekly TV series, *The American Jewish Hour*. It was a variety show and some of my good pals including Milton Berle, Don Rickles, and Bob Newhart had been guests. Linda kept calling and pestering me to get Lucy on the show.

"Please Paula, make it happen," she said desperately. "I'll always be grateful." Where had I heard that line before? I was convinced she was related to Gary Morton.

Even in the midst and turmoil of the divorce/bankruptcy rollercoaster, I finally gave in. I called Lucy to tell her about the requested interview and she agreed, but only if I went with her. The day of the interview I was running late and told Lucy I would meet her at the studio. It was on Sunset Boulevard and not far from my soon-to-be-ex home on Foothill. Lucy had Frank Gorey, her chauffeur, drive her and we met there.

Linda was overjoyed and very accommodating. When it came time for Lucy's interview, I saddled back at the bar lounge where I watched the performers through a glass partition. I then downed a few double gin martinis to drink my current problems away. I got smashed. Lucy was done with her interview and rushed out, waving good-by, as she dashed out the door with Frank to another appointment.

"Paula, thank you so much for showing up. I'll call you later."

Right after she left, I fell off the barstool. I somehow stumbled to my car and drove home, figuring I could get there quickly. Just my luck, the Beverly Hills police had tailed me.

After what I am sure was an erratic drive, I made it to my house. The police parked their car, got out and arrested me. I was dragged down to the police station where I immediately called Linda to tell her of my predicament. After all, I had just left her and had done her a huge favor. But Linda told me she was in a pressure bind and didn't have time to deal with me.

I couldn't call Lucy for help. How would that look for a headline? "Lucille Ball bails out three-time broke divorcee best bud from the brink!"

I used my charm on the butchy jailer and got a second call. I dialed the famous showbiz lawyer to the stars, Harry Weiss, a well-known gay lawyer who discretely handled problems of the rich and famous when they *didn't* want publicity. Harry was short, full of charm—a diminutive fashion plate who wore a trademark fedora and carried a bejeweled walking stick.

He was a real character and a longtime friend of Mae West, who had accompanied her to the opening of *Dinah East*. She was outraged at the inferences made that she was the main source of the story and wanted to see if there was some way she could have Harry sue me. He talked her out of it, saying it was too difficult to prove and she should just laugh it off, which, to her credit, she did.

Because of my pending bankruptcy, I had no resources and I paid Harry with my Steuben Glassware, a wedding gift from my previous marriage to Burt Bacharach. It was one of the few things I managed to keep from that divorce. Through Harry's finesse, I was able to delay my ultimate court date for the D.U.I, which resulted in the suspension of my driver's license for three years. I still had my pilot's license but a lot of good that was going to do me.

The boom was finally lowered and that awful day had come when I was forever locked out of my beloved Foothill residence. Everything had been moved into storage. I had no money and no place to go. Lucy came to my rescue. I know she was fearful of my sanity, so after my bankruptcy I moved into her guesthouse with my little dog Red to allow me time to recover from my personal devastation and to shield me from people who were dunning me for money owed to them by Chuck. He had disappeared. Lucy was always there for me. I stayed in her guesthouse for many months until the next phase of my life.

★ ★ ★

The friction between Gary and me was obvious and did not lessen over time. He was jealous of anyone that was close to Lucy. Not that his position was threatened, but he needed to maintain a certain control over her, which he did in a somewhat charming passive-aggressive way. He played a game with her and he was the adoring clown. The one the queen would forgive if he continued to amuse her. He was allowed to step over the line as long as he groveled like a favorite pet waiting for her to rub his ego.

Over time he understood how fond Lucy was of me, dependent on my observations and basic intelligence. After he married Lucy, it was clear there was no getting rid of me and this increased his resentment toward me. He would try to put me down every chance he got, but Lucy wouldn't allow it, which only fueled his competitiveness with me.

"Don't you dare ever talk to her like that!" Lucy would scream at him often at the dinner table.

On a side note, Lucy also had something to say to Milton Berle's wife, Ruth Cosgrove, who was a publicist and a one-time company commander and captain of the Women's Army Corps in the 1940s. Ruth and I didn't hit it off since she was Jack Carter's first wife, Joann Mann's best friend and unfairly felt I had something to do with their breakup. Ruth and I paid each other only the slightest acknowledgment in Lucy's presence. Personally, I always felt Ruth was more jealous of my longtime friendship with Milton.

I had first met Milton when I was the understudy for Anne Crowley in *Seventeen*, the Booth Tarkington musical that he was producing on Broadway. Milton was disruptive, constantly giving his notes during rehearsals. Once he came in and the girls in the chorus, which included me, were doing a number in front of the curtain. Milton didn't like it and he came up on stage and showed us some new moves, which for the time were pretty inappropriate for females. He wanted us to have cigars in our hands. Then Milton left and our director Richard Whorf, stager Hassard Short, and our choreographer Dania Krupska came in and said, "Now forget everything Milton just showed you. Go back to how you learned it."

Over the years, Milton and I developed a parlor trick of sorts that we would perform at parties. Lucy loved this and she would always insist, "Paula, do that incredible trick with Milton!" Well, Milton would go into one room and I would go into another. Milton would start chatting up the guests and then he would ask them to give him a title of a song. Milton would then call out to me and say, "Hey, Paula..." and Milton would talk in a secret code and I would start singing the song the party guest had recommended. It was always a hit. Nobody could figure it out. Not even Lucy. Milton made me swear never to tell, and to this day I've kept it a secret.

Lucy and Ruth came to near blows one day over a snide remark Ruth made about me. I heard this through Milton.

"Ruth, what are you carrying on about? Paula had nothing to do with Jack and his former wife breaking up," Lucy said. "Paula didn't even know he was married. It wasn't her fault that Jack didn't tell her that his divorce wasn't final when they got married in Florida. Get over your misdirected anger at Paula. If you want to be angry with someone, be angry with Jack, not her."

At first I was stunned that Lucy would take on Ruth who was a longtime friend. I was flattered that Lucy had defended me again. She was my vocal bodyguard.

But back to Gary. He would shut up as long as I seemed to fill Lucy's life because he played a lot of golf and was happy that I was there to play backgammon with Lucy, go shopping, and spend time with her when he wasn't there.

★ ★ ★

Lucy was certainly considerate of Gary's position in the beginning as a "nobody." She taught him about the industry and gave him steady employment. Gary started as the warmup comedian for her shows and later made him executive producer, for which he was paid handsomely. As long as Lucy was alive and working, Gary had some clout in the entertainment community. She made him Vice-President of Lucille Ball Productions. He didn't deserve it, and he made a lot of enemies wielding his power as producer of Lucy's shows.

His growing pomposity and failure to respect past dues to agents and former associates rubbed a lot of people the wrong way. Behind his back they laughed and called him "Mr. No Balls."

When I was still in New York living at the San Remo, one of the first things Gary did after he moved in with his new bride, was to completely renovate his closet/bath. I was amazed when I saw the amount of effort that went into it. It was huge and I must admit, quite spectacular. It rivaled the finest men's stores in Beverly Hills. Everything was brass, marble, and polished woods, complete with a sauna and paneled closets for all the suits he was having tailored by the top clothiers. Lucy often joked about how that end of the house was sagging under the weight of Gary's closet.

Because of his addiction to golf, he was able to socialize with celebrities who wouldn't have hired him as a caddy without Lucy's stamp of approval. His "best friends" were big money people like real estate tycoons, Marvin Davis and Lew Rudin, themselves widely regarded as notorious climbers and users.

Lucy leased space for her future productions at Fox Studios, which Marvin owned. Gary was constantly playing golf with Marvin and hobnobbing with all the big-time money. Lucy could have cared less. Marvin was able to get Lucy for his charity benefits, which she despised, because of Gary. Lucy had no liking for Marvin. She found him both physically and personally gross.

She told me how Marvin's son had insulted her at dinner at Chasen's one night.

"I'll never forgive fatso for not slapping his own son for disrespecting me." "Fatso," one of Lucy's favorite adjectives, would always precede Marvin's name in conversation. Marvin lost any standing he might have had in her eyes from that day forward. She wanted nothing more to do with him socially, so what did Marvin need with Gary after that?

It was rumored that what really broke up the Davis-Morton friendship was another one of Gary's hobbies—clothes. Marvin had admired one of Gary's suits so Gary took him to his tailor, Carmen Lamola. Marvin bought a slew of suits from Carmen at a subsequent fitting. One day, Carmen told Marvin that he couldn't afford to make suits for him anymore. He reluctantly admitted that he had to give Gary a percentage of everything he ordered. There was no way Carmen could make a profit working for Marvin anymore. When Marvin found out, he cooled his golf game with Gary for good.

★ ★ ★

I was shocked when Lucy told me she was letting go of Mickey Rudin, her longtime legal representative. Somehow Gary convinced her he was not doing right by her. Mickey Rudin was Frank Sinatra's lawyer for godsake and stood by him through all his troubles. Gary's inflated ego at this point, now that he was an "established producer," fueled his need to establish control over Lucy's financial decisions with people who were loyal to him as opposed to those who were loyal to the old "Desi" regime.

I first thought to myself, *what is it with these guys and their control of women*? Give them a slice and they want the whole pie. Personally, I felt Gary was no more equipped to handle Lucy's business affairs than Tinkerbell. His legal replacement choice for Lucy was not an improvement from my perspective, not that I was an expert. I was very nervous for Lucy because I knew Mickey was much smarter than Gary. Bottom line, Lucy didn't ask me for my opinion. This was a business decision, which she hated, and had to go along with her husband. Respect for him also lacked in their household. The kids never liked Gary. They just put up with him. At the dinner table, he would make some stupid remark that always began with, "Hey Loose," (that is what he called Lucy at intimate settings, like dinner) and the kids would roll their eyes, which I would catch. Lucy would tell me the kids balked anytime he tried to wield his authority over them.

"What can I say, Paula? They already have a father they adore." I could relate to this because Michael had similar reactions to Ron and Chuck. Gary also didn't appreciate interference in money matters. Desi, Jr. had borrowed some money from his mother, and he wanted to pay her back.

"No need," Lucy said. "Just the fact that you offered is enough."

"No!" was Gary's response. "Take the money. It'll teach him some respect for it." Gary wasn't wrong, but it simply wasn't his business to say anything. Desi, Jr. had been on his own, playing with a rock group, "Dino, Desi and Billy" in the 1960s and later morphed into acting. Desi, Jr. knew about earning a living. He wasn't living off a rich wife and playing golf every day. These things did little to endear Gary to the kids. On one of Desi, Jr.'s birthdays Gary tried to give him some of his old cashmere sweaters, which Desi, Jr. wisely declined.

Gary had the impression that he was something of a financial guru and would constantly lecture me about what I didn't know about business. This from a man who owed his success given to him by a woman, as opposed to someone who earned $6 million dollars on a $20,000 investment, ME! Herbert Solow also wrote about a "European Street" that Gary demanded be built at the Desilu Studio for use in some of their proposed future shows. It never came to pass, because it would have been a complete waste of money.

We women have to remember one thing when it comes to our girlfriends with their men—if the lady is happy, butt out! We can only hope the male figure that enters their lives is one we will get along with, whether it be a one-night stand, a rebound from a recently ended relationship, an ex-boyfriend, a current boyfriend, or especially a husband.

"Paula, you've given me the best thing I could have wanted," Lucy often told me. I knew what she meant. Gary. He *did* make her life happier than Desi had. She loved Gary in an easy, uncomplicated way she couldn't love Desi. Plus, she'd been so lonely. Gary filled that void for her. She thanked me and would remind me almost daily, "I know Gary didn't love me in the beginning, but I think he's learned to after all these years." He was a good husband and Gary made Lucy laugh.

★ ★ ★

Shortly after I had moved into her guesthouse, Lucy wanted to cheer me up with a ski trip. She had purchased three condominiums in Snowmass. Lucy loved the cold weather and thought a change of scenery would be good. I couldn't have agreed with her more.

She also invited Lee Tannen and his lover, Tom Wells, to come along. Lee was indirectly related to Gary Morton, and befriended Lucy in the last seven years of her life. He worked in advertising, had a wild sense of humor and was a great backgammon player. Rounding out the roster on that trip was Jeanine Foreman, who was married to comedian Joey Foreman. Lucy invited her because she was an excellent backgammon player and loved to ski. Also included was Lucy's driver Frank from California. Frank Gorey was a nice man, loyal to Lucy. I never heard him say a bad thing about anybody. He was respectful and very Irish, I might add.

Our daily routine started with Tom and me cooking breakfast and then a ski run for Jeanine and me, while Lucy and the boys would start the games. We'd break for lunch to do some shopping in Aspen which was a short drive from Snowmass. Aspen was a celebrity friendly town. They were so used to seeing all the famous faces, and respectfully left the rich and famous alone. That's why it remains a favorite playground for the stars.

We would just mill around, have fun, drink a few hot toddies and make our way back to the condo for more games and dinner. Lucy was banished from the kitchen. She was not a great cook. Since Tom and I were gourmet eaters and cooks, we relegated her to the dishes.

"You can clean up now, Lucy," we'd joke. She would of course, good naturally do it, although she got a helping hand from Frank.

After dinner, it was back to the boards for Lucy and the boys, while Jeanine and I strayed off for some local weed and a little bar hopping. Lucy knew I needed the relaxation and distraction. She encouraged me to go out and let off some steam.

"Now, Paula, you go and have a good time," she would say. I knew Lucy was content to stay in and play backgammon all night with the boys. After all, that's what they were there for.

By the time we got back, they were still at it. One time, I had brought some fun Eva Gabor wigs, courtesy of my dear friend Eva Gabor, of all colors and shapes for us to wear, which Lucy loved.

Those days remain some of my most cherished times with Lucy, and I knew she felt the same way.

★ ★ ★

VII
Interior Designer

1980

New career.

Spring, 1983. Lucy and Gary had been discussing for a while about being a bicoastal couple. There were talks of doing a future movie in the Big Apple but more importantly, Little Lucie was living in New York with her husband, Larry Luckinbill, and the kids. Naturally, Lucy wanted to be closer to her grandchildren.

As luck would have it, one of Gary's golfing buddies was Lew Rudin, the enormously wealthy New York real estate magnate. The Rudin family empire owned over forty buildings valued at $2 billion, including more than 3,500 apartments in New York City. Lew Rudin was previously married to Gladyce Rudin, a well-known bicoastal hostess, à la Edie Goetz. Gladyce later married movie studio executive David Begelman.

Lucy and Gary were able to lease a fabulous two-bedroom apartment in one of Lew's buildings on the Upper East Side of Manhattan. The apartment overlooked the East River and literally, the world. The building also housed so many celebrities, if there had been a cataclysmic disaster, half of the showbiz elite would have been wiped out.

When the deal was finalized, Lucy excitedly said, "Paula, I want *you* to decorate our apartment." She told me Gary thought he was going to put his dream of decorating back on the table. She told me how she quietly laughed when Gary could hardly wait for each new issue of *Architectural Digest* to arrive. Gary had a Bloomingdale's designer mock up a complete room-by-room rendering of what he envisioned. When he presented the final work-ups, colors and costs to Lucy, she was furious.

"How much did THIS cost me?"

"$5,000," he muttered.

"You pissed away $5,000 when we have the best possible decorator ever? And she's right here—Paula!" I'm sure that went over smoothly with dear old Morton. She had already told Gary the whole New York move was aborted until he agreed that I got the job as "the decorator of choice." Also, she didn't want a repeat of the Palm Springs fiasco from years before.

"I've already talked to Lew and as soon as a single opens up in the building you'll be moving in, too." Lucy told me. "Meanwhile, we'll have to find a place for you to stay until then. I'll take care of all your travel and moving expenses. Don't worry about Red, Paula. She can stay with me until you're settled in. I'll also look after your plants."

Wouldn't that be great? I thought. It would be a chance to get away from all the recent unpleasantness of the bankruptcy and divorce. I wouldn't have to worry about driving and I knew Michael would be fine because he was still in high school and living with Jack. I had a lot to think about when I went to bed and I fell asleep dreaming about a new chapter in my life. The next day was the real challenge.

"Lucy, where am I going to stay in the meantime?"

"How about Swen's place?"

"Lucy, are you kidding me? You've seen how cramped that place is. Do you expect me to sleep on one of those carousel animals?"

"Oh yeah, right. Well, how about Dorothy Strelsin's? She still owns that beautiful duplex penthouse on Fifth Avenue, doesn't she?"

Dorothy Strelsin was still heavily involved in the New York social scene and used every opportunity to weasel into the spotlight. When I was married to Jack and starring on Broadway, Dorothy was always ingratiating herself with me. I never realized that social status was the only thing that made her heart pump. I had even gotten her a part in Harry's movie when she came along with me to Positano.

At this low point, if I had called Dorothy, she never would have taken me in. She knew all about my woes and by now, in her eyes, my social status had plunged.

"Lucy, I know her," I said. "She's not about to let me stay at her place."

"Get her on the phone," Lucy said. "I'll take care of it."

Dorothy liked backgammon and was a big fan of Lucy's. All it took was a phone call from Lucy to do the trick.

"Dorothy, could Paula stay with you for a while?"

"Oh, of course," Dorothy gushed. "I'd be happy to do that for you, Lucy, no problem at all."

Dorothy was hoping for acceptance into one of Lucy's gaming coteries that hovered around the fringes and believed they were more than backgammon fill-ins. I felt bad that I had committed Lucy to playing backgammon with Dorothy—Lucy would now have to listen to her bullshit. As far as I was concerned, Dorothy should have gotten an award for being the all-time queen of ass kissers.

I packed enough clothes for a couple of months. Who knew when my apartment would become available? Dorothy was in good spirits when I arrived and even threw a party for me in May that included Rex Reed, Swen Swenson, Sondra Lee, Janie Kipness (Joe's wife), and Broadway producer Harry Rigby. I personally invited Lee Tannen and Tom Wells to the party and everyone had a great time.

Once I got settled, I immediately threw myself into the whirlwind feat of putting together Lucy's apartment. Everything needed to be updated including the bathrooms, the kitchen, closets, window treatments, lighting, wallpaper, and carpeting. All of this had to be done in record time of five months and, mind you, I hadn't been in New York in over fifteen years. I had to start from scratch to find the appropriate technicians to do all the jobs and re-acquaint myself with the wholesale decorating houses.

I also flew back to Los Angeles where I could easily locate contemporary furniture and items that had a lighter, more uplifting feel rather than the darker, heavier antiques popular with New Yorkers at that time. I made several trips back and forth, checking with Lucy on fabrics and wallpapers. Lucy was aware of all the stress I was un-

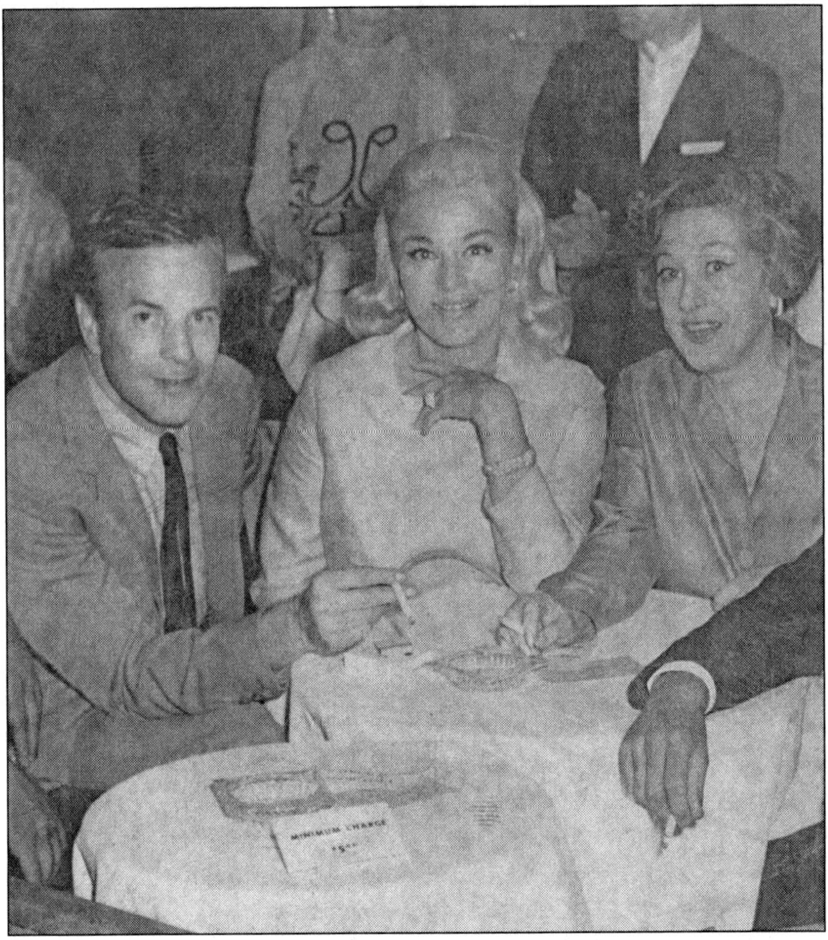

Both Franco Zeffirelli and I were houseguests at various times of Dorothy Strelsin's who owned lavish homes on both coasts.

der, and during my short visits she would always remark how grateful she and Gary were for my commitment and dedication to getting the task done so quickly. Personally, I was glad to be so involved and focused on something other than my recent woes.

★ ★ ★

Ben Franklin once said, "Fish and guests smell in three days." By the summer, I was beginning to feel as if I was imposing on Dorothy even though I was hardly in the apartment. Luckily, Lee and Tom were leaving for Greece and needed someone to take care of their apartment. They were happy to have Michael and me stay and watch their place while they were away. When they returned, Lucy's apartment was still in the finishing phases and the boys allowed me to stay on until her apartment was ready.

Lucy came for a brief visit checking in at the Hotel Westbury on 69th Street. Gary was off on a golf tournament and left Lucy alone. Lee, Tom and I would stick around to have some laughs and had marathon backgammon sessions.

During her stay at the Westbury, she often remarked about the beautiful hangers, and impressive silverware with the large monogram "W" that Lee pointed out could easily stand for Morton. I told her, "Lucy, your hangers are going to be even more exquisite. I've already ordered them from Henry Hanger, 'Hanger to the Stars'."

"Oooooh, really?" Lucy responded.

"They're pale lavender Lucite, with your initials on them." More oooohs.

Not to be outdone, upon checking out of the Westbury, Lee and Tom thought it would be funny to stuff one of the oversize pillows with some of the silverware and hangers. As they began clattering down the hallway, Lucy pulled up short and said, "Hey guys, do you really want to see this in the news: 'Lucille Ball caught stealing hangers and silverware from the Hotel Westbury'? No, no, I don't think so!"

While I was staying at Tom's and waiting for my apartment to open up, I had to fly back to Los Angeles for a post-bankruptcy hearing. I stayed in Lucy's guesthouse. Upon returning to New York, Lucy handed me a letter, sealed with a big lipstick kiss on the envelope which I still have and treasure. In big bold letters she instructed me to open it only on the plane. Frank drove me to the airport. I could hardly wait until we took off to read it. In it she assured me I would be missed and to feel free to call her anytime night or day. She reiterated how much she and Gary loved their "pad." She advised me to not worry about the future, telling me she would help me get back on my feet. This after my disastrous financial collapse. Lucy advised me to take care of my health, let go of "justified" rage and for everyone's sake I should be "kinder" to myself.... "*take the time to relax, control your feelings. ... You have been through a lot, and you have survived, now ease up and help yourself. Get happy. But for Christ's sake and yours, don't marry everyone who asks you!!*" When I read it, I burst into tears.

What a classy, classy lady. I was truly blessed to have her as a friend.

★ ★ ★

I finished decorating Lucy's apartment and it was magnificent. Lucy was so impressed that she contacted *Architectural Digest*. They were excited to get the exclusive and the photo spread was featured in the May 1984 issue. As mentioned, I designed all the furniture. Lucy had given me carte blanche. She knew I was cost conscious. She also knew I was "Lucy conscious." The apartment would not be another one of "Gary's closets."

To be honest, my taste and Gary's didn't differ that much. The main thing was that he was predictable and uninspiring. A true dilettante. That said, I was very accommodating to his preferences. I made an absolutely fabulous closet for him and even made sure the elements he wanted were implemented in their home entertainment center. Per Gary's request, I had several VCRs in different formats that could be accessed in a variety of ways and be shown on any monitor throughout the apartment. That was considered high tech back then.

I had the wall unit in the den bleached in pine while the living room housed a high-gloss almond lacquer cabinet for the television that was hydraulically controlled. It resembled a simple console when the television was lowered.

To continue with the California look, a flowing floor plan, large windows and mirrored wall panels did the trick. I chose vertical string blinds in the dining area, which controlled the remarkable views. I centered on a predominantly beige theme, lightened with soft pastel touches through pillows and accent pieces.

The furnishings were a graceful blend of softly combined contemporary and period styles. I used aqua and mauve accent colors for the living room that I knew Lucy loved. I used more mauve

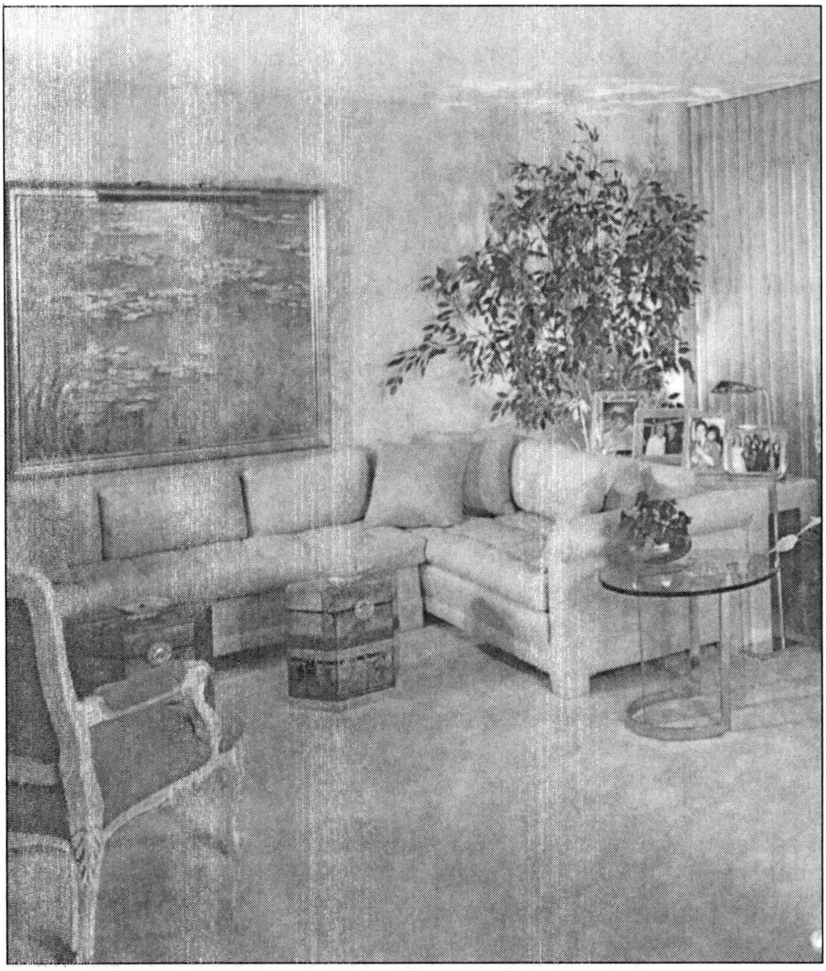

Lucy's New York apartment I designed. Here in Home Entertainment Magazine *with her favorite "Monet" painting. - Photo credit Doug Hanewinckel.*

colors in the bedroom. A soft-toned fabric airily strewn with blossoming branches evoked a lighthearted garden atmosphere. Lucy would walk around saying, "Mauve, I'm in a *mauuuuve* mood."

I also knew artist Jacques Harvey, whose work was in the style of many classic painters, particularly Impressionist artists. I had him paint a Monet-inspired oil of the water lilies. Lucy adored it.

When Jaime Adriles-Arce photographed the apartment, I tried to steer the shots away from the oil painting offering that we didn't want people to know Lucy had such valuable art in the place. I also didn't want the world to know that one of the richest women had fakes! Interestingly enough, an original Claude Monet water lily painting, "Le Bassin Aux Nymphéas," was stolen a year later out of an Upper East Side townhouse that was home to Imelda Marcos and the Philippine Consulate.

Considering my recent financial and public implosion, the articles about the apartment featured in various magazines, particularly the *Architectural Digest* spread was a tremendous boost to my self-worth. It felt great to express myself in another artistic medium. I have to give Lucy full credit for that. She helped me regain my confidence and the accomplishment lifted me from the doldrums.

Everyone loved the outcome of my decorating. So I was surprised when Lucy told me that Little Lucie felt the apartment was not "child friendly."

"She's worried that if she brings her kids over and they spill something or have an accident I would be upset," Lucy confessed. I understood Little Lucie's concern and wasn't offended. Simon was probably three at the time and Joe was around two, but I had already taken this into consideration.

"Lucy, I know it looks pristine, but I had everything pro sealed," I said. Pro sealing is a form of scotch guarding and I had everything from the fabrics on the sofas and chairs, to the carpeting and even the wallpaper treated. They could crawl over the furniture and vomit on it and it wouldn't have made a difference.

"I don't understand her, Paula," Lucy said. "I told her the main reason I got this apartment was so I could be closer to the kids. She's overly sensitive anytime I correct them. I told you about that time when I had Ambrose drive me to her place in upstate New York and the boys were running around barefoot. She went bananas and screamed at me when I insisted they should be wearing shoes. I feel like I have to walk on eggshells."

"She's a new mother, Lucy," I interjected. "You know we all have different ideas on how to raise our children. Maybe you should go a little easier on her."

"Ha! It's more like the other way around."

It wasn't the last time the subject matter came up.

★ ★ ★

We had already installed the fake Monet in the New York apartment when I read about an auction featuring a real Monet. When I mentioned it to Lucy she surprised me.

"Oh, we have to go," she said.

"Lucy, it's going to go for big money."

"So what? It will be fun to watch. And who knows, maybe I'll get lucky. Like shooting craps!"

"It's more like being at the race track. Coming down the last bidding stretch does have some serious excitement."

"Now I really want to go. Let's do it!"

It was an early sale and we were to have dinner afterwards. So off in the limo we went, dressed to the nines to the auction. For an elite, reserved, formal bunch they were excited no end by Lucy's presence. We were ushered to prime seats, smack in the middle for everyone to see. Next to me was a distinguished foreign gentleman, wrapped up in his list of intended buys, oblivious to the rest of the surrounding dignitaries. Though he did glance up when our arrival caused a mild sensation with flutter and whispers all around.

Usually at a prestigious auction, people are much too poker faced to show any emotion, but Lucy's presence was an exception. There is a big difference in auction houses all the way from a stockyard group in the boonies to the pampered elite at Sotheby's; from the unintelligible spiel that sounds like a babble of gobbledygook to the refined sing-song of "Do I hear a raise?"

Lucy gave me a look that said, "What do I do now?" We hadn't talked about bidding and I know she had used a paddle or two in her life, but I wondered to myself if she was really serious about buying this thing.

"You're safe opening the bid because it will be low to start," I whispered. I had a fairly good idea what it would fetch in the end from past history. "Keep in the action for the first few raises if you want to be safe." Before the auction began, she sat there fanning herself with the paddle, smiling around and acknowledging adoring yet strangely silent glances and winks. The auction started with a few minor art treasures. Then the Monet was brought out. It was displayed behind a velvet cloth which was lifted and spot lit for a few breathless moments before the bidding began. The auctioneer announced the provenance, then the opening price, and the bidding started. It was a low come on and I bumped Lucy's knee to spur her on, and up went her arm.

There were others who joined in. Lucy's arm kept going up. Seemed as if she got the hang of this real fast. I wondered, *Is she serious*? I held my breath. She had the means, so why should I worry.

Then the bidding got really hot, fast, and fell into a stratospheric range, and luckily she stopped. I let my breath out slowly as the sold price and winning bidder was pointed out. The price inspired a round of applause and the painting was carried off like royalty. We looked at each and shook our shoulders. *Oh well, we tried.*

We quietly made our way out and laughed as we drove off to Danny's Hideaway where Gary was waiting to be told that Lucy passed on a chance to be the owner of a treasured piece of art. Gary of course was thrilled the money wasn't spent on anything but himself or his clothes. Lucy in the end was her own work of art that would live forever.

★ ★ ★

While Frank was driving Lucy in Los Angeles, her New York chauffeur of choice was Ambrose Hartley, another Irishman who was a very large fellow with a sense of humor to match. We shared a lot of laughs together. When Lucy was in New York, Ambrose devoted all of his time to her but he did have other clients, namely businessman Hugh Michaels. While Lucy was back in Los Angeles for a time, Ambrose introduced me to him. Besides being a financial genius, he was a very wealthy real estate mogul from Chicago. Hugh was big, most attractive, with a great sense of humor. He owned major property in Chicago and, at the time, was in the process of making an offer to buy the Gotham Hotel in New York City.

When he came to town he would take me out and over a short period of time, we had an affair. Part of his appeal was his wackiness. While staying at his huge suite at the Park Plaza, he would have the hotel chef lay out a spread of champagne and caviar, incredible hors d'oeuvres and mountains of exotic fruits. I would invite Swen and a few of my friends to feast on what was a banquet fit for a king. They all thought he was somewhat eccentric but a hoot.

He was extremely generous with me. We would drive all over New York City in this huge limousine that he insisted Ambrose use. No matter where we were, he would have Ambrose stop while he impulsively jumped out to buy me a bauble. He'd take me shopping and we'd go to Saks Fifth Avenue and buy his and hers watches. He also declared that I would be the decorator for the Gotham Hotel. He was most impressed that my work was going to appear in *Architectural Digest*.

While assessing the cost involved in refurbishing the Gotham Hotel, we spent hours there holding numerous meetings with the architects he had hired. We walked through the building's empty spaces, rooms and floors, stepping over steel beams and rubble from a former grandeur. I was excited at this new opportunity to delve into architecture and design of this expansive nature.

All of this was overwhelming for me. Here I was a fifty-five-year-old woman, still attractive despite all the trauma inflicted by Chuck. I was being pursued by a suitor five years my junior, and it felt good. He was beyond infatuated; he was crazy in love with me. It seemed strangely unreal. I was truly swept off my feet, and although I was flattered, I didn't trust myself. I was really taken by him, but I wasn't in love. That much I realized. This man was offering me the moon, but how did I know what the outcome would be? Could I trust his protestations?

I was hesitant about telling Lucy. I knew she didn't want me to have another failure. I didn't want to worry her unnecessarily. I needed to be sure. He told me his wife was institutionalized and intended to divorce her. He insisted I fly with him to Chicago to meet his grown daughters. It was something I found as strange as they did. And I found out he had lied about his wife being confined. She was just as surprised to meet me as I was to meet her. She was very much okay.

I was terribly upset with Hugh, and flew out on the next plane, wanting nothing more to do with him. He chased right after me. He wouldn't stop until he begged me to let him talk to Lucy, who was in as much shock as I was at his wild ravings about how he would kill himself if I wouldn't marry him. He even got down on his knees to Lucy, swearing his undying love to me. The whole thing was a farce. All the while Lucy stood wide-eyed, looking at me like I had rocks in my head.

After he left, I was so embarrassed I wanted to die. Lucy sat me down and gave me the required lecture.

"Now listen to me, Paula, this is for your own good. You're going to have to choose between being my friend or continuing with this romance. He is a married man and you know that I don't approve. Not only that, but I think you're making a huge mistake. This man isn't by any means sane enough in my opinion. You just have to make a decision."

As she said this, I flashed back to the story she told me during our out of town *Wildcat* try out, about her relationship with Pandro Berman. Pandro was a major producer who worked his way up the ranks at RKO Pictures, producing such classics as *Morning Glory* with Katherine Hepburn and *Top Hat* with Fred Astaire and Ginger Rogers. He was the one who was responsible for Lucy being promoted from being an extra to small parts while she was at RKO. He saw her potential and got her into *Stage Door* starring Katherine Hepburn, which was her first big break.

Pandro was her champion, but she felt guilty that he wanted to divorce his wife to marry her. Lucy was crazy about him. In fact, Desi even resembled him. She certainly liked that type it seemed. But her morality won out in the end. When she broke up with him, he became very vindictive and her career suffered as a result.

They eventually made up years later, in 1953 when he was a producer at MGM and produced Lucy's and Desi's movie, *The Long, Long Trailer*. I bring this up because I, too, was not about to cause a divorce, let alone continue any relationship with Hugh.

"There's no way I'm going to have anything more to do with him," I responded. "I don't love him, even if it means my career and the potential of tremendous opportunities and untold financial gains. I won't be responsible for a divorce, any more than you would have with Pandro. The only difference is you loved him. I don't love Hugh. But I have to admit, you really hurt me with your ultimatum, Lucy. You know there's no other decision. So why be so harsh on me?"

"I'm sorry, Paula," Lucy said. "I should have given you more credit, but you know I've witnessed your poor judgment in the past when it comes to your choice in men. Forgive my overreaction but I care for you too much to stand by and say nothing."

Lucy could see that I was still a little shook up.

"I know this little drama scene was pretty heavy," I said. "This calls for a nightcap so we can both rest better." Ambrose drove us to Elaine's, a celeb eatery for some much needed diversion. Elaine was overjoyed to see Lucy and me. She made sure we were seated away from the sightseeing looky-loos. After a few greetings from the local patrons, including my ex-tenant, Woody Allen, we settled in and placed our order. Over drinks, the atmosphere had lightened to the point where I questioned Lucy about something that had puzzled me for years.

"Lucy, how is it that you married Gary, who is so different in type than Pandro and Desi?"

"Well, that's easy. I didn't want to make the same mistake again," she chuckled as she waved back to Dustin Hoffman, who was seated close by. Dustin was starring on Broadway in *Death of a Salesman*. "We've got to go see that show, Paula. I love Dustin. He's such a good actor." By the time dinner was over, we seemed to have resolved our little drama. On the ride home, Lucy couldn't help but rebuke Ambrose with a dig. "Hey Ambrose, keep the nutsos away from my girlfriend!"

★ ★ ★

Lucy's favorite designer was Halston. I remember the love affair between Ball and Halston began when we were shopping for Lucy's wedding dress. When it came to Lucy's veil, an up-and-coming designer was suggested. Halston was fresh from Lilly Daché, the renowned milliner, and running the millinery department at Bergdorf.

Halston was extremely handsome and blurted out to Lucy, "Let me make something that is light and airy that won't upset your hairdo." Lucy didn't need the big circus on her head that Daché was known for, but Halston was so accommodating that Lucy was impressed. When he transitioned over to clothing, Lucy followed. She and I frequented Halston's studio often. His showroom was spectacular. He had done it in a deep high-gloss red burgundy.

When my studio apartment opened up in Lucy's building, I moved out of Tom's apartment. My apartment had finally become a reality, allowing me to stop living out of boxes and other people's closets for a change.

The first thing I did was paint the ceilings and walls in the burgundy of Halston's studio. I had to copy it. It was cozy and soothing. By doing the walls and ceiling in the same color, it made the place appear cavernous—and to me it was like a womb. Lucy loved it, "You made it work beautifully, Paula."

I drilled holes in my walls as I snaked the picture light wires for my artwork. Illuminating the dark burgundy walls this way made them come alive. Since I had no view except the tall buildings across the way, I often imagined the white clouds in the distance as the mountains of my recent life in California, for which I now longed. I had my baby grand, my bookcases, and my favorite desk which had traveled cross-country four times.

I called it my cocoon. It was a place where I could heal myself after my terrible experiences with Chuck and the bankruptcy; where I could begin to mend emotionally; catch up with life and reflect on where I was going. Mainly I pondered, what kind of future did I have?

I decided to get my New York real estate license which was easy and always a good thing to have. I went to work almost immediately. But, my healing was cut short with something I couldn't have anticipated—and had always been a silent threat. It finally surfaced after all these years. I felt I had to tell Lucy about this new looming crisis.

I have always been basically healthy and physically active with the one exception of a precancerous scare. I had successfully given birth to Michael with no apparent problems. But I was starting to experience some "lady problems." After consulting several mystified doctors, I called Irma Bacharach, my former mother-in-law and go-to person for her list of specialists. She had been the one who recommended the doctor who initially treated me so many years ago. What a small world. As I was staring at my deep red Field's carpet, I remembered it was Doctor Feldman (Freddie's Field's brother) who had been my gynecologist at the time of my first cancer scare. I figured he must be retired by now, but Irma still had his telephone number. He lived in the Bronx in a baronial estate and generously invited me to join him and his wife for the weekend. While I was there he examined me and gave me a dour diagnosis of something called leukoplakia, a skin cancer also known as lichen sclerosis. Swell!

He wanted me to have a biopsy done to be sure, which I eventually did. In simple language, I had a kind of cancer for which there was no known treatment or cure. It wasn't always fatal, but the worst part was that it was very uncomfortable because of its location, especially the skin of the vulva. Sitting and walking aggravated it and sex was out of the question. My list of boyfriends had dwindled to zero, so there were no explanations due to anyone. There was no way I could avoid the subject with Lucy, who when I told her was shocked and went into mother-hen mode.

"Oh my god, we have to solve this somehow," she said. I begged her not to tell Gary, as if he would give a damn anyway. Irma on her part insisted I see her healer, Dean Kraft, who had been treating and curing her for various ailments for years.

Dean had become a well-known phenomenon. He practiced a form of "energy healing" that captured the imagination of some skeptics. Supposedly he had killed cancer cells in test tubes by using his own personal energy. I really didn't believe in that sort of thing, but when you're desperate, you'll try whatever there is. Dean treated me and I actually went into remission within a couple of months.

During this time Lucy had Ambrose take me to these sessions, and she was as amazed as I was by my improvement. But the fact remained that she was more worried about this cancer than I was. She tried not to show it, but I could tell her concern in little ways.

Suddenly she wanted to know what I was doing and where I was at all times. She knew I was seeing a bunch of other doctors and questioned me constantly for progress reports.

With the *Architectural Digest* issue finally on the stands, my job prospects were kicking into high gear. Already two of the building tenants were eager for me to redo their apartments. During all of this I was still seeing cancer specialists and having Dean Kraft work his magic on me, which consisted of me lying on a table with him passing his energy through his hands by waving them over my afflicted area. The sessions usually lasted fifteen minutes and then I was off with Lucy for lunch or dinner or a show. She was as curious and open-minded as I was, and possibly as skeptical. It certainly wasn't invasive and at this point I'd try anything. Over and over she'd say, "Thank God, you're getting better. I don't know what I'd do without you in my life!"

When Lucy and I weren't off shopping, visiting her grandkids, she'd be engaged with her backgammon ladies. I vaguely remember them as we had little in common. They were mostly the wives of Gary's golfing buddies. Lucy knew better than to try to engage me in this group.

I've never been a game player. I couldn't sit for too long. I guess I was too kinetic, energetic and restless. I always had to be doing something constructive with my hands, painting, sewing, and building or crafting. It was torture for me to sit for hours playing endlessly and for what? Lucy early on had taught me to play backgammon and I became really good. So good I would constantly beat her, which only made her more desirous for us to play together.

I'd often ask her why she liked this particular game as opposed to Scrabble, which at least stimulated the mind. Her answer was enigmatic, "Because it's a new game each time."

★ ★ ★

One evening in the fall of '84 when Gary was out of town and shortly after my apartment was completely finished, Lucy, Tom

Wells, Lee Tannen, and I were headed out to a local place for a quick dinner and possibly some backgammon afterwards.

Lee was in a hyper foul mood and out of left field, he started in on me. Lee was going on and on about, "Paula does this and Paula does that. Why is it always about Paula? Paula can do no wrong." Both Lucy and I were stunned and honestly had no idea what he was ranting on about, or what had set him off. Uncharacteristically, Lucy was outraged.

"Stop the car, Ambrose. Lee, get out of the car! I can't stand it. That's it. I won't put up with your disrespect and nasty remarks about Paula anymore. She doesn't deserve your abuse. I've had it with you and your mouth. Out! You too, Tom. Get out!!"

Ambrose pulled the limo up to the curb and they were unceremoniously dumped somewhere Midtown. Ambrose was as astonished as I was. We held our breath while Lucy continued screaming. "That bastard! Enough already! No more bitching from that asshole! Jesus! I'm so sorry, Paula. I know how he treats you and you don't deserve that from anyone. And I don't need to hear anymore either. Ambrose, take us back to the apartment. We'll order in. I'm too upset to eat right now anyway. Christ almighty! Who can stand that? How does Tom put up with him?" She went on and on, "I never want to see or hear from that piece of shit again. You hear, Ambrose? You tell him that from me. I mean it. No more. It's over. Forever."

By this time I was crying because I felt bad about being the reason for her outburst and distressed over something I had sparked. Here she was, protecting me again from an all too common treatment I had experienced since my bankruptcy. I was vulnerable and an easy target. Lee had grown comfortable with Lucy, and over time had shown his true colors. He was a sarcastic man and when he smelled blood, he went for the jugular. Lee's humor was edgy and he overestimated Lucy's tolerance for his acerbic humor. His diatribe was mean and repugnant and Lucy reacted in kind.

My guardian angel had jumped to my rescue once again. When we got back to the apartment, we downed a couple of heavy Jack

Daniels while we waited for Ambrose to fetch us a couple of burgers from around the corner.

Lucy didn't speak to Lee for several years until he wormed his way back into her life again.

★ ★ ★

An old friend of mine appeared on the scene, socialite Celeste "Cici" Huston, now divorced from John Huston. She was in town for a visit and we both wanted to get re-acquainted after all these years. Having successfully paired a host of my other friends over the years, I just couldn't resist trying to connect this gorgeous woman to one of the available men I knew. I mentioned my plan to Lucy and she was game.

"The only rich man I know is Lew Rudin, but he's dating this airhead." Lucy liked to call her "Miss Boom Boom." She didn't suffer fools lightly and felt that Lew deserved better. Cici was perfect, also smart and had celebrity status. So Lucy arranged for Lew and Cici to meet, both of us placing bets on their future. But love is strange. To our surprise, they didn't click. It was a shame, because Cici would have made a wonderful follow-up to his former wife, Gladyce, the ultimate hostess. "BoomBoom" won that round.

Lucy loved having me in New York. Before she came to town, she had her secretary dispatch a large to do list ranging from food, liquor and how the beds were made. I didn't mind check-ing them after the maid was finished to make sure they were done correctly.

Lucy also depended on me to recommend any shows she might want to see. I was her girl Friday in the Big Apple and I didn't mind one bit. When Lucy wasn't in town, I was very lonely since most of my showbiz friends now lived in Los Angeles where all the work seemed to be in those days. I didn't like living in New York the second time. In the 1960s you could walk in Central Park without getting mugged. But now it had become too dangerous.

Lucy's trips included lots of clothes shopping at all the large department stores and chic boutiques. Lucy always looked like she stepped out of the pages of Vogue. She loved Ciner Jewel-ry, a high-end costume store run by a very sweet woman, Jackie Rogers.

Lucy was also fond of Lucille de Paris, a very expensive brand of alligator bags. I suspect it was because the name was Lucille. Her preferred perfume was "Tatiana" by Diane Von Fürstenberg, and Somper Furs were her favorite.

Lucy and I were accustomed to doing our own hair and makeup like most actresses do out of sheer necessity. She would, however, have professional makeup artists and hairdressers work on her when she had important engagements. Over the years, Lucy had me do her makeup and hair like good girlfriends do. It became more frequent in her later years. I remember many times being called over to her home in Beverly Hills.

"Paula, can you come over? I've got to go out tonight and Irma isn't available and I don't have time to go to the beauty parlor." Irma Kusely was Lucy's longtime hair stylist since the days of *I Love Lucy*.

So off I went and I'd set her hair exactly the same way. Each curl had to go in a specific direction and then I'd work on her makeup and help dye her hair. All of her dyes and hennas were in a room out in the back of her Beverly Hills home. It had everything you'd find in a top beauty salon, including a special sink to soak her hair. On those occasions when Lucy knew she was performing or was going where there would be lots of cameras, she'd wear one of her wigs that allowed her to use lifting tape that took up the loose skin on her face, a trick not unknown to savvy makeup artists and most aging stars.

Lucy didn't like to go out in public without makeup, so I would be the one to do her cosmetics. She had given me a special little diagram of how she wanted her makeup done. It was very specific and in stages as to how it would be applied, the coloring, the shading, and so on. Once she was dolled up, we'd hit various showrooms including Halston's, where he would have his gorgeous models parade his latest fashions for us. She still had the body of a model and when she would see a model walking by with a particular outfit, she'd say, "I'll buy that one." She'd try it on and it would fit perfectly. However, Halston insisted on making it specifically to her measurements. When she would return in a few days for the outfit, it never fit as well as the first time.

On one occasion, Lucy and I were shopping at Halston's studio for an event she had to attend. The Museum of Broadcasting (now The Paley Center for Media) had planned a gala dinner and retrospective of Lucy's career in April of 1985. Lucy wanted me by her side. As we were looking at the gowns on the models, Halston came running over and asked Lucy if everything was okay. He was acting erratic and hyper. Lucy whispered to me as he sped on by, "He's gonna kill himself on that shit!" By now, I knew what she meant.

Lucy settled on a beautiful, light aqua, diaphanous gown. Halston insisted that he make it especially for her and that it would be delivered in time for the occasion. On the night of the gala when we were leaving, Lucy said, "Paula, I can't walk in this dress." And she literally couldn't get into the limo either.

Thinking quickly, and being no stranger to costume 911 emergencies, I released the seam of the kick pleat far enough for her to move. It was a fashion statement as it showed off more of Lucy's gorgeous leg than planned. People commented on it all night.

Lucy leaned over to me and said, "I can't believe they went to all this trouble to honor me, Paula." Then she looked at her exposed leg and added, "Well you've certainly done it again." The dinner was a classy affair. The crème de la crème of the industry were there, including Wallis Annenberg.

Wallis, a renowned philanthropist, now serves as Chairman and President of The Annenberg Foundation, a multi-billion dollar philanthropic organization. Her father, Walter Annenberg, was a US Ambassador to the United Kingdom in the early '70s. He had an enormous estate near Palm Springs called "Sunnyland," where he entertained royalty, presidents, and celebrities - including Lucy and Desi. Walter was also a publisher. His empire included *TV Guide*, which upon its initial launch in April 1953 featured the first photos of Lucy with newborn Desi, Jr.

Lucy had known the family for years and when I lived on Foothill, Wallis or "Wally" as she preferred to be called, was my neighbor. Wally knew I was close to Lucy and after meeting one day, we all hit it off. Wally was either at my house for parties or I was over at hers. I enjoyed playing the clown for her and her kids, making them laugh. Wally was married to Seth Weingarten and they had

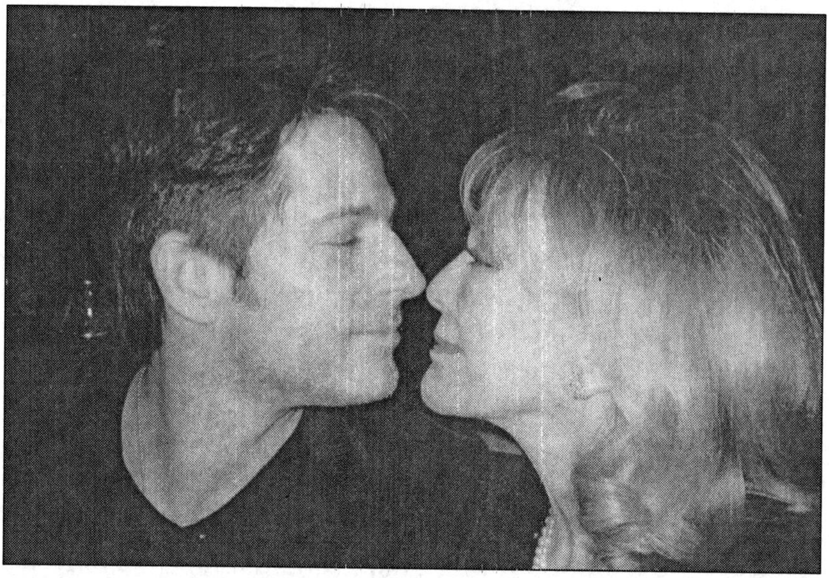

My darling son, Michael and I nose to nose. We saw things eye to eye, too. He never disappointed. He successfully followed me into real estate after a brief entry into show business. Celebrity children face a rare crapshoot for their own success.

four children. Their son, Charlie, and my son, Michael, practically grew up together, starting with their nannies walking them up and down the streets of Beverly Hills in their strollers.

Charlie and Michael remained friends all through college, and later worked together on a film that Charlie produced featuring Michael. After that endeavor, they both chose entirely different careers, which better suited their individual ambitions.

That night Lucy remarked, "Paula, does Wally seem different to you? I detect sadness. What's changed?"

"Beats me. Unfortunately, we've been out of touch for years."

I figured it must be the heavy burden of her new responsibility running the foundation and loss of privacy. That's enough to dampen a free spirit.

Lucy said, "Get her over here for a picture. Let's see if we can cheer her up."

Lucy and I enjoyed the rest of the evening and chatted with Lucy's longtime publicist Charlie Pomerantz along with Robert Batscha, the president of the museum and the museum's publicist,

Lettie Aronson, who was Woody Allen's sister. We complimented them on their amazing evening. It was really wonderful.

★ ★ ★

Made for television movies of the 1980s—who can forget them? More than 100 million people viewed 1983's *The Day After*, about a nuclear holocaust. Hollywood watched Farrah Fawcett's dramatic performance in 1984's *The Burning Bed*, an account of spousal abuse that was based on a true story, garnering Farrah her first Emmy nomination for Outstanding Lead Actress. And, 1985 was the first year a television production or theatrical film dared to touch the subject of A.I.D.S with *An Early Frost*.

Gary was making all the creative decisions for Lucy these days, why I'll never know. He wasn't even talented as a standup comic and yet he was now telling Lucille Ball what was best for her...or was it him? Lucy did trust and defer to his guidance for her career, as was her right. For some reason, Gary was pushing Lucy to do a movie made for television. That movie was *Stone Pillow*. Lucy had great qualms about it from the beginning and for good reason.

Ironically, I had been consulting with a psychic for the last year. His name was John Monti, a young Steve McQueen look-alike and very well-respected by the FBI and local police for leading them to kidnappers and murder suspects. We would meet and tape our sessions a couple times a year. Whether you believe in them or not, I've always been fascinated with psychics.

John came over on my birthday in April of 1985 to give me a reading. The way he worked was he would look at someone's picture and then talk about them. He was a naïve, simple soul who didn't know a lot about show business and was also very shy. But he was spot-on with his readings, past, present, and future.

John happened to see Lucy's photo on my piano and told me that she was very ambivalent about something that was soon to occur. He said she was thinking of "taking a walk" and not at all happy with a current working situation. He discussed her medical condition among other things. I had never mentioned Lucy to

him, let alone my conce
Then, the phone rang. It
“Paula, call me right away
John hold the session while I ca
come to her apartment right away.
she said, “Bring him along, too.”

When we arrived Lucy was in a very agitat
out of the movie.

“Paula, I don’t know about this *Stone Pillow* that Gary’s pushing me to do. I’m not at all sure I want to do it with George Schaefer. Plus, I don’t like the script and it’s going to be shot in just a few weeks.” At this point, John in his unsophisticated way, out of nowhere started in on Lucy and her health, and how she was completely out of whack. Here was this baby-faced, sandy-haired doll lecturing Lucy about her health. Lucy and I were stunned. As shocked as we were, we sat still and listened.

Lucy didn’t believe in psychics but she knew and trusted me. She was paying close attention and I knew it had to do with the fact that she witnessed my remission through the energy healings of Dean Kraft; otherwise she probably would have just changed the subject and then politely dismissed him.

John said there was fluid retention in her body and she wasn’t on a correct diet. He told her she wasn’t sleeping well and that she needed to get her blood checked (I still have this on tape, so I’m repeating his choice of words).

“I see unusual activity around your thyroid that would indicate that things aren’t balanced in your system, and that’s making you feel depressed,” John said. “You shouldn’t be smoking and you need more exercise. It’s going to be important. In some parts of your body, the blood isn’t getting there right away so you need to exercise. Your arm will go to sleep and you have a shoulder ache that’s caused by lack of circulation. You have to stop taking your medications. I think they’re throwing your system a little bit off. I think you’re taking too much or the wrong type.”

He had no idea how true this was. For example, prior to Lucy moving in to the New York apartment, she sent boxes of her clothes and personal things for me to organize and put away for [illegible] ized and after years of [illegible] she liked them arranged. [illegible] medicine cabinet, I couldn't [illegible] s. I was astonished at the assort- [illegible] *all* these, I thought. There were so [illegible] names. I wondered if they ever consulted [illegible] me medications were conflicting and some [illegible] ed dates on them.

I had no idea she was taking Dexedrine and sleeping pills. They were large doses and plentiful. Lucy had so many drugs that she could have opened a pharmacy. I couldn't even find room for all of them, even though I had built a very oversized medicine cabinet for her. I knew she had high blood pressure but all these pills? I grew alarmed and tried to quietly discuss it with Gary once or twice.

"Gary, I don't think all these things are good for her," I said.

"She's got the best doctors in the world, don't worry," he said.

Lucy employed many doctors. She went to several of them, including Dr. Rex Kennamer, known as "Doctor to the Stars" who only treated the biggest celebrities—Frank Sinatra, Rock Hudson and Elizabeth Taylor.

"Gary, you should really take a look at this, it's not right," I said. He was completely unaware of the extent of the seriousness of her conflicting medications. Being the caring human being he was, Gary blew me off. There wasn't even one vitamin in the lot. I was concerned, but one did not confront Lucy with such things. However, now was a perfect time with John present.

"Well, Lucy, maybe you could make sure the meds are all up to date," I said, hoping my voice didn't crack.

"I will, Paula," Lucy said rather deadpan. It was not taken well and we could hear a pin drop.

"Anything else I should know, John?" Lucy asked.

"That's just what's coming to me right now, Miss Ball."

"John, could you have predicted that I would ask you to call me 'Lucy'?!"

We all laughed. That was a sigh of relief. But in the days and years to come, it would prove to be no laughing matter.

★ ★ ★

Production on *Stone Pillow* commenced a few weeks later in April of 1985. Lucy played a character named "Florabelle," an elderly woman who gets caught up in the system and winds up a bag lady struggling to survive on the streets of New York City. Lucy was initially attracted to the character because it was a chance for her to break out and do a dramatic role after all those years of comedy.

Stone Pillow was set in the middle of winter and although April seemed a good bet to be cold, New York experienced a record-breaking heat wave. Lucy, all bundled up and sweating, losing precious fluids, only aggravated her fragile physique and caused her to faint several times during filming. On top of this, her left shoulder pain was becoming unbearable.

She called it the FS ("fucking shoulder") and often couldn't even raise her arm. One night when Lucy and I were out to dinner with Gary, Lew Rudin and Boom-Boom at the Hamburger Hamlet, Lucy jumped up from her seat backwards, as if someone shot her in the arm with an electrode. It hurt so badly she let out a blood-curdling scream. Everyone in the restaurant was concerned. After that incident, she admitted there was a problem.

"Paula, I've got to bite the bullet," Lucy said. "Make me an appointment with Dean." She saw Dean through the entire shoot on a daily basis.

I actually had a small part in the movie at Lucy's insistence.

"Look George, there has to be a part for Paula in this. She plays great hookers!"

George Schaefer, a well-respected director of classics and a dignified man, said, "Lucy, there are no hookers in this movie, but I'll find a part for her."

He did and it was a small but juicy role. I portrayed a matron in one of the shelters and I chose to play her in a very masculine way, which Lucy got a kick out of. I also knew Lucy wanted me around for moral support, and to play backgammon in between set ups.

I was like a watchdog for Lucy. I protected her from the myriad of fans and hangers on that pestered her. She couldn't say "no" but I did. Lucy was forever gracious, signing autographs for anyone approaching her. That could be dangerous for more than her well-being. This was New York 1985, not New York 1960.

For the scenes in the desolate Bronx, trailers and equipment trucks surrounded her trailer, so there was not much need for greater security. I rustled up some snacks at the catering truck and as I was walking back to Lucy's trailer, I noticed a man acting strangely. As an actress, I'm very aware of body language and this person's movements were definitely not normal—furtive is the word I would use. I stopped and pretended not to see him. He was slinking down as if he didn't want to be seen. He was close to Lucy's trailer and her door was open. I took a chance and screamed, "Fire!" which got everyone's attention. Crew members ran toward me as I pointed to the man and yelled, "Get him." They held him down to the ground until security came and found a huge knife under his jacket.

Turns out he was a mental patient with a long list of offenses. Lucy saw the tail end of it all and was shaken up when she heard I had saved her from that lunatic's mayhem.

"Paula just saved my life," she screamed. "She could have been killed instead of me. Oh my god, my brave little sister. How can I ever repay you for this?"

Even though Lucy struggled with the heat, she still gave the production her all. Such a professional —she had all her lines memorized. Lucy loved walking around as that character because nobody recognized her.

I remember when Little Lucie gave birth to her daughter, Katharine Desiree, in January of that year, Lucy wanted to go to the hospital. She called me.

"Bring your camera, Paula," she said. "We're going to the hospital to take pictures of Little Lucie's new baby." Lucy didn't want to draw attention at the hospital, so she wore a large fur hat and sported big sunglasses so nobody would recognize her.

We got to the hospital and entered an elevator with a pregnant lady who was just about to "drop." I don't know how she recognized Lucy in her disguise but she did.

"Oh, Lucille Ball, you've got to give me your autograph!" she said. Just as she completed her sentence, her water burst. It got even more surreal.

Production wrapped on *Stone Pillow* in May of 1985 and it aired six months later. Reviews for *Stone Pillow* were disastrous across the board. Lucy was in shock and stayed in bed for days. We were all concerned because she had no appetite and walked around in a daze. I'd take a tray of food to her into the bedroom and it would remain untouched. I worried about the "pill factory" in the bathroom and worried she was medicating herself to deal with the pain. Gary was no help. Typically, he threw his hands in the air and said, "What can I do? Listen, Lucy, I tried to do the best that I could for you. It's not my fault they didn't like it." Then, he was off on another golf trip.

I stayed with her and even tried to get her to play backgammon to get her mind off the criticism. It didn't work. She would often rant, "Desi was right. I never should have tried to change my image. He was right about *Mame* and he was right about this. My fans only want the ditsy 'Lucy' they know. They won't let me stretch myself."

"But Lucy, it was one of the highest rated shows of the week," I pleaded with her.

"Bullshit! So what?" she answered. "I can't even be allowed to grow old like everyone else. No one gives a damn about the social statement of playing an elderly homeless woman. All they want is that goofball. I can't even be me. Must I wear these fucking red wigs and pull up my sagging jowls for eternity? I hate growing old, Paula. Wait, you'll see what I mean. You're still young."

She cried hard, filling those lovely blue, red-rimmed eyes, as I wept with her. I knew how hurtful all this was for her at this time of her career and at her age.

"I've had it with this town," she said. "I hate the weather and as far as Little Lucie is concerned, she's made it obvious she doesn't care if I'm here or not. She has her own life now with Larry and the kids and she doesn't even want to bring them over here."

Lucy packed her bags quickly and was back in Los Angeles just in time for the holidays.

★ ★ ★

Shortly after Lucy left, my mother phoned me.

"Paula, you know Red is about to give birth. When are you coming back?" Swen had bred my Yorkie and my mother was looking after her. I assured her I would be back before the puppies were due. I had to attend to some of my client's needs. I was now an established and respected interior designer.

Women in my building like Kaye Ballard, a well-known actress/comedian whom I had known forever, happened to have the same layout as my apartment and it was easy for me do over. Nicci Gamache also had an identical apartment as mine and she loved what I had done, so I just repeated what I had with lighter colors.

I phoned Lucy to tell her I was coming back to LA for a short visit, staying with my friend Devra Hill, who had a large house with lots of rooms to spare. Devra is married to Irwin Zucker, a big press agent for authors.

When it came time to whelp the puppies, Lucy insisted on being there for this special event. She was no stranger to birthing animals from her days on the Desilu Ranch, and came dressed for the occasion in old sweats. We went to my room where my beloved Red was resting comfortably in a large cardboard box I prepared for her. Lucy knelt down, stroking Red's fur.

"When are they coming?" Lucy asked.

"Any minute now," I replied. "Her temperature has dropped low as is usual just before whelping time." Sure enough, Red started labor and soon what appeared to be a little balloon was protruding from her rear and zip, there it was.

Small dogs often have a difficult time tearing open the sacs so we assisted in the processes. I remember it well because there was my friend Lucy, rubbing the first pup, warming it up in her beautifully manicured hands and then removing the slime out of its mouth and nose so it could breathe. Lucy and I were relieved as it all went so smoothly, teamwork and a job well done. We watched as the tiny babies, three in all, eagerly crawled to Red's teats as she lay exhausted and content with her precious litter.

"Well, now that Red's got her job done, I have one for you, my dear," Lucy said. I could tell by her demeanor she was about to give her own special delivery. "Finally, after all these years, I've decided to do some updates on the house. I'm tired of listening to Gary moan and groan about the bald carpet in the lanai. You did such a great job on the New York apartment, who else am I going to use?"

At first I was elated, but then I realized I would have to be in Los Angeles to do the work. Paying two rents made no sense, not to mention moving my life across the country again. I just wasn't ready at this point in my life. I didn't even have a place to store my stuff. I had to keep the New York apartment even if I accepted the job. Lucy was aware of this.

"Don't worry, Paula, you can stay here," Lucy said. "I'll talk to Devra about a payment arrangement." Lucy looking out for me again. I knew she didn't want me to take a loss. It took me some time to get back on my feet but I would have quickly lost a lot of that momentum. I would continue to pay the rent in New York and Lucy was going to take care by paying Devra. I told Lucy it shouldn't be more than a couple of months. I would be living out of a suitcase again, but for my mentor and my best friend, I didn't mind. Besides, her home certainly could use that long overdue makeover.

★ ★ ★

The décor of Lucy's house, which I often joked was early Desilu prop shop, was a constant thorn in Gary's side. He was honestly embarrassed by the pedestrian look of the house. Meanwhile, it was Lucy's house and where she and Desi had resided. Lucy hated change. She loved the familiar: friends, music, makeup and clothes. Change was a threat. She had resisted Gary's pleadings for years with her own insistent, bellowing, "Noooo waaaaay!" But finally she was willing, only on the condition that I was to be the decorator.

Lucy had allowed Gary to redo his bathroom when he first moved in and Gary made a stab at redoing Lucy's to some extent. I now discovered the marble tub Gary put in had not been done up to code. It was dangerously unsupported. It was a miracle that it didn't fall through the ceiling into the living room below.

When I began the project, I corrected all the problems that literally had been swept under the tub. I installed a pink marble tub with gold plated fixtures. I commissioned an artist to paint a fabulous sunset on the ceiling with clouds in muted colors of pinks and mauve, her favorite. It was heavenly soaking there, to be sure. The olive drab shag carpet with the famous bald spots that Gary had complained about was replaced with beautiful off-white plush carpeting. I had actually sent her samples while I was still in New York for her to approve. I bought a lot of things for her down at Abell's Auction House. Knowing Lucy's penury, I wasn't about to spend a lot of money going to showrooms and buying items for retail when I could get practically brand new things down at Abell's, which pleased her to no end.

I chanced on a pair of exquisite chairs and a coffee table that had belonged to Rona Barrett whom Lucy adored. Rona was a gifted designer as well as a syndicated columnist. Unfortunately, no amount of coercion could convince Lucy to get rid of the big Formica table that was in the formal dining room that she had custom made at the studio.

I once asked her, "Why don't you have just a beautiful antique table that you can put leaves in? Like a refectory table."

"Oh nooo," Lucy said. "This is much better. It's more serviceable. I could care less about the looks."

She was more concerned about how practical it was. Here she hosted script sessions or sent out photographs to her fans. The dining room was really more her office. That was function over fashion.

The same went for Lucy's wine cellar. I discovered she actually had one when I first stayed with her before moving to New York. It was behind a door under the backstairs of the house. Lucy had given me the keys because I needed a place to store all my wines. When I opened the door, instead of the cool chill one would expect when entering a wine cellar, I was greeted with a blast of hot air. *What in god's name?* I thought to myself as I walked in, nearly pinching my nose from the pungent vinegary smell of heated grapes.

As I inspected some of the bottles, the corks were all dry from the heat and some of the wine had seeped out of the bottles, leaving a syrupy residue on the floor. It was certainly no place to store a Lafitte Rothschild, which deserved a cold setting. I told Lucy, "What good is a wine cellar if you don't have any refrigeration?"

"Oh Paula, you know I don't drink wine," she said. "They've been sending me bottles of it since *I Love Lucy*. That's the wine cellar, so I just figured to put them in there. There's plenty of room for yours."

"Oh no, Lucy, I'll find an alternative."

Yes, my precious wines escaped the fate of Lucy's inferno of a wine cellar, but little did I know I would lose them all together.

Fess Parker, best known for playing "Daniel Boone" on television, had become a wine connoisseur and later owned the Fess Parker Winery. Fess also had storage places where you could store your wines in chilled rooms, which certainly was a more attractive option than the sauna lurking under Lucy's backstairs.

I checked out his facilities, which were quite sophisticated. I had all my precious wines sent there before I took off to New York. When I returned to California, I called up the storage facility and discovered my wines had been sold! They gave me some lame excuse that they couldn't get in touch with me when I had clearly left more than adequate information. I sued Fess Parker and Co. and easily won. It was obvious to the judge when I presented Lucy's address and phone number, that I had left adequate means to get in touch with me.

I received ample remuneration but one can't help feeling cheated in situations like this. It was a hobby after all, a much enjoyable one—now being imbibed by someone other than me. It's almost like having a favorite pet stolen. Lucy didn't quite empathize with me on this one. She wasn't into the nuances of vintage wine. After all, one bottle of Jack Daniels is pretty much like the next.

★ ★ ★

I remember one time I was redoing Little Lucie's bedroom, another print on print, since Lucy loved that in the New York apart-m … liked it. I took her a…

… this!" she said. My m…

… elieve me, you ap- p…

… ay, I'll change it! I'm s…

… before. I was quite t… . The next day Lucy c…

"I want you to come here right away," she said with a sense of urgency.

Lucy was waiting for me at the side door when I pulled into the driveway.

"Paula, I'm so sorry," she said. "I went in there and looked in Little Lucie's room again. It's beautiful. I don't know what possessed me. You're right, it's quite exquisite. Forget what I said last night. It stays. You don't have to change a thing."

Lucy explained that she was withdrawing from some medication and the doctor told her that she might experience strange behavior. She had actually taken what I said to heart, and her doctor took her off almost everything.

She had become so dependent on the meds she wasn't aware of how difficult she had become and was fighting with everyone at the drop of a hat. She would be up one minute and down the next. I connected this with the wallpaper incident.

For anyone who has experienced a loved one going through withdrawals, you know what I'm talking about. It is not easy, no matter what kind of substance your loved one is addicted to. That person needs all the support that can be garnered, and everyone should be aware of this. Well, almost everyone, except Gary.

I went downstairs to the kitchen after Lucy apologized. Gary was there and he pulled me aside off to the den.

"I see you too are feeling the wrath of Miss Ball," he said sarcastically.

"What the hell are you talking about, Gary?" I asked.

"Paula, she's impossible. I can't take it anymore. She's unbearable. I heard her yelling at you. Everyone can hear her yell from one end of the house to the other. I just can't deal with it anymore and I'm thinking about divorcing her."

If there were a sound made when someone's jaw actually hit the floor, you would have heard it then. I was speechless. I had to process exactly what Gary said before I could respond. I pointed my finger straight at him as my emotions rushed through my body.

"You ungrateful moron," I started off. "Don't you see what's happening? This is all because of Lucy's change in medication. She's having withdrawals. It will pass. Lucy needs our support and understanding, not condemnations." I wish I had a camera because the look on Gary's face was priceless, actually comical. I had never spoken to him in that tone and he was stunned beyond belief. I really wanted to laugh, but I was too outraged.

"You're going to leave the most beloved person in the world? Is that it, Gary? Sure, now that you're financially secure. She loves you, Gary. She made you the star you think you are in this town. I'm warning you. You better think twice, because they're going to hate you, *everyone* is going to hate you and I can't wait till they all take pot shots at you. And you're damned lucky I don't go now and tell Lucy that I've warned you all these years about her medications and how you just blew me off to go play fucking golf!"

At this point I was shaking. I lost all respect for that man. It just confirmed what I had suspected all those years: Gary Morton was a first-class prick.

★ ★ ★

One of my favorite memories of Lucy was spending time with her in the rehearsal studio, which was right next to the guesthouse. Lucy enjoyed walking around, pointing here and there, "Paula, look how I took care of all your plants." They were all practically dead.

Red would often run beside us begging for attention, whereas Lucy's antisocial Tinkerbell was tucked under Lucy's arm most of her life. Come to think of it, all of Lucy's Tinkers were just one-woman dogs. We'd chat about all the things in our lives while wandering through the storage room, checking on abandoned gifts and toys with myriads of extra golf sets found resting around waiting to be donated to charity. Our visit usually ended in the rehearsal studio.

The studio contained a small stage and piano with a dance bar and mirrors. It reminded me when we first started working together on Broadway and I helped Lucy with her songs. Little Lucie and Desi, Jr. created their own plays in that same space when they were very young.

Lucy usually wound up sitting at the piano bench even though she didn't play herself, and request that I sing for her.

"Paula, sing me 'Rainy Day.' "

"Here's That Rainy Day" was everyone's favorite cry-along song. Written by one of Lucy's good friends, Jimmy Van Heusen, and lyrics by Johnny Burkel, the song was the stand-out ballad from the all-too forgettable musical *Carnival in Flanders*. Garland would sing it, Sinatra made it famous, and I used it in my act all the time, where Lucy saw me perform it a million times. It was special singing for Lucy.

"Funny how love becomes a cold rainy day, funny that rainy day is here."

After I sang that lyric, we both would dissolve into tears about our past loves.

★ ★ ★

I knew Lucy trusted my taste and Gary *loved* what I had done especially when the new carpet arrived and was finally laid. One of the strange things about decorating for Lucy was that she had a real phobia about birds, bees and butterflies, anything that had wings. They couldn't appear anywhere, not in the fabric, the wallpapers, nowhere.

Lucy explained that when she was a young girl, she was frightened by a bird that had flown into her bedroom. It left a lasting impression on her, and her reactions were sometimes hard to fathom.

In the course of my decoration duties, I had purchased some Chinese ceramic bowls for the house. They were painted with flowers and called fish bowls, or sometimes egg crates. I hadn't noticed any birds in the pattern probably because of all the flowers.

We were having dinner one night and watching *Wheel of Fortune*. Lucy loved game shows and she adored Vanna White. Just as Vanna appeared on the screen, Lucy started screaming and all of us where aghast. She jumped up like a mad woman and screamed, "Get that out of here!"

I had not seen the tiny bee print on the Chinese bowl. How Lucy could see that from clear across the room was just amazing. Frank had to take it back into the kitchen before we could sit down to finish dinner and our game shows.

I knew Lucy loved what I was doing with the house. There was no major remodeling, just fluffing up what was already there. The one room I didn't touch was the den. It didn't need it. It had the most beautiful wood paneling and shelves. Lucy's portrait hung over the gorgeous fireplace with her two grandkids on both sides.

At one point I had taken a picture of Simon, Little Lucie's son, with his blanket. He was about a year old and Lucy blew it up into a large poster and it hung on the opposite wall. Over the years I had become the family photographer. I had a nice array of fabulous cameras and Lucy always insisted on paying me for the film, so naturally I always gave her the negatives.

I had just put the final touches on her bedroom and I really outdid myself this time. I was so pleased that she had a room as exquisite and glorious as she was. The colors were an impressionistic watery swirl of flowers of pale lavender and aqua tints that all blended and flowed together. The silky sheen of the fabric gave it a luminous glow like that of a heavenly haze.

The curtains were also fabulous. Unfortunately, her closets were impossible to expand after Gary had taken all the available space. Lucy's things were parceled around the various guest rooms adjacent to the master bedroom so that he could have room for his stuff. Somehow it just didn't seem fair.

★ ★ ★

I had just come back from a full day of shopping and I had some fabrics for Lucy to approve. I noticed that someone had just pulled out of the driveway as I was coming in.

"Who was that, Lucy?" I asked as I laid out the materials for Lucy to look at.

"Another goddamn interviewer!" she said. "I'm so tired of them asking the same questions over and over. How did you meet Desi? How did you get into show business? What's your favorite *Lucy* episode? What's it like being a legend? Christ, aren't there enough books already out there with all this information? I'm sure they'll still be writing about the same stories when I'm dead."

"Lucy, stop talking like that," I said instinctively.

"No, Paula, I am so tired of it." I could tell by Lucy's tone that she wasn't up to approving any fabrics at the moment. "Why don't I interview you, Paula?"

"What? Lucy...?"

"Yeah, let me be the interviewer for once. Let's start with how did you get into show business?" Something most people don't know is that Lucy loved playing interviewer. She did this with a lot of her close friends and surprised them with her questions. She once told me she played this game with a couple of her students, like Carole Cook, back in the Desilu workshop days. Carole became a favorite of Lucy's and Lucy had her on her shows several times. I decided to indulge her when she asked the first question.

"So tell me something about yourself that I don't know," she said.

"Well, you know I went to Northwestern University, but did you know that some of their well-known alumni include Warren Beatty, Charlotte Rae, Garry Marshall, Cloris Leachman, Karen Black, Ann-Margret and Tony Roberts?"

"Ohhhh?" Lucy's eyes went wide.

"Also, NU ran the prestigious Waa-Mu, an annual original Northwestern musical show for all the theater students. It's been dubbed the greatest college show in America." Lucy loved this, so I continued on.

"I was in a sorority, Gamma Phi Beta and when the mothers of my sorority sisters found out I was half-Catholic **and** half-Jewish, it was too much for them—they wanted to kick me out, until they found out that I had the lead in the Waa-Mu Show. I guess it was okay for a 'star' to be amongst their daughters rather than a half-breed religious kid."

"So that's where you started?"

"Yes, but I came down with a severe case of laryngitis and couldn't perform." It probably was a psychological reaction caused by the fact that Poppy wouldn't cancel his European vacation for my first major performance. In fact, it was the only time I ever lost my voice. Many years later, I found, through analysis, his dismissal of my talents was crucial to my self-esteem.

"Oh," Lucy said as she fidgeted in her chair.

"Are you alright, Lucy?"

"Now come on, I'm the one asking the questions here."

"Oh, right. Yes, of course." I explained further. "When I finally achieved recognition, Poppy gained respect for my choice of a theatrical profession. But because of my failure to perform in the Waa-Mu, my voice teacher insisted I audition to regain my confidence. There was an open casting call for the National Touring Company of *Brigadoon* in Chicago. And she handed me all the information.

"Well, I thought, why not? So I hopped into my yellow Mercury convertible and joined the other aspirants. I auditioned and was hired on the spot for an opening in the chorus. The next day I told my teacher that I was dropping out of school. She asked me if I thought that was wise.

"What good is a diploma going to do for me two years from now when I can have the experience of touring with an original Broadway production?" I asked.

Lucy thought about my answer and said, "I certainly can't argue about that."

"But against my father's wishes, I dropped out of NU."

"Naturally, then what happened?" she prodded.

"Funny thing, the first day of rehearsal I showed up late. As you know I've never been a morning person so I just strolled in. I was immediately reprimanded and was told if I showed up late again, don't bother coming back.

"Wow, I thought, this is serious. From that day forward, I was never late for rehearsal or anything again. I changed my attitude about being on time since it was just that important enough."

"Well, I know that's definitely true from first-hand experience... Now what have you got to show me in the way of fabrics?" We spent the rest of the afternoon talking about my early days, intermittently going over fabric choices and reluctantly on my part, a couple of games of backgammon.

Now that I look back on it, that was truly a special day.

★ ★ ★

During my real estate glory days of the 1970s, I had rented one of my properties on Gloaming Way to Dennis Edwards of The Temptations. Through Dennis I met the Pointer Sisters, in particular Ruth Pointer. Ruth and Dennis were an item at the time, and later married. I met Ruth, Anita and June at a time when things were not going well for them. I liked them a lot.

I thought they were extremely talented and tried to be instrumental in helping them get back on their feet again by introducing them to Mickey Rudin, Lucy's lawyer. He in turn introduced the Pointer Sisters to Jerry Weintraub, a tour-de-force in entertainment.

I ran into Jerry all the time at parties in New York when he was dating singer Jane Morgan, a major star then. Jerry later married her and went on to manage musical acts like John Denver and Neil Diamond; and he produced classic films like *Nashville, Oh God!,* and *Oceans Eleven.* Sadly, he passed away in 2015. Jerry introduced the Pointer Sisters to Richard Perry, an equally prominent music producer, more in alignment with their talent. Richard worked with Ringo Starr, Carly Simon and Diana Ross. The Pointer Sisters got a whole new lease on life when their album *Energy* launched Perry's new record label, Planet Records, in 1978. They scored a huge hit with their cover of Bruce Springsteen's "Fire" and the album went gold. It breathed new life into their career and The Pointer Sisters and Richard Perry went on to make music history.

I remained very close with the ladies over the years. When I came back to Los Angeles and was redoing Lucy's house, I found

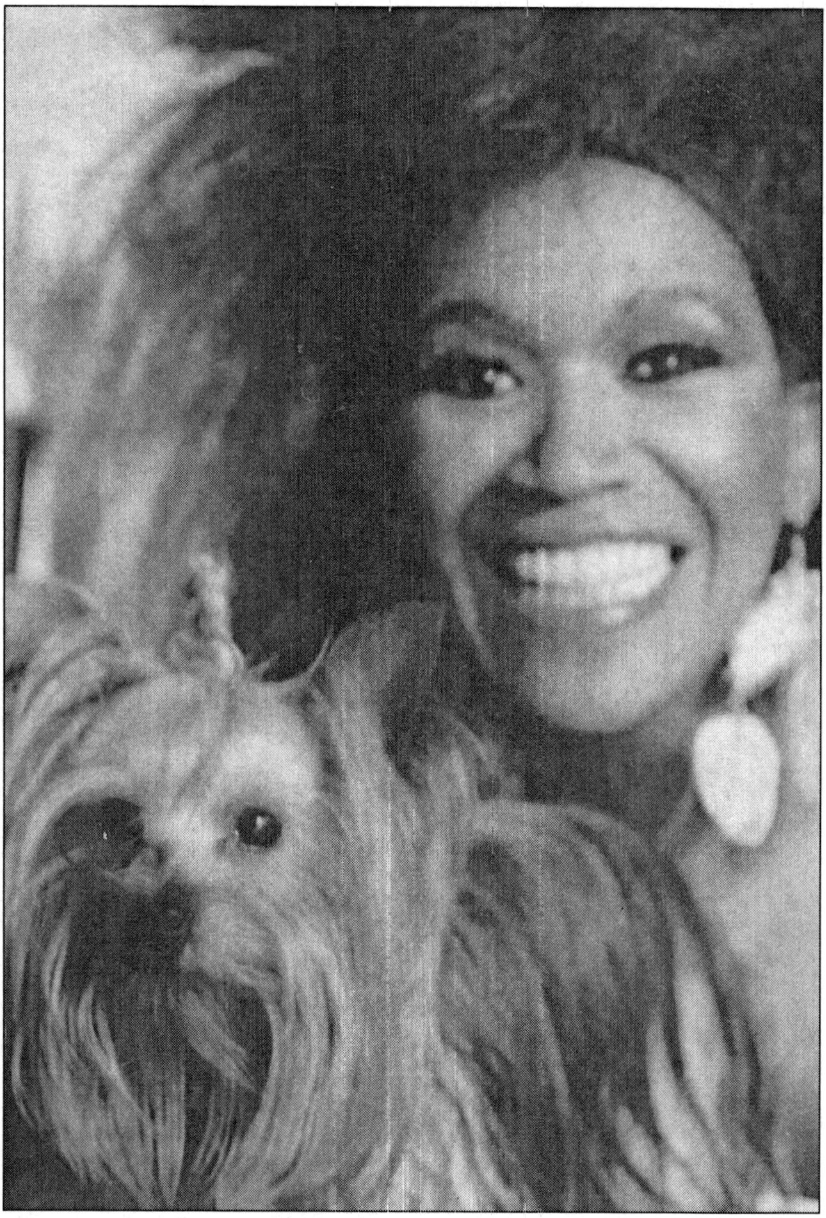

Ruth Pointer with my Yorkie, Red.

Ruth a beautiful two-acre estate in Malibu. It needed some major fixing up and Ruth allowed me to have free rein.

"Paula, since we're going on tour this summer, why don't you live at the house and redecorate it while I'm gone?" Ruth suggested. "You

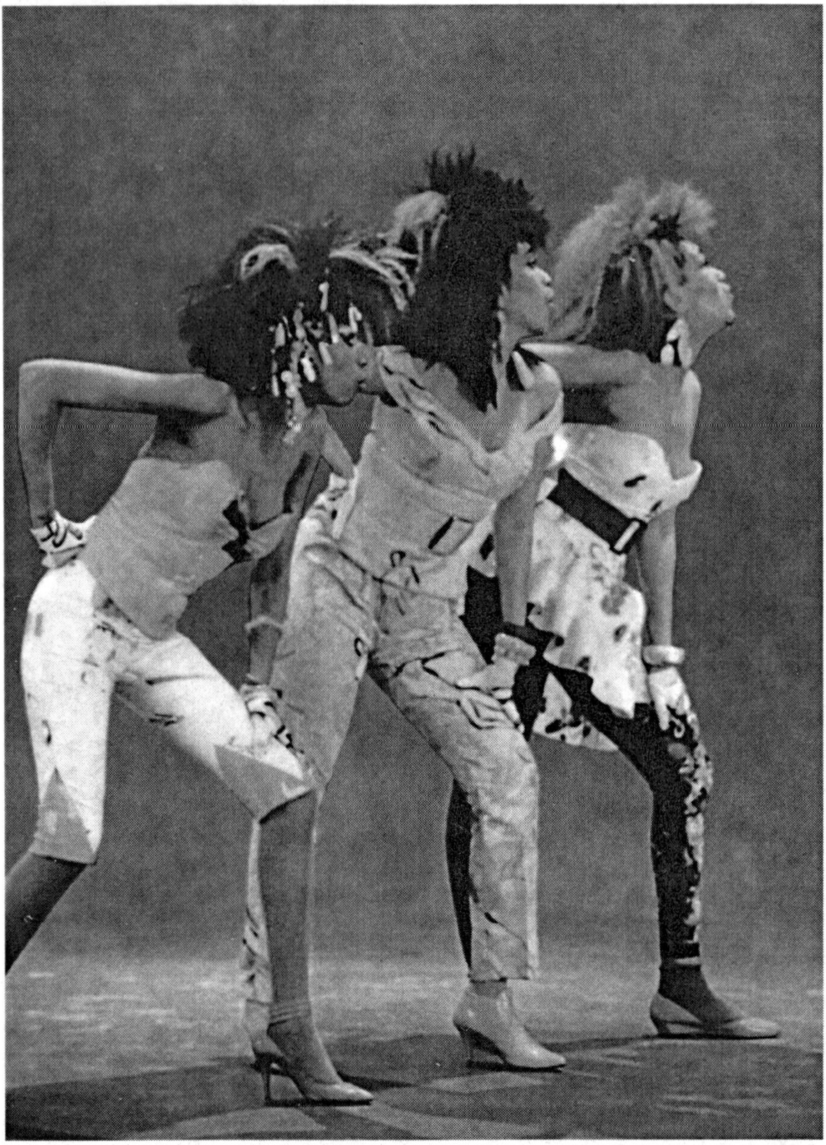

The Pointer Sisters, (from left to right) June, Anita and Ruth.

can have carte blanche." Two things I loved hearing. Red and I could move out of Devra's house and Lucy could stop paying my rent.

This worked out perfectly because there was practically nothing left to do at Lucy's. One afternoon, Gary called me into the den.

"Hey Paula, you got a minute? Lucy wanted me to talk to you about your bill." I wasn't sure I heard him right.

"What bill?"

"You know, what we owe you."

"She already paid me."

"Oh come on, Paula, you know you expect something."

"Not from her," giving him a look.

"Well, how much from me then?"

"Aren't you lucky? You get the family discount as her spouse. We're even."

Lucy appeared at the side door with hugs and kisses with reminders to call right away as soon as I got there. I began working on Ruth's house in Malibu and a couple of days later a package arrived. It was the Kentia Palm in the Chinese Bowl with the bee in the pattern. Attached was a note from Lucy: "Enjoy the new digs. I know Ruth will love what you do. Please come to dinner tonight. Love Lucy." Believe it or not, that palm is still in my life.

I liked to be on site when doing a job, and with Ruth's house, there was a lot of ripping and tearing. The place looked like a palace when I was finished. It went from a rustic cabin to a sophisticated beach house.

While I was staying at Ruth's place, I found a little house in Malibu that was up on Trancas Canyon that was for sale for about $190,000. I had enough money for the down payment but my credit was terrible because of the bankruptcy. I didn't want to ask Lucy if she would co-sign for me (hadn't she done enough?) so I asked Ruth, who generously agreed.

I remember the first time I took Ruth to meet Lucy. Ruth was a big fan and I said to Lucy, "My friend Ruth Pointer is dying to meet you." Lucy knew who the Pointer Sisters were. She knew all about Mickey Rudin's help, and she knew how friendly I was with them so she said, "Bring Ruth by one day." Lucy was a little stunned at first when Ruth came over to the house. I don't think she expected to be met by this six-foot tall black woman with flaming red hair, who was so excited to meet Lucille Ball. Lucy was gracious as always.

We spent the afternoon with Ruth regaling Lucy with "Sister stories" that had her in stitches. Ruth is an amazing raconteur and animated performer, and easily held Lucy's attention. Lucy found

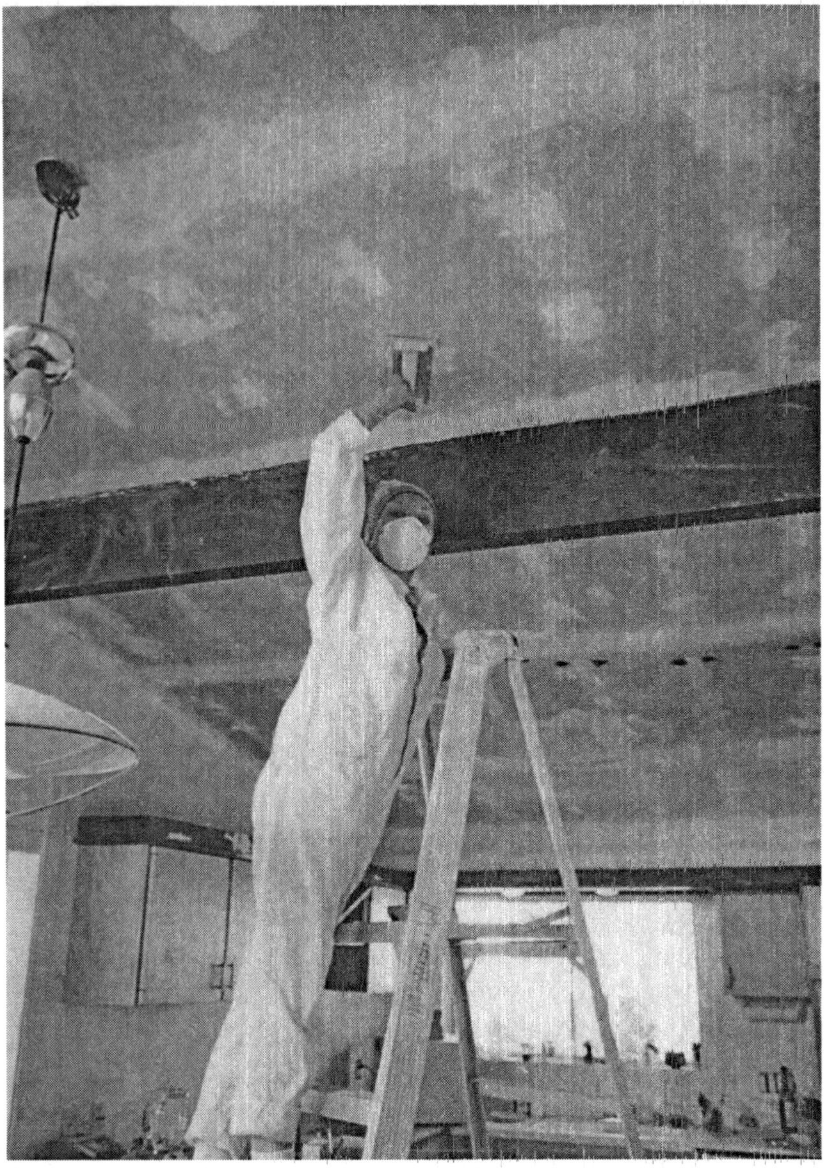

Loved plastering.

her highly amusing and valued their friendship. She was the first to come out to Ruth's house to check on my progress and add her approval to the renovations. When I had completed Ruth's house and all the legal things had been hammered out, I finally moved into my property on Trancas Canyon and began fixing it up.

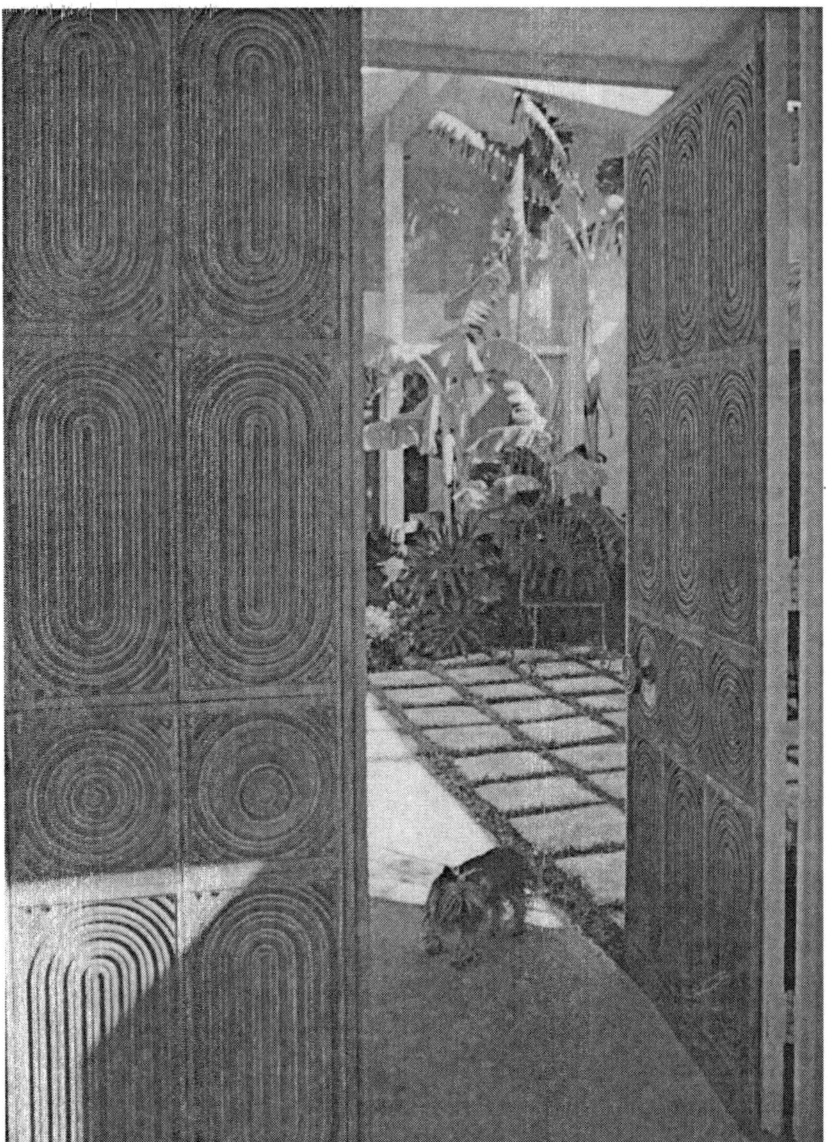

My Yorkie, Tushie, in the entry of my house in Trancas Canyon, Malibu.

I now had a place to relocate all my furniture back from New York and begin a new life after a couple of rough years. Truth is, I had no more interest in living in New York. I wasn't motivated to hook up with any of my old show business friends. I felt that I had ended that part of my life and moved on. I was really lonely there. For me, the magnetism of show business, of that need for applause was gone. I had been weaned away from that big tit. The charm no longer existed and I had no desire to perform.

Long gone were my weeks on stage or hanging out in Greenwich Village where Barbra Streisand, Bobby Short, Joan Rivers, Johnny Mathis were all first getting their feet wet in front of live audiences all those years ago.

I returned to Los Angeles continuing with my decorating for several other celebrities including Jan and Toni Murray's Beverly Hills hilltop home. They were dear friends of Jack's and mine for years back in New York. Although decorating had been profitable, my goal was to get back into real estate. That I felt could only happen in California.

Lucy was delighted I was moving back. After I purchased the Trancas property, she visited often, if only to sit and watch me plaster the ceilings and refinish kitchen cabinets or fabric the walls. She gladly made the trek. There were many backgammon parties I hosted and we had a lot of fun.

★ ★ ★

Despite Lucy's trips to Trancas Canyon, she was becoming more and more reclusive. If Lucy didn't have to venture out, she wouldn't. The thing of it is, Lucy couldn't stand to be alone. She might have read a book every now and then, but that was not her favorite thing to do. Since Gary was away most of the time playing golf, she preferred staying at home and playing backgammon. She started hosting an annual tournament down at Pips, a famous disco/backgammon hall in Beverly Hills.

The club was started by Stan Herman and his pal Hugh Hefner. Stan was a westside real estate broker and old beau of mine. Backgammon was their favorite game and the club caught on quick with the famous and the jet-set. Dean Martin, Vince Edwards, Henry Winkler, and Sylvester Stallone frequented the dance club there; and members paid a $3,000 monthly fee.

I remember at one of her events Lucy got so anxious because nobody was playing the game. They were all hanging out at the bar drinking. Lucy had to go in there and shoo everybody to the backgammon room, which had custom-made tables and mirrored walls. When they started playing, everybody got into the swing of things and had fun. Lucy had become so fixated with the game it engulfed her whole existence. She needed players for her tournaments, and the more famous, the better. Some of her personal favorites included comedian Mary Wicks, Altovise Davis (Sammy Davis' widow), Jeanine Foreman, Polly Bergen, and Thelma Orloff, Lucy's oldest showbiz starlet friend who was now selling real estate with the nickname "Realty Royalty." But her all-time favorite player was a gentleman by the name of Gaby Horowitz.

Gaby was movie-star handsome and a champion backgammon player, referred by some as the "Bobby Fisher of backgammon." He was also a backgammon instructor at Pips. When Gaby finally met Lucy, she immediately took a liking to him, so much so that he became a fixture at her favorite backgammon table in her home.

One day while I was helping Lucy with her fan mail, Gaby showed up and Lucy couldn't resist the temptation to play backgammon with him. She left me with a stack of her publicity photos which we had been searching through. I had always expressed to Lucy my desire to have a photo of her that nobody else had. Out of this mass of photographs scattered all over the dining room table, my eye caught one I had never seen. And it was the only one. Special to my mind.

"Aha! At last." I thought, "This is it!" I grabbed the photo and interrupted her game.

"Lucy, I found the photo I want." And without looking up or missing a beat, she waved me aside and said, "Of course, Paula," never taking her eyes off the board. Thrilled with my trophy, I was almost out the door when she called out after me, "Make me thirty more copies!" I was crushed, my bubble was burst. The only consolation was in knowing that this photo became the one she chose for her special friends. Unfortunately, it was also the one Lucy gave to "asshole" Lee Tannen years later after their long estrangement.

Early on, Lucy dubbed Gaby Horowitz, to be henceforth referred to as Gaby "Monet." He was that beautiful. The nickname

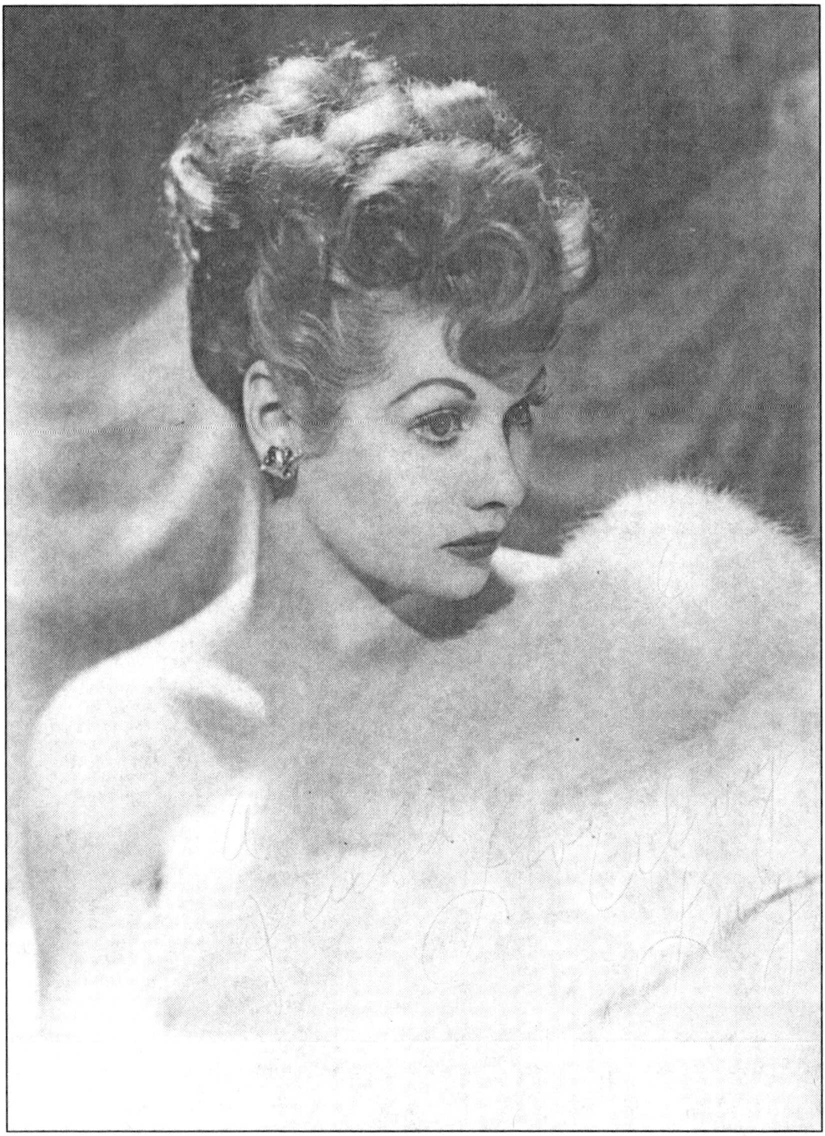

This is the photo I chose for myself and later the one she ended up giving to close friends.

was in honor of her love for the artist Monet, and it fit. I'm sure he benefitted from the association. She never nicknamed anybody *else* that I can recall.

I later introduced Gaby to Ruth Pointer, who was smitten with him, too. They became the best of friends. Gaby was living the Hol-

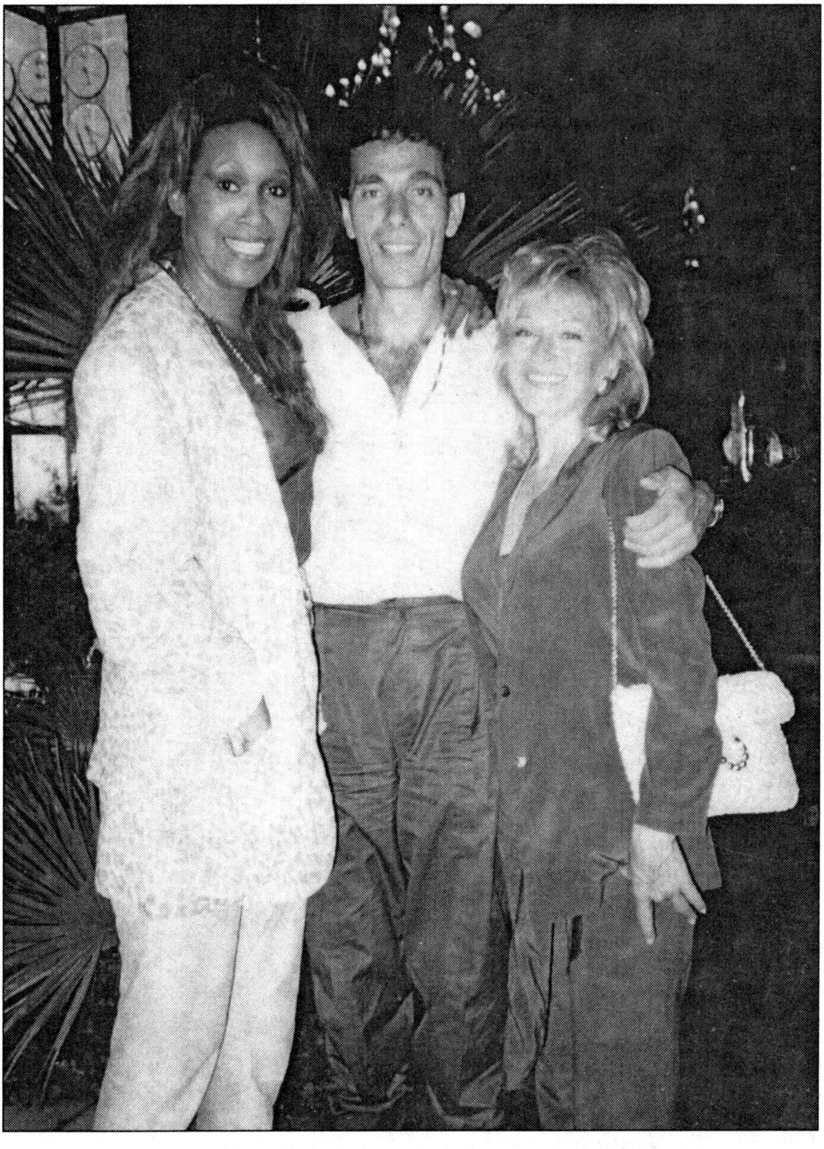

Ruth Pointer, Gaby "Monet" Horowitz and I in Beverly Hills.

lywood dream—a dashing guy who drove fast cars, dated beautiful women and made great money playing backgammon until tragedy struck. He was hanging out with Bruce Roman, a Scientologist and then friend of Gaby's wife, attorney Marcia Clark. Both men were gun collectors and cleaning their firearms when the gun Bruce had in his hands went off. The bullet ricocheted and accidentally found its way into Gaby's head. He was in the hospital for a long time and, as far as I know, never really regained his senses.

★ ★ ★

If Lucy's taste for decorating was abysmal, her cooking was even worse. She was adept at making hot dogs, baked beans and potato salad. She had fondness for Chinese food, and hired a husband and wife Chinese couple to cook and clean full-time. It was Gary's idea to hire them, a dream come true for a Jewish kid from the Bronx.

Kung was the cook and Chou was the upstairs maid. Kung was not a big fan of mine because on his days off I would cook in *his* kitchen. Lucy was happy to have a break. She loved my spaghetti. In fact, everybody loves my spaghetti. The secret ingredient is anchovies, which appealed greatly to Lucy's palate. I never told her exactly what I put in there, although I told her she could have the recipe anytime.

"Oh no. I'd rather have you do it," she said. "Just make up a whole batch so we'll always have some in the freezer."

When Kung came back from the weekends, he'd glare at me like I'd killed his prize duck. And Kung always knew when I cooked. He resented my presence in his "work space" and never failed to notice even when I scrubbed them meticulously—his pots had been tampered with.

Kung didn't have the greatest personality in the world and got testier with old age. Chou didn't fare much better. She started having problems with her knees and could no longer climb the stairs. Lucy cared for them as long as possible until they could no longer handle the work.

The next couple Lucy and Gary hired were Russian, Roosha and Chris. They were very nice but later got divorced. When Lucy died, Roosha went with Gary to Palm Springs and took care of him at the Thunderbird house.

Gary didn't really care much for Tinkerbell, or animals in general. He would have had Roosha take care of Lucy's dog as she had done in the Beverly Hills home. Gary later married a golf pro after

Lucy died. I was aghast, but what was so surprising about that? He had to marry someone that would do him some good and she must have because she looked like Gary in a dress.

This new wife didn't particularly care for Roosha and had her fired. And cruelly, would not let Roosha take Tinkerbell with her. It broke poor Roosha's heart. One other person who worked at Lucy's house was Gary's nephew, Michael Maurer. He served as a gofer and was always creeping around. Lucy constantly complained about him, but he kept his job until she died. I understand that Gary put the poor fool through the wringer after Lucy's death. What a surprise.

★ ★ ★

In 1986 it was announced Lucy was headed back to television in a new ABC series called *Life with Lucy* produced by Aaron Spelling. Aaron had an impeccable track record with such hits as *Dynasty, Charlie's Angels, Hart to Hart* and *The Love Boat*. Since the network was impressed with the previous year's numbers from *Stone Pillow*, they believed Lucy still had the goods for a hit show. But Lucy wasn't so thrilled. She felt the script and concept was sub-standard.

"I don't like it, Paula, what am I going to do?" Lucy said.

When I read the script, I felt it was *Stone Pillow* all over again. It had no zip. She was basically going to play an older version of herself. I knew she couldn't do the physical comedy anymore, and didn't have much mobility since her ski accident.

"Lucy, do you really want to do this?" I asked. "You obviously don't need the work."

"Everyone's pressuring me. Gary's pressuring me. I can't ask Desi for his opinion. He's too sick. I know what he would say anyway. It's too late. Gary's already finalized everything."

Lucy told me that she didn't mind not working but hated that the industry kept piling her up with awards.

"It's like, 'We better give this to her before she dies because she's getting old,'" Lucy said. She hated getting ready for these events and resented attending them even more.

"The worst was that Harvard Pudding thing I was dragged into," she said. "Ugh, what a stinker!"

Even though she surrounded herself with some familiar people like Gale Gordon, and her writing team of Bob Carroll, Jr. and Madelyn Pugh Davis as cornerstones for assurance, the show just wasn't funny. As much as I wanted to, I could barely muster up a laugh. Gary ran around as if he had no idea what he was doing, which wasn't far from the truth. But, he was right there with Aaron Spelling as Executive Producer of the series, being paid top dollar. Lucy looked exhausted and I could tell she wanted to be anywhere but there. It reminded me of when I first met her and she sang for the first time in front of the cast for *Wildcat*. I felt so sorry for her once again. Even though everyone around her was pretending it was wonderful, Lucy knew the magic was gone.

Life with Lucy ended November 1986, and in December, Desi Arnaz passed away from lung cancer. Lucy was devastated. Her relationship with Desi and his wife, Edie Hirsch, was very amicable. There was never any reference to any of their previous problems, and they both held great respect for one another.

Desi had eased up on his drinking at the end of his life, having come to the realization that he was killing himself. Edie was a delightful lady and kept him in line as best as she could. He was a strong-willed, reckless, risk-taking, gambling Latin for most of his life. I knew how much he meant to Lucy. Gary was her husband now, but no one could ever replace what Lucy and Desi had all those amazing years together despite the disappointments in their personal life. They could never be ignored or swept out of her memory. Gary knew where he stood in her priorities and could only step back and let her grieve, silently in her own space. As a friend, I knew she didn't want overt sympathy, just to be left to her private thoughts.

The couple made television history, had two kids and their partnership had meant so much to millions of Americans. None of this was lost on Lucy.

★ ★ ★

In 1987 I sold my property in Malibu. While deciding what to do with the money I made, I needed a place to live. While I was looking for another house to buy, a friend of mine, Phyllis Morris, called me up one day.

Phyllis was a successful furniture designer and decorator, and a fellow native from Chicago. Phyllis took art classes in Los Angeles and quickly made a name for herself when she designed a lamp modeled after her pink-dyed poodle. She drove around town in her signature mink coat and pink Cadillac convertible, and her celebrity status skyrocketed.

Her business, the Phyllis Morris Furniture Company, dealt in high-end furniture and was often featured in *Architectural Digest*. Her clients consisted of Joan Collins, Liberace, and Joan Crawford. Phyllis loved to tell the story of how Crawford had stopped by her showroom once and Phyllis offered her a Coke. The very next day, dozens of cases of Pepsi showed up with a note from the screen legend telling Phyllis to dump the Coke down the drain. Joan still held a position on the board of directors at Pepsi, and it was in her financial interest to cheer for Team Pepsi. Phyllis was married to Nathan Goller and they had two children, James and Jaime, whom I later helped in remodeling their houses. Phyllis was also a very smart businesswoman and made wise investments in real estate and eventually practically owned Hollywood.

Phyllis convinced me to move into one of her buildings, a place called "The Lotus" on La Cienega. It resembled a Chinese village and was very unique, which appealed greatly to me. Because it had interesting architectural features, I decided to stay there for a while until I could figure out what to do next. Ironically years earlier, Phyllis had encouraged Lucy to come to one of her design forums. Lucy realized that was the least of her talents and figured it couldn't hurt. But it also didn't help. Phyllis was a larger than life character and Lucy told me she figured there were laughs to be had. Phyllis told me later that when Lucy showed up for class they asked her, "Who is your favorite decorator?" Lucy replied, "My set designer and the prop room at Desilu!"

I showed up at Lucy's house to play backgammon one day, and she was dressed to the nines.

"I'm sick of playing games today. I need to get out of the house for a change," she said. "I haven't even been to that new Beverly Center since they tore down the Kiddyland Park. What will all those anxious divorcees do now that it's gone? Oh well, that's not my problem. But hey, I hear they have great hot dogs over there!"

So off we drove in her tan Mercedes, minus Frank. She was raring to go and I was delighted to see her so energetic. I hadn't seen her like this for quite a while. She looked happy and eager for an adventure. When we arrived at the food court, it took me a few minutes before I realized that something was about to happen. There was a sense the moment had been frozen in time.

It was like a small earthquake had occurred and everyone was looking for the epicenter. No one moved as it became apparent that Lucille Ball was actually in plain sight. Of course, she looked older, but all the trappings were there: the incredible hair color, the perfect fitting suit and perfect nails. Sure, it was like maybe an imposter was filling in for her, when a particularly brave woman stepped forward in a very hesitant manner and asked a question.

"Didn't you used to be Lucille Ball?" she asked.

"In a former life, yes," Lucy laughed.

We went over to the railing where you could look down on every floor in the wide-open space. I noticed Lucy's breathing got more rapid, like she was having a panic attack or perhaps she got vertigo from looking down.

"Paula, I feel dizzy," she said, grabbing my arm. "Get me out of here!"

In the flutter of an eyelash we were gone. Too late to mention the hot dog at that point, we were back home in a flash at her secure surroundings. I don't recall her ever attempting another trip to the Beverly Center, or many public outings after that day.

★ ★ ★

In May of 1988 tragedy struck. Lucy suffered a stroke and was rushed to Cedars Sinai Medical Center. It was all over the news. Lucy didn't stay long. She hated hospitals and they scared her. The stroke had caused paralysis to her left side and her mouth drooped a little at the corner. She didn't want anyone to see her in this state, but I rushed over as soon as she was home.

I was greeted by the imposing presence of Trudi Arcudi, a private nurse hired to help Lucy recover. She was well-respected in her industry, caring for many big stars who nicknamed her, "Trudy Arcudi Private Duty."

"How is she?" I asked.

"She's doing better, Paula, and she's been asking for you." I quickly went upstairs to Lucy's bedroom where she was resting in bed. Lucy was not in a good mood; she was impatient with any kind of illness. Her speech was slurred, but she made an effort to talk despite her discomfort and appearance.

Trudi joined us and Lucy complimented her.

"She's something, Paula, isn't she?" Lucy said. Trudi was one of the most caring and diplomatic people I had ever met. A true gem. She and Lucy hit if off greatly. Trudi wouldn't take shit from anyone. God couldn't intimidate the woman. She did her job well and saw to it that everyone followed her orders.

Trudi and I watched over Lucy like a hawk because she had high blood pressure. We were constantly concerned about the cook's innocent disregard for salt in her food. Lucy loved spicy food, a killer for her condition. Everyone was warned about it, but Lucy couldn't be dissuaded from her love of salt and salty foods.

Trudi told me later she caught Lucy drinking a margarita with a ton of salt on the rim. Lucy knew it was bad for her and didn't give a damn.

"Gary made it for me and I'm going to drink it," she said.

"The hell you are," Trudi told her with a smile, "not as long as I'm around here." Whereupon she removed the salt and returned the drink. I honestly don't know where Lucy ever acquired a taste for margaritas, but they definitely were not good for her.

Trudi had a granddaughter, Shannon, that she took care of. I had found a small baby grand piano at Abell's Auction House and Lucy right away said, "Get it! Get it!" I bought it for maybe $400. Lucy gave it to Trudi and Trudi was thrilled that Lucy would be so kind and thoughtful towards her. Thanks to Trudi, Lucy was on the

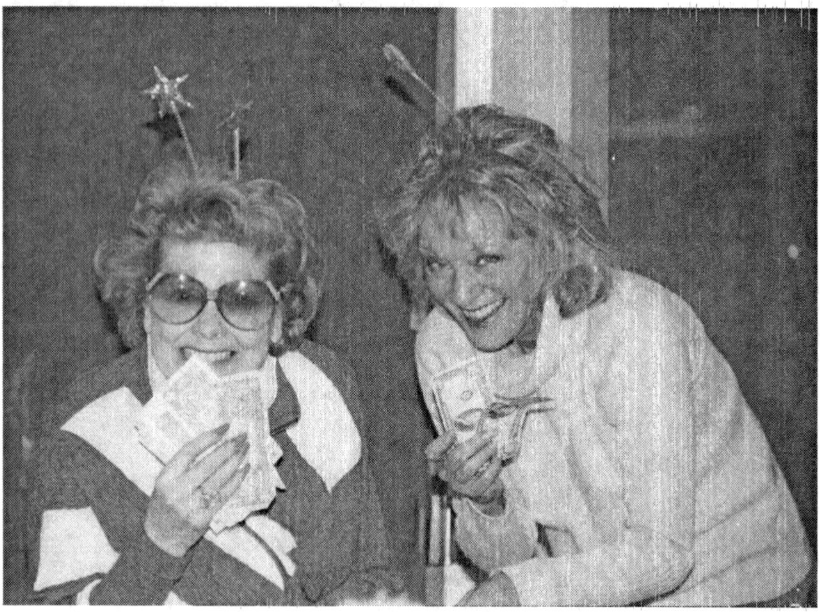

Lucy and I big winners at pig.

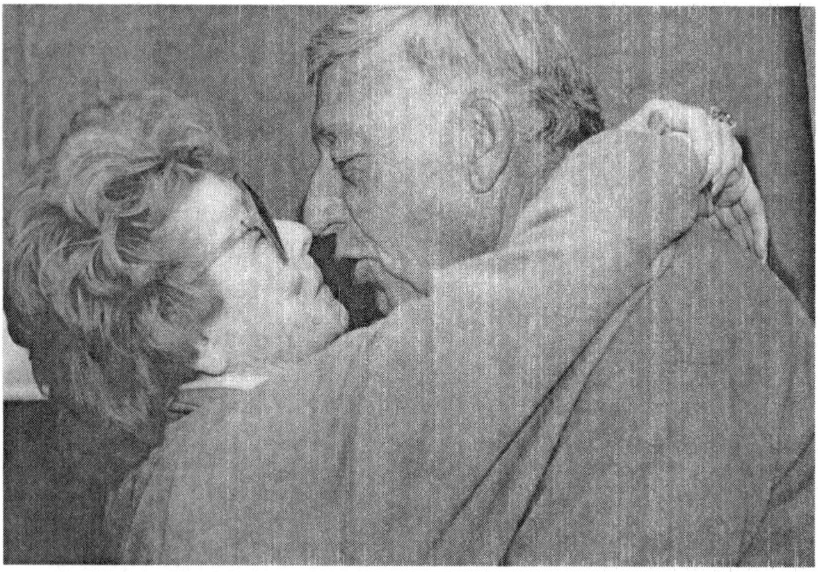

I was grateful for the last New Year's Eve weekend in Palm Springs with Lucy.

mend in record time. Not too long after her recovery however, Gary let Trudi go.

I could say I was shocked but at this point, it was what everyone expected of Gary.

"Why are you letting her go, Gary?" I asked.

"Oh, she's too expensive," was his reply. His answer made no sense since Lucy was quite wealthy and certainly SAG or her insurance paid for Trudi's services. I personally believe Gary's dismissal of Trudi was instrumental in Lucy having her second fatal heart attack. Who else was going to put a stop to those ridiculous margarita drinks with all that salt?

Trudi had an unimposing presence and gained Lucy's confidence and she also became a good friend. When Lucy went back into the hospital at the very end, she insisted on having Trudi there as her night nurse, for which I was most grateful.

★ ★ ★

During this time I was extremely concerned for Lucy's health. It started with all the medications I was privy to when I remodeled her New York apartment. Earlier that year in January, Lucy had gone to the hospital for some routine tests and wound up staying for a few days when she had to have a cyst removed next to her thyroid gland.

It wasn't anything nearly as extreme as the stroke. However, when Lucy returned home she called and asked me to come over. I raced to her house and went up to her bedroom where she was resting. She looked good and appeared happy.

"You know, Paula, when I go, I want it to be from this room," she said. "I'm just so happy with what you did with it."

"Now Lucy, back to what happened in the hospital," I said.

"Oh, Paula, it was nothing major."

"Anytime you're in the hospital for a few days, it's major, Lucy."

"I was reminded about something that young man said."

"Who, Lucy?"

"You know, that psychic fellow from New York."

"You mean John Monti?"

"Yes, yes, him. He predicted this." That was true to some extent. I remember John saying there was unusual activity around the thyroid area. The truth is, Lucy's health was failing. She continued to smoke heavily. Both she and Gary smoked and there was no way Lucy could quit because Gary said he never would. Ironically, that's what killed him—he died of lung cancer. Being a witness to, and watching your best friend's health decline is heartbreaking. After the stroke I didn't want to let Lucy out of my sight.

★ ★ ★

On the morning of April 26, 1989, my phone rang yet again, at an ungodly hour. *Jesus Christ*, I thought as I struggled for the receiver. It was Kevin Thomas.

"Paula, I'm so sorry," he said. I was foggy because of the early hour phone call, and I tried to focus on what Kevin was saying.

"What do you mean you're sorry?" I asked, the words barely escaped my mouth.

"Oh, you don't know?"

"Know what?"

"Lucy passed away this morning." Silence. It felt like an eternity. "Hello, Paula, are you there?"

"I'll have to call you back, Kevin." I felt the room spinning. I was trying to absorb the reality that was quickly settling in about my best friend. Lucy had been rushed to the hospital just a week earlier when she was experiencing severe chest pains. She was in critical condition when she arrived and underwent hours of surgery to repair a tear in her aorta. Some parts of the aorta and aortic valve had been replaced with tissue from a donor, a young man in his twenties as I recall. Lucy spent the next week in the hospital. Now that I look back, Trudi and I were some of the last people to see her alive. Very few people were allowed in and you had to have specific passes (I still have all of mine).

Little Lucie and Desi, Jr. stopped by that week. Lucy seemed to be getting much better after her heart surgery and I think we all believed she was going home. I remember Desi, Jr. and his wife felt they could safely return to their home in Nevada and stopped by for one last visit.

Little Lucie was there and I felt she and Lucy reconciled during that last visit. The hurt and anger of the past disappeared immediately. Both said they loved each other and neither would let go of the other's hand. Lucy hugged Little Lucie one last time and said, "I guess this means I'll have to stop fighting with Larry." Little Lucie's eyes filled with tears. The only words she could get out were, "Oh, Mom!" Everyone started crying, even the nurse.

Her fans had put up a great big sign across the street. It read: "Lucy Get Well, We Love You!" They didn't know if she could see it or not, but Lucy was thrilled that they were there for support.

The last time I saw Lucy, she was complaining about her hair roots and her nails. She hated for anybody to see her without her nails done properly.

"Well, Lucy, do you want me to get somebody—a manicurist in here?" I asked.

"Oh no, that's alright," she said. "I won't be in here much longer."

I sat down on the bed with her. As she had done so often in the past, Lucy held my hand.

"Paula, it's no fun getting old," she said softly. I tried not to let her see me fighting back the tears. She looked so frail. I desperately wanted to hug her and tell her how much I loved her, but I was afraid it might alarm her to see me be so emotional.

I didn't want to confirm both our worst fears that time was running out. She suspected it but didn't know the seriousness of her condition. It still breaks my heart. I never really got to say goodbye. And now my best friend, my mentor, my sister was gone.

Trudi told me the first thing Gary did was contact his attorney. He did not call her children or loved ones. He called his lawyer. Typical Gary.

Back at the house, I asked Little Lucie, "Where's Gary?"

"He's in the den," she said. "He doesn't want to see anybody."

"I'd like to talk to him."

"Well, he's in seclusion." No doubt talking to his lawyer, I thought. I finally saw Gary a day or so later. What he said was very telling.

"Well, I guess she's happy now, she's back with Desi," he said. Gary knew deep down that Desi was the love of her life, and had to live in Desi's shadow all through their marriage.

After Lucy died, I contacted the doctor to get specific details on what happened.

"I'd liken it to having an old frayed garden hose that could blow at the base," he said. "There is no way to repair it. It has to be replaced, which is what we did with a twenty seven-year-old male donor, using his tissue to replace the vessel going into her heart. Because the operation took eight hours, it was too much of a strain on her system. We had to stop. We planned to replace the other valve descending from the heart as soon as she recovered from this latest procedure. However, in the middle of the night, the other valve blew and it was impossible to repair. She died before we could get to it."

Twenty-two years later I survived this same surgery when these procedures had been greatly approved upon and the survival rate was much higher. It was another example of the chance coincidences between our lives.

★ ★ ★

On that following Mother's Day, Little Lucie held a memorial for her mother. It was a picnic of sorts including a very short list of invitees: family, close friends and former Desilu employees. It was held at the estate of Robert Taylor. Lucy had a fondness for Robert, who had been her good friend.

It was a cheerless, overcast day, as I made the drive through Brentwood in my trusty Mercedes. I was already numb and definitely not in a send-off kind of mood. I honestly don't know how I made it there. But thanks to Michael and Swen, they kept me distracted with small talk until we arrived to be greeted by Wanda who was checking every single person, making sure the hounding tabloids would not gain access to what would have been a major scoop for them.

When I looked around, I was shocked by the "new guard" that were gathered. I could count the number of people I thought belonged there–Trudi, Mary Wickes, Onna White, and Thelma Orloff—and other folks Lucy felt close to. There were a lot of johnny-come-latelies who happened to weasel their way into the last few months of Lucy's life.

I didn't want to be there. I had to put on one hell of a face to be around these people. I decided it was easier for me to hide behind my camera. I had been the family photographer for years, so I began snapping away. I was in a daze. The overall mood was grief and sadness. It was low key with not a smile in view. I somehow got through it.

I spent much of the time talking with Trudi. I got the impression that she shared my feelings. I know it was a tribute to Lucy. She would have wanted something more up-beat. I couldn't imagine anyone was having a good time. Lucy would have hated it. Little Lucie tried her best and I applaud her effort, but even her cheerful demeanor and attempt at a picnic atmosphere were no help.

After a couple of hours, Mike, Swen and I made it back to my car, where I turned on the radio to distract myself from being anymore depressed. We drove away from the ranch. As I was maneuvering down through the canyon turns, I thought I heard a familiar voice on the radio. It was Frank Sinatra. I knew in an instant as I turned up the volume that Lucy was there with me. A thin river of tears began streaming down my face. I listened as Frank crooned, *"Funny how love becomes a cold rainy day, funny that rainy day is here."*

★ ★ ★

I couldn't stop thinking about Lucy in the following weeks after she passed. I just kept going over things in my head those last few weeks before she was rushed to the hospital. I thought about how uneasy she was about appearing on the Academy Awards, but was finally okay with it because it was with Bob (Hope). I watched the show and was very proud of Lucy. Not only did she look gorgeous, but she sailed through the presentation like a pro, as if she did it every night. The only thing I noticed was that her wig was bothering her and she would scratch behind her ear as she often did when it was too tight. Later she remarked to me how much she enjoyed being there and the overwhelming response she received from her peers.

I had dinner with her almost every night, not suspecting they would be the last. As I look back now, Lucy continually called me to come over, as if she knew she didn't have much time left. We had just celebrated my birthday with Michael on April 9th and Gaby Monet had been shot on April 14th. Lucy was saddened with that news. Ruth Berle died on the 19th. Lucy wanted me to send Milton a note when I saw him next. I know she called him, too.

At one of our dinners, Lucy asked me how Swen was doing. He had contracted the HIV virus. It was a devastating epidemic that widely impacted the gay community earlier in the decade. It was beginning to reach more awareness when people who were not gay became infected; disproving ridiculous theories that AIDS was a "gay" disease. But for 1989, it was still a subject that people found uncomfortable to talk about, but not Lucy. She was well-informed about the subject.

"Swen is doing fine," I said. He had purchased a house on Angelo Drive in Beverly Hills. He still had the house of carnival fun on Minetta Lane in New York, but didn't go back that often.

"Will you give him my love the next time you speak with him?" she said. "Tell him to come over to play some backgammon and I'll cook him a big dinner here at the house." *Lucy cook* I thought? That just might kill him.

"Tell him I want to smother him with nothing but big kisses!"

Swen did pass away four years later from complications from A.I.D.S. Lucy adored him, as did I.

That encounter reminded me that first day I met her at rehearsals. So beautiful. So graceful. So accommodating. That fiery mane of red hair, down to the heartiness of her laugh. Her well-manicured nails that suited her elegant taste in clothes.

Lucy was truly one of a kind. She was my sister, she was my mother, and she was my best friend. You're only lucky to have one of these in your life. I was lucky it was Lucy. I did love Lucy, and Lucy loved me.

★ ★ ★

VIII
Epilogue

I knew finishing this book would be hard because the first person I would have wanted to read it was Lucy. Hopefully, she would have loved it and had a few laughs. I can just hear her say, "Well now, Paula, you've certainly outdone yourself this time. Is there anything you can't do?"

Lucy would have watched every episode of *Dancing with the Stars* while still remaining faithful to *Wheel of Fortune*, watching Vanna White turn those bright white and black letters. She would

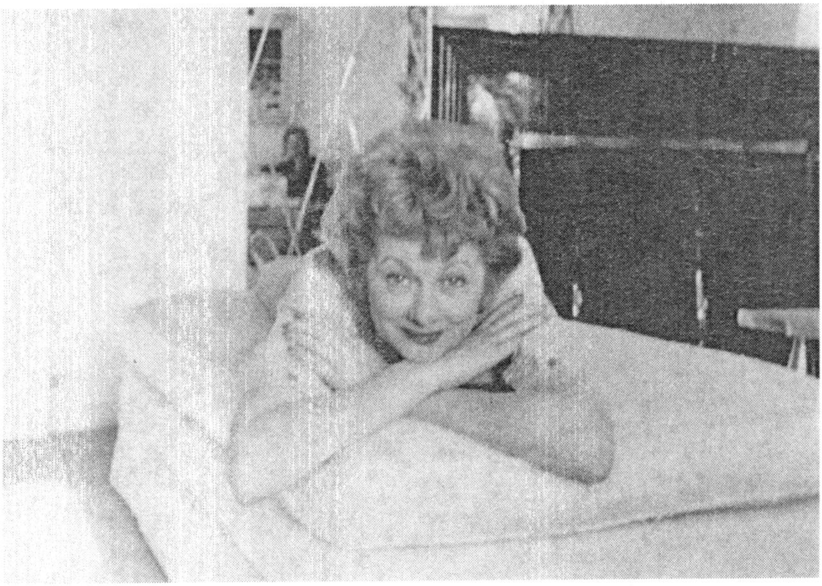

Photography has been my lifelong hobby and Lucy didn't mind me taking photos. I took this during rehearsals of Wildcat while she was staying at the Imperial House in New York City. You can see me in the mirror.

have gotten a big kick out of my son Michael's marriage to Victoria and having twins, both redheads!

Despite her death nearly three decades ago, Lucy is never out of my memory, not even for a minute. Sometimes when the phone rings early in the morning, I expect it to be her. I wouldn't mind being woken up at an ungodly hour just to hear her voice again.

I find it hardest to finish this book because it means saying a final goodbye to my dearest friend, on paper that is. She is with me in my heart and mind constantly but for now, it is the end.

But it's not forever.

★ ★ ★

Acknowledgments

I want to thank especially my son, Michael Carter, and his lovely wife, Victoria, my nieces Lisa, Paula, Rebecca, and Alexandra; and to all the people who put up with my writing this memoir, not in the order of their importance to me or the book, rather for my deep gratitude with whatever help, guidance, insights, support, and patience they gave me so generously: Neile Adams, Jill Arnold, Neil Barry, Burt Bacharach, Josette Banzet, John Bowab, Janie Brady, Slim Brandy, Basil and Carol Collier, Iris Davis, Angie Dickinson, Nancy Dussault, Margie Duncan, Alan Eichler, Jonathan Freund, Sandy Glabman, Nate Goller, Devra Hill, Paul Horner, Cici Huston, David Hughes, Saif Ilderem, Sirena Irwin, Laurie Jacobson, Dr. Robert Koblin, Sondra Lee, Sue Main, Valentine Mayer, Anne McDermott, Marc Meshekow, Daniel Molheran, Quinn O'Hara, Chris Ostrow, Kit Parker, Debbie Pinthus, Anita Pointer, Ruth Pointer, Rex Reed, Sally Sherman, Angela Stark, Michael Stern, Stu Shostak, Marshall Terrill, Kevin Thomas, Alicia Van der Veer, Jaime Vermeulen, Christine Wagner, Seth Weingarten, Rob Weise, Sheryl Woodley, and Irwin Zucker.

★ ★ ★

This book is a memoir. It reflects my present recollections of events and experiences over time. My memories, thoughts, and musings are solely my own and are not intended to offend or harm anyone.

All photos are from the author's collection unless otherwise noted.

CPSIA information can be obtained
at www.ICGtesting.com
Printed in the USA
FSOW02n2114090118
43236FS

9 781629 332260